The learning disabled adolescent

Program alternatives in the secondary school

The learning disabled adolescent

Program alternatives in the secondary school

GEORGE E. MARSH II, Ed.D.
University of Arkansas

CAROL KOZISEK GEARHEART, Ed.D.
University of Northern Colorado

BILL R. GEARHEART, Ed.D.
University of Northern Colorado

with 41 *illustrations*

The C. V. Mosby Company

Saint Louis   1978

Printed in the United States of America

The C. V. Mosby Company
11830 Westline Industrial Drive, St. Louis, Missouri 63141

Library of Congress Cataloging in Publication Data

Marsh, George E
    The learning disabled adolescent.

    Includes bibliographical references and index.
    1.   Mentally handicapped children—Education
(Secondary). 2. Learning disabilities. I. Gearheart,
Carol K., 1937-   joint author. II. Gearheart, B. R.,
joint author. III. Title.
LC4661.M29   371.9'2   77-18050
ISBN 0-8016-3118-1

GW/CB/B 9 8 7 6 5 4 3 2 1

Preface

Parents and professionals of various disciplines have invested talent and resources as part of a commitment to the learning disabilities movement. We can reflect with pride on the progress of the last decade. Hundreds of classes have been initiated in public and private schools, teacher-training programs have kept pace with the demand for competent specialists in the field, research activity has increased dramatically, and there is a growing social awareness concerning the needs of students whose lives are affected by learning disabilities. However, much remains to be accomplished if we are to fulfill the needs of students with learning disabilities.

Although there are numerous programs, a variety of remedial methodologies, and a wealth of teaching materials available for use in an elementary program, the educational needs of adolescents with learning disabilities have been neglected and their futures compromised. As American society becomes inevitably more complex during the age of technology, secondary education for students with learning disabilities is increasingly important. New approaches to education must be developed for this special population. Many authorities seem to agree tacitly about the rudiments of a secondary program, but basic textbooks that are suitable for use in college training programs are difficult to find. Therefore, we have endeavored to organize and present a book containing what we believe to be the most effective components of secondary programming.

We are convinced that secondary education of students with learning disabilities requires a different orientation than that which may be successful in the elementary school.

The status of secondary school programming is such that it would be impossible to present a comprehensive approach relating to teaching methods. However, we have attempted to analyze and describe both a theoretical base and the educational components for such a program. The next decade will undoubtedly usher in new ideas, innovative approaches, and exemplary programs. We eagerly await these events! Nevertheless, we believe that it is necessary to provide meaningful direction *now* for college students who are preparing to teach adolescents with learning disabilities. This is our primary target group.

We also direct this text to the varied group of secondary teachers with whom the learning disability specialist will work—the "regular classroom" teachers. The success of any program and the impact of special programming on the lives of students will be determined, in large measure, by the knowledge, acceptance, and cooperation of these secondary teachers. We would hope that our efforts may assist them in conceptualizing the unique problems of students with learning disabilities so that they may better understand why professional attitudes, skills, and capabilities must serve as the foundation for a successful program. The secondary program for students with learning disabilities is inextricably bound to the regular program. The direct involvement of all teachers—involvement that is based on understanding the nature of learning disabilities—will benefit those students who have long been regarded as "losers" in our society.

Literally thousands of students leave our secondary schools each year, as graduates or dropouts, who are unable to function adequately in our society because they have no marketable skills and are not prepared for the myriad demands of adulthood. We must train *all* students for living in our society, yet schools persist in maintaining a system that rewards primarily the college-bound student; this occurs with the knowledge that only one student in four will graduate from college. Moreover, some students with learning disabilities would be capable of meeting the challenge of college if they were given special provisions and alternatives. However, they are denied educational advancement by a system of rigid, pedantic approaches to learning.

The first section of this text presents a concise overview of the field of learning disabilities. We then discuss the two major factors that dictate a different approach to the education of the adolescent with learning disabilities. These factors are: (1) the adolescent has different personal and social needs simply because of maturational and cognitive change, and (2) the secondary school has a legacy of concern for academics, grades, credits, and preparation for college, all of which are based on the presumption that students entering the secondary school have—or should have—mastered basic skills. Implications that may be extrapolated from these two factors are the bases for unique program needs.

The second section encompasses the program emphases that we believe to be the most important for the student with learning disabilities in the secondary school, along with suggestions relating to assessment practices. Although learning disabilities can be formidable and perplexing problems that have stimulated the development of some elaborate remedial strategies, accommodation and compensatory teaching exceed in importance in the secondary school. Remediation *is* important, but we believe that its utility begins to diminish with the increasing age of students. The emphasis *must* become focussed on the use of whatever skills and abilities the student may have. This requires adaptations and accommodations that permit learning through the use of these

existing skills and abilities. The objective is to encourage learning and academic achievement free from traditional academic requirements. Herein lies the greatest problem. Educators have long been accustomed to employing certain methods of evaluating achievement, time-honored and venerated methods that resist change. In an effort to treat students with learning disabilities fairly, we are likely to be accused of "undermining" the system and advocating "lowered academic standards." But we believe that well-conceived change will yield meaningful programs that maintain standards of academic excellence although traditional practices may not be retained.

In addition to the central concern of maintaining balance between remediation and accommodation, motivational techniques, career education, and counseling needs of students are considered.

The final section of this text presents descriptions of public and private school programs. We have stressed the components that we believe to be essential in a complete program for secondary students. In the last chapter, we consider briefly the status of postsecondary programs. Although limited in scope and applicability, some programs do exist and must be considered when one is planning for some secondary students who may wish to continue formal education beyond high school.

We have attempted to prepare a text with a practical orientation, although theoretical considerations are essential to our discussion of some issues. It is our earnest hope that this book will focus the attention of professionals on educational programs that will become the capstone of a continuum of educational provisions for secondary students. The needs of these students demand a change in current educational practices. We hope that this text will contribute in some small way to that change, a change we believe to be part of the movement toward social equality for all people.

George E. Marsh II
Carol Kozisek Gearheart
Bill R. Gearheart

Acknowledgments

A fine group of high school students, and their teachers, deserve our special gratitude because they have provided us with the photographs used to illustrate this book. The talent and accomplishments of these students serve as a testimony to the highest hopes we have expressed in this volume. The following persons associated with the Pre-Career and Occupational Training Project (Pre-COT), Title IV-C, ESEA, of the Bryant High School in Bryant, Arkansas, deserve special recognition for their outstanding assistance:

Director: Judy Connor

Associate director: Elizabeth McAllister

Student photographers
Jebby Abbott
Myles Bell
Mark Croy
Fred Cochran
Robert Garner
Roy Hall
Steve Meeks
Bobby Sheridan
Carmine Tieri

Tutor photographers
Steve Edwards
Andy Briebel

Darkroom technicians
Roy Stanley
Billy Speer
Charles Watts
Steve Watson

G. E. M.

Contents

SECTION TWO
Components of a secondary program

4 Assessment, 59

5 Accommodation and compensatory teaching, 85

A review of learning disabilities, views of adolescence, and the secondary school

A major crisis in special education has been triggered by the lack of adequate secondary programs for learning disabled students. Effective programs have been developed for preschool and the middle age range of children, but the growth of related programming at the secondary school level has been much slower and has tended to follow patterns that are more appropriate for younger children. This is unfortunate because services at the secondary school level are urgently needed to keep students in school and to prepare them for social and vocational adjustments. Secondary school programs and preparation of secondary learning disabilities specialists should be predicated on the fact that the secondary school is an entirely different environment from the elementary school and the nature and needs of adolescent are much different.

The major objective of this book is to stress the importance of specialized approaches to the education of learning disabled adolescents. Of central importance was the development of a rationale on which to base recommendations for the emergence of programming in learning disabilities at the secondary school level. The first section has been completed with this purpose in mind.

Therefore, Chapter 1 briefly reviews the historical development of the field of learning disabilities, identifies the major educational approaches, depicts the trends, and reviews the characteristics of adolescents with learning disabilities. Chapter 2 presents a summary of views of adolescence with the ultimate aim of distinguishing this period from childhood, per se, to emphasize the need for a different sensitivity, and, in general, a different approach to the problems of boys and girls approaching adulthood. Chapter 3 includes a discussion of the history, structure, and functioning of the secondary school in America. Hopefully the major differences between elementary and secondary schools will be appreciated by those who must implement secondary programs because many educational approaches to secondary school students must take into account such differences if they are to be effective.

CHAPTER 1

An overview

Professionals of various disciplines have long been concerned about children described as *perceptually impaired, neurologically handicapped, aphasic, dyslexic,* or *language handicapped.* Terminology describing such children is peculiar to each profession because of the unique orientation of each profession. Although the umbrella term *learning disabilities* (LD) has not reduced controversy over etiologies and the definition of learning disabilities remains the subject of debate, it has been the antecedent for extraordinary educational change and a remarkable increase in public school programs for children with a variety of learning problems. Thousands of children who had significant learning and behavioral problems but who could not qualify for the traditional categories of special education were quickly embraced by the learning disabilities movement. It has been concerned parents who have played the major role in promotion of learning disabilities as a new category of special education which could account for school failure by explaining learning disorders as caused by factors beyond the control of the learner.

Since about 1970 college-level programs for preparing special educators to teach the learning disabled in public schools have increased dramatically. Books and journals have been dedicated to the study of learning disabilities, and various professional and lay organizations have been organized. The special education subdiscipline concerned with learning disabilities has become very prominent in a very short period, and its recency may account for some of the problems associated with labeling, diagnosis, and effectiveness of educational strategies.

Although most practitioners seem to accept the use of the common term *learning disabilities*, it is actually a category that entails many diagnostic entities and is applied to a heterogeneous group of children. The development of a useful and accurate definition was a major effort of professionals in the 1960s, and it is apparent that considerable disagreement still exists between disciplines. Most states have incorporated similar definitions because state statutes tend to imitate federal guidelines, but many issues have not been resolved between professional groups concerned with the more rigorous definitions necessary for conducting meaningful research. The importance of definitions may very well depend on one's profession and specific interests.

One important concern involves the sensitive area of the use of labels. Special education has recently undergone a purge of traditional practices in the identification and labeling of mentally retarded children. The stigma effect that is associated with some terms and labels in education is also believed to be responsible for inhibiting the opportunities of students. The main points of contention are related to issues concerning the necessity of labels, the nature of definitions, and the potential for harm. While many groups became actively involved in defining the parameters of learning disabilities, others were questioning the meaningfulness of applying a new label to children who exhibit such diverse characteristics.

HISTORICAL REVIEW

The historical antecedents of learning disabilities have been traced to the works of a few prominent persons who have influenced educational practice, research, and theory. Observations of neurologically impaired adults with disturbances of language, read-

ing, writing, and arithmetic led some to conclude that parallel relationships existed in children with learning disorders. Learning disorders were thought of as manifestations of neurological dysfunction that was caused by either a genetically determined developmental disorder or acquired brain damage.

Morgan (1896) speculated that the inability of a bright school boy to read was caused by defective development of the left angular gyrus, which he called *congenital word blindness.* Hinshelwood (1917), an ophthalmologist, believed that congenital word blindness was a rare condition that should not be confused with reading disorders caused by environmental factors. A later theoretical postulation, proposed by Orton (1937) had a profound impact on educational practice. His belief that language disabilities are related to disorders of cerebral dominance (identified as mixed dominance) led to the development of the *Orton-Gillingham method of remedial reading instruction.* The Orton Society continues to conduct research and to develop special education materials and programs for children today.

Orton believed that language problems and specific reading disorders were caused by the lack of fully established cerebral dominance. According to his theory, if cerebral dominance is fully established, or lateralized, then the dominant cerebral hemisphere controls language functions. In mixed dominance, the subdominant hemisphere may inconsistently exert primary influence on such acts as reading and writing, which is manifested as the ubiquitous reversals found in young children and in many children with mild to severe reading disability. Orton ultimately investigated not only language disorders but also a wide range of academic deficiencies and motor and speech development.

Over the years, many characteristics have come to be associated with developmental conditions. Motor problems and perceptual disturbances have been used in diagnosis. These same characteristics have been assigned to the category of acquired damage. This issue is central to differences that still exist between many theorists. A preponderance of reading, writing, and arithmetic disorders in members of certain families has led some investigators to the conclusion that the problems are neurologically based and genetically caused (Hallgren, 1950; Thompson, 1966; and Critchley, 1970). This is disputed by those who believe that the same learning problems and characteristics are associated with neurological dysfunction caused by brain damage or that they can be attributed to inefficient learning caused by environmental factors.

Serious behavioral changes were noted in children who had been stricken by a severe form of encephalitis that swept the North American continent and Europe during the 1920s (Schain, 1972). Many of these children who had not experienced behavioral problems before the onset of the disease were apparently disturbed after the disease ran its course. This condition was evidenced by violent and destructive behavior as well as several forms of motor abnormalities and was viewed as a brain damage syndrome. The existence of such syndromes in children across widespread geographical areas directed medical attention toward central nervous system pathologies in young children. Atypical behavior noticeable by physicians, parents, and educators led to the acceptance of conditions in children that could interfere with learning and that could be explainable in terms of central nervous system disorders. This would have important implications for future development of the field of learning disabilities.

Strauss and Lehtinen published a classical book, *Psychopathology and Education of the Brain Injured Child* (1947), that is regarded by many as the cornerstone of the field of learning disabilities. Like Orton, Strauss and Lehtinen have influenced educational practice and many educational professionals.

Strauss and Lehtinen investigated the behavioral manifestations of children who were generally so atypical that they were considered to have severe emotional problems. They considered the behavioral abnormalities of their subjects to be the result of le-

sions to the brain that were caused by injury during development. Behavioral differences were believed to be caused by exogenous factors (infections, toxins, blows to the head, and so forth) rather than some inherited trait. A familial history of mental deficiency was reason to consider the possibility of endogenous factors (genetic inheritance) as the probable cause of disability, and Strauss and Lehtinen maintained that the different etiologies led to different behavioral characteristics. Strauss and Lehtinen proposed that exogenous damage to the brain culminated in characteristic behavioral, perceptual, and thinking disorders. These characteristics were identified as abnormal responses to environmental stimuli, distractibility, perseveration, higher levels of motor activity, hyperactivity, disorganized behavior, perceptual disturbances, and motor problems. The diagnosis became sufficiently well accepted that the child possessing these characteristics was said to exhibit the *Strauss syndrome*.

Educational plans for the brain-injured (Strauss syndrome) child emphasized reduction of stimuli, carefully regulated motor activity in learning, limited color to enhance visual perception, planned concrete-manipulative materials, and a structured classroom environment. Vestiges of these teaching strategies are still evident in some classrooms and advocated by some authorities.

Objection has been made to Strauss and Lehtinen's terminology and assumptions. The assumption that brain injury exists without objective evidence of its existence remains a point of contention. Schain (1972), a neurologist, supported earlier critics of the assumption of brain damage in children by stating that no behavioral syndrome is pathognomonic of the presence of brain damage. Confusion over terminology has persisted because of the lack of agreement about what constitutes a learning disability. The inability to replicate some of Strauss' research and the unwieldiness (if not inaccuracy) of the term, *brain injury*, led to the demand for better descriptive terminology and a refinement of symptoms that would differentiate among the several conditions of childhood disorders as well as specifying etiologies and teaching practices.

Semantical disputes have been sustained by practitioners who do not have medical degrees although their controversies have raged over medical terminology and medical syndromes. The original symptoms of brain damage syndromes, typically of a severe nature, were attributed to children with only minor deviations or "soft" neurological signs of disturbances. This fact led Schain (1972) to conclude that the early workers who described brain damage syndromes caused by epidemic encephalitis would be surprised at its present prevalence in a less severe form. This less severe form has been called *minimal brain damage, minimal cerebral dysfunction*, and *minimal brain dysfunction*. Gesell and Amatruda (1947) were among the first to use the term *minimal cerebral injury* to refer to infants with various developmental problems. The term was widened over 20 years to include various forms of symptomatology found in children who did not have severe forms of anomalies, but who were believed to have organic damage (Eisenberg, 1957; Paine, 1962; and Clements, 1966).

As children with learning problems began to receive the attention of various disciplines (in the days before the evolution of the term *learning disabilities*), it became obvious that interdisciplinary communication and cooperation would have to rely on some form of commonality in descriptive terminology. Many individuals began to suggest alternative terminology that might be applied to children who were viewed in specific ways and described in terms unique to various disciplines.

Several conferences were held during the 1960s that considered terminology. Kirk (1963) proposed the term *learning disabilities* to the group of parents who organized the Association for Children with Learning Disabilities. Clements (1966) suggested the term *minimal brain dysfunction* (which had been used by Strauss) to differentiate between children with serious neuropathology and minimally affected children. Chalfant and

Scheffelin (1969) in an extensive review of research used the term *central processing dysfunctions* to refer to numerous types of learning disorders relating to a range of skills in the neurophysiological use of information. One of the early texts on learning disabilities was written by Johnson and Myklebust (1967) who used the term *psychoneurological learning disabilities;* this referred to the disruption of the psychological process of learning as a result of neurological deficiency. The current term, *learning disabilities*, has been well established by its use in federal legislation. However, it is still a very broad term that focuses attention on educational factors while avoiding the emphasis on medical terminology although medical and/or psychological data are typically synthesized in the diagnosis.

From the educational point of view, learning disabilities may be identified as a failure of an otherwise apparently capable child of meeting educational criteria (achievement in reading, writing, arithmetic, and so forth) considered necessary for adequate learning and growth. Diagnosis attempts to uncover the reasons for failure so that educational strategies may be implemented to counteract failure.

Although *learning disabilities* is a broad term encompassing many diagnostic entities, most practitioners have accepted it with some degree of agreement about its meaning. In reality, there is considerable variability in the description of learning disabilities according to the influence of various authorities and differences in state laws. Some states still refer to these children as neurologically handicapped, educationally handicapped, and perceptually/communicatively disordered. There is frequently more latitude in the definition and diagnosis for educational purposes than in research. To illustrate the distinction between authorities, a brief discussion of definitions follows.

DEFINITIONS OF LEARNING DISABILITIES

Kirk (1962) provided what may be considered the original definition:

A learning disability refers to a retardation, disorder or delayed development in one or more of the processes of speech, language, reading, spelling, writing, or arithmetic resulting from possible cerebral dysfunction and/or emotional or behavioral disturbance and not from mental retardation, sensory deprivation, or cultural or instructional factors. (p. 263)

Bateman (1965) defined learning disabled children as:

Children who . . . manifest an educationally significant discrepancy between their estimated intellectual potential and actual level of performance related to basic disorders in the learning processes, which may or may not be accompanied by demonstrable central nervous system dysfunction, and which are not secondary to generalized mental retardation, educational or cultural deprivation, severe emotional disturbance, or sensory loss. (p. 220)

Johnson and Myklebust (1967) focused on neurological functioning in their term psychoneurological learning disabilities. They defined the condition by indicating the conditions that do not exist concomitantly with learning disabilities and by excluding various handicapping characteristics. The National Advisory Committee on Handicapped Children under the leadership of Kirk (1968) offered the following definition:

Children with special learning disabilities exhibit a disorder in one or more of the basic psychological processes involved in understanding or using spoken or written languages. These may be manifested in disorders of listening, thinking, talking, reading, writing, spelling, or arithmetic. They include conditions which have been referred to as perceptual handicaps, brain injury, minimal brain dysfunction, dyslexia, developmental aphasia, etc. They do not include learning problems which are due primarily to visual, hearing, or motor handicaps, to mental retardation, emotional disturbance, or to environmental disadvantage.

More recently, Cruickshank (1976, p. 114) has suggested the term *perceptually handicapped with specific learning disabilities*, which refers to children who have a demonstrable deficiency of academic achievement that is the result of perceptual or perceptual-motor handicaps. Furthermore, the definition would accept children in this category without concern for etiology or other contributing factors. In Cruickshank's view, acceptance of this term would focus attention on perception and more clearly define a target group. This would require legal changes in current definitions and would extend special education to any child who experiences perceptual impairment, which would include mentally retarded children.

Gallagher (1976) suggests that the population must be better defined. He estimates that only a small group, less than 1%, of school children have specific learning disabilities, and they should be the special responsibility of special education. Such children would be described as having outstanding discrepancies in individual development, which leads to academic problems. Gallagher further contends that there are still major gaps in the knowledge about the nature of such children and, consequently, what must be done about them.

Kirk (1976) also expressed concern about the growth of the field of learning disabilities and believes that the mildly handicapped child should be educated in the regular education program with special education reserved for the more hard-core learning disabled children. He also considered "collapsing" the legal and definitional barriers that separate learning disabilities from mental retardation. This would pare down the current population that is being served by special education because the underachievers and mildly handicapped children would be removed from special programs and educated by the regular classroom teacher.

Some definitional clarification did take place late in 1975. In 1975 the Congress of the United States passed a highly significant new law, Public Law 94-142, which mandated comprehensive services for all handicapped children. (see Appendix A.) This law provided that, to prevent the states from attempting to call an unreasonable number of children "handicapped" to receive more federal funds, only 12% of the school-age enrollment could be served, at any one time, as handicapped with federal funds. The various handicapping conditions were named, and no restriction was placed on how many (what percentage) could be served under any of the handicapping conditions except learning disabilities. Because of the variations in interpretation of what the term *learning disabilities* really meant, schools were limited to serving no more than one sixth of those served as handicapped in programs designed for the learning disabled. In other words, no more than 2% of the *total* school population could be served as learning disabled. The congressional committee that worked on this law was openly concerned that too many children would be called *learning disabled*, and thus other handicapped children (mentally retarded, speech handicapped, and so forth) would not receive appropriate services from educators or their fair share of federal dollars. This unusual congressional action effectively illustrates the degree of very real concern for this definitional difficulty and some of the possible results.

As a part of this same law, the Office of Education was directed to better define learning disabilities and indicate how learning disabled children should be identified. Various proposals were made after extensive conferences with learning disabilities specialists throughout the nation. When it appeared that consensus had been reached on a new, more restrictive definition in late 1976, an official proposal was drafted and submitted for public review and comment. The proposal was criticized by many individuals and organizations and led to such disagreement and confusion that officials of the Bureau of Education for the Handicapped decided to retain the original, broad definition that had been the source of earlier controversy. As a result, the regulations for the implementation of P.L. 94-142, which were published in August, 1977, include only one significant change from the original definition—for purposes of receiving federal entitlements under P.L. 94-142, a maximum of 2% of the total school population can be included in the handicapped group of students who may benefit from federal funding. However, a recent change in rules and regulations re-

moves the 2% cap on learning disabled children while requiring new methods for evaluating such students.* The issues are still unresolved and definitional problems are certain to surface again. The problems of how to diagnose learning disabilities are serious.

Perhaps we will eventually agree that some definitions must be established primarily for the purpose of providing programs, rather than for the conciseness required to provide obvious focus for research efforts. At the very least, a practical definition could be used by the schools for purposes of assignment to special education programs. This would be a dispositional procedure that would de-emphasize the label, and the stigma associated with it, but that would permit programmatic variations to assist a portion of students greatly in need of special services. Professionals interested in research would be operating under a different set of definitional principles recognized in the need for sound experimental design and restrictive sample selection.

Disputes over terminology have been important in the history of learning disabilities because they have led to increased use of both research and theoretical speculation to question and/or defend various theories or points of view. This activity has led to a better understanding of what different theorists really believe and has generated benefits that have surpassed the immediate polemical concerns by increasing total available knowledge in the field. It is also obvious that there will continue to be controversy over definitions and that final decisions will inevitably affect the direction of special education. Most practitioners will undoubtedly cope with circumstances as they presently exist, attempting to serve students as effectively as possible and await future events.

In any event, the modern concept of learning disabilities has fused various categories as traditionally conceived, such as brain damage and developmental dyslexia, and eliminates the distinctions. As an *educational* concept, *learning disabilities* has focused atten-

---

*Federal Register, 1977, 42 (250).

tion on the remediation of learning problems of children, while allowing a continuance of the debate over etiology and more specific syndromes.

CHARACTERISTICS OF CHILDREN WITH LEARNING DISABILITIES

As is the case of mentally retarded children, certain characteristics have been associated with children who have been called learning disabled and have been employed as significant factors in screening, identification, and diagnosis. Some of these characteristics have been mentioned briefly in the section on definitions. The only common trait to be found among all children with learning disabilities is a discrepancy between apparent ability to learn and actual academic achievement. The characteristics of the learning disabled are generally considered to be either the reasons for or the results of the learning disability, but the presence of one or more of the characteristics discussed in this section does not "prove" the existence of a learning disability. Confusion and disagreement over terminology, semantics, and etiology have caused the group of learning disabled students (as they are presently defined) to be very heterogeneous with variations attributable to different theoretical viewpoints or to emphasis on some specific problem among the various educational problems exhibited by children. It is, therefore, not surprising that there is disagreement as to what should be considered as accepted characteristics that can be associated with learning disabilities. The suggestions of Cruickshank, Gallagher, and Kirk cited previously (p. 7) would delimit the group of learning disabled students to a more homogeneous group of children with many common characteristics as a result of the definition. But for the present, these are only suggestions.

Many of the characteristics to be discussed in the following section have been associated with other conditions of childhood such as mental retardation and certain highly specific organic brain pathologies. It may be presumptuous to assume that these characteristics are group characteristics, but they are characteristics often found among children presently considered to be learning disabled. Recent studies of such specialized areas as adulthood aphasia tend to disregard much of the old research in this field because new technology clearly indicates that most research designs were incapable of eliminating the confounding factors of diagnosis. For example, an aphasic with left temporal lobe damage cannot necessarily be compared with other aphasics who seem to have left hemispheric damage because the location of a lesion may be so different among the subjects that differing behavioral effects would make comparisons essentially useless. In a similar way, comparing groups of children with various types and/or degrees of hyperactivity may lead to faulty conclusions because of the difficulty in diagnosing hyperactivity. Connors (1971) has accumulated convincing evidence that indicates that there is more than one type of hyperactivity, thus any research conducted with children simply labeled hyperactive could offer results of questionable value. It may be wise to consider the emerging evidence about mental retardation that, in effect, cautions the acceptance of characteristics as individual or situation-specific until research proves otherwise. However, as indicated before, there are certain characteristics that appear to be found more often among those children and youth who have been called learning disabled than among the population as a whole. These characteristics are discussed as follows.

Hyperactivity

This characteristic has long been associated with learning disabilities. It has caused some confusion because of the variability of definitions, because there is no single test for hyperactivity, and because several methods of treatment have been proposed for its management. The literature uses the terms *hyperactivity*, *hyperkinesia*, and *hyperkinetic syndrome*. Physicians seem to prefer the term *hyperkinesis*. Unless other definitions are forthcoming, *hyperkinesis* and *hyperactivity* will probably continue to permeate the literature and will be used interchangeably.

Medical dictionaries make little distinction between the terms.

Hyperactive children appear to demonstrate inappropriate and abnormal levels of physical activity that may stem from a variety of factors including chemical imbalances, organic factors, or learned behavior. The condition has been controlled in certain children by diet, amphetamines, biofeedback, yoga, and behavior modification, but no one approach is effective in all cases. Although not as common a problem among students in the secondary schools (as among younger children), it is one characteristic usually associated with learning disabilities.

Short attention span

Many learning disabled children are described as being unable to attend to learning tasks for any length of time. Attention seems to wane rapidly, and the child tends to react abnormally (overreaction as compared with others his age) to any novel stimulation. Attention is easily distracted, and children so affected have difficulty finishing tasks because of such difficulties. Tarver and Hallahan (1974) reviewed 21 studies and concluded that learning disabled children do tend to be more distractable than normal children under certain conditions.

Perceptual disorders

Perceptual disorders have received considerable attention as factors in learning disabilities. Disorders of perception are manifested in the various sensory channels—visual, tactual, auditory. Whether caused by genetic inheritance, actual brain damage, or certain (presumed) learning factors, perceptual disorders are believed to result in disruption of the interpretation of sensory information by the brain. The functional integrity of the sensory organ is not questioned but, rather, the manner in which the subject perceives sensory information. A visual perceptual disorder is usually believed to account for the difficulty a child experiences in reversal of letters and numbers, inadequate reproduction of geometric designs, and poor handwriting. Auditory perceptual problems involve difficulty in discriminating between gross sounds, speech sounds, and separating or centering on target sounds in a noisy background. Cacophonous sounds in a classroom are believed to interfere with learning for some children with auditory perceptual problems.

Numerous tests and treatment methods for perceptual disorders have been developed in the last several years. Concentrated efforts of educators to correct perceptual disturbances of children have more recently created a controversy because some authorities believe that little educational benefit can be derived from noneducational strategies. Recent sophisticated research of the type reported by Ross (1976) reveals how simplistic certain educational conceptions of visual perception have been. It is, therefore, not too surprising that some remedial methods have been relatively ineffective.

Motor problems

Significant discrepancies in motor development and motor integration have been noted in some children with learning disabilities. These children are described as clumsy or awkward and seem to experience difficulty with many school-related tasks demanding motor coordination. The motor coordination problems have been largely divided into two groups for diagnosis and remediation—gross and fine. Some learning disabled children have gross motor incoordination that interferes with their ability to participate in normal physical education activities. Others have difficulty with fine motor problems, an obvious factor in writing and postulated as a problem in reading.

Many of the earliest learning disability programs were heavily based on the presumption of motor problems and on efforts to correct such problems. For very young children, an excellent case may be made for the belief that serious motor difficulties may inhibit the use of normal modes of environmental exploration and thus may retard the development of a sound basis for further learning. For older children this may not be true, but to the extent that motor problems reduce acceptance by other children and thus reduce ego development and normal self-respect, improvement in motor ability may be effective in enhancing learning (Cratty, 1969). As with other characteristics related to learning disabilities, etiologic and diagnostic controversies lead to considerable professional dispute and to differences in accepted remedial procedures.

Mixed lateral dominance

The development of the prehensile hand and the appositional thumb, the facility for language, and the asymmetry of the brain are major characteristics that separate the human being from the lower animals. In the adult human being, there is typically a development of preferential use of one side of the body. Unilateral hemispheric dominance for language functions has been recognized for some time as a result of investigations of brain damage in adults that have provided useful information about the nature and operation of the central nervous system. Much of this information is, however, of restricted use in the study of children.

It is widely accepted by medical authorities that the left hemisphere of the brain is the base of language functioning for most persons. It has also been considered important for a person to establish complete dominance (handedness, eyedness, footedness) on one side of the body. Consequently, many intervention programs in learning disabilities, particularly those in the early years of learning disabilities programming, stressed the importance of assisting young children to develop complete, unilateral dominance. However, as a result of more recent medical evidence, these assumptions are being questioned because many children and adults seem to have mixed-dominance without any particular problems in reading or academic achievement.

In cases in which a hemisphere has been diseased from early infancy or early childhood and later removed, there is often no evidence of language impairment (Lennenberg, 1966). This has led some to conclude that the hemispheres may have equal ability to develop language function. In any event, much remains to be learned before sound educational applications can be developed.

Memory disorders

Learning disabled children have noticeable and measurable difficulty with the basic process of memory. Memory has been investigated by many authorities, and it is still not clearly understood. Attempts to remediate disorders of memory have been mostly unsuccessful. The consequences of a memory disorder are among the most devastating for the learner, because any specific inability to acquire and retain information that is necessary in problem-solving behavior and long-term academic growth will eventuate in a persistent educational handicap. Many LD students demonstrate an inability to assimilate, store, and recall information.

Language disorders

Many children with learning disabilities have normal or near normal *spoken* language, although some have difficulties in this area. However, language disorders can relate to a number of areas of language. *Inner language* refers to a preverbal ability to internalize and organize experiences to provide a basis for later spoken and written language. Although it is unlikely that this will be seen at the secondary school level, it is altogether possible that a teacher may deal with a student at the secondary school level whose other language functions have been seriously impaired by early difficulties of this nature. However, *expressive language disorders* or *receptive language disorders*, which may be evidenced in either *oral* or *written language*, may be more evident in secondary school level students. In extreme cases, these disorders may be called *expressive* or *receptive aphasia*, when dealing with spoken language; these, too, are not very common disorders. Disorders of written language are the usual kind found in learning disabled adolescents. These are most often thought of in terms of lack of ability to write or read. Although not often conceptualized as such, severe reading disabilities are equally well described as severe written language disorders. In fact, if learning disabilities specialists think in terms of language development in addition to thinking of "reading skills," additional in-

sights may be garnered, in some cases, as to needed remedial or developmental approaches.

It is commonly agreed that language difficulties that are primarily caused by *speech disorders* (such as articulation, voice, or fluency difficulties) or by a lower-than-average mental ability are not considered learning disability correlates.

Many other characteristics have been associated with learning disabilities, a number of them developing out of the assessment practices used by school psychologists or diagnosticians. Children may show specific patterns of response on tests that seem to typify identifiable diagnostic entities, and it is not uncommon to encounter such descriptions as *auditory closure problems, sequential memory disorders*, or *coding problems*. Such terms derive from the jargon of professionals who frequently deal with learning disabilities and who tend to describe children in terms of the instruments they employ in assessment.

It must be reiterated that the characteristics usually related to learning disabilities are not necessarily group characteristics. Learning disabled children may have one or more of these characteristics, but in different combinations. It is not accurate or appropriate to regard two children with different patterns of abilities and disabilities as being diagnostically similar even though both are identified as learning disabled. Confusion over the label or the definition must be understood and appreciated by the practitioner because there is considerable potential for future problems because of the broad scope of the label or definition (Cruickshank, 1972). Perhaps the only learning disabilities definitional problem that would be more serious than making assumptions about similarities between children, just because they were both considered learning disabled, would be to assume that learning disabilities do not exist just because of such variations. If differences in the rate of learning and levels of achievement could be established as nothing more than predictable and natural developmental variations, then the concept of learning disabilities would be meaningless. However, if it is possible to isolate specific syndromes that have diagnostic and educational relevance, then the concept of learning disabilities has meaning and value transcending the confusion of the multitude of symptoms found with underachieving children.

Rutter and Yule (1973) compared groups of subjects who shared the common experience of poor reading achievement but who could be differentiated on the basis of other characteristics. Using probability theory, they estimated that only 2.28% of the students in a school-age population should be expected to read at levels as low as or lower than two standard deviations below the mean on tests of reading achievement. When the investigators used reading accuracy as a criterion, they discovered that 6.3% of the students in their sample actually had scores that low. When the criterion was reading comprehension, the incidence was as high as 9.3%.

It was concluded that there is a "large abnormal hump" on the normal distribution that is caused by the existence of a group of students having normal intelligence and severe reading disabilities. This evidence lends support to the concept of a specific reading retardation syndrome characterized by severe reading difficulties not accountable for in terms of low intelligence nor predictable in terms of the lower end of the continuum of a normal distribution of reading skills. The "severe reading disabilities group" with normal intelligence revealed a greater incidence of speech and language disorders, showed a highly disproportionate number of boys, and appeared less likely to improve in reading with experience. The "general backwardness group" evidenced developmental lag, showed only a slightly higher preponderance of boys, and tended to improve in reading with experience.

Although definitions that artificially set the cutoff point for classification of students at some low level of achievement will undoubtedly increase the likelihood of identifying students with severe problems, the nature of these problems will not necessarily be clear. Furthermore, intense research is necessary in the field of learning disabilities to ascertain specific syndromes in as much as this will be possible. Such findings would augment the efforts of diagnosticians and educators and would contribute to a general body of understanding that might hasten the development of an acceptable definition. The recent trend toward use of an ecological model (behaviorism and task analysis) is welcome in the classroom but perhaps should not be supported with such fervor that the expansion of knowledge in etiologies is abandoned.

THE TREND TOWARD SECONDARY PROGRAMMING

The wide acceptance of the field of learning disabilities is evidenced by the remarkable growth of programs at the elementary level since the early 1960s and the recent stress on preschool screening and intervention. By contrast, the development of programming at the junior and senior high school levels has been much more restricted. Scranton and Downs (1975) conducted a national survey of school districts to determine the scope of learning disability services. Of 37 reporting states it was revealed that although 40% of the districts offered elementary programs, only 9% offered educational programming at the secondary level. There are many possible causes for the slow rate of development of such programming, but it is apparent that the emphasis has been on early childhood and elementary programs. The various states have not differentiated between the certification of elementary and secondary specialists, and differences in the orientation of teachers and the focus of curricula at the two levels have been minimal.

The most distinctive feature characterizing secondary education that distinguishes it from elementary education is the emphasis on acquisition of knowledge in content areas of study. Few teachers in a typical secondary school have any formal training in teaching tool subjects. More important, perhaps, is the fact that few secondary teachers are experienced in methods of adapting the cur-

riculum or implementing accommodation techniques for students lacking in skills necessary for the accomplishment of course work. The elementary school program is expected to prepare each student with the basic training sufficient for more advanced educational pursuits. For the most part, secondary teachers are not likely to assume responsibility for the amelioration of basic academic deficiencies. Their training and their interests relate to subject areas, concept development, or specific vocational skills, rather than to reading skills, number concepts, or underlying factors in the environment and/or the student that might interfere with learning.

Special education practices at this level must be rooted in different competencies and a different orientation than would be expected in the elementary school. The specialist at the elementary level is usually able to communicate easily with regular classroom teachers because they share common training and a conventional purpose to teach students to acquire skills in basic reading,

writing, and arithmetic. The most common type of service delivery system in the elementary school seems to be the resource room. This arrangement is a natural extension of the regular classroom, the activities of the resource room can be integrated with the regular curriculum, and there is a great deal of carry-over from one setting to the other.

Several problems are associated with this approach at the secondary level because teachers tend to be divided by areas of specialization; they do not focus on individual differences of learners and they may misunderstand or question the value of special education. Many programs for the learning disabled at the secondary level appear to be imitations of the elementary school resource room. This approach is not usually satisfactory because it fails to involve the many regular classroom teachers and disregards the realities of the curriculum. The efforts of the specialist should be directed toward the immediate problems of the learner and provide for close interaction with the teachers and the specific course of study of each student.

Because there have been few models for delivery of secondary services to LD students and because university training programs have prepared specialists with an elementary emphasis, it is understandable that many fledgling secondary programs have relied on the elementary resource room as a pattern for imitation. If the school accepts a rather circumscribed purpose (to assist students only in the acquisition of basic skills in reading, arithmetic, and communication), then the traditional resource room might be sufficient. However, if the school recognizes and takes into account the special demands of the school curriculum on the learner, as well as the unique needs of adolescents, then a quite different type of programming may be needed. This is a very important consideration that is likely to be the pivotal point of controversy in secondary programming. Until such time that many options are explored and research is conducted on a wide scale, we shall have to rely on informed opinions and trial-and-error experimentation to design and implement appropriate secondary services.

The goals of the secondary LD program

To clarify the issues pertaining to the goals of the secondary LD program, consideration of the opinions of writers in the field who have taken positions about the nature and extent of secondary services is helpful.

Lerner (1976) suggests that the secondary school needs several options for delivering educational services. For some students it may be desirable to offer a self-contained classroom, while for others a special resource room may be more beneficial in providing services because the specialist can act as a liaison between teacher and counselor, student and parent. Moreover, the school may offer a variety of specially designed courses for students. Lerner asserts that resource teachers in high school learning disabilities programs "must be familiar with the entire curriculum of the school" (p. 38). This famili-

arity would enable the teacher to assist the students in a variety of courses because the students will not be satisfied with services that are not "directly" related to academic problems. Lerner concludes that "remediation must be closely tied to what is happening in the classroom" (p. 39).

Goodman and Mann (1976) take an opposite view. They propose a "basic education program" at the secondary level that restricts the activities of the specialist to the teaching of basics in mathematics and language arts. They would restrict enrollment of students to those who lack a full sixth-grade competency. The goal for the secondary specialist would be to ensure that all students reach mastery in mathematics and language arts, which is defined as sixth-grade achievement. They believe that when a student reaches the beginning of seventh-grade level performance integration in the regular program is possible. Furthermore, Goodman and Mann would delimit the activities of the specialist as clearly indicated in their remark that "specialists rarely have much to offer for problems in secondary school content areas. Let them shy away from areas where their training and skills are not relevant" (p. 46).

It should be clear that program options are somewhere between these two extremes, and the decision to develop one program or another may very well be determined by one's conceptualization of the goals of the secondary learning disabilities program and perception of the needs of the students. It would appear that if one approaches the problem from the students' point of view, at least two subgroups can be identified and that services for these subgroups should be somewhat different although each individual should be separately evaluated. One group of students, from a functional point of view, are so severely affected by deficiencies in basic skills that they are totally unequipped to function with any degree of proficiency in regular classes and content areas of study. Another group may be close to being able to function in content areas because of a higher level of achievement and academic ability. Both groups would find it very difficult, if not impossible, to function without assistance. There are many approaches, but generally it appears that an exclusive emphasis on continued remediation in reading and arithmetic is patently unsatisfactory. Students with normal intelligence, a prerequisite under current definitions, must be able to function in many classes if efficient and sufficient methods of instruction are employed. The overriding objective should be *to provide a system of instruction that reduces complexity without sacrificing quality.* If accommodation can be made for such students, as in the case of visually impaired students who succeed in school, then the problem of delivering services takes on a different meaning.

Since reading is a critical survival skill in school, it is not surprising that so many secondary programs will probably continue to emphasize remediation in this area. Many adolescents with histories of learning disabilities may develop sufficient skill in reading to manage some of the required reading. Typically, however, the student is very deficient in reading comprehension. Technically his reading may seem adequate but unless he is able to attack his assignments with understanding then his demonstrable achievement in reading, as determined by some test score, is of little importance. Lengthy reading and homework assignments begin to take their toll of the learner's limited ability and patience. The student simply cannot maintain the pace that his peers effortlessly keep as they respond to the demands of several teachers in different courses. Students with lower levels of reading ability are unhappily trapped in a situation in which they devote their energies to *learning to read* while their course work requires that they use *reading to learn.* We see limited value in the practice of students visiting the resource room for the single purpose of receiving remedial instruction in reading or arithmetic while they are expected to cope with the rigorous demands of several teachers and to glean meaning from textbooks that are far too difficult.

Moreover, the inability to successfully

pursue the traditional liberal arts education should not be used to justify assignment to a "manual arts" curriculum. Some learning disabled students *may* benefit from a "manual arts" program, but such an assignment must be based on a variety of factors, not simply on low-level reading or arithmetic skills. Equal educational opportunity should permit each student to benefit from academic training and career education to the maximum extent possible. Insufficiency in reading should not automatically deny a student the opportunity to participate and learn in an academic class nor should it limit the student to training that usually leads to entry-level skill in a low-status job.

A carefully balanced program would include the provision of specific remediation in addition to assistance in dealing with course work through accommodation to the learner's individual needs. We would suggest that the secondary specialist in learning disabilities be a person who is well-trained in the remediation of learning disabilities, who is familiar with the breadth and extent of the secondary curriculum, who can assume leadership as an advocate of students, who can act as a liaison between the students, school authorities, and the home, and who can assist in the modification and adaptation of learning experiences in the secondary curriculum. Such a person would *not* accept the premise that the *only* goal of education is to teach secondary learning disabled students to reach minimal levels of academic proficiency. This is only part of the purpose. Each student should also have the opportunity to profit from instruction in a variety of courses by means of alternative learning strategies. The verbal bias of our schools and our society should not artificially limit the pursuits of intelligent but inefficient learners.

The remainder of this book is devoted to the purpose of expanding the concept of LD programming at the secondary level as well as the opportunities and horizons for students who are unfortunately afflicted by learning disorders that too frequently create needless suffering.

Characteristics unique to adolescents with learning disabilities

Some might expect that adolescents with learning disabilities would be more readily identified because of blatant discrepancies in achievement over a period of years. It is true that older students have more opportunity, as a function of time, to demonstrate many problems that may come to the attention of teachers and parents. The confusion over the definition and the lack of interest in secondary learning disabled students has created a paucity of research relating to this issue. It is difficult, without explicit criteria, to review the histories of secondary students and confidently separate the learning disabled from other groups of students with lagging achievement.

It is also true that the lack of active case-finding efforts at the secondary level and the absence of services has created a situation in which many regular classroom teachers have become accustomed to the acceptance of most nonachieving students in their classes unless they exhibit disturbed or disruptive behavior. Without appropriate services the teacher would ordinarily tolerate the presence of underachievers because it would be unproductive to make a referral.

The prevalence of learning disabilities at the secondary level cannot be estimated with any degree of confidence until precise definitions based on research are developed. For now, it will be necessary to use general guidelines to identify LD students from among the general population of underachievers.

The concept of underachievement is historically tied to the concept of the achievement quotient (AQ). Using the student's capacity to learn (usually assumed to be the IQ), it was possible to compare actual achievement with expected achievement and determine significant discrepancies. This process has been popular with some learning disabilities specialists as well. This issue will be discussed at greater length in the chapter on assessment, but it should be stated briefly that (1) it is not possible to estimate with absolute accuracy a student's capacity to learn, (2) the IQ score cannot predict achievement expectancy with consistency even assuming that it can estimate capacity to learn, and (3) use of this system does not guarantee that the groups of underachievers and learning disabled students can be separated. Also, much of what has been learned about learning disabilities in younger children may simply not apply to older students. It is also unlikely that the use of arbitrary cutoff points, such as 4 or more years of academic retardation, using the grade level as the criterion, will do much more than ensure that the most seriously deficient students will be identified, thus sacrificing a number of mildly disabled students who could benefit from services.

Until we are able to use information that hopefully will result from further research, we may need to be content with the prevailing definitions with the added assurance that students appear to have inexplicable reasons that interfere with learning. Much remains to be accomplished as the following discussion should demonstrate.

In one of the earliest publications devoted to the subject of the adolescent with learning disabilities,* a number of writers expressed opinions about the special problems of the adolescent. Wilcox (1970) asserted that adolescents should be reidentified at the secondary level and stated that the criteria for identification change because maturity masks many overt mental and emotional traits and some primary symptoms tend to disappear at puberty. Wilcox noted the changes in characteristics for the older student as follows:

hyperactivity—The teenaged student responds to a number of influences (such as discipline and personal dignity) and controls the urge to engage in constant movement by restricting movement to tapping of fingers and feet, grimacing, or tics.

perceptual-motor impairments—Maturation is said to cause a form of compensation for dis-

---

*Anderson, L. E. (Ed.). Helping the adolescent with the hidden handicap, Los Angeles: California Association for Neurologically Handicapped Children, 1970.

ability in the sense of time, differentiation of size, and distance.

emotional lability—The adolescent persists in overreacting to stimuli. Although less aggressive, less restless, and less variable in mood, they are still unaware of their impact on others.

general coordination deficits—Although fine and gross motor coordination improves, handwriting remains poor.

attention—Although attention span lengthens, the student is unable to benefit from lecture periods and foreign language classes. The students are divided into "goof-offs" who distract others and the anxiety-ridden student who freezes and cannot concentrate for long.

impulsivity—Overreaction to stimuli persists with manifestations recognized in behavior such as the "loudest clapper" or the "uncontrolled sneezer."

memory and thinking—This may be the most marked and easily recognizable trait in adolescence. The student cannot think things through to completion, is disorganized in study routines and general school work, and should have a special study routine and a memory-training course.

specific learning disabilities—Specific language disorders are evident in reading, writing, and spelling and it is recommended that the student should be given help in spelling because this may be the most frequent residual difficulty after reading and writing skills are established.

equivocal neurological signs and EEG irregularities—Handedness should be established by adolescence and difficulties are usually noticed only in physical education activities. (pp. 7-9)

Weiss and Weiss (1974) approach the problem of the adolescent from the point of view of a developmental lag in learning abilities and have stated that subtle lags may be found in gross motor development, sensorimotor development, perceptual-motor development, language development, and conceptual skills. "All of the general symptoms noted in the child at an earlier age appear in a somewhat *altered manner* in the older child" (p. 4).

Thompson (1970) recognizes the developmental lag as an important factor in relationship to diagnostic practices because reliance on norm-referenced instruments inflates the incidence of students placed in special programs. Thompson contends that a developmental lag in reading of 1 to 3 years is not sufficient reason to regard a student as having a learning disorder and suggests that the school should permit students to develop at individual rates. Failure of an immature student to perform at levels beyond innate capacity during the developmental period is, according to Thompson, not truly a learning disorder but rather an unfortunate consequence of adherence to the norm-referenced system.

de Hirsch (1963) identified two major groups of adolescents with learning difficulties. One group experiences severe psychological disturbances that interfere with learning after initial success in the early grades of school. School performance begins to diminish in quality because of poor ego strength and physiological immaturity. The second group exhibits vestiges of language disorders recognized in early childhood. These subjects tend to show a higher performance ability than verbal ability on the Wechsler Intelligence Scale for Children (WISC), experience difficulty in written work, are inarticulate, defiant, and hostile, and have a low-frustration tolerance.

Hagin (1971) implicates specific language disabilities as evidence of persistent problems in adolescents who present the following characteristics: lack of neurological organization relating to cerebral dominance, visual-motor problems, auditory problems, poor concept of body image, and tactile figure-ground problems.

Lehtinen-Rogan (1971) believes that the adolescent with a perceptual handicap will experience a lessening of the problems most noticeable in childhood (i.e., reversals). The central nervous system is mature by the time the student is in secondary school, which enables the individual to develop compensatory behavior. Characteristics of LD students include distractability, inability to sustain attention, discontinuity of thought, poor feedback, poor organization, and deficient memory.

Nall (1969) identified the characteristics of adolescents with learning disabilities as short attention span, perseveration, deficient auditory memory, problems in visual perception, and distractibility.

Rourke et al (1973) selected a group of adults with known cerebral lesions and compared them with adolescents who demonstrated similar lateralized motor deficits. The adolescents were then given psychological tests and performed similarly to adults on psychometric measures. Because the performance of the adolescents with learning disabilities was comparable to that of adults with known lesions, it was concluded that learning disabilities in adolescents may be related to cerebral dysfunction.

Strother (1971) discussed divergent views on etiology and definitions of learning disabilities and concluded that diagnosis at the secondary level is confused by the overlap of emotional characteristics found in students with primary learning disabilities and those who are actually emotionally disturbed or whose *primary* difficulties relate to behavior problems. He suggested that the teacher should investigate learning disabilities by observing behaviors indicated by visual and auditory problems, hyperactivity, problems of conceptualization, and speech and writing disorders.

Dykman and Ackerman (1975) re-examined hyperactive adolescent boys who were originally identified as such while they were children and contrasted them with other groups. They concluded that many still showed problems of self-control and had experienced serious adjustment problems including the use of drugs, involvement in thefts, aggressive behavior, and family conflict. Achievement still lagged. Normoactive LD subjects (LD subjects with normal activity levels) tended to demonstrate a developmental neurological lag that began to disappear during adolescence. However, hyperactive and hypoactive groups continued to exhibit behavior that might be explained by longer lasting lags or structural dysfunction. All LD groups demonstrated depressions in performance on the Arithmetic, Coding, Information, and Digit Span subtests of the WISC.

Mendelson et al (1971) and Weiss et al (1971) conducted follow-up studies of adolescents previously diagnosed as hyperactive during childhood. They concluded that many of the characteristics found during childhood tend to disappear. Cohen et al (1972) examined cognitive styles in adolescents who were previously diagnosed as hyperactive and concluded that the subjects showed a pattern of inefficient approach to problem solving similar to the approach of younger hyperactive subjects. Training in impulse control and attention was considered important for adolescents.

The only defensible generalization that may be made about the preceding research is that results tend to be ambiguous and present conclusions must be considered tentative. There appears to be considerable support for the opinion that when we speak of adolescent learning disabled students we are in fact speaking of a variety of groups, not one discrete group. Perhaps this is unavoidable, given the present definition(s) of learning disabilities.

SUMMARY

Learning disabilities has different meanings to different segments of the population because of the broadness and vagueness of the currently accepted definition. Much of the history of the current learning disabilities concept relates to perceptual disabilities, brain injury (or at least the symptoms usually related to brain injury), and/or hyperactivity. However, the presently accepted definition is related more to the educational manifestations of learning disabilities than to causal factors—a fact that many research oriented professionals find difficult to accept.

Nearly all of the early programming for learning disabled students was provided at the elementary school level, and thus the diagnostic tools, educational methods, and service delivery patterns were developed for this age group. Secondary school programs have been initiated, but there is even less agreement as to what to do and how to do it than at the elementary age level. Many secondary programs are simply carbon copies of the elementary programs in the same school district and, in most cases, this has been something less than satisfactory. The nature of the secondary school and the nature and characteristics of the adolescents it serves seem to dictate a different type of program.

Despite the fact that there is little research relating to adolescents with learning disabilities, certain definable trends of thought are present concerning the characteristics and the nature of the adolescent with learning disabilities. Present conclusions are based on either limited research evidence or authoritative opinion. A summarization of these trends is as follows:

1. *One major point of view is that many adolescents seem to overcome learning disabilities as a result of maturation of the central nervous system.* This is based on the assumption that learning disabilities are caused primarily by delayed development of the central nervous system and may logically lead to the conclusion that if we are to serve such students (as learning disabled) we are serving the "leftover" academic deficits, not a basic, provable learning disability. Other writers indicate that most of the learning disabilities characteristics disappear with age but do not assume central nervous system maturation as the cause for this disappearance. Educational implications for this point of view are essentially the same as if the delayed developmental assumption is made.

2. *A second major point of view is that learning disabled adolescents exhibit vestigial remains of characteristics recognized in childhood that can be attributed to central nervous system damage or dysfunction that does not appreciably improve.* This view leads to a somewhat different system of identification of learning disabilities in adolescence and may or may not lead to different programming than that based on the point of view discussed in the preceding paragraphs. Other writers indicate that most characteristics of learning disabilities remain at maturity, although in some altered form. These writers base part of their belief on re-

search and part on "expert opinion" and subjective observation.

3. One minor view suggests that learning disabilities may actually begin during adolescence after a normal childhood. This may be related (causally) to any of a variety of factors such as body chemistry, purely affective components, or actual brain insult.

We would suggest that all three trends are quite feasible and that whichever group, groups, or subgroups are eventually called *learning disabled* for programmatic purposes may depend more on factors such as funding, parent power, and the availability of other adapted programs within the secondary school than on unequivocal research results. Be that as it may, teachers of learning disabled students must have a basic understanding of these variables to be more effective in their assigned educational tasks, particularly if, during their professional career, they may work in different parts of the nation where considerable variations may exist.

The remainder of this book provides the teacher with practical information that will be useful in the development and implementation of programs regardless of future developments in the debate over the nature of learning disabilities in adolescents. We believe that it is essential that any teacher who elects to work with secondary school students should have knowledge and specific competencies related to the period of adolescence in human development and to the nature of the secondary school. The secondary learning disabilities specialist must have a functional knowledge of the variety of course offerings at the secondary level, deal effectively with the learning, social, and emotional needs of students, coordinate programs for individual students among several teachers, work closely with the parents and ancillary personnel, modify the regular curriculum and offer a variety of accommodation techniques to each student, and relate the remediation of basic skills to regular classroom instruction.

The following chapters discuss the nature of the adolescent, the secondary school, assessment, remediation, accommodation, behavior management, career education, and counseling. A final section about existing secondary school programs, both public and private, and attempts to provide for the learning disabled student at the postsecondary level concludes this book.

DISCUSSION QUESTIONS

1. What factors contribute to the confusion that exists in defining learning disabilities?
2. Discuss why the definition of learning disabilities that might be used for determination of school placement would be inadequate in research.
3. What implications for school programming and allocation of resources would follow from the acceptance of Cruickshank's proposed definition of learning disabilities?
4. Why might the characteristics used to describe young children with learning disabilities be inappropriate for adolescents?
5. Contrast Lerner's view of the role of the secondary teacher of learning disabled students with that of Goodman and Mann.

REFERENCES AND READINGS

Bateman, B. An educator's view of a diagnostic approach to learning disorders. In J. Hellmuth (Ed.), *Learning disorders* (Vol. 1). Seattle: Special Child Publications, 1965.

Chalfant, J., and Scheffelin, M. *Central processing dysfunction in children: A review of research.* (NINDS Monograph No. 9). Washington, D.C.: U.S. Government Printing Office, 1969.

Clements, S. D., and Peters, J. E. Minimal brain dysfunctions in the school-age child. *Archives of General Psychiatry*, 1962, *6*, 185-197.

Clements, S. D. *Minimal brain dysfunction in children: Terminology and identification, phase one of a three-phase project* (NINDS Monograph No. 3) Washington, D.C.: U.S. Government Printing Office, 1966.

Cohen, N. J., et al. Cognitive styles in adolescents previously diagnosed as hyperactive. *Journal of Child Psychology and Psychiatry*, 1972, *13*(3), 203-209.

Conners, C. Recent drug studies with hyperkinetic children. *Journal of Learning Disabilities*, 1971, *4*(9), 476-483.

Critchley, M. *The dyslexic child* (2nd ed.). Springfield, Ill.: Charles C Thomas, Publisher, 1970.

Cruickshank, W. M. Some issues facing the field of learning disability. *Journal of Learning Disabilities*, 1972, *5*(7), 380-388.

Cruickshank, W. M. (Personal perspectives). In J. M. Kauffman and D. P. Hallahan (Eds.), *Teaching children with learning disabilities*. Columbus, Ohio: Charles E. Merrill Publishing Co., 1976.

Cratty, B. *Perceptual-motor behavior and educational processes.* Springfield, Ill.: Charles C Thomas, Publisher, 1969.

de Hirsch, K. Two categories of learning difficulties in adolescents. *American Journal of Orthopsychiatry*, 1963, *33*, 87-91.

Dorney, W. The effectiveness of reading instruction in the modification of attitudes of adolescent delinquent boys. *Journal of Educational Research*, 1967, *60*, 438-443.

Dykman, R. A. and Ackerman, P. T. Hyperactive boys as adolescents. Unpublished paper, 1975.

Eisenberg, L. Psychiatric implications of brain damage in children. *Psychiatry Quarterly*, 1957, *31*, 72-92.

Gallagher, J. J. (Personal Perspectives). In J. M. Kauffman and D. P. Hallahan (Eds.), *Teaching children with learning disabilities*. Columbus, Ohio: Charles E. Merrill Publishing Co., 1976.

Gesell, A., and Amatruda, C. S. *Developmental diagnosis* (2nd ed.). New York: Hoeber Publishing Co., 1947.

Goodman, L., and Mann, L. *Learning disabilities in the secondary school.* New York: Grune & Stratton, Inc., 1976.

Hagin, R. A. How do we find him? In E. Schloss (Ed.), *The educator's enigma: The adolescent with learning disabilities.* San Rafael, Calif.: Academic Therapy Publications, 1971.

Hallgren, B. Specific dyslexia ("congenital word-blindness"): clinical and genetic study. *Acta Psychiatrica Scandinavica*, 1950, Suppl. 65, 1-287.

Hinshelwood, J. *Congenital word-blindness.* London: M. K. Lewis & Co. Ltd., 1917.

Johnson, D., and Myklebust, H. *Learning disabilities: Educational principles and practices.* New York: Grune & Stratton, Inc., 1967.

Kirk, S. A. *Educating exceptional children.* Boston: Houghton Mifflin Co., 1962.

Kirk, S. A. Behavioral diagnosis and remediation of learning disabilities. Proceedings of the Conference on Exploration into the Problems of the Perceptually Handicapped Child, First Annual Meeting, Vol. 1, Chicago, 1963.

Kirk, S. A. (Personal Perspectives). In J. M. Kauffman and D. P. Hallahan (Eds.), *Teaching children with learning disabilities.* Columbus, Ohio, Charles E. Merrill Publishing Co., 1976.

Lehtinen-Rogan, L. E. How do we teach him? In E. Schloss (Ed.), *The educator's enigma: The adolescent with learning disabilities.* San Rafael, Calif.: Academic Therapy Publications, 1971.

Lennenberg, E. Speech development: Its anatomical and physiological concomitants. In E. Carterette (Ed.), *Brain function,* (Vol. 3). Berkeley: University of California Press, 1966.

Lerner, J. W. *Children with learning disabilities* (2nd ed.). Boston: Houghton Mifflin Co., 1976.

Mendelson, W., et al. Hyperactive boys as teenagers: A follow-up study. *Journal of Nervous and Mental Diseases*, 1971, *153*, 273-279.

Morgan, W. P. A case of congenital word blindness. *British Medical Journal*, 1896, *2*, 1378.

Nall, A. The adolescent with learning disability. In *Progress in parent information, professional growth, and public policy.* Proceedings of the Sixth Annual Conference, ACLD, Fort Worth, 1969.

National Advisory Committee on Handicapped Children, *Special Education for Handicapped Children.* First Annual Report, Washington, D.C.: U.S. Department of Health, Education and Welfare, 1968.

Orton, S. T. *Reading, writing, and speech problems in children.* New York: W. W. Norton & Co., Inc., 1937.

Paine, R. S. Minimal chronic brain syndromes in children. *Developmental Medicine and Child Neurology,* 1962, *4,* 21-27.

Penfield, W., and Roberts, L. *Speech and brain mechanisms.* New York: Atheneum Publishers, 1966.

Peters, J. E., and Clements, S. D. Multiple causality: Toward clarification of the diagnostic dilemma in child guidance (Part 2). In J. Hellmuth (Ed.), *Learning Disorders* (Vol. 1), Seattle: Special Child Publications, 1965.

Ross, J. The resources of binocular perception. *Scientific American,* 1976, *234*(3), 80-87.

Rourke, B. P., et al. Neuropsychological significance of lateralized deficits on the grooved pegboard test for older children with learning disabilities. *Journal of Consulting and Clinical Psychology,* 1973, *41,* 128-134.

Rutter, M., and Yule, W. The concept of specific reading retardation. Unpublished manuscript, 1973.

Schain, R. J. *Neurology of childhood learning disorders.* Baltimore: The Williams & Wilkins Co., 1972.

Scranton, T., and Downs, M. Elementary and secondary learning disabilities programs in the U.S.: A survey. *Journal of Learning Disabilities,* 1975, *8*(6), 394-399.

Strauss, A. A., and Lehtinen, L. E. *Psychopatholgoy and education of the brain-injured child.* New York: Grune & Stratton, Inc., 1947.

Strother, C. R. Who is he? In E. Schloss (Ed.), *The educator's enigma: The adolescent with learning disabilities.* San Rafael, Calif.: Academic Therapy Publications, 1971.

Tarver, S. G., and Hallahan, D. P. Attention deficits in children with learning disabilities: A review. *Journal of Learning Disabilities,* 1974, *7*(9), 560-569.

Thompson, A. Moving toward adulthood. In L. Anderson (Ed.), *Helping the adolescent with the hidden handicap.* Los Angeles: California Association for Neurologically Handicapped Children, 1970.

Thompson, L. J. *Reading disability.* Springfield, Ill.: Charles C Thomas, Publisher, 1966.

Weiss, G., et al. Studies on the hyperactive child: A five-year followup. *Archives of General Psychiatry,* 1971, (24), 409-414.

Weiss, H. G., and Weiss, M. S. *A survival manual.* Great Barrington, Mass.: Treehouse Associates, 1974.

Wilcox, E. Identifying characteristics of the NH adolescent. In L. E. Anderson (Ed.), *Helping the adolescent with the hidden handicap.* Los Angeles: California Association for Neurologically Handicapped Children, 1970.

Zangwill, O. The current status of cerebral dominance. In D. McKrioch and E. Weinstein (Eds.), *Disorders of communication.* Baltimore: The Williams & Wilkins, Co., 1964.

CHAPTER 2

Adolescence

INTRODUCTION

An examination of the period of adolescence in human development can contribute much to an understanding of learning disabilities in secondary school–age students. The educators who plan to work with adolescents with learning disabilities must first understand them. They must not confuse the characteristics of younger children with those of adolescents. The older student must be understood initially as a person with different needs, interests, abilities, and problems than his younger counterpart. Educational practices must be carefully differentiated from those that are applied with younger children. Many of the traditional approaches to educating the young child with a learning disability (for example, process training, certain aspects of behavior modification) may be inappropriate or need to be substantially altered for use with older students. The hierarchy of needs and the applicable reward system for any particular adolescent may be highly complex. The nature of adolescence should be carefully considered when shaping educational plans.

Growth of the study of adolescence has been slow and erratic primarily because most early investigations in psychology became sidetracked by the growing preoccupation with the study of childhood and infancy. Psychoeducational research in this area must be increased because much more information is needed to understand the adolescent and especially because of a lack of knowledge about the adolescent with a learning disability.

VIEWS OF ADOLESCENCE

As with other concepts in sociology and education, it is difficult to offer a definition of adolescence that would be commonly accepted. This relates in part to the variety of orientations of the theorists who study adolescence and the purposes for which definitions are made. For example, some have investigated adolescence as a period of significant physiological change and development of sexual roles occurring with puberty. Many investigators have been concerned with such diverse aspects of adolescence as cognition, morality, delinquency, and the so-called adolescent subculture. Psychological theories dominated early theoretical speculation about adolescence, but sociological studies have become more prominent in recent years because of such phenomena as delinquency, drug abuse, and the new sexual morality. As the culture has changed, it has been necessary to adjust our views of adolescence.

Adolescence has been defined operationally, and rather simplistically, as a period of significant biological change. It is a time when the body of a child is transformed into that of an adult by natural processes of maturation. This straightforward definition has remarkable validity because it centers on observable changes that are easily identified and measured. The comparatively gradual growth pattern of childhood erupts into furious development with dramatic changes in body size and shape as well as the appearance of secondary sexual characteristics. These changes have interested many investigators who have amassed tables of normative data concerning the age at menarche (the first menstrual period), rate of weight gain, phases of growth spurts, and numerous other facts. Normative data of this type clearly distinguishes the period of adolescence from other stages of human development. However, there are many ways of viewing adolescence and the description of the maturational processes of this period are insufficient to fully describe or to define it.

Physiology of adolescence

Physiologically it is possible to delineate specific stages of growth and development along a continuum from birth to death. It is interesting that the period of adolescence is commonly regarded as a unitary span of time even though there is ample physiological, psychological, and social information to support the division of adolescence into two general periods. Eichorn (1966) calls the period between 10 and 13 years of age *transescence*. Adolescence, per se, begins after this period.

Transescence is a stage of development that extends from the time just prior to the beginning of puberty to the early phases of adolescence. Children in this group tend to share common physical, emotional, social, and intellectual characteristics. The most important aspect of the period is transition. The sudden transition from childhood to pubescence is unsettling. The transescent experiences rapid physical change; a relatively stable period of development is not regained until the early phases of adolescence at which time the rate of change is similar to the slower rate experienced prior to transescence. The different characteristics and psychological aspects of transescence seem to justify the organization of such groupings as the middle school and the junior high school.

Although research has been limited because of an apparent emphasis on the investigation of other age groups, some very interesting information became available as a result of the Boyce Medical Study (1969). Medical examinations were conducted at the Boyce Middle School of Upper St. Clair, Pennsylvania. Ten physicians, aides, nurses, and technicians administered a variety of examinations to 232 boys and 255 girls. The subjects ranged in age from 10.1 to 14.0 years. The major purposes of the study were to determine the level of biological maturation and condition of health for each subject and to evaluate the medical findings.

Developmental age was determined by measurements of skeletal age, blood samples, urinalysis, height and weight, and development of the reproductive systems. Developmental status for each subject was determined through a classification system that assigned each subject to one of five categories based on a continuum from no evidence of secondary sexual characteristics (Level I) to complete development of secondary sexual characteristics (Level V). Although there was significant individual variability, that is, some younger children surpassed older ones, remarkable differences were found between boys and girls. Two distinct groups emerged within this chronological age range comprised primarily of relatively mature females in one group and immature males in the other. Sixty-two percent of the boys were classified in Levels I and II, whereas only 14% were classified in Levels IV and V. Fifty-seven percent of the girls were classified in Levels III, IV, and V. Although these results are not surprising, confirming, as they do, other research concerning the maturational superiority of females, they do reveal that such differences

continue to exist even though the subjects in this study were from families in which they undoubtedly benefitted from a high level of health care and nutrition. Such data as these should clearly indicate that there are, in fact, two distinct groups (maturationally) within the middle school and the junior high school. The majority of males develop at a slower pace, as measured by developmental age, and this rate of development may account for the higher incidence of school "failure" as unrealistic academic expectations are made. Stated another way, it may be reasonable to expect significantly lower levels of academic achievement in boys and regard such performance as normal. Therefore, it seems reasonable to anticipate and accept lower than average levels of academic achievement from many boys and some girls, especially during the time from the fifth through the ninth grades. In any event, teachers should be very cautious about the use of chronological age alone for classification purposes because it is relatively unreliable and fosters unrealistic expectations.

The period of transescence is, therefore, a short time period during which the transescent experiences significant growth and rapid physiological changes. The period ends when the subject reaches a level of stabilization during the early part of adolescence when physiological development is relatively complete.

In a more technical sense, physiological changes during transescence result from increased, rather than new, hormonal activity (Kulin, 1974). The endocrine system secretes larger quantities of hormones into the bloodstream, which dramatically affect development of the body and the personality. Although much of the activity of the endocrine system is not fully understood, it is clear that the activity of the pituitary gland, the hypothalamus, and the gonads cause changes that alter the structure and functioning of the human body.

Puberty is generally measured by signs of sexual change, however. This is more clearcut in girls than in boys. In the female, enlargement of the breasts is usually accompanied or preceded by the appearance of pubic hair. Authorities in the area of human development tend to accept menarche as indisputable evidence of puberty although the individual may not actually be sexually fertile. Most girls reach menarche by 11 or 12 years of age.

There is no primary sign in the maturational process of males. An increase in the growth of the testes and scrotum are indicative, as is the appearance of pubic, body, and facial hair; but these events do not usually coincide. There is much variability in the appearance of these signs, and pubertal development tends to occur more slowly in males.

Maturation also brings about a final development of the brain and this complex organ plays an important role in the functioning of the person, in development, and in the ability to interact intelligently with the environment. It is known that the brain responds to hormones in the bloodstream that are released during puberty, but this, along with other mysteries of the brain, is not fully understood.

Growth stages of the brain became more fully understood following the studies of Dobbing and Smart (1974), who examined human brains in fetuses, neonates, and young children. The brain grows in two major identifiable stages. Initially, there is a spurt of growth between the tenth and eighteenth weeks of gestation and from the twentieth week of gestation until 2 years after birth. Both stages are obviously important in intellectual development, but the second stage is believed to leave the organism most vulnerable to damage as a result of nutritional deficiency.

The brain is, in a sense, two functioning brains because of the discrete processes associated with each hemisphere (Sperry, 1975). The hemispheres are connected by an intricate network of fibers, the *corpus callosum*. Cognitive functions believed to be associated with the left hemisphere are calculation of difficult arithmetic problems and logic involving verbal reasoning and mathematics. By contrast, the right hemisphere

processes spatial relations, creative and artistic thinking, and simple arithmetic computations. Luria (1973) contends that higher order specialization of the hemispheres does not occur until about 10 years of age, at which time language functions are firmly associated with the left hemisphere.

The effects of nutritional deficiency are especially devastating in brain development as Cragg (1974) discovered in the examination of brain tissues of nourished and malnourished animals. He determined that malnourished animals experienced a reduction of significant proportions in synaptic development. If synapses, the interconnections of neurons in the central nervous system, do not function properly, serious consequences for intellectual development can follow.

The primary nutritional concern in adolescence is that the individual take in sufficient quantities of protein and other nutrients to sustain and maintain final growth. There has been considerable concern about the quality of teenage diets. Certain dietary factors may diminish development and functioning with serious consequences for health and learning. In the Boyce study, it was determined that as many as 8% of the students had extremely high levels of cholesterol.

The results of some controversial research (Hoeffer, 1971; Cott, 1971, 1972; and Powers, 1974) have identified dietary substances that may contribute to hyperactivity and other conditions that interfere with learning. It is believed that food additives, such as food dyes, and other natural substances may cause metabolic imbalances and allergic reactions. Caffeine and sugar have been indicted by a number of investigators. The ingestion of coffee, chocolate, candy, soft drinks, and junk foods has been implicated because these foods may cause excitement, irritability, overactivity, nervousness, headaches, and a variety of other physiological reactions. At least in theory, many substances that appear in the diet of today's adolescents may have profound adverse influences on the chemistry of the brain and the body.

In this area, as in so many others relating to adolescents and those with learning disabilities, there is simply very little information to clarify important issues about the symptomatology and characteristics of various conditions. For example, the authoritative remarks that occasionally appear in the literature about the transformed nature of the hyperactive child during adolescence cannot be supported by research. The studies to date are equivocal. There is such a paucity of research that it is necessary to draw only tentative conclusions about many characteristics of adolescents.

It would undoubtedly be of great value if more medical research were conducted for use in educational planning and programming. Schools tend to classify students in age–grade groups and to expect similar levels of achievement. It is obvious that this practice will not ensure the derivation of logical groupings for educational purposes. In another vein, there is little or no significant physiological research with the learning disabled adolescent. There is a critical need for much more research in the immediate future.

An evolutionary view of adolescence

Hall (1904) has been celebrated as the originator of the psychology of adolescence. His views were strongly influenced by the theories of Darwin. In rejecting psychoanalytic theories of infantile sexuality, he sought a rationale to explain the development of the human being from infancy to adolescence. The evolutionary concept seemed to satisfy his requirements, because the stages of human development could be neatly ordered along a continuum of phylogenetic development that had been promulgated by Darwinian theorists of his time. Whereas it was believed that the human being evolved from lower forms of life, it was accepted that the intrauterine growth of the unborn child reflected the many stages of phylogenetic development recapitulating ancestral history through the various stages of nonhuman life forms.

Hall introduced the concept that the many stages of development after birth were also reflective of ancestral history. The infant was likened unto a primate, the child to a more primitive form of early man, and the adolescent represented the transition to civilization. This transitional period was depicted as one of "storm and stress" and, if nothing else, the storm and stress characterization of adolescence has remained as a predominant factor influencing contemporary views of adolescence. Hall's preoccupation with adolescence was a result of his belief that the period of childhood was controlled by a rigid biological plan that could not be greatly affected by intervention. However, adolescence was regarded as more flexible and subject to the influence of training.

It is noteworthy that when the field of psychology began to emerge with many theories about the nature of intelligence and learning, emphasis was placed on the study of animals, infants, and *young* children. The development of behaviorism soon shifted attention away from theoretical constructs to observable, measurable behaviors. The psychoanalytic theories of Freud soon embraced a host of followers who stressed the importance of infantile sexuality and regarded adolescence as a less significant period of development. Hence, Hall's evolutionary concept of development fell into disuse.

Psychoanalytic theories

Adolescence was viewed by Freud as a period of turbulence, or storm and stress, but for different reasons than Hall. According to Freud, the greatest adjustment problem of the adolescent is to accommodate to the re-emergence of long suppressed sexual instincts that were originally managed in childhood as a result of the incomplete resolution of the Oedipal complex. Adolescence is a new battleground for old struggles. Adjustment in the adult is determined more by the conflicts of childhood than those of adolescence. The stressful nature of adolescence is simply the result of the resurgence of primitive instincts created by the imbalance stimulated by biological change. The ego needs to develop a new strength to check the stirring, primitive drives. It is therefore regarded as normal for the adolescent to be troubled, aggressive, uncertain, and to engage in conflict with parents and other adults because of the turmoil over sexual instincts and the need to seek emancipation from the domination of adults.

Neopsychoanalytic theories invoke an elaboration of the older theories to explain the turmoil of adolescence. The greatest challenge *to the individual* is to develop a sense of identity at the same time that resolution of sexual drives is accomplished by attaching sexual impulses to individuals outside the family unit. Erickson (1968) contends that the primary task of the adolescent is to develop autonomy that allows development of relationships with others. The adolescent must also accept a system of values, learn to engage in *intimate* relationships with others, enter into partnerships, and develop an individual sense of identity and relate this meaningfully to the world. With regard to the discussion of transescence earlier in the chapter, application of Erickson's view would lead one to believe that the major task of transescence is to establish a sense of sexuality while adolescence continues the process with a more complete development of self-identity.

Cross-cultural views

Many writers consider adolescence to be a period of turmoil. Since Hall's characterization of "storm and stress," many different theorists have accepted this trait although frequently with different explanations. The psychoanalytic view, for example, considers stress to be normal because of the underlying natural causes for it. Presumably, the absence of turmoil and stress in an adolescent would be indicative of abnormal development. Regardless of professional speculation, it seems that many lay persons would consider the adolescent to be in a troubled and volatile stage of development. Parents are distressed by the frequent arguments and emotional outbursts in the home, teachers often complain about the aggressive behavior of students, delinquency and vandalism are pervasive problems, and the inter-action between boys and girls is often less than placid.

Mead (1928) questioned the validity of the storm and stress characterization as a result of her observations of the Samoan culture in which she concluded that children entered adolescence and then adulthood with remarkable calm rather than stress. This shattered the ethnocentric view that traits of adolescence were universal, which in turn refuted the basic tenets of the predominant theories. Physiological change and the development of sexual maturity and desire seem to be the only universal features of adolescence. Sex roles are learned, however, and the concepts of femininity and masculinity are quite different among cultures. There is a dissimilarity in the relationship of children to parents when comparisons are made; hence, a difference in the status of the adolescent.

The influences of a particular culture dictate the nature of sex roles and the status of individuals; mores define and shape acceptable behavior. Therefore, depending on the culture, the social mix of mores and folkways can apparently cause adolescence to be stressful or quite placid.

Storm and stress may very well be associated with adolescence in the industrialized nations for reasons peculiar to economic factors. The adolescent in America is financially dependent on the family long after emotional dependence is weakened. If young adults were able to secure gainful employment (as they once could in America and still can in many nonindustrialized nations), independence might be more readily achieved and adolescence would be more purely a matter of biology.

Adolescents in urban–industrialized nations tend to acquire a sense of identity as preparations are undertaken for occupations and careers. Erickson (1968) speaks of identity in abstract terms that have practical application. Although his theories are relevant it should be recognized that one's identity is determined, to a great extent, by one's vocational status. Green (1973) notes that we tend to ask children, "What do you

want to be when you grow up?" rather than "How do you expect to make your living?" Identity for the adult is largely determined and dominated by occupational endeavors and professional status.

This may explain the difficulty associated with the inability to earn significant amounts of money. Parents must finance the major portion of all adolescent activities, and he who controls the finances exerts other forms of control. This relationship establishes a power structure that is superimposed on the natural control parents assume as a responsibility of parenthood. The adolescent's quest for emancipation is curtailed by the inability to earn money that would permit inde-

pendence even though all other forms of dependency on the family unit may be resolved. Child labor laws, the need for advanced education and training, and other limiting factors (not the least of which may be the need of society to artificially limit the size of the labor force) prolong adolescence.

If identity is related to occupational preparation, then a critical consideration for the LD student is whether school practices (for example, requirements for specific levels of achievement for graduation or permission for advanced training) may contribute to the identity crisis. The prerequisite for entry-level credentials (a diploma) in the labor market is particularly problematic for some students. The work–study program has been promoted in some schools for the educable mentally retarded student so that most students can earn a diploma or its equivalent as well as gaining vocational competencies. Learning disabled students have not universally enjoyed this option but it is presently under consideration by some schools. Poor achievement denies academic success, academic failure prevents the acquisition of academic credentials, and this shuts off many avenues of occupational potential. This may lead to the ultimate identity crisis in our society that is so often counteracted by engaging in crime, drug abuse, and other forms of behavior regarded as deviant. Such a result obviously depends on many personal and environmental factors, but it should be obvious that failure in school is related to forces that drive students away from acceptable social goals.

In any event, the behavior of adolescents is best understood in terms of the cultures in which it is displayed. Although there are remarkable similarities in the *biological* development of adolescents in various parts of the world, the rich variety of social customs forces the acceptance of a wider view that defies simple definition or description.

Social learning theory

Social learning theory, based on the work of Rotter (1954), proposes that an individual learns through social reinforcement in accordance with the internal–external loci of control. Reinforcement may occur as a result of a sense of personal determination (internal locus of control) or as the result of external factors such as luck, providence, or the control of others (external locus of control). Theoretically, this approach can be applied to the study of the development of the personality and to the instructional setting of the secondary school. Since the formulation of this theory, a number of studies have been conducted with adults, children, and handicapped children. A great deal of interest has been stimulated by research contrasting mentally retarded subjects with normal subjects (Kolstoe, 1972; Lawrence and

Winschell, 1975), but very little research has been conducted with learning disabled persons.

In essence, social learning theory proposes that young children tend to develop a view of the world as it pertains to success and failure. Eventually, the child must develop a conceptualization of standards and then compare himself with them. Before this occurs the child has no real concept of success or failure. The young child interprets success in terms of adult standards. The child is externally controlled and will engage in activities that are defined and rewarded by adults.

As children mature, they seek other avenues of approval (primarily from the peer culture) and accept peer values. As the child matures and internalizes the locus of control, the criteria for success or failure become more personally determined although the individual remains aware of externally established standards. Continuous and unrelenting failure may force the student into withdrawal from any situation that tends to be competitive. This may have a strong, detrimental effect on learning disabled students who continually meet with failure and failure-producing situations. In a study of elementary LD students, it has been demonstrated that failure reduces the performance activity of externally controlled subjects (Hisama, 1976).

The tendency to develop success-striving activity or to avoid failure by refusing to take risks is determined by a complex set of factors that includes the relationships of the ability to perform, the nature of the learning task, feedback information, and reward systems. The child who attempts learning activities that are challenging but not impossible and who is informed of failure and rewarded for success, will have an opportunity to develop a realistic self-concept, be aware of personal strengths, and rationally view the world. Because of the many factors that prevent academic success, the LD adolescent may suffer a retardation of development toward internal locus of control. This may cause the student to be more vulnerable to the influences of the peer culture and, later, of the counterculture.

Festinger (1954) proposed that is is important for a person to verify information to develop a sense of identity and a stable image of the world. We can verify certain kinds of information rather directly by experimenting with physical objects, an activity that occupies much of a child's time. Verification of more abstract concepts, such as beliefs, judgments, and values, must be made by comparison with others. A person may toss a ball far into the distance, compose a poem, or paint a picture, but there is no way of determining how "well" one has done unless there is a standard for comparison. Standards are generally determined by other persons and by records. Less explicit, but certainly understood, are standards of beauty and excellence that are determined by the interaction of tradition and cultural imperatives. People seek out others who are like them in some way such as race, social status, cultural background, and psychological states to confirm their beliefs.

The nature of learning disabilities is such that comparisons with others can leave one with a sense of inferiority unless such inadequacies can be compensated for or offset by success in other areas. A very poor reader is obviously academically inferior to others in the school. The myriad of academic tasks that can be successfully managed by normal students are extremely difficult for the LD adolescent. Important questions about self-esteem should be asked about the kind of feedback such a student receives through comparison.

Modeling

Bandura (1971) expanded a method of behavior modification based on the principle that people tend to imitate the behavior of others. Early work in behavior modification showed that subjects could overcome extreme fears of animate and inanimate objects (for example, snakes) by participating in directed imitation of models who demonstrated no fear. The power of the modeling influence is evident from models who are not even physically present, as in the case of television characters (Baran and Meyer, 1975).

Stephens (1973) reviewed a number of studies dealing with social modeling and delinquents and concluded:

1. Behavior is more readily imitated by subjects when the model has a similar physical appearance to the subject.
2. Hostile–aggressive behaviors are more quickly imitated than other types.
3. Behavior that is rewarded is imitated and retained more readily than behavior that is punished or not reinforced. (p. 336)

Cullinan et al. (1975) reviewed research in modeling with implications for special education and concluded that the technique has value for use in behavior problems, counseling, classroom skills, language development, and other areas.

Modeling is a very useful approach to understanding adolescent behavior as well as changing it. Imitation can occur as a result of chance relationships with a model who influences an individual. The peer group may maintain and reinforce certain types of behaviors that are undesirable (for example, teasing, fighting, and profanity). The faddish styles of dress, slang, and modes of conduct are well known consequences of social modeling. It seems that at least part of the cause for drug abuse, crime, and negative attitudes toward school can just as easily be explained by the natural process of social modeling.

The adolescent subculture

Most persons do not deny the existence of a peer culture of adolescents. Social modeling explains the influence of adolescents on each other and is most dramatically represented in certain modes of conduct, styles of dress, and rituals. The recent phenomenon of nostalgic reflection on the 1950s in movies and television programs causes young adults to remember, perhaps with amusement, that it was once "cool" to wear a black leather jacket, a duck-tail hair style, or jeans with the loops removed. These manifestations of peer influence are of interest but are not as significant as the way in which the peer culture relates to the larger society.

Coleman (1971) asserted that the values of students are at odds with the values of adults. Students are generally more concerned with social popularity than academic pursuits. A boy would rather be remembered as an athletic star than a scholar, and girls would rather be popular than scholarly. The school is valued as a social setting rather than a place of learning. He further believes that the industrial society has allowed the adolescent subculture to flourish even though it is at odds with the goals of adult society that are inculcated in the school. The subculture determines what the student should achieve and this defines the social environment.

If we can accept these conclusions, it can be seen that adolescence is a most difficult time because of the various pressures on the teenager. The peer group (and larger peer subculture) and the school and family present sources of pressure that may not be balanced.

The social fabric of the adolescent subculture is determined by standards that exert influence on the interaction of individuals. A child is born with certain innate abilities that serve to differentiate potential for development and acceptance in the society. Most persons are endowed with sufficient talent to adapt to the culture and to lead relatively well-adjusted lives. Experiences in life are composed of success, failure, frustration, stress, competition, and anxiety, all of which contribute to individual development. Race, sex, income, social status, religion, and physical attributes are related to adjustment. Each adolescent must develop a sense of identity. The adolescent subculture is an important proving ground. The presence of a learning disability cannot make the process any easier.

The peer group and the adolescent subculture have been topics of interest to a number of investigators over the years. It is not surprising to find a great deal of controversy among investigators about the importance and the limits of influence exerted by the peer group. However, it is generally accepted that the peer group provides each adolescent with a frame of reference for comparison and social feedback. The rapid physical and chemical changes that occur in the body of an adolescent are sometimes unsettling, but this experience is shared by others and this knowledge can be supportive. Standards of conduct provide the individual with structure in activities outside the family unit and the trials encountered in relating to others provide training for the adult world.

It is conceivable that later adult behaviors are greatly influenced by the nature of adolescent adjustment. A boy who excels in sports may be greatly surprised when he finds that the adult world is not very impressed with a high school athletic letter. If he can demonstrate sufficient athletic prowess to enter a professional sport, a career may result; but most high school stars must find other avenues of occupational endeavor. At the other end of the spectrum are individuals who are socially isolated and who enter adulthood with bitterness and trepidation. There is no clear evidence that maladjustment in adulthood (for example, alcoholism, deviant sexual behavior, psychoneurotic disorders) is directly related to maladaptive processes begun in adolescence, but this certainly seems possible. Psychoanalytic theorists believe that the roots of maladjustment begin in childhood but because of the unique nature of adolescence in the American culture, it seems reasonable to expect that serious maladjustment for some individuals may begin after a relatively normal childhood.

As noted earlier, most writers acknowledge the existence of the adolescent subculture but many dispute its significance. The main point of contention seems to concern the conflict that exists between peer and family values. The importance and impact of peer values may be influenced by the type of child rearing practices employed by parents. Elder (1962) identified seven types of parenting practices ranging from autocratic to ignoring. Although the extremes of this continuum might be undesirable for healthy

development, a home that balances structure with affection may produce a child that is less affected by peer values, especially if those values run contrary to modes of conduct and laws of the society. Children who are parent dominated and raised in a dictatorial environment, as well as those who are virtually ignored by their parents, may readily accept a peer group as a kind of surrogate family.

The self-fulfilling prophecy

Another influence that may be important in understanding adolescence (this is presumably more important to understanding deviant behavior) relates to a theoretical view expressed by Rosenthal and Jacobsen (1968) who reported the results of a study in which the performance of students was compared with the expectations of their teachers. In brief, the theory presupposes that students will perform poorly in school if their teachers expect them to. Although the study on which the theory rests has been rather severely criticized for its design, it has had quite an impact on special education and has been used to condemn labeling and other practices in special education. It is not surprising to find frequent reference to the self-fulfilling prophecy in the learning disabilities literature.

An examination of this theory in contrast with the discussion concerning social learning theory may be of value. Although children, at a very young age, may be induced to perceive themselves in much the same way as their teachers perceive them, the influence of peers and the emergence of self-determined behaviors are much more important to the adolescent. A teenager develops an image of himself or herself and of the world that is to a great extent determined by relatively accurate information gathered through strict and rigid comparison.

For the most part, comparisons tend to be made early in life and students develop rather accurate perceptions about how they are ranked. Most third-grade children know who is the best runner or who can be trusted by the teacher to take an important message to the office. For anyone who has watched children "choose-up" sides for a game of softball, it becomes obvious that young children are about as capable of selecting the best players as are the varsity coaches. The point is that standards define status. Some are vague, such as beauty, but there is sufficient consensus on most points. Gallagher (1976) succinctly summarized this point by stating that children who do not perform up to teacher expectations are very aware that they are not doing well. Although this may lead to a low self-concept and feelings of inferiority, they are often rather accurate perceptions. Gallagher maintains that feelings of inferiority cannot be easily eliminated because they are "adequate perceptions of an unfortunate set of characteristics" (p. 196).

Whether students show poor academic performance because they have accepted teacher expectations for poor performance or because of more concrete causes is of little consequence by the time they have reached secondary school. It is extremely important that teachers recognize the realities of poor performance and the associated factor of low self-esteem as germane to remedial strategies.

Cognitive structures of adolescence

Inhelder and Piaget (1958) and their students, such as Elkind (1975), have contributed significantly to our understanding of the period of adolescence and have elevated its status in psychology as a distinct and significant period of human development. Piaget developed a theory of cognitive development that conceptualizes a natural maturational process through which intelligence emerges in various stages, a non-random organization of sequences in which the child develops systems of mental operations. In this theory, early cognitive structures are prerequisite to the sequential development of later structures; the child's thinking is distinctive and different from that of the adult. Rather than acquiring intelligence in a uniform, discrete, and continuous sequence or as an accumulation of content, the child acquires and discards ways of thinking as he progresses to maturity. According to Piaget, during the stage that precedes adolescence (which Piaget calls the *concrete operational period*) the child engages in thinking that is characteristically tied to the concrete world. Although egocentrism is an important aspect of each level of development and continues to affect even the most intelligent individuals, the child is able to appreciate another person's point of view, communicate his ideas and understand those of others, make judgments concerning physical reality, and engage in games and enterprises requiring rules and incorporating several roles.

The peer group has a natural attraction for the child as an avenue of social activity partly because of the qualitative differences between adult and childhood abilities in cognitive development. Gradual assimilation into the peer culture begins during the concrete period (Elkind, 1975) and culminates in the latter stages of adolescence. Recognition of the qualitative aspects of the emergence of intelligent thinking is important if we are to understand not only the development of intellectual abilities but also the importance and influence of the peer group.

The child, who is a concrete thinker, is limited to the use of certain facts in the solution of problems whereas the adolescent is capable of using a combination of facts (combinatorial thinking). The adolescent develops a refined system of symbolism for problem solving that reflects the structures of *formal thought* described by Piaget.

The child may solve problems by means of concrete thinking, which entails the reduction of a problem to basic elements. Adolescents are capable of using symbols and have the capacity to deal with hypothetical situations and topics that have no concrete referents or which transcend the boundaries of time constraints. With this ability, comes the realization that there are many ways of viewing situations and many alternatives. A problem may have many outcomes, and each decision has many consequences. Therefore, the increasingly abstract nature of thinking comes to typify the ability of secondary students to engage in much more difficult content such as algebra, geometry, and critical reading.

Elkind (1975) notes that the capacity to think about thinking is another structural feature of adolescence. The adolescent can consider himself or herself to be an object, evaluate himself or herself as others might, and make highly complex comparisons. This may explain the self-consciousness of the individual who, for the first time, becomes aware of the thoughts and opinions of others. This may also explain the power of peer influence. Moral thinking changes because the adolescent is aware that his or her thoughts are private and sometimes at variance with what he or she professes to others. The ability to maintain a private point of view and not share personal feelings and beliefs with others can create a real dilemma. Moreover, the adolescent is able to conceptualize idealistic situations relating to religion, politics, or any other topic. Comparing reality with the invented ideal leads to much of the conflict between adults and adolescents according to Elkind. A certain superiority of thinking develops although the adolescent is not yet fully aware that the world is not simply divided between black and white, right and wrong, good and evil. Severe criticism can be directed internally by a student who fails to meet ideal requirements in appearance, social interaction, and academic achievement.

Ausubel and Ausubel (1971) have reviewed pertinent studies that support the emergence of increasingly abstract thinking among adolescents. Yudin (1971) has shown that younger adolescents are less efficient than older adolescents in concept attainment and the acqui-

sition of logical operations is related to idiosyncratic aspects in which different individuals progress at different rates.

This evidence and its many implications should be understood by all teachers at the secondary level. LD adolescents are likely to have specific problems in reading or arithmetic ability but this does not mean that they will have inadequate cognitive ability. The mentally retarded student, by contrast, may show similar levels of achievement at the secondary level, but the differences in cognition are remarkable. The mentally retarded adolescent will tend to reach upper levels of concrete thinking ability (Kolstoe and Hirsch, 1974) but will apparently show no ability to enter formal operational thinking.

The LD adolescent is capable of dealing with any of the abstract concepts found in the content of the secondary school curriculum just as any other adolescent with normal intelligence. However, the restrictions of poor reading ability inhibit learning and lead to the *appearance* of inability to deal with abstract concepts.

Deviancy and adolescence

So much has been written and aired in television broadcasts about adolescent deviancy that it certainly requires little documentation. Since World War II there has been a steady rise in the rate of crimes committed by adolescents. In recent years drug abuse and alcoholism have increased dramatically in this age group, and certain forms of personality disorders have increased in prevalence.

Of particular interest to the field of learning disabilities has been the trend to correlate delinquency with learning disabilities and to assume a causal relationship. Many authors report a positive association between learning disabilities and delinquency (Miller and Windhauser, 1971; Hurwitz et al., 1972; and Hogenson, 1974). Dorney (1967) reported that the rate of recidivism in a group of delinquents was reduced by direct instruction in remedial reading. Berman and Siegal (1976) reported that delinquents tend to be deficient in verbal, perceptual, and nonverbal conceptual spheres. Violence-prone individuals have a clear history of disturbance stemming from childhood that is associated with brain abnormalities (Rosenthal, 1970).

It is still premature to assume that learning disabilities cause delinquency because there are so many other obvious contributing factors. It is also rather simplistic to think that by simply improving the academic ability of students it will be possible to alter crime rates and prevent delinquency. This is a matter that will continue to receive more attention in the future as more investigators turn their attention toward the relationship between learning disabilities and delinquency.

The definition of adolescence

It may be perplexing that the definition of adolescence comes at the end of a chapter dealing with the topic of adolescence. It should be evident that the development of a definition is not a simple matter. For our purposes, *adolescence* may be defined as *the period that begins with the onset of puberty and ends when the individual is relatively independent of the emotional and financial bonds of the family unit and is able to function in the adult society.* This definition is admittedly lacking in explicitness, nonetheless it is the only definition that may be applicable across cultural lines because of the considerable variations that exist regarding the termination point of adolescence. In earlier, less industrialized societies, adolescence was often quickly terminated by the excision of the foreskin in the circumcision ritual or through tatooing of the female body. Adolescence in America is an extended period that is primarily shaped by economic factors and may vary widely in individual cases. Our major concern in this book is the adolescent in the secondary school.

If the reader accepts our view, then the intellectual and physiological aspects of adolescence are merely extensions or culminations of natural developmental processes. However, the difficulty of transition experienced by many adolescents is not primarily determined by biology but rather by social and cultural factors.

SUMMARY

An understanding of programming for learning disabled students in the secondary schools requires an understanding of learning disabilities—what they are and how they may be remediated; an understanding of the secondary schools—how they are organized, their goals, and their idiosyncrasies; and an understanding of adolescents—the "raw materials" with which we must work. This chapter discussed adolescents physiologically, evolutionarily, psychoanalytically, and culturally. We have considered the work of social learning theorists, behaviorists, and developmental theorists, as they relate to a more complete understanding of adolescence. Effects of the existence of an adolescent subculture, including possibly serious effects on the motivation to achieve academically, have been reviewed. The established fact of measurable differences in the maturation of males and females and the potential effect of generalized academic expectations on the part of educators has been noted. All of these factors must be considered in planning for learning disabled students in the secondary schools, and for the most part, consideration must be made on a student-by-student basis. These factors are a major part of the reason why planning for the learning disabled student in the secondary school remains such a tremendous challenge.

DISCUSSION QUESTIONS

1. Contrast social learning theory with psychoanalytic theory as they relate to the explanation of adolescent development.
2. Discuss the various theories applied to the study of adolescence and indicate the strengths and weaknesses of each in the examination and treatment of learning disabilities.
3. Consider how "storm and stress" may complicate the treatment of learning disabilities in an academic setting.
4. List the other influences that might cause adolescents to become delinquent in addition to the possible interaction of learning disabilities.
5. Discuss the concept that traits of adolescence are universal.

REFERENCES AND READINGS

Ausubel, D. P., and Ausubel, P. Cognitive development in adolescence. In M. Powell and A. H. Frerichs (Eds.), *Readings in adolescent psychology*. Minneapolis: Burgess Publishing Co., 1971.

Bandura, A. *Social learning theory*. New York: General Learning Press, 1971.

Baran, S. J., and Meyer, T. P. Retarded children's perceptions of favorite TV characters. *Mental Retardation*, 1975, *13*(4), 28-31.

Berman, A., and Siegal, A. W. Adaptive and learning skills in juvenile delinquents: A neuropsychological analysis. *Journal of Learning Disabilities*, 1976, *9*(9), 583-590.

Boyce Medical Study. Unpublished paper. September, 1969.

Coleman, J. S. The adolescent subculture and academic achievement. In M. Powell and A. H. Frerichs (Eds.), *Readings in adolescent psychology*. Minneapolis: Burgess Publishing Co., 1971.

Cott, A. Orthomolecular approach to the treatment of learning disabilities. *Schizophrenia*, 1971, *3*(2), 93-105.

Cott, A. Megavitamins: The orthomolecular approach to behavioral disorders and learning disabilities, *Academic Therapy*, 1972, *7*, 245-259.

Cragg, B. Plasticity of synapses. *British Medical Bulletin*, 1974, *30*(2), 141-144.

Cullinan, D. et al. Modeling: Research with implications for special education. *Journal of Special Education*, 1975, *9*(2), 209-221.

Dobbing, J., and Smart, J. Vulnerability of the developing brain and behavior. *British Medical Bulletin*, 1974, *30*(2), 164-168.

Dorney, W. The effectiveness of reading instruction in the modification of attitudes of adolescent delinquent boys. *Journal of Educational Research*, 1967, *60*, 438-443.

Eichhorn, D. H. *The middle school*. New York: The Center for Applied Research in Education, 1966.

Elder, G. H., Jr. Structural variations in the child rearing relationship. *Sociometry*, 1962, *25*, 241-262.

Elkind, D. *Children and adolescents* (2nd ed.). New York: Oxford University Press, 1975.

Erikson, E. *Identity: youth and crisis*. New York: W. W. Norton & Co., Inc., 1968.

Festinger, L. A theory of social comparison processes. *Human Relations*, 1954, *7*, 117-140.

Gallagher, J. J. (Personal Perspectives) In J. M. Kauffman and D. P. Hallahan (Eds.), *Teaching children with learning disabilities*. Columbus, Ohio: Charles E. Merrill Publishing Co., 1976.

Green, T. F. Career education and the pathologies of work. In L. M. McClure and C. Buan (Eds.), *Essays on career education*. Portland, Oregon: Northwest Regional Educational Laboratory, 1973.

Hall, G. S. *Adolescence: Its psychology and its relations to physiology, anthropology, sociology, sex, crime, religion, and education*. New York: Appleton-Century-Crofts, 1904.

Hisama, T. Achievement motivation and the locus of control of children with learning disabilities and behavior disorders. *Journal of Learning Disabilities*, 1976, *9*(6), 58-62.

Hoeffer, A. Vitamin B_3–dependent child. *Schizophrenia*, 1971, *3*(2), 107-113.

Hogenson, D. L. Reading failure and juvenile delinquency. *Bulletin of the Orton Society*, 1974, *24*, 164-169.

Hurwitz, I., et al. Neuropsychological function of normal boys, delinquent boys, and boys with learning problems. *Perceptual and Motor Skills*, 1972, *35*, 387-394.

Inhelder, B., and Piaget, J. *The growth of logical thinking from childhood to adolescence*. New York: Basic Books, Inc., Publishers, 1958.

Kolstoe, O. P. *Mental retardation*. New York: Holt, Rinehart & Winston, Inc., 1972.

Kolstoe, O. P., and Hirsch, D. F. Convergent thinking of retarded and nonretarded boys. *Exceptional Children*, 1974, *40*(4), 292-293.

Kulin, H. E. The physiology of adolescence in man. *Human Biology*, 1974, *46*, 133-143.

Lawrence, E. A., and Winschel, J. F. Locus of control: Implications for special education. *Exceptional Children*, 1975, *41*(7), 483-490.

Luria, A. R. *The working brain: An introduction to neuropsychology*. New York: Basic Books, Inc., Publishers, 1973.

Mead, M. *Coming of age in Samoa*. New York: William Morrow & Co., Inc., 1928.

Miller, W. H., and Windhauser, E. Reading disability: Tendency toward delinquency? *Clearinghouse*, 1971, *46*, 183-186.

Powers, H., Jr. Dietary measures to improve behavior and achievement, *Academic Therapy*, 1974, 203-214.

Rosenthal, A. Violence is predictable. *Today's Health*, 1970, *48*, 56-57.

Rosenthal, R., and Jacobsen, L. *Pygmalion in the classroom*. New York: Holt, Rinehart & Winston, Inc., 1968.

Rotter, J. B. *Social learning theory and clinical psychology*. Englewood Cliffs, N.J.: Prentice-Hall, Inc., 1954.

Sperry, R. Left-brain, right-brain, *Saturday Review*, 1975, 30-33.

Stephens, T. M. Using reinforcement and social modeling with delinquent youth, *Review of Educational Research*, 1973, *43*, 323-340.

Yudin, L. W. Formal thought in adolescence as a function of intelligence. In M. Powell and A. H. Frerichs (Eds.), *Readings in adolescent psychology*. Minneapolis: Burgess Publishing Co., 1971.

CHAPTER 3

The secondary school

INTRODUCTION

In this section, we have thus far considered an educational phenomenon, *learning disabilities*, and a stage of human development, *adolescence*. The final element for developing a total perspective and a frame of reference for understanding the environment of the adolescent is to consider the secondary school. Some authors use the term *secondary school* as restrictive to the high school while others more liberally include the junior high level. Regardless of the various organizational arrangements (for example, middle school, junior high, senior high, ungraded, and so forth), we shall use *secondary* as an adjective to refer to the various organizational arrangements, curricula, methods, students, and other factors traditionally associated with grades seven through twelve.

The secondary school must be carefully considered when planning for learning disabled adolescents because the special program will be administered as part of a larger, comprehensive secondary school educational program. The formal school program is organized to promote and enhance the educational progress of students who are enrolled in the school; this is the major purpose of the various local educational agencies located throughout the United States. There will likely be continuing debate about the overall effectiveness of the school, but most persons usually agree about the intended purpose. We shall review the structure and practices of the secondary school, the curriculum, the manner in which students are expected to learn, and some of the major issues facing the secondary school in an effort to determine how these issues relate to the provision of services for learning disabled adolescents.

STRUCTURE AND PRACTICES OF THE SECONDARY SCHOOL

The wide acknowledgment of learning disabilities is evidenced by the remarkable growth of programs at the elementary school level. However, the pace and scope of programming at the junior high and senior high school levels have been much more restricted. Scranton and Downs (1975) conducted a national survey and determined that of 37 reporting states, 40% of the school districts offered elementary school level learning disabilities programs while only 9% offered similar programs at the secondary school level. The complex organizational structure of the secondary school may be the cause of peculiar barriers to the development of programming; but, whatever the cause or causes, it is obvious that the emphasis has been on early childhood and elementary school programs in an apparent effort to prevent learning disabilities. States have not ordinarily differentiated between the certification of elementary and secondary teachers in special education although there is now a trend to do so. This is important because the differences in basic orientation of teachers and the focus of curricula at these two levels are most remarkable.

In schools where attempts have been made to establish secondary LD programs, they have often resulted in imitations of the elementary resource room model staffed by specialists who have primary training for elementary programs. This approach is not typically satisfactory because it fails to involve the many regular classroom teachers and disregards the realities of the secondary school curriculum.

To be successful, programming at the secondary school level must take into account many factors associated with the characteristics of adolescents, the peer subculture, the structure of the secondary school, environmental influences, and the very demanding content-oriented curriculum. Provision of special education for secondary school students with learning disabilities requires that the teacher understand the differences between childhood and adolescence as well as the differences between elementary and secondary schools.

The historical perspective

Education is controlled and supported by the state. Although numerous requirements and limitations are imposed by federal legislation and case law, the nature and maintenance of public education is ultimately directed by the state legislature. In theory, each state may set specific standards for the curriculum, the hiring of personnel, and all other aspects of administration. However, the board of education is granted discretionary powers in the control of the school district at the local level. The rise of power in the hands of teachers and the establishment of students' rights have diminished the authority of the school board and administration in recent years, but the mechanism of control is still managed by the board.

Patterns of school organization are remarkably similar throughout the nation. These patterns have evolved through the influence of political philosophy, public attitudes and mores, economic conditions, and the pressures of special interest groups as expressed through state legislation and local policies.

Early schools originally served small numbers of children in isolated areas, and the local community exercised complete control. As the population increased, schools became more numerous and compulsory attendance laws assured a larger student population. By 1920 half of the nation's population resided in urban areas and special problems confronted the schools as educational goals shifted from needs associated with agrarian concerns to those created by industrialized urban centers.

The first high schools were instituted to prepare a few, elite individuals for a college education. The organization, curriculum, and administration of the high school was patterned after that of the college, and most people seemed to accept the college-bound premise of secondary education.

As society continued to change and as more students of diverse backgrounds entered secondary schools, it became evident that the purposes of the secondary school were not necessarily appropriate for all students. The scope of the secondary school was re-examined by the Commission on the Reorganization of Secondary Education beginning in 1913. The report of this Commission (issued in 1918) is famous for its declaration of the Seven Cardinal Principles of Education—health, command of fundamental processes, worthy home membership, vocation, citizenship, worthy use of leisure time, and ethical character.

Less recognized but just as significant were the recommendations of the Commission that altered the scope of the secondary school from that of a prep school to that of an institution that would also serve the students who were less concerned with college than with securing successful employment in the community. However, the high school has always maintained the aura of its ancient, priveleged purpose, and college preparation (liberal arts) and vocational training have not always coexisted in peace and harmony in the American high school.

In recognition of the needs of younger adolescents, the first junior high school was begun in 1909 (Grambs et al, 1961). As the high school was patterned after the college, so was the organization, curriculum, and administration of the junior high school patterned after that of the senior high school.

Today's technological society has created a wide range of problems for the schools. The diversity of the student body is very great, the value of an education is too often measured in terms of its gatekeeping function rather than preparation for a career, and the local community struggles to maintain local autonomy while even the state legislature finds it must yield some of its control of the schools to the federal government.

There has been continuing public discontent with the practices, efficacy, and accountability of secondary education. The decrease in student achievement scores has been of sufficient public interest to become the subject of a television documentary.* The quali-

tative nature of school programs has also been criticized. The curriculum has been viewed as: (1) too narrow, (2) too broad, (3) unrealistic in preparing modern youth for the demands and careers of the technological society and (4) totally inadequate as preparation for any quality university program.

Kiernan (1976), the executive secretary of the National Association of Secondary School Principals, maintains that secondary schools reflect the forces of change in society more than most institutions and believes that schools are continuously modified in each succeeding decade by the flow of American life. The same questions are being asked now as were asked in 1913. What is the purpose and function of the school? What should be the substance of the curriculum? How should students be instructed?

These questions have been asked formally and informally at all critical junctures in American history. The original response to the needs of an industrialized society demonstrated the flexibility of the school as it attempted to change from strict college preparation to a more expanded, generalized purpose. The challenge of the international space race stimulated significant change in the math and science curricula of the schools. The phenomenal turmoil during and after the Vietnam conflict once again tested the flexibility of the secondary school to adapt to a stronger voice of parents, teachers, and students in the determination of policies, to adapt the curriculum, and to submit to innovations in administration and evaluation.

Schools are still adjusting to the dramatic social changes of the 1960s and early 1970s, and they appear to be subjected to a new round of scrutiny and modification as the demand for "greater accountability" emanates from power centers.

Criticism of the public schools seems to be related to their visibility and a need of patrons to exercise local control. Citizens feel distant from most other governmental institutions; they believe that they have little control over the national government. They react to and feel more a part of political issues at the state level, but cherish, and at times, fiercely protect their relationship with the

---

*American Broadcasting Company; American Schools: Flunking the Test, May 27, 1976.

neighborhood school and the local school system. It is an institution over which their control is immediately obvious—control exercised through interactions with teachers and administrators and support or opposition voiced at board meetings. Patrons follow minute details of school-related issues in the newspaper and are highly vocal in supporting or defeating local tax issues that affect the operation of the school.

During the 1960s the schools changed many practices, included more relevant options in the curriculum, and permitted greater student participation in the policymaking decisions of the schools. There were many changes in physical plants, moves toward open schools and open classrooms, and the addition of nontraditional activities.

Although many of these changes occurred as a result of the growing social movement of the 1960s, many professional educators, called *education's romantic critics* by Schrag (1967), published stinging criticisms of the schools that had an impact on many segments of society. The schools were said to be too structured, were accused of dehumanizing children, and were said to stifle true learning in the interest of conformity. In response to the many forces demanding change and criticism from all sides, sweeping modifications were introduced. The curriculum in many schools became more concerned with Black studies, with sociological concerns, and with values. But, as part of the same movement, there was an insistence on academic achievement, an issue that has become the most important concern of the 1970s.

The scholastic attainment of students, as measured by standardized achievement tests, has been declining, and, as a consequence, the changes that were introduced in the 1960s are now regarded as "frills" that are partly responsible for the poor performance of students. Alternative schools open their doors promising to "get back to basics." Voters in some states (such as Oregon in 1976) actually closed the schools by refusing to permit an increase in taxation with the argument that schools are not accomplishing their assigned task—teaching basic skills.

Significant drops in the scores of students on tests of the American College Testing Bureau have been central to the raging controversy over the adequacy of American education. The Associated Press (February 15, 1976) carried an article, *High School Preparation Weaker*, that discussed the results of the American College Testing (ACT) program and indicated that a significant trend toward a national decline in test scores of students was apparent. The ACT was reported to have attributed reasons for the drop to a change in the nature of the college-bound student and poor high school preparation. Factors cited to support these conclusions were (1) the greater use of electives in high school, (2) the lowering of teacher expectations of students, and (3) schooling directed more by students than teachers. Many of the reputed "causes" might be attributed to changes in the school that had been asked for by critics a decade before.

A number of authors have joined in the debate over these events. Wilhelms (1975) acknowledged that scores seemed to be dropping but attempted to explain them as fluctuations not truly reflective of a massive slide-off in basic skills. Mueller (1975) was convinced that such data are indicative of slipping standards. Other explanations have emphasized a variety of factors, but the majority of critics appear to be convinced that there is a serious problem.

It appears that the schools have attempted many adaptations in a continuing effort to educate a heterogeneous student population in a highly technological society. The diversity of students is the greatest problem. Unlike many European schools where all but the most academically talented students are excluded from secondary schools, American education attempts to meet the needs of all students while heralding the standards of academic excellence. On the whole, most students can be considered literate. It is absurd to regard students with achievement scores above the sixth or seventh grade level as "illiterate." Most persons with this ability can function in society, although their living standards may not be in conformity with middle class values. Granted, these students would not be able to excel on a college entrance examination; but, the schools have attempted to adjust to the diversity of the student body by expanding and humanizing the curriculum so that the total educational program would be relevant to all students. Even though the need to alter the curriculum for these very purposes was recognized in the final report of the Commission on the Reorganization of Secondary Education, critics in the 1970s persist in their demand for the type of academic excellence used to gauge the acceptability of the few, elite, college-bound students.

The reality is that schools continue to be evaluated in terms of achievement scores in tool subjects and content areas of study, and these circumstances reinforce the rigid, traditional patterns of academic expectation that militate against all students who fall below the median on standardized tests and especially against learning disabled students. Although society expects the schools to produce students who can grapple with the demands of the modern technological society, demands that are far more complex than 50 or 100 years ago, the schools must also promote the highest levels of academic excellence in the liberal arts and this must be accomplished in approximately the same length of time as at the turn of the century.

The central question becomes whether the schools can prepare students who can effectively meet the demands of a complex society by training students in job entry skills, while at the same time maintaining the highest levels of liberal arts–oriented scholastic achievement. This issue will continue to be a significant problem for the schools as they attempt to respond to the demands of several groups. If the schools can be permitted to operate a system that provides for more than one type of training, a system that rewards students of diverse abilities, the issue may be resolved. The educational significance of the school should not be measured by the academic or intellectual ability of its students nor should schools be ranked by the academic achievement of students. This dilemma in modern American education diminishes the probability of success for students

such as the learning disabled who have considerable talent but inadequate basic skills.

Career education has been introduced as a concept that may improve the lives of all children but especially the handicapped, many of whom will not benefit from a liberal arts curriculum nor be able to attend college. Career education has been criticized, as have most innovations, but if attitudinal changes in society continue to permit the acceptance of the handicapped then career education can be a viable alternative for many students. These issues will be more fully considered in a later chapter.

The purposes of the secondary school have gradually emerged, altered, and expanded as differing economic and social factors predominate in the society. The final report of the Commission on the Reorganization of Secondary Education, concluded in 1918, provides an interesting contrast to the purposes of education espoused in 1976 by the Bicentennial Conference Report on America's Secondary Schools (Chaffee and Clark, 1976), which are as follows:

1. Personal self confidence (self-image); flexibility; ability to cope
2. Basic language and computation skills; human "survival" skills, including consumer skills, family and parenthood training, career exploration; skills to understand and to use political, economic, and social systems
3. Civic education, including the concept of social cohesion
4. Moral development
5. Occupational competency; employability
6. Aesthetic development; skills for lifelong learning and leisure time (p. 16)

Organization and administration of the secondary school

Most secondary schools are organized in a traditional, bureaucratic manner with authority vested in a principal by the board of education. The principal is expected to carry out rules, regulations, and policies as directed by the local board of education in accordance with state laws. The principal is accountable to the superintendent and, in larger districts, may be subject to the authority of one or more assistant or area superintendents. Most larger secondary schools have assistant principals who handle specialized administrative areas under the direction of the principal.

The alignment of administrative personnel (line authority) and their responsibilities for various instructional and noninstructional personnel are derived from the traditional bureaucratic structure so characteristic of military, business, and governmental organizations. The bureaucracy operates under the principle that the objectives of an organization can be met most effectively by a clear distinction of official duties logically divided between various positions for specialization and accountability. In the strictest sense, bureaucratic theory is minimally concerned with persons who fill the roles but emphasizes the hierarchy or chain of command wherein each succeeding administrator is held responsible to a superior for the quality and quantity of work conducted at each level. Such a structure has been traditionally accepted in the United States as the most efficient system by which organizational objectives can be met. An early, widely accepted description of bureaucratic theory can be found in the works of Weber (Gerth and Mills, 1946).

A portion of the total spectrum of problems experienced in the schools may be attributed directly to the struggles that exist between the administration and the instructional staff. Traditionally, as we have just described, the principal has exercised considerable authority and enjoyed the use of centralized power in the administration of the school and in the supervision and direction of student and teacher activities. This power base has been eroded significantly in recent years as a result of law suits in which courts have rendered decisions defining the rights of teachers and students and limiting the scope of the school's authority. Collective bargaining and unionism have also played a role in taking some of the power from the hands of school administrators. Whether or not the newly developing balance of power may cause the schools to improve and to operate more efficiently remains to be seen. But presently, such

events have tended to cast administrative and instructional personnel into opposing camps.

Specialists in learning disabilities at the secondary school level must be aware of these issues because they can have a significant impact on the ultimate success of the special education program. Harmonious relationships would be most advantageous to the functioning of many components and activities in a special program. A specialist must be aware of the climate in the school before making any attempts to implement various programs and activities that might lead to antagonism or anger on the part of various special interest groups. Under prevailing conditions in most secondary schools, the principal still wields considerable authority. If a secondary specialist "sells" the principal on a certain idea or programmatic change without soliciting the support of the faculty, the instructional staff may be resistant to the change and the entire program can be jeopardized. Understanding the bureaucracy and the potential for conflict is essential.

Anderson (1974) investigated the effects of the bureaucracy in a study of school administration in 18 secondary schools and determined that bureaucratization is related to students' feelings of alienation from the school and tends to become more entrenched in schools of lower class neighborhoods. An LD specialist will quickly discover that the attitudes of students may be more negative in a highly structured school and planned program changes in a rigidly controlled school will collide head-on with institutional inflexibility.

The balance of power between teachers and principal is of utmost importance. The morale of the teaching staff is greatly affected by the personality and administrative style of the principal. Administrators may predetermine the success or failure of a program depending on how they view it. It is highly desirable to secure the support of both the administration and the instructional staff and to prevent any issue from becoming a point of contention between the administration and the faculty.

Secondary teachers are not necessarily aware of the goals, objectives, and intentions of the secondary program for learning disabilities and may not be sympathetic because there is good reason to believe that many of the students served in any such program will be the same ones that teachers have considered as disciplinary problems. Also, many secondary teachers may resent the "freedom" they witness in the activities of special personnel who are not tied to the type of regimentation demanded in the normal school subjects. Specialists at the elementary level have experienced public relations problems because of the rich variety of materials and equipment frequently found in their classes. A special class with carpeting may appear to be luxuriously furnished especially if regular classes meet in drab rooms with tile floors. The organization of the school, the relationships of staff members, and the by-products of any type of conflict are potential pitfalls for special programming.

Gullet (1975) maintains that an organization must adapt to the challenge of the environment or cease to exist; it may be necessary to deemphasize the hierarchy, status, and rank of individuals in favor of a system that incorporates the talents and energies of all employees in decision-making procedures. Until this happens, conflict will result from the forces that collide over the issues of school organization and administration. The secondary LD specialist must be cognizant of these issues because the support of the the faculty and administration may be as significant as instructional methods and materials in the success of a program. A sense of diplomacy seems to be a major prerequisite for teaching secondary learning disabled students unless the teacher is content to teach remedial reading or remedial mathematics as separate "subjects," uncoordinated with other curricular efforts, a practice we would reject as ineffective.

The school and community power structure

Many problems can arise as a result of the interaction between administrators, teachers, and students under the bureaucratic structure of organization. Significant informal sources of power and influence exist in addition to the formal sources subsumed under the administrative structure of the school. These subelements of the informal power structure should be fully understood to appreciate the nature of the secondary school.

Power is related to the ability to make and implement decisions that affect an organization; persons with this ability form the power structure. The state legislature, the state department of education, the local board of education, and the administrative personnel hold decision-making authority and comprise the formal power structure. However, it must be recognized that many special interest groups and influential individuals share power and influence over the schools although they are not a part of the formal structure. They may be considered, in total, as the informal power structure.

Where the informal power structure and the formal administrative structure do not coincide, forces may exist that attempt to exert unethical influences. An example would be the purchase of property for a new school in a location that would enrich a private citizen in the community. In other cases, individuals may be especially interested in obtaining contracts for food, supplies, furniture, transportation, and other school-related consumption because thousands of dollars are involved. The unethical nature of this facet of the power structure will be of greatest concern to upper level administrators, but there are examples of the influence of informal power at the school level that may concern the classroom teacher.

Principals of secondary schools may command considerable respect or be despised by the faculty. Some principals exhibit certain administrative styles that relate to power. A democratic principal may attempt to involve all teachers in decision-making practices. An authoritarian principal will more likely retain complete authority in important matters, thereby seriously affecting the morale of the faculty. Some principals may abdicate power to informal sources as they ignore important functions or allow themselves to be influenced by key individuals on the faculty or outside the school. Such influences should concern the LD specialist because of the implications for program effectiveness.

The internal workings of a secondary school may be affected to some degree by informal sources of power outside the school district, but it is more common that individuals within the school exert power through relationships with important community figures, board members, or administrators. Some teachers have considerable prestige through such factors as their right of tenure or excellence in teaching. Where such prestige or power exists, either adverse or beneficial results may occur. From a public rela-

tions point of view, the LD specialist should make an effort to identify these individuals and to assess their attitudes toward the special education program. If possible, it may be important to "court" such individuals to ensure program acceptance. A disgruntled remedial reading teacher or a language arts teacher who is threatened by the existence of a secondary LD program, for whatever reason, may be able to undermine program support and reduce its effectiveness.

A political reality is that a learning disabilities specialist may have to spend considerable time in securing the support of individuals inside and outside the school. The specialist should try to circumvent conflict with any individual if possible and attempt

to foster relationships that work in the best interests of the program goals and the students.

The curriculum

As noted previously, there is remarkable similarity in the organization of the junior and senior high schools because, in most instances, the structure of the senior high school has been modified and applied to the junior high school. It remains logical to refer to both as simply secondary schools because the differences that exist are minor. The curriculum is very similar partly because of imitation and partly because of the uniform standards established by the national organizations that accredit the schools.

The curriculum of the secondary school is usually departmentalized so that teachers conduct planning and teaching in a manner not unlike the college. Each secondary teacher is trained to teach in specific content areas. Each state requires that secondary teachers have much different credentials than elementary teachers. Unlike the elementary teacher, the secondary teacher is concerned with a particular field of study, such as science or history. Very few states require secondary teachers to have any training in the methods of teaching reading, arithmetic, and writing. Until recently, state certification requirements have not demanded that secondary teachers have exposure to course work reflecting the needs and training of handicapped students. It is not surprising, then, that secondary teachers are often frustrated by students who fail to learn. They do not understand them, are likely to feel threatened by student failure, and do not know how to help them.

Typically, the curriculum is not integrated because of division into content areas. In many elementary programs, the curriculum is integrated so that students may simultaneously experience training in social science, reading, and mathematics. Most secondary schools use the *separate subjects curriculum.* Under this system, each facet of the curriculum is treated as a separate content area with the subject matter sequenced in a hierarchy

designed to lead to mastery of the content. Other content areas are similarly organized and each area is presented individually by teachers who are trained in that content area. The LD specialist should be aware that the curriculum is hierarchically arranged by sequences graded by levels of difficulty within specific content areas and that the interaction between components (or teachers) of the curriculum is difficult to arrange and requires considerable planning.

A curriculum for junior and senior high school students consists of *required* courses, and *elective* subjects. The tradition of the Carnegie unit is maintained. A student must earn credits in required and elective courses to be promoted and earn a diploma. A unit of credit is, in most cases, equivalent to two semesters of work. Some schools also require students to earn activity units that do not carry academic credits such as working in the cafeteria or acting as an aide in a kindergarten class.

There is variability in the courses that are offered in different schools, but most schools require a certain conformity in the number and type of required courses because of accreditation standards. The uniformity of required course work is most interesting because it typically reflects the basic competency one would associate with a liberal arts education. Under a 3-3 arrangement, students in the seventh, eighth, and ninth grades of junior high school and the tenth, eleventh, and twelfth grades of senior high school may be required to earn 15 to 18 units of study at each level. The required courses ordinarily consist of three units of English or language arts, one to two units of history or social studies, two units of mathematics, and two units of science. Many schools permit "basic" courses in the required areas to suffice for credit. Some schools offer basic arithmetic, practical English, or applied science and math, which are courses with simpler content but which can be used to qualify for graduation credit. Some junior high schools may offer as many as 130 or more courses, and many high schools offer a curriculum with 200 to 250 different courses.

A student who enrolls for the required and elective courses and who earns enough units is eligible for a high school diploma. Successful completion demands that the student attend classes regularly, maintain acceptable behavior, and complete course assignments to the satisfaction of the instructors. Some states are also beginning to require that, in addition to course completion, a student must have a demonstrable level of achievement in tool subjects such as reading and arithmetic computation. California now permits students to graduate without completion of specific units if they can successfully pass a state examination of basic skills (a proficiency exam) that requires the student to apply concepts to the solution of problems relating to consumerism and practical life situations.

Many secondary students value the school as a social setting more than as an educational endeavor. Extracurricular activities are also a very important part of school. They consume much of the teachers' time and sometimes seem to compete with other aspects of the secondary program for the attention of students as well as for financial support.

Course demands

Most academic courses require extensive reading, written and oral reports, and written tests. Some teachers are much more demanding than others. Moreover, the learning characteristics of a particular student may very well determine which courses are the most difficult. There is no way to rank courses by difficulty, except within a given school, because of the many variables involved. Some courses are more difficult than others because of the abstract way in which the content is presented. A senior high school course in social studies may be conducted as a discussion class in one school with a liberal use of films and field trips. In another district, a course with the same title may involve extensive reading of current texts and periodicals. A learning disabled student with unique learning problems may find many courses difficult; but, as a rule, most courses are relatively difficult because of the abstract way

in which the content is presented and the heavy reliance on reading for basic instruction and acquisition of information.

Instructional methods

Traditional instructional techniques require that students participate in classes. A typical class in language arts, history, or mathematics is ordinarily steeped in lecture-type instruction by the teacher. Homework assignments usually require considerable completion time after regular school hours. Students who attend classes regularly, take copious notes, and possess basic reading skills are capable of dealing with the demands of course work. Individualization of instruction, a common practice at the elementary school level, does not usually occur in secondary schools.

A secondary instructor of an academic subject may have as many as five classes a day with a minimum of 30 students in each period. The objectives of the course demand that the instructor cover a predetermined amount of material in the semester. Therefore, the instructor is not usually concerned with the individual problems of students nor with the homework and related demands of other courses the students are taking. Deviation from the lecture is not a usual practice in a class with 30 or more students so that individual attention may not be offered by the instructor nor requested by the student.

Current trends in the provision of special educational services at all levels have been toward some form of integration in the regular classroom (the principle of the least restrictive environment—mainstreaming). Aside from the legal pressures creating this trend, many educators believe that greater educational benefits can be realized in a regular setting as opposed to a self-contained class. Two significant problems in secondary education are the attitude of teachers and time. The size of classes, the limited amount of time for interaction with individual students, the conceptual style of teaching, and the attitudes toward students with limited abilities diminishes the chances of academic

...vival for LD students without planned intervention.

Long-standing evidence supports the belief that teachers tend to adhere to and participate in the social "pecking order" of students by according more respect to socially popular students (Polansky, 1954). Teachers tend to (1) interact with students who are ranked highly in the peer group, (2) use expository methods of teaching, (3) use most of the class time with a lecture-type format, and (4) ignore students who are poor achievers.

In the intermediate grades it is probably quite clear to most students just who is ranked highly in various social-value dimensions. Status-ranking becomes a serious problem for low-ranking students and is probably the most intense in the secondary school setting. Cohen (1972) has reviewed research in the sociology of the classroom and has addressed the issue of achievement status as a basis for rank-ordering in the classroom as follows:

> Over time, students develop an achievement pattern which is known to themselves, to other students and to the teacher, operating like any other status ranking. Many teachers and students seem to believe that there is one general human ability with smart high-achieving students and "dumb" low-achieving students at opposite ends of the continuum. There are also measurable achievement differences in these two groups; no doubt some of the performance differential is due to individual differences in ability and skills, but the sociologist hypothesizes that some of the variance in performance is due to the expectations for competence held by the teachers and students for high-achieving smart students as compared to low-achieving dull students. (p. 445)

Classroom learning is a phenomenon based on the interaction of many variables. Differences between two classrooms may be remarkable if the teacher in one class is willing to modify the tempo and mode of instruction and the other is not. Obviously, changes should be made early in the elementary grades to try to counteract the strong influence of the peer group in making status judgments based on academic performance, although students at the secondary level may be able to overcome such stigmatization by cultivating status in other areas.

Recent professional disagreements over issues of mainstreaming appear to be misdirecting the attention of special educators to very simplistic conceptualizations of learning. The mere presence of a student in a regular class or a more traditional special education setting will not ensure learning. We desperately need more intense investigation of many variables that contribute to or detract from learning with regard to the dimensions of instructional techniques, materials, and individual characteristics.

In the meantime, it makes little difference whether or not one would attribute poor achievement in LD students to a self-fulfilling prophecy, to innate characteristics of the learner, or to specific environmental factors of the classroom. By the time a complex combination of adverse conditions are operating at the secondary level, it is absolutely essential that multifaceted intervention be made by the LD specialist. In many respects, traditional practices of the secondary school create unnecessary problems that must be effectively dealt with to afford every possible opportunity for learning. We cannot be timid about assuming a position of advocacy because time is running out.

Grading

In most secondary schools conventional letter grades still predominate. The National Education Association (1974) conducted a survey of secondary schools and estimated that 82% of junior high schools and 84% of senior high schools employed a letter grading system to evaluate the performance of students. Typically, schools report student progress in the familiar symbols A, B, C, D, and F.

Letter grades bear a relationship to normative data, although many factors can influence the grade, most important of which is the teacher's attitude toward the student. In many settings the letter grade is derived from a multiplicity of factors such as class participation, attendance, completed assignments, and test performance. The letter grade does not necessarily reflect the student's level of academic achievement nor mastery of an area of content.

Letter grades have been promoted because the grade point average (GPA) is believed to be a good predictor of college performance, the GPA and the rank in class sort out students who may be awarded scholarships, grades are believed to be motivating for students, and the American economic system is based on competition.

Evans (1976) has reviewed research that strongly indicates that grades (1) cause many students to cheat, (2) encourage students to view the teacher as a manipulable object, and (3) reduce or in some cases prevent the individualization of instruction. Grades are often subjective, may be unrelated to the objectives of education, and may serve to diminish the self-esteem of students. Some schools have introduced alternatives such as pass–fail or contracting for grades. A viable approach seems to be mastery or criterion-level systems that take into account the abilities and individual learning differences of the students. In any event, the letter grade system is firmly entrenched as a practice of the secondary school and will continue to pose many problems for learning disabled students.

A complete and informative review published by the Association for Supervision and Curriculum Development (Simon and Bellanca, 1976) presents an overview of the research relating to grading systems and discusses several alternatives. This topic should be of great concern to the special educator.

Learning and verbal ability

Practices of the school reflect educational demands and priorities valued by the culture. This is demonstrated by the stress placed on certain kinds of courses and areas of study, as in the emphasis on science and mathematics after the Soviet Union launched Sputnik. One uniform practice has been the emphasis on learning that requires verbal ability. This priority is typified by the concern about slipping achievement scores. Also, it should be apparent that the school is concerned with the fundamental skills of reading and arithmetic computation. Many special classes are provided for remedial reading and arithmetic, but there are no such classes for remedial art or music. Sperry (1975) has discussed hemispheric specialization of the brain as such specialization relates to learning in the school. The left hemisphere specializes in those abilities that permit the development of logic and abstract ability whereas the right hemisphere is mute, handles simple arithmetic computation and spatial relations, and controls artistic creativity. Sperry contends that the school ignores the right hemisphere by stressing skills associated with the left hemisphere, predominantly reading, mathematics, and abstract reasoning.

The *verbal bias*, as it might be termed, is at the root of the thinking that requires minimum levels of academic achievement as a prerequisite for graduation and for accelerated levels of achievement necessary for entrance into college and graduate school. This practice has had a long tradition in both Eastern and Western nations. Although law and medicine could be practiced in early America after a period of apprenticeship, most prestigious professions have traditionally required advanced training rooted in academic competition. In modern America, it is well known that many businesses and industries use high school diplomas and college degrees more as a technique to sort the applicants than for the competencies they imply.

Reading ability at the lower elementary levels is much easier to determine than in the secondary grades because instructional programs are based on hierarchical sequences of acquired skills. After the basic skills are entrenched, reading becomes more a matter of proficiency, speed, and increased skill in the acquisition of vocabulary. Skilled readers can read a passage, discern its meaning, analyze its content, postulate questions, offer interpretations, and relate it in a meaningful manner to themselves and their environment.

A bright student who is *unable* to read efficiently is ordinarily capable of processing and analyzing information with the same efficiency as a good reader. However, the school typically requires students to gain nearly all information from textbooks and to perform in a manner that requires writing. Too many secondary school educators are unable or unwilling to reduce the complications involved with reading through accommodation techniques. Accommodation implies that the student is expected to learn and achieve just like other students, but the methods of learning, responding, and evaluation are adjusted to the student's learning style. This is not accomplished in most schools because of the verbal bias in education.

Authors have become aware of the difficulty many students encounter when using textbooks in increasingly complex subject matter. The information explosion of this decade is phenomenal requiring students to learn much more than any previous generation. The reading level of many high school and college textbooks has been lowered because the highly abstract content and sheer volume have interfered with learning.

Few persons would question the need for competent and well-trained persons to serve society in a variety of vocational and professional roles. It seems logical that preparation of scientists, physicians, and other professionals should demand the most capable candidates. These requirements, however, should not be used to artificially restrict the career opportunities of capable young persons who are not able to read efficiently.

This discussion does not concern the current controversy over lowering admission requirements or the open admissions policy of universities. It concerns those individuals who can demonstrate ability in some alternative manner without the traditional need to prove it through reading and written examinations. This is an important and necessary distinction as it pertains to the learning disabled adolescent. Traditional standards may be maintained, but traditional methods of learning and assessment may be altered without jeopardizing educational programs and without diminishing the quality of education for the individual. The best analogy is

that of the blind student who is allowed to earn the same certificate as other students but without meeting the same requirements as nonhandicapped persons. However, verbal bias constrains the mobility of learning disabled students and limits academic options.

The LD specialist should be aware of these issues because of the dramatic problems they cause. An LD student, although capable of learning, is frequently saddled with numerous textbooks and written assignments that cannot be managed. Viewing the education of the LD secondary student as a simple matter of the continuation of elementary level remedial reading and arithmeitc is narrow and unrealistic. Even if students can make significant gains in reading achievement through special education, it is unlikely that they will be able to apply these skills to the demands of the curriculum in the same manner as nonhandicapped students.

Learning disabilities programs in the secondary school

It is impossible to fully explore the local special education programs without referring to federal and state leadership. Laws and guidelines that result from federal and state activity in special education ultimately affect the decisions of the local board of education that govern the nature and extent of programming. One of the greatest concerns is the financial support of the local program.

The federal government has demonstrated an active interest in the scope of special education for many decades and recently enacted P.L. 94-142. This law and the several state acts, written in accordance with federally approved guidelines, mandate educational opportunity for all handicapped children and create a mechanism for financing the excess costs of special education.

It is difficult to determine the exact costs of an average program, and averages are misleading. The expenses involved in educating a child in a particular state or district may be quite different from other states and districts. However, it is generally estimated that a special education program for a mildly handicapped child costs approximately 1½ to 2 times as much as that for a nonhandicapped youngster. Children with more severe handicaps require as much as 3 or more times the average amount to provide adequate services.

The breadth of the secondary school special education program may range from limited assistance to students in tool subjects to highly organized services in academic subjects, career education, and work experience programs. (In later chapters several examples of these approaches will be presented.) In keeping with the premise that handicapped students should be provided equal educational opportunity in the least restrictive environment, the secondary LD student should be allowed a rich variety of opportunities in academic and career-oriented instruction similar to the educational options accorded nonhandicapped students.

In most school systems, special education services are coordinated by a special education administrator. This individual may be called a *director of special education, coordinator,* or *supervisor.* In some districts, special education is supervised by an assistant superintendent, but the growing complexity of special education makes it feasible to employ a specialist to manage the scope and sequence of special education throughout the entire system. Many special education administrators do not have line authority but function in staff relationships with administrators and teachers. The primary duties of the special education administrator involve general administrative duties, supervision, public relations, and in-service training. Although the special education administrator may be the key person in the district to handle administrative problems, the LD specialist may need to assume extraordinary responsibilities in the performance of duties because of the many unique problems associated with special education in a secondary school. The LD specialist cannot "be all things to all people" but the complex demands of the secondary program may require unusually competent teachers.

Secondary teachers are trained to be con-

tent oriented because of the subject-centered curriculum; they sometimes lack the skills and sensitivity to accommodate the student with specific learning disabilities. The LD specialist must be able to develop rapport with the secondary teachers, be familiar with courses in the curriculum, be knowledgeable about adolescent psychology as well as competent in remediation of learning disabilities, be able to assist teachers in the modification of the curriculum and materials, be thoroughly capable of using task analysis, be able to use a variety of commercial assessment instruments in addition to being capable of developing and utilizing informal methods of assessment, and be sufficiently trained to direct programs in career education and work-study. The secondary specialist must be trained to work in a variety of service delivery systems, from self-contained to the consultation model and may utilize several different systems in providing an appropriate program for students with a wide variety of needs.

THE FUTURE OF SECONDARY EDUCATION

The LD specialist who enters the field at the secondary level in the next few years will be participating in a new and exciting experience that will most certainly yield both rewards and frustrations. The challenges to secondary education will test the courage of both regular classroom teachers and special education teachers in the decades ahead because education appears to be at a turning point. The learning disabilities teacher has to experiment with many variables until the most effective models, materials, and techniques emerge. At the same time, the inevitable change facing the secondary school will be unsettling to teachers, administration, students, parents, and the community.

The traditional system has been attacked by educators, legislators, and lay persons. In spite of the fact that society has created a dilemma for the school by expecting it to accomplish too many tasks without clear definition of the objectives and without providing adequate human and economic resources, the educational community has recognized many of its shortcomings and is apparently willing to make the adjustments necessary for a meaningful and relevant educational process. Issues confronting the educational system include systems of teaching, financial problems, student participation, and educational outcomes.

Systems of teaching

Regardless of content orientation, each teacher is faced with the very real problem of effective teaching. In an effort to improve systems of teaching, several university training programs have experimented with competency-based instruction that is often heavily field based. There are conflicting opinions about the value of this type of instruction because there is often a question about the characteristics desired in a teacher and about the lack of differences in the learning behavior of students who are subjected to instruction by teachers who have been trained in both traditional and innovative programs. If a student fails to learn more efficiently in either type of program (or more than other students as demonstrated through quantification on some measure), then the differences in the training programs are significant in only one respect—the cost. It will become the obligation of university training programs to subject training programs to strenuous investigation in an effort to maximize the training of "the best" teachers, to identify the best candidates, and to continue in-service programming after teachers have graduated.

The educational technologies that seemed to hold so much promise just a few years ago have been disappointing. Literally thousands of dollars were spent on the development, purchase, and use of teaching machines and other forms of commercial hardware. Yet, it was realized at least 10 years ago that the shiny, electrical gadgetry would not substantially improve learning for most students because of the underlying problems related to group instruction as compared with individualized instruction (Oettinger and Marks, 1968).

Teachers encounter a formidable barrier when attempting to promote individualized learning in a group setting. The teacher is restricted by the need to cover certain areas of instructional content in specific time periods with large numbers of students. It is therefore most practical to hold all students to the same pace with uniformly scheduled evaluations. Any deviation from this customary approach is difficult for the teacher because it necessitates proliferation of paperwork to keep track of as many as 150 students in a day. Oettinger and Marks (1968) reviewed research indicating that effective monitoring of students in a continuous progress curriculum would be extremely burdensome because in a population of 900 students there would be about 30 to 40 transfers between courses necessitating 300 mastery tests each day. The administrative factors alone would be almost impossible for teachers to handle under current structure and conditions.

One of the provisions of P.L. 94-142 requires the explicit development of an Individualized Educational Program (IEP) for each handicapped student complete with goals, objective criteria to evaluate progress toward the goals, and other information concerning the placement of the student. It is very possible that IEPs will be required for *all* children in the future whether or not they are handicapped. Although this is desirable, commendable, and easily supported as an educational procedure, it certainly has the potential of creating an educational crisis of monumental proportions unless teachers are given additional specialized assistance, time, and training. This additional support would require budget increases at a time when school budgets are subject to inflation and reduction because of the unwillingness of patrons to support increases.

Whether or not teachers will be restricted to teaching large groups of students with equipment little more sophisticated than a blackboard may be determined by the commitment of universities to new, exemplary programs of training and by the willingness of society to provide the resources for small-group and individualized instruction as well as for long-term, relevant in-service training for teachers to ensure that the teaching community can keep abreast of the latest in educational philosophy, research, and technology.

These issues are of more than passing interest to the special educator because of a variety of implications that may be inferred. The growing problems faced by the regular classroom teacher may contribute to a breach that sometimes exists between specialists and the regular classroom teachers. Specifically, the requests made of regular classroom teachers by the specialists in addition to the requirements mandated by legislation and litigation in special education may become very difficult to handle and may cause regular classroom teachers to assume defensive attitudes. *Special educators must put forth increased effort to understand the roles and problems of regular classroom teachers because they are usually shared concerns.*

In the next several decades, the teaching profession will experience many pressures—accountability, collective bargaining, and dwindling enrollments among others—that will inevitably change the direction and nature of teaching. It is in the best interests of students for administrators, teachers, government agencies, and patrons to work together to optimize effective teacher training, improve teaching methods, and support in-service and preservice programs with adequate resources. Special educators must understand and support this cause.

Financial problems

The most significant and serious problem facing education is competition for the tax dollar. It is impossible to ignore that inflation continues, the tax base has been challenged in various court cases as a method of support for schools, and there has been a growing trend of voters to defeat tax issues. Zero-based budgeting may very well become basic to the administration of education in the near future. Educators will have to keep faith with school patrons, to improve education to the maximum extent, to use each dollar wisely,

and to make priority decisions about the rank and importance of various functions and activities of the school.

Classroom activities must take precedence over any other school-related endeavor, even if that means reduction of the budget in other areas. Resolution of the financial problems is essential. The schools should be held accountable for educational goals and effectiveness should be demonstrated; but, society should make reasonable demands of the school and should be held accountable for financial support.

Student participation

As the traditional modes of school administration have been criticized and challenged, it has become apparent that sweeping changes must occur in this area and in the relationship of students to decision-making procedures. Neill (1976, p. 25) lists the rights and responsibilities of students as follows:

Student rights
The right to all constitutional guarantees
The right to learn
The right to pursue an education without interference
The right to be respected and accepted as a human being
The right to be appropriately involved in one's own education on an equal basis

Student responsibilities
The responsibility to respect the constitutional rights of others
The responsibility to learn
The responsibility to be involved in setting up and observing necessary constraints to freedom
The responsibility to participate in governance

The school, as a bureaucratic organization, may need to yield to more flexible structures that incorporate the input of persons traditionally outside the power structure. Teachers are forcing concessions from the school by forming unions and by collective bargaining. Demands of students voiced in the 1960s were initially met with opposition but eventually brought about a number of curriculum changes that are now generally accepted.

To continue the process of integrating students, Dr. Terrel H. Bell (1976) the former U. S. Commissioner of Education has recommended that we need to "dejuvenilize" secondary education. The process of "dejuvenilization" entails participation of students on school boards and other important decision-making groups in the community, involvement of students in community businesses and agencies, and more direct involvement of students in the development of rules, regulations, and disciplinary codes. Miller (1976) has indicated that the demand for students to improve their behavior has been one-sided and that it is reasonable to expect pupil productivity to increase with improvements in administrative behavior. If research in effective leadership demonstrates that the involvement of all persons in the organization can improve productivity, then student involvement of the same magnitude would seem to be logical.

Educational outcomes

A major issue that is related to those mentioned above is the ultimate expectations of society for the school. This topic has been indirectly addressed in a previous portion of this chapter, but it is significant because it is a periennial problem as society changes. The current re-emergence of this issue might be called *back to basics*. The school responded to the demands of the 1960s for reform, but now many of those innovations are blamed for the drop in average achievement scores. It would seem that the school must be given a clear definition of societal goals as well as the resources to accomplish them. Perhaps, with the acceptance of career education, society will be able to make a distinction between college-bound and noncollege-bound students. If this "distinction" means the recognition of vocationally-oriented education as an education of equal value to the traditional college preparatory orientation of the past and not as some sort of second-class educational program, one issue will be on its way to resolution. Then, as a result of such recognition, there may be a variety of programs, including alternatives that will benefit the learning disabled, that will be accepted

as appropriate, valued components of the secondary school.

A related issue involves basic competencies and the high school diploma. If we broaden societal/educational goals, we must re-examine the purpose of the diploma. We must question the logic of the current trend that would equate the possession of a diploma with an established level of basic achievement, a requirement that would discriminate against many students who would not be able to meet such standards. How much relationship should the diploma have with academics? Should the development of a criterion for graduation be established as a single goal for a heterogeneous student population? Should a diploma be equated with a proficiency examination? Could the diploma be expanded to reward students of diverse backgrounds and career preparations without a single standard for obtaining it? These issues must be faced.

SUMMARY

Our concern in this chapter has been the nature of the secondary school and how this may influence the effectiveness of special programming for the adolescent who is learning disabled. Most of the early secondary school programs for the learning disabled were practically carbon copies of elementary school programs. These tended to be remedial in nature and were based on such assumptions as the relatively close contact that elementary regular classroom teachers have with their students. The elementary school learning disability specialist had only one primary (professional) person with whom to communicate regarding recommended procedures, need for coordinated efforts, and the like. In addition, the elementary school student was not nearly as subject to peer influence as was the secondary school student. The predictable result was that secondary school programs based on the elementary school model were not very effective.

The only reasonable conclusion, considering the preceding information, is that secondary school programs must be based on careful analysis and consideration of the unique characteristics of the secondary schools. In this chapter, the structure and educational practices of the secondary schools were discussed, with emphasis on those practices and characteristics that would likely have the greatest influence on the effectiveness of educational provisions for the learning disabled. The traditional liberal arts, college-oriented nature of the secondary school, the present concern with "slipping" achievement scores, the tendency to use the lecture method and assume average reading skills, and the general concern about any program that might be interpreted as "lowering academic requirements" were reviewed. The bureaucratic organization of secondary schools, the acknowledged and the hidden power structures, and the need for the learning disabilities specialist to be aware of these and other similar factors were stressed. The separate subjects curriculum, the letter grade system, and the accreditation-based requirements for graduation are all factors that are very relevant for providing a meaningful program for the adolescent learning disabled student.

Four issues that confront the secondary school—systems of teaching, financial problems, student participation, and changing (or indefinite) educational outcomes—were related to the needs of the learning disabled student. The resolution of these issues can be critical to the school's capability to provide adequate programs for the adolescent student who has learning disabilities.

Secondary level teachers of the learning disabled student must be aware of all of the preceding factors, dilemmas, and influences if they are to develop and maintain a program that is of maximum benefit to students. These factors must be considered in addition to those that relate to the unique needs of the adolescent and the various educational techniques and approaches that are appropriate for learning disabled adolescents.

DISCUSSION QUESTIONS

1. Contrast the Seven Cardinal Principles of Education with the purposes of education proposed in 1976 at the Bicentennial Conference on Secondary Schools.

2. In what ways does P.L. 94-142 change the decision-making process in the school?
3. What are the pros and cons of competency examinations required for high school graduation? What impact might this policy have on the lives of learning disabled students?
4. What might be the reaction of organized teachers (unions) to the requirements of such laws as P.L. 94-142?
5. What might be a viable alternative to traditional grading practices for learning disabled students?

REFERENCES AND READINGS

Adams, R. S., and Biddle, B. J. *Realities of teaching: Explorations with videotape.* New York: Holt, Rinehart & Winston, Inc., 1970.

Anderson, B. D. An application of the bureaucratic model to the study of school administration. *Journal of Educational Administration,* 1974, *12*(1), 63-75.

Bell, T. M. Let's "dejuvenilize" secondary education. In J. Chaffee, Jr., and J. P. Clark (Eds.), *New dimensions for educating youth.* Denver: U.S. Department of Health, Education and Welfare, 1976.

Chaffee, J., Jr., and Clark, J. P. (Eds.). *New dimensions for educating youth.* Denver: U.S. Department of Health, Education and Welfare, 1976.

Cohen, E. G. Sociology and the classroom: setting the conditions for teacher-student interaction. *Review of Educational Research,* 1972, *42,* 441-452.

Evans, F. B. What research says about grading. In S. Simon and J. Bellanca (Eds.), *Degrading the grading myths: A primer of alternatives to grades and marks.* Washington, D.C.: Association for Supervision and Curriculum Development, 1976.

Gearheart, B. R. *Organization and administration of educational programs for exceptional children.* Springfield, Ill.: Charles C Thomas, Publisher, 1974.

Gerth, H. H., and Mills, C. W. *From Max Weber: Essays in sociology.* New York: Oxford University Press, 1946.

Grambs, J. D., et al. *The junior high school we need.* Washington, D.C.: The Association of Supervision and Curriculum Development, National Education Association, 1961.

Gullet, C. R. Mechanistic vs. organic organizations: What does the future hold? *The Personnel Administrator,* 1975, *20*(7), 17-19.

Kiernan, O. B. Reflecting the forces of change. In J. Chaffee and J. P. Clark (Eds.), *New dimensions for educating youth,* Denver: U.S. Department of Health, Education and Welfare, 1976.

Lerner, J. *Children with learning disabilities.* Boston: Houghton-Mifflin Co., 1976.

Miller, W. C. Can a principal's improved behavior result in higher pupil achievement? *Educational Leadership,* 1976, *33*(5), 336-338.

Mueller, S. American education standards are slipping. *Today's Education,* 1975, *64*(4), 50-53.

National Education Association. What research says to the teacher: Evaluation and reporting of student achievement, Washington, D.C.: National Education Association, 1974.

Neill, S. B. Two R's for students: Rights and responsibilities. In J. Chaffee and J. P. Clark (Eds.), *New dimensions for educating youth*, Denver: U.S. Department of Health, Education and Welfare, 1976.

Neill, S. B. Why not admit you need help? In J. Chaffee and J. P. Clark (Eds.), *New dimensions for educating youth*. Denver: U.S. Department of Health, Education and Welfare, 1976.

Oettinger, A., and Marks, S. Educational technology: New myths and old realities, *Harvard Educational Review*, 1968, *38*, 697-717.

Polansky, L. Group social climate and the teacher's supportiveness of group status systems. *Journal of Educational Sociology*, 1954, *28*, 115-123.

Schrag, P. Education's "romantic" critics. In S. Dropkin, et al. (Eds.), *Contemporary American Education* (3rd ed.). New York: Macmillan Inc., 1975.

Scranton, T. R., and Downs, M. C. Elementary and secondary learning disabilities programs in the U.S.: A survey. *Journal of Learning Disabilities*, 1975, *8*, 394-399.

Simon, S., and Bellanca, J. (Eds.). *Degrading the grading myths: A primer of alternatives to grades and marks*. Washington, D.C.: Association for Supervision and Curriculum Development, 1976.

Sperry, R., Left-brain, right-brain, *Saturday Review*, 1975, 30-33.

Sumption, M. R., and Engstrom, Y. *School-community relations*. New York: McGraw-Hill Book Co., 1966.

Wilhelms, F. T. What about basic standards? *Today's Education*, 1975, *64*(4), 46-49.

Components of a secondary program

Recognizing that the field of learning disabilities is in a state of transformation as secondary level programs are being developed, this section discusses important considerations for program developers and learning disabilities specialists, many of whom will assume leadership in program development. We are fully aware that some of the recommendations will be of temporary help because the status of secondary programs will change rapidly as progress is made. However, it is imperative that we recognize and confront certain issues so that effective programming might have an auspicious beginning.

First, there is little reason to believe that the self-contained classroom will be of much benefit to the majority of students at the secondary level. There may be some students in some settings for whom this delivery system is appropriate, but we have elected to concentrate on the resource room as the most efficient and reasonable method of providing educational services for LD students. Second, the value of remediation diminishes as students near the end of their schooling. It is true that any particular student may require specific remediation in the tool subjects, but there is little evidence to justify any system that would segregate learning disabled students who, by definition, are quite intelligent and capable of academic progress. Many students, although unable to read proficiently, are able to learn in the variety of courses of the secondary school if sufficient accommodation and compensatory teaching techniques are provided. The trend toward a "back to basics" movement notwithstanding, students who are incapable of learning in the traditional manner because of legitimate learning disabilities must be accorded alternatives in the curriculum that permit equal educational opportunity, Third, the needs of learning disabled adolescents are best served by specialists who are well-grounded in the field of learning disabilities and who also have training in managing adolescent problems, in coping with the complexities of the secondary curriculum, in relating to other professionals, and in providing assistance to parents. Finally, the secondary program should be designed so that it will offer the student a variety of career options among which might be the opportunity to enter college.

Chapter Four represents an effort to cover the myriad issues relating to assessment. There is little consensus about what tests should be used in a minimum battery, but assessment has many purposes and educators hold a special responsibility to employ methods that are relevant to the daily demands of the curriculum and to the objectives of education that are realized after graduation. Chapter Five presents ways and means of making the secondary setting responsive to the needs of LD students through accommodation and compensatory teaching. Chapter Six is a presentation of our view of remediation. We recognize the importance that has traditionally been attached to this general area because this has been a central focus of the field, but the program that limits services to remedial aspects at the secondary level will be of minimal help to most students. Chapter Seven is a presentation of practical approaches to behavioral principles. Chapter Eight concerns career education and vocational preparation that is of vital importance but that has been neglected. Chapter Nine reviews the principles and practices of the school counseling program and suggests ways of improving the negative attitudes and poor self-concepts of students.

Undoubtedly, as we move into a new era and a new phase of special education, many issues and problems will unfold. We realize that the suggestions of this section may not provide solutions to all of the most pressing problems, but we hope that they will provide a grasp of the problems confronting us today and that they will be useful in supporting meaningful educational efforts for the LD adolescent in the future.

CHAPTER 4

Assessment

INTRODUCTION

Any discussion of assessment must account for different viewpoints about intelligence and achievement tests and about the shortcomings of the definition(s) of learning disabilities. This is evidenced by the criticisms of psychoeducational testing that have been so prominent in both the professional literature and the popular press. The controversy involves issues about the validity of intelligence and achievement tests, misuse of these instruments, and the potential harm to children. An inadequate definition of learning disabilities creates significant problems in assessment because it is not possible to identify a specific group of persons who share certain, clear-cut characteristics.

The assessment of *any* student is complicated by the fact that courts have rendered decisions altering or restricting the use of tests by school personnel. Assessment of a secondary student for learning disabilities presents many problems because there is little agreement about identifying characteristics nor is there consensus about an acceptable battery of assessment instruments.

As noted in Chapter One (p. 8), concern among federal lawmakers about the nonrestrictive definition of learning disabilities led to the belief that great numbers of learning disabled students would be identified, which might have the effect of diminishing the amount of federal funds under P.L. 94-142 available to other types of handicapped students. To counteract this, a ceiling was originally established to limit the number of LD students who would be eligible for funding but this plan was later abandoned. Until the issuance of further regulations for P.L. 94-142 in August, 1977, there was an attempt by the Bureau of Education for the Handicapped to meet federal requirements of the law by developing a specific evaluation procedure to be used in determination of which students are truly learning disabled. This effort was finally abandoned because of disagreement among many professionals who would not support the plan. As a result of these regulations, all handicapped students, including the learning disabled, are to be evaluated in accordance with the following procedures:

State and local educational agencies shall insure, at a minimum, that:

(a) Tests and other evaluation materials:

(1) Are provided and administered in the child's native language or other mode of communication, unless it is clearly not feasible to do so;

(2) Have been validated for the specific purpose for which they are used; and

(3) Are administered by trained personnel in conformance with the instructions provided by their producer:

(b) Tests and other evaluation materials include those tailored to assess specific areas of educational need and not merely those which are designated to provide a single general intelligence quotient;

(c) Tests are selected and administered so as best to ensure that when a test is administered to a child with impaired sensory, manual, or speaking skills, the test results accurately reflect the child's aptitude or achievement level or whatever other factors the test purports to measure, rather than reflecting the child's impaired sensory, manual, or speaking skills (except where those skills are the factors which the test purports to measure);

(d) No single procedure is used as the sole criterion for determining an appropriate educational program for a child; and

(e) The evaluation is made by a multidisciplinary team or group of persons, including at least one teacher or other specialist with knowledge in the area of suspected disability.

(f) The child is assessed in all areas related to the suspected disability, including, where appropriate, health, vision, hearing, social and emotional status, general intelligence, academic performance, communicative status, and motor abilities.*

Although these general procedures incor-

porate regulations pertaining to the appropriateness of tests and the competencies of examiners, procedures that can be embraced by most professionals who assume responsibility for all handicapped students, there were no practical approaches suggested for the assessment of learning disabled students relating to the broad definition of the condition and the need to limit or greatly reduce the number of students who should rightfully be considered to have learning disabilities. Such determination is to be left in the hands of a collective group, the multidisciplinary team, at each local level. Therefore, it can be reasonably expected that different interpretations of the definition will be made by the various examiners because of variance in experience and professional judgment. This circumstance may be especially problematic at the secondary level.

In December, 1977 the Office of Education announced final regulations to help states identify children who might have specific learning disabilities. The final regulations expand the procedure of utilizing a multidisciplinary team to determine learning disabilities. A synopsis of the regulations follows.*

Evaluation team

In evaluating a child who is suspected of having a specific learning disability, each public agency shall include the following professional persons on the multidisciplinary team:

1. The student's regular teacher or, in the event the student has no regular teacher, a regular classroom teacher qualified to teach a student of the age of the referred student.

2. A child of less than school age will be represented by a person who is qualified by the state to teach children of that age.

3. At least one person qualified to conduct individual diagnostic examinations such as a school psychologist, speech-therapist, or remedial reading teacher.

Criteria for determination of learning disabilities

The team may determine that a child has a specific learning disability if the child does not

---

*Federal Register, 1977, 42(163), 42496-42497.

*Federal Register, 1977, 42(250), 65082-65085.

achieve commensurate with his or her ability (in the defined areas) when provided with learning experiences appropriate for the child's age and ability levels; and, if the team determines that a child has a severe discrepancy between achievement and intellectual ability in one or more of these areas:

1. Oral expression
2. Listening comprehension
3. Written expression
4. Basic reading skill
5. Reading comprehension
6. Mathematics calculation or reasoning

The team may not identify a child as having a learning disability if the severe discrepancy may be attributed to a visual, hearing, or motor handicap, mental retardation, emotional disturbance, or environmental, cultural, or economic disadvantage.

Observation

At least one team member other than the child's regular teacher shall observe the child's academic performance in the regular setting and, in the case of a child of less than school age, a team member shall observe the child in an environment appropriate for the child of that age.

Written report

The team shall prepare a written report of the results of the evaluation, which must include whether the child has a specific learning disability, the basis for the determination, the relevant behavior noted during the observation of the child, the relationship of the behavior to academic functioning, educationally relevant medical findings, whether or not there is a severe discrepancy between achievement and ability that is not correctable without special services, and the determination of the team concerning the effects of environmental, cultural, or economic disadvantage. Each team member must certify that the report reflects his or her opinion and, if not, the team member who disagrees must submit a separate statement presenting his or her conclusions.

This is the summary of the operational procedure to be used in the evaluation of students referred with possible learning disabilities. It is apparent that the extent of procedural changes in the new regulations relates primarily to the nature or composition of the multidisciplinary team. This procedure does not concern issues that have been at the center of the controversy over the definition of learning disabilities, does not clarify these issues, and places responsibility for decision making on a group of professionals at the local level. As noted before, the problems involved in determination of learning disabilities at the secondary level may prove to be very troublesome to examiners and the incidence of the condition may vary greatly from one school district to another.

Many of the problems associated with the definition, the diagnostic features, and the estimation of the incidence found at the elementary school level are also evident at the secondary school level. The practice of estimating the incidence at any level may be viewed as "pulling figures out of the air" in as much as they are based on a certain amount of guesswork. We urgently need to turn professional attention to these problems at the secondary level.

In view of the limited information from research investigations, the criteria used to place a young child into special programming may not be of much relevance with older students. *Initial* diagnosis of an adolescent may present different problems than those presented in reconfirmation of a condition with a long history. It is quite possible that some students may be able to cope rather effectively with mild disorders until the extreme difficulty and demands of an increasingly complex curriculum become overwhelming. Assessment of students at the secondary level who may have learning disabilities will be an interesting and challenging area of professional concern.

CATEGORIES OF ASSESSMENT

There are many purposes for and levels of assessment. From the broad perspective, however, assessment can be classified according to *administrative* and/or *instructional* needs. Some types of assessment may be important to assist in the attainment of instructional objectives and also be required to meet some administrative need. Assessment may also be classified by the nature of the instruments used. These include but are not necessarily limited to:

A. Formal tests
   1. Intelligence

2. Achievement
3. Diagnostic
4. Personality and projective
5. Interests and/or aptitude
B. Informal methods
    1. Observation
    2. Behavioral sampling
    3. Interview
    4. Teacher-constructed tests.
C. Criterion-referenced, or mastery, tests
D. Task analysis

Formal tests are used by schools for many purposes, but their use in diagnosis and classification is paramount. Beyond initial diagnosis, however, formal tests may be of little value to many teachers because they fail to yield information that is applicable in meeting instructional objectives. Too many examiners are not able to convert such information into relevant educational information and teachers, who are often not trained in the administration and interpretation of these instruments, find diagnostic reports to be meaningless. This may be a result of the gap between administrative and instructional needs, but teachers who are trained in informal methods, mastery tests, and task analysis realize that assessment is a never-ending process that must rely on daily evaluation. This places the use of formal tests in proper perspective as assessment approaches are balanced in a comprehensive educational effort.

THE NEED FOR INFORMATION

Special education programs at the local level are affected by numerous legal requirements of federal and state legislation or regulations that grow out of such legislation. Agencies *require* information. Children who have special education needs must be identified (child-find) and classified for fiscal support to be extended to the local program. This reality is recognized in state policies determining eligibility for special program service and related special funding.

Although the main purpose of assessment should be to determine the learning needs of students and to provide evaluative measures for making appropriate decisions, the need to determine eligibility is also a serious concern

for the school. Because of legal and social forces, some state guidelines appear to avoid arbitrary cutoff points related to test scores and are rather vague about eligibility.

Many problems can arise because of the administrative needs of local, state, and federal education agencies. Recent state and federal actions have caused an impact on assessment practices because the psychological examiner and other assessment personnel are responsible for evaluating or re-evaluating many students. This limits available time for interpretation of evaluative measures that might be useful for instruction. Accountability has also increased the demand for assessment by requiring additional testing, the results of which are used for justification of program existence, if not effectiveness. Special education personnel are caught between opposing forces because it is necessary to collect psychoeducational data for administrative and instructional purposes while social and legal forces restraining the use of standardized instruments have caused school personnel to be reluctant to use tests.

The Council for Exceptional Children has addressed this problem (Nazzaro, 1976):

Awareness of the need for comprehensive assessment was triggered by the court cases of the early 1970's which dealt in part with the placement of minority children in EMR classes on the basis of single IQ scores, (*Larry P.* v. *Riles*, 1972; *Diana* v. *State Board of Education*, 1970). . . . Although the initial reaction was in response to the use of tests judged to be inappropriate for certain minority group children, the need for comprehensive assessment has been generalized to all children. (p. 37)

The Council for Exceptional Children continues by reviewing the recommendations of the Bureau of Education for the Handicapped and concluding that a comprehensive assessment is one that uses a full range of instruments and observations that includes diagnostic tests and other "appropriate" formal and informal measurements.

A multifactored or multiple-assessment procedure is recommended because it is apparently believed that a wealth of data and scores from a variety of sources will allow examiners to make better decisions about students based on a broad sample of behaviors. Presumably, this can prevent the undesirable practice of classifying students erroneously. Many students have been misclassified on the basis of single test scores or limited observations. This was a major argument in the litigation of *Diana* v. *The Board of Education*. However, it would seem that examiners who tend to make judgments later considered to be erroneous may still do so in spite of multifactored assessment. Improved competence on the part of psychoeducational examiners is essential. The use of teams tends to impose a balance in assessment decisions. Nonetheless, it is possible that the greater volume of test data may increase the possibility of variant scores appearing on various instruments that may fit the biases of examiners.

Another factor that will increase the frequency and quantity of evaluations is P.L. 94-142, which requires each local educational agency (school) to prepare and update an individualized written program for each handicapped child. The law defines the Individualized Education Program (IEP) as:

A written statement for each handicapped child developed in any meeting by a representative of the local educational agency or an intermediate educational unit who shall be qualified to provide, or supervise the provision of, specially designed instruction to meet the unique needs of handicapped children, the teacher, the parents or guardian of such child, and, whenever appropriate, such child, which statement shall include (A) a statement of the present levels of educational performance of such child, (B) a statement of annual goals, including short-term instructional objectives, (C) a statement of the specific educational services to be provided to such child, and the extent to which such child will be able to participate in regular educational programs, (D) the projected date for initiation and anticipated duration of such services, and (E) appropriate objective criteria and evaluation procedures and schedules for determining, on at least an annual basis, whether instructional objectives are being achieved.

The responsibility for the development and maintenance of the educational plan will be a major responsibility of the special educator. The teacher will find it necessary to use psychoeducational data from the psychologist or psychological examiner as well as to conduct further evaluations, some of which will likely be standardized tests, to satisfy the need for "objective criteria and evaluation procedures" in monitoring the child's progress.

The need for information is increasing as more tests are required in the assessment of various components of a student's behavior and personality to meet diagnostic, instructional, and administrative requirements. The great numbers of test scores available to teams of examiners may increase the probability that individual examiners and teams will tend to "find something wrong" with a child because of orientation-bias to certain theories of learning disabilities.

Teachers should be aware that tests provide no magic solution to learning problems of children. There will always be an opportunity for errors in the diagnosis and classification of students. Expecting too much from test information is a mistake. Improper diagnosis can be tragic. Tests are frequently misunderstood and some professionals tend to ignore elementary statistical concepts relating to tests.

At best, tests can offer clues or probable insights into the functioning of a student and, as such, can be used as hypothetical bases for educational provisions. Tests can be helpful in diagnosis and educational planning as long as the limitations of the various instruments are recognized. Patient observation and behavioral samplings should direct the activities of examiners who should be reluctant to make decisions that expeditiously categorize children. The *need for information* can be classified as follows:

1. Test information is required for diagnosis and initial classification (administrative needs).
2. Test information is helpful in generating educational plans and making decisions about children (instructional needs).
3. Test information is important for the evaluation of the results of instructional

activities (an administrative and an instructional need).

THE DECISION TO TEST

It is true that tests have been misunderstood and misused. Controversy surrounding test-use causes problems for examiners. Therefore, the decision to test a student should be made in accordance with clear, established objectives. The following considerations might be helpful in establishing testing practices at the local level:

1. A child should not be subjected to a test unless there is a clear reason why other data-gathering practices will not be sufficient.
2. Diagnostic and intelligence tests should not be used as screening instruments.
3. Specific tests must be selected because the results may answer questions posed by professionals; tests should not be administered simply because they are available.
4. Tests should be administered by examiners who are fully qualified to administer and interpret them.
5. Tests should not be administered unless there is a clear need to use the results in the immediate future.
6. The best use of test information is in the process of making decisions about a student.

A student should not be subjected to a battery of tests just because the school has the tests. The decision to administer each test should be made because it has the potential to help clarify or resolve some problem concerning the student. Efficient screening procedures should be used to identify students considered at risk. Some schools use a variety of diagnostic instruments to serve as a screening battery. This is not necessary and is certainly expensive because of the direct cost and the indirect expense of removing personnel from other more productive activities in the school.

If the judgment is made that a student requires further testing, assessment procedures should be implemented with the expectation that the new information will be valuable in clarification of some problem and in its potential amelioration. Test information should be carefully interpreted with particular attention devoted to statistical properties. Test information is of little value within the files of a school officer. Test scores can be transmuted into valuable educational information.

The Council for Exceptional Children makes recommendations about the uses of group tests and individual assessment pertaining to students and parents (Nazzaro, 1976):

1. A description of the test with some sample of the items should be provided.
2. The parents and student should be given a statement concerning the purpose of the test.
3. An explanation should be given of how the results will be used.
4. The parents should be informed as to whether or not the results will become a part of the permanent record.
5. A list of rights should be explained, they are:
   a. to review all records related to referrals for evaluation.
   b. to review the procedures and instruments to be used in the evaluation.
   c. to refuse to permit the evaluation.
   d. to be fully informed of the results.
   e. to get outside evaluation at public expense if necessary.

The Bureau of Education for the Handicapped, as reported by Nazzaro (1976), has recommended that any instrument used should meet the test of reasonableness (a legal concept):

Evaluation materials and procedures used for purposes of classification and placement of handicapped children should meet a test of reasonableness in the eyes of competent professional persons and informed laymen. Such procedures should be administered by qualified persons under conditions conducive to the best performance of the child. (p. 39)

LEGAL CONSIDERATIONS

All programs for handicapped children in the latter half of the 1970s must be planned and implemented within a framework of legal regulations and restraints that did not exist in the 1960s. These grew out of certain ethical considerations and interpretations of the role of the public schools under state and federal statutes but were not implemented in most parts of the nation until the conclusion of a variety of court actions directed against schools and resulting state and federal legislation. This litigation did not typically include actions related specifically to the learning disabled but tended more to be concerned with the mentally retarded. Nevertheless, it had a number of effects on programs for the learning disabled. These court actions, the way in which they were handled by professional educators and boards of education, and the role of a variety of parent and professional groups makes fascinating reading for those who are legally inclined and historically oriented. The general effects may be summarized as follows:

A. All handicapped children have a right to an appropriate, free, public education.

B. Identification and placement of children in special programs for the handicapped must include careful consideration of racial, ethnic, and language differences, and dictates modified assessment practices in many instances.

C. A possible stigma effect, resulting from special education placement, and the labelling that such placement seems to require, must be avoided if at all possible.

1. A first corollary of this principle is that the least restrictive educational alternative (which may likely be effective) must be used. The first choice would be retention in the mainstream of public education with consultive help to the teacher; second choice might be some type of resource room help; and last choice would be the self-contained special class.

2. A second corollary is that if a label must be used to initiate assistance through special programming, the label with the least negative connotation should be used.

D. The principle of *due process* as it relates to making decisions about all of the above has received national attention, and due process, a term that was virtually unknown among rank and file special educators in 1970, is in common use today. This principle was given a strong boost by Public Law 93-380, the Educational Amendments of 1974, which included the requirement that *all* states provide certain basic aspects of due process in their state plans. It was further strengthened by P.L. 94-142 as illustrated by the following excerpt from Section 615:

(b) (1) The procedures required by this section shall include, but shall not be limited to—

(A) an opportunity for the parents or guardian of a handicapped child to examine all relevant records with respect to the identification, evaluation, and educational placement of the child, and the provision of a free appropriate public education to such child, and to obtain an independent educational evaluation of the child;

(B) procedures to protect the rights of the child whenever the parents or guardian of the child are not known, unavailable, or the child is a ward of the State, including the assignment of an individual (who shall not be an employee of the State educational agency, local educational agency, or intermediate educational unit involved in the education or care of the child) to act as a surrogate for the parents or guardian;

(C) written prior notice to the parents or guardian of the child whenever such agency or unit—

(i) proposes to initiate or change, or

(ii) refuses to initiate or change,

the identification, evaluation, or educational placement of the child or the provision of a free appropriate public education to the child;

(D) procedures designed to assure that the notice required by clause (C) fully inform the parents or guardian, in the parents' or guardian's native language, unless it clearly is not feasible to do so, of all procedures available pursuant to this section; and

(E) an opportunity to present complaints with respect to any matter relating to the identification, evaluation, or educational placement of the child, or the provision of a free appropriate public education to such child.

(2) Whenever a complaint has been received under paragraph (1) of this subsection, the parents or guardian shall have an opportunity for an impartial due process hearing which shall be conducted by the State educational agency or by the local educational agency or intermediate educational unit, as determined by State law or by the State educational agency. No hearing conducted pursuant to the requirements of this paragraph shall be conducted by an employee of such agency or unit involved in the education or care of the child.

P.L. 94-142, then, provides a legal mechanism for settling disputes that may arise between parents and school officials concerning identification, evaluation, or placement of a child. This is a most dramatic event in education and places many new demands on school officials.

Most schools have begun to respond to these demands. Assessment should be made with regard to the student's educational functioning, which is, in turn, related to the academic program of the school. The results should be expressed in terms that take into account the student's strengths and weaknesses. A variety of observations and instruments should be used so that determinations are not made on the basis of a single criterion. Parents should be informed in writing and in the primary language of the family about the intention to change or alter the educational status of the child. Permission must be sought for testing. Test results must be explained to the parents. Lastly, a grievance procedure should be clearly established and described so that parents may appeal any decisions or actions of the school.

GATHERING INFORMATION

The assessment process is actually concerned with the gathering of information with which it may be possible to make important decisions about students. Some authors recommend that the school should collect information under the categories of (1) case history, (2) clinical observation, (3) formal and diagnostic testing, and (4) informal testing. (Lerner, 1976).

The process of taking a *case history* is very time consuming and difficult. Social workers are thoroughly trained in the technique of taking a case history, while very few teachers have learned the technique in teacher preparation programs. A topical survey or interview might be conducted with the parents of the student by the interviewer, but any such procedure should have clearly identified purposes because a great deal of information may emerge that is actually of little value to the school and that may be embarrassing to the family because of its sensitive nature. Some parents tend to "bare all" about interpersonal relationships with their spouses that is of little significance to the school beyond a certain point. Such information can be dangerous in the records of the child because of the potential for a breach of confidentiality. Also, getting parents to speculate about when accidents might have occurred to a child may cause feelings of guilt if the parents believe that parental negligence and the resultant "damage" to the child are causing current educational difficulties. Schools should be cautious in this type of data gathering and should institute procedures for selecting important information and maintaining the confidentiality of records.

Clinical observation is the process of collecting data from various informal sources under the direct supervision of a specialist in some field. Educational specialists in learning disabilities should be able to make observations and interpret such information subjectively for the purposes of identifying characteristic behaviors that might not be sensitive to test instruments. The ability to develop this skill is directly related to experience that cannot be gained readily. With the propensity to rely on standardized tests, either because they are convenient or they disguise inexperience, a valuable source of information is lost when clinical observations are not made. One limitation of this process is that the work load and other responsibilities of the educational specialist curtails the opportunity to make consistent observations. This can be remedied to a certain extent by assisting classroom teachers in developing observational techniques.

Informal methods of assessment are rich in significant information that can be readily employed by the diagnostician in making decisions about the performance of students and in erecting educational plans. The informal reading inventory is a familiar technique to many teachers. It is possible that a regular classroom teacher can use similar forms of assessment to provide additional information supporting the efforts of the diagnostic team. The orientation of the secondary school is such that many teachers are not concerned with teaching tool subjects, nor do they have formal training in these areas. Therefore, it is important that the examination systematically include assessment of these areas that are so important to functioning in content areas.

THE ASSESSMENT PROCESS

The school must follow a logical sequence of events in the assessment of students. This process must be designed to focus on the needs of students and to meet legal requirements rather than to be convenient for the school administration. The following areas have been identified as potential areas of evaluation (Walker, 1976, p. 21):

A. Educational functioning
   1. Achievement in subject areas
   2. Learning style
   3. Strengths and weaknesses
B. Social-emotional functioning
   1. Social/psychological development
      a. Attending/receiving
      b. Responding
      c. Valuing
      d. Organizing
      e. Characterizing
   2. Self-help skills
C. Physical functioning
   1. Visual
   2. Hearing
   3. Speech
   4. Motor/psychomotor
      a. Gross motor
      b. Fine motor
   5. Medical health
D. Cognitive functioning
   1. Intelligence
   2. Adaptive behavior

   3. Thinking processes
      a. Knowledge
      b. Comprehension
      c. Application
      d. Analysis
      e. Synthesis
      f. Evaluation
E. Language functioning
   1. Receptive
   2. Expressive
   3. Nonverbal
   4. Speech
F. Family
   1. Dominant language
   2. Parent-child interactions
   3. Social service needs
G. Environment
   1. Home
   2. School
   3. Interpersonal
   4. Material

The functions of the examiners (team, committee) in obtaining this information should be guided by professional and ethical standards as well as all legal requirements, which includes due process procedures. To gain maximum effectiveness, the activities of the examiners must be streamlined because poorly planned assessment procedures cause significant delays that create "waiting-lists" and interfere with educational placement. When the assessment process is established, it should be viewed as a system (using systems theory) and carefully analyzed to identify and eradicate any bottlenecks. Efficient and appropriate forms should be developed to document all activities of the examiners. The functions of a team or committee for placement are detailed in Fig. 1.*

The functions of the examining team are directed by one overriding objective—to gather pertinent information about a student with which to make decisions. When the data are amassed, the team must agree about the placement of the student. If agreement is

---

*A resource manual, *Functions of the Placement Committee in Special Education,* has been published by the National Association of State Directors of Special Education. It is such an excellent publication that any school should find its contents of significant value for organizing and monitoring a local assessment program.

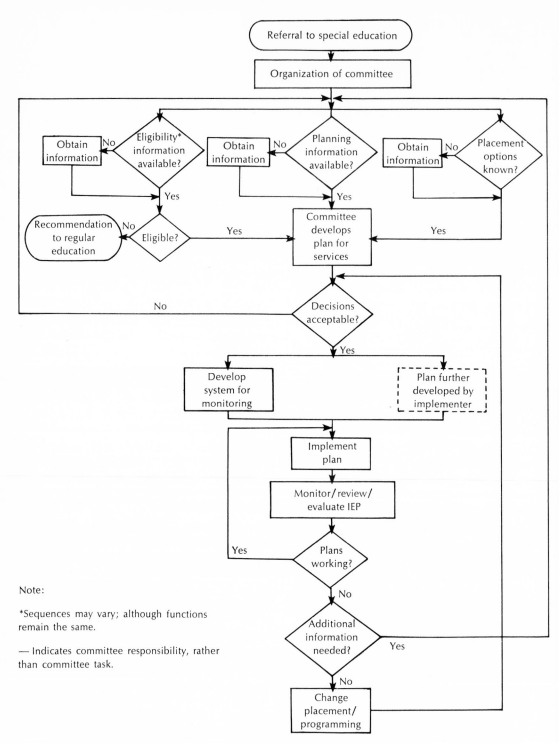

Fig. 1. Flowchart: placement committee functions. (From Walker, J. [Ed.]. *Functions of the placement committee in special education.* Washington, D.C.: National Association of State Directors of Special Education, 1976.)

Individual Education Program: Total Service Plan

Child's name _____

School _____

Date of program entry_____

Prioritized long-term goals:

_____

_____

_____

Summary of
present levels of performance:

_____

_____

_____

_____

_____

Short-term objectives	Specific educational and/or support services	Person(s) responsible	Percent of time	Beginning and ending date	Review date

Percent of time in regular classroom	Committee members present _____
	_____
	_____
	_____
Placement recommendation	Dates of meetings _____
	_____

Committee recommendations for
specific procedures/techniques, materials, etc. (include information about learning style)

Objective evaluation criteria for each annual goal statement

Fig. 2. Individual Education Program: total service plan. (From Walker, J. [Ed.]. *Functions of the placement committee in special education*. Washington, D.C.: National Association of State Directors of Special Education, 1976.)

Individual Education Program: Total Service Plan
(Complete one of these for each goal statement specified on total service plan)

Child's name _____   Goal statement:_____

School _____   _____

Date of program entry_____   Short-term instructional objectives: ___

Projected ending date_____   _____

Person(s) completing form_____   _____

Behavioral objectives	Task analysis of objectives	Strategies and/or techniques	Materials and/or resources	Date started	Date ended	Comments

Fig. 3. Individual Education Program: individual implementation plan. (From Walker, J. [Ed.]. *Functions of the placement committee in special education.* Washington, D.C.: National Association of State Directors of Special Education, 1976.)

reached, if it can be determined that a student is eligible, and if placement is made in accordance with due process procedures, the most important concern of the team and teachers is the development of an IEP. The IEP should be a natural extension of the decisions reached in the assessment process. The National Association of State Directors of Special Education has recommended that the placement team should develop a *total service plan* that states long-term objectives, the percentage of time a student is to attend regular class, and other required information. A total service plan is shown in Fig. 2. The regular classroom and special teachers are responsible for development of the *implementation* IEP, which is a series of responses to the major objectives developed by the placement team. Fig. 3 is an example of an IEP form for one objective of the implementation phase. This part of the process requires the completion of several forms pertaining to the total number of objectives in the plan for a particular student. The completion of these forms constitutes the IEP (total service and implementation plans) in accordance with the directives of P.L. 94-142.

THE NATURE OF STANDARDIZED TESTS

The core of many diagnostic efforts is the interpretation of formal tests because they are standardized on normative groups, which allows the examiner to make comparisons on the basis of the scores the tests yield. Standardization implies that all subjects have an opportunity to answer the same questions, that they receive identical and unambiguous instructions, that no subject has an advantage, and that a predetermined system of scoring is employed (Nunnally, 1964). Test scores can clarify a student's abilities in relationship to common standards established on large groups of subjects. Standardization is important because there is a need to understand the behaviors of students in measurable terms in much the same manner that it is necessary to have a standard system of weights and measures for such measurements to be meaningful to all people.

Scores that are derived from standardized instruments are useful because they permit an examiner to appraise differences in achievement and growth. The numerical score allows for other forms of treatment of differences between students such as statisti-

cal comparison in descriptive analysis and educational research. Human differences are not clearly understood nor can they be measured with the same precision as physical quantities. Intelligence and other hypothetical constructs are developed to explain behavior. Test developers attempt to provide examiners with instruments that are valid (measuring traits for which they are developed) and reliable (providing uniform results with consistency).

The major types of norms used for educational purposes are age, grade, percentile, and standard score norms (Thorndike and Hagen, 1969). Norms contain certain properties that approach the desirable qualities sought in standardization so that uniformity in the expression of results and in comparison can be made. Most educators are aware of these concepts but may tend to ignore caution about test use, may disregard error, and may not consider statistical properties.

SELECTED TESTS
Introduction

A variety of standardized tests and informal methods of assessment have been used with learning disabled children. The diagnosis may depend in part on uneven patterns of development or "scatter" that occurs in the appearance of test profiles. It is generally expected that assessment of student performance and ability will reveal comparable intelligence and achievement test scores. If a student appears to have adequate intellectual ability yet significant deviations in achievement and/or other specific skills, then a diagnosis of learning disabilities may be one possibility.

The basic assumption in education that a student should perform near his ability is the premise for the conceptualization of *underachievement* and *learning disabilities*. Underachievement is believed to result from the inability of a student to "work up to capacity" because poor teaching, lack of motivation, or other vague factors interfere with the normal learning process. Learning disabilities are believed to be distinguished from other cases of underachievement be-

cause of presumed dysfunctions of the central nervous system or abnormal development of processes that disrupt learning.

The first step in the process of determining either underachievement or a learning disability is to estimate the individual's expected or anticipated level of functioning by means of an intelligence test, which is then contrasted with achievement scores or *levels of performance.*

Tests provide examiners with measures of current behaviors. They cannot accurately predict or estimate potential or ultimate functioning, although they are extremely useful in the hands of competent examiners who can make informed judgments.

An assortment of statistical methods have been used with younger children in the determination of discrepancies between potential and actual achievement. Most of these methods have incorporated the mental age (MA) to fix expected achievement. The MA is, of course, derived from an intelligence test. In its most basic form the MA is estimated and reduced by five to arrive at grade expectancy (GE) (MA $- 5 =$ GE). Myklebust (1968) has employed a more elaborate method to identify learning disabilities based on a learning quotient (LQ) that is related to the MA.

An intelligence test score is an approximation or a rough estimate of what might be reasonably expected. Some of the discrepancy between the results of an intelligence test and those of an achievement battery can be explained, not so much as failure of the child to work up to capacity, but as inability of the test instrument to predict achievement.

Thorndike (1963) has addressed this issue directly by attacking the basic assumptions of MA and the predictive ability of intelligence tests. Because the correlation between intelligence and reading and other skills is not perfect, other factors must influence achievement. The artifact of the regression effect causes brighter students to have reading scores that are below expectations while students at the other end of the continuum tend to exceed them. These and other factors should encourage examiners to exercise caution in making decisions about students. Tests can be helpful if they are regarded as tools, and if test results are tempered with sound judgment.

It becomes increasingly confusing as the intelligence test is applied in prediction of different academic subjects. Whereas reading tends to demonstrate a curve of gradual and continuous development, arithmetic does not because it is closely tied to the school curriculum (what is actually *taught* in the schools). After acquisition of fundamental skills, a student may make remarkable progress in reading without further instruction. With arithmetic, however, a student is unlikely to be exposed to more advanced concepts without direct teaching. Therefore, a student may tend to show an arithmetic achievement score that is at or somewhat below grade level and that may be erroneously interpreted as a deficit, especially if reading achievement is high. Many quite normal high school and college students have rather low scores in arithmetic or mathematics that are a function of limited exposure to advanced instruction and the fact that skills that fall into disuse tend to diminish. Predicting achievement in content areas is very complex because poor achievement can be attributed to so many different variables.

As a consequence, there has been a recent, dramatic revolution in assessment that has led to the adoption of criterion-referenced measurements and mastery tests. Although these instruments are useful in many ways that norm-referenced tests are not, they still lack the qualities that are necessary in the differentiation of the learning disabled group from other underachievers.

Thorndike (1963) has insisted that another statistical technique, regression analysis, using both the chronological age and the IQ as predictors, is a more defensible approach to the examination and estimation of discrepancies between actual and expected achievement levels. Using regression analysis in reading, arithmetic, and other areas may provide superior estimates of what should be expected for students of various

ages and/or levels of intelligence. But, even with more precision in estimating expectations based on the interaction of these variables, the field of learning disabilities must still focus on the causes and factors that delineate specific groups of underachievers. As results from this line of endeavor accrue, it will be essential that learning disabilities in specific academic areas, (reading, arithmetic, and writing) and specific process disabilities (visual perception, auditory perception, motor systems, language, and so forth) be investigated as distinct entities.

Because of the controversy over the use of standardized tests, the trend toward criterion-referenced measures, the limited number of tests developed for use with older students suspected of being learning disabled, and the lack of specificity about characteristics associated with older LD subjects, it is clear that the selection and use of tests at the secondary level is not a trivial matter. It should also be clear that any decisions based on test results, especially at the secondary level, are speculative because in most instances it is necessary to make assumptions that the causes of scholastic failure are the result of learning disabilities. As mentioned earlier, the term *learning disability* is a rubric that encompasses many diagnostic entities which leads to professional disagreement about characteristics and the lack of a restrictive definition. It is important to focus on factors relating to academic achievement, success in the content areas, and general adjustment, rather than engaging in activities that direct attention away from the functional problems of students into theoretical exploration of process deficits and etiologies. Assessment must be aimed at pragmatic considerations that are relevant to the immediate educational needs of students as well as to posteducational adjustment.

The concerns and issues just discussed are of prime importance, but until they have been resolved to the satisfaction of all (or nearly all), we must deal with the students who are presently experiencing difficulties with the tests currently in use. Awareness of the concerns and issues should lead to caution in application of test results, but students in need of help cannot wait for the provision of perfect assessment tools. We shall therefore proceed with a review of what is now available and how such tests may be used.

Intelligence tests

The most popular intelligence test is the *Wechsler Intelligence Scale for Children* (WISC), which was revised in 1974 and is referred to as the WISC-R. For older adolescents, the *Wechsler Adult Intelligence Scale* (WAIS) is used. The outstanding feature of these tests is that they are comprised of two universal measures of intelligence, verbal and nonverbal. The tests yield three IQ scores—the verbal IQ, the performance IQ, and a full-scale IQ. The mean IQ for each scale is 100 with a standard deviation of 15. Descriptions of the WISC subtests are:

Information—measures associative thinking and general comprehension of facts that are acquired in the home and school.
Comprehension—measures the use of common sense, reasoning, and judgment.
Arithmetic—measures the ability to apply arithmetic processes in problem solving, abstract concepts of number and numerical operations, and numerical reasoning.
Similarities—measures abstract and concrete reasoning that involves verbal concepts and the capacity for associative and remote memory.
Vocabulary—measures the ability to understand words. This test reflects the level of education and the environment. It measures the accumulated verbal learning ability of an individual and the range of ideas, information, and qualitative levels of reasoning ability.
Digit Span—measures the ability to repeat auditory information in sequence and detail and to hold attention.
Picture Completion—measures the ability to detect essential and nonessential visual stimuli from common objects in the environment.
Picture Arrangement—measures the ability to conceive a total situation using visual comprehension and organization.
Block Design—measures the ability to perceive, analyze, and reproduce abstract designs. Requires concrete and abstract abilities and visual-motor coordination.
Object Assembly—measures the ability to see spatial relationships and to synthesize concrete parts into meaningful wholes. It measures visual-motor coordination and simple assembly skills.
Coding—measures the ability to learn visual-motor skills in new situations, dexterity, speed, and accuracy.
Mazes—an alternate test that measures the ability to plan, attend, and use foresight.

Language tests

Although theories of learning disabilities relating to language and psycholinguistic processes can be traced to Myklebust and Orton, among others, the explicit study of language development has been conducted by many investigators who have had little interest in learning disabilities per se. The phenomenal amount of research with the *Illinois Test of Psycholinguistic Abilities* (ITPA) in recent years encouraged many authorities to investigate this aspect of human development as a factor in learning disabilities. The ITPA is not generally suitable for use with adolescents.

The *Detroit Tests of Learning Aptitude* constitute a battery of aptitude tests formed by 19 subtests. The tests have been used as a measure of language development although many other abilities are tapped. The subtests can be grouped in accordance with varying permutations for assessing specific students or groups of students. They are used extensively with older students.

The *Hiskey-Nebraska Test of Learning Aptitude* was originally developed for deaf persons, but a revision of the test is now available for hearing persons. It is used by some examiners to fill the need for a measure of language development. As in the case of the Detroit Tests, various combinations of subtests can be administered for different purposes. At least one state (South Carolina) recommends this test in the assessment of adolescents with learning disabilities. A more complete discussion of this approach is presented later in this chapter.

Another test familiar to practitioners who work with younger children is the *Picture Story Language Test* that was developed by

Myklebust. The test is also suitable for older children with norms extending to the age of 17. Essentially, the test requires a subject to compose and write a story about a picture. Three scales measure the productivity, syntax, and abstractness-concreteness of the response.

The *Malcomesisus Screening Test of Specific Language Disability* is another test that can determine a subject's strengths and weaknesses in processing language and written work. The examinee is required to listen to a paragraph, isolate essential facts, recall them, and put them in sequence. The content of the organization as well as the nature of the written work can be evaluated.

A valuable instrument for use in assessing more complex forms of language usage of appropriate interest to the secondary teacher is the *Illinois Index of Scholastic Aptitude*. It measures the precise language skills of students in understanding the use of synonyms and antonyms and in reading comprehension.

Achievement tests

Aside from the traditional achievement batteries that are routinely administered to all students by the schools, one individual achievement test has frequently been used by special education personnel in the assessment of adolescents. The *Wide Range Achievement Test* (WRAT) provides scales in reading recognition, arithmetic computation, and spelling that are appropriate for adolescents and adults. The test is easy to administer, takes little time, and is easily scored. Scores can be reported as grade equivalents, percentiles, and standard scores that can be related to deviation IQ scores.

Many group achievement tests are extremely valuable in use with secondary students, but day-to-day encounters of students with specific content areas (history, science, and so forth) should be evaluated in terms of the specific course objectives and/or text-related materials actually used. Task analysis and criterion-referenced tests, or mastery tests, are absolutely essential. These topics will be considered in a later section.

Other tests

There are of course many tests that might be used with secondary students. We have not intended to recommend any specific tests but have attempted to mention some that may be at the core of many diagnostic batteries. Some tests, such as the *Halstead-Reitan Battery* might have application to these subjects but would ordinarily not be included in a typical secondary school assessment program. Again, we wish to emphasize the point that tests should be selected for specific purposes associated with making important decisions about students. Therefore, if a student appears to have problems that alert the examiners to the possibility of social maladjustment or atypical personality disorders, it might be desirable to extend testing in those areas if the results can be anticipated to resolve questions about the student. Close coordination between the family, physicians, and other members of the professional community outside the school should be maintained.

TESTS USED IN CHILD SERVICE DEMONSTRATION CENTERS

The Bureau of Education for the Handicapped funds 29 learning disabilities model centers under ESEA, Title VI-G. Although many of the centers provide educational programs for elementary and secondary students, seven centers clearly serve secondary students exclusively. The following information was taken from the *Catalogue of Child Service Demonstration Centers: 1975-76*, a publication of the National Learning Disabilities Assistance Project. Based on the programs that differentiate between tests used at the elementary level and those used at the secondary level and those programs that are exclusively for secondary students, the following information indicates the tests that are used in the seven centers. The number in parentheses after each test designates the number of centers that actually use that particular instrument. These are:

Auditory Discrimination Test (revised (1) edition)

Bender Visual Motor Gestalt Test (5)

Benton Visual Retention	(2)
California Achievement Test	(2)
Columbia Test of Mental Maturity	(1)
Detroit Tests of Learning Aptitude	(5)
Developmental Test of Visual Perception (3rd edition)	(1)
Diagnostic Reading Scales (revised edition)	(3)
Durrell Analysis of Reading Difficulty	(5)
Gates-MacGinitie Reading Tests	(2)
Gates-McKillop Reading Diagnostic Tests	(1)
Goldman-Fristoe-Woodcock Auditory Skills Test Battery	(1)
Gray Oral Reading Test	(1)
Hiskey-Nebraska Test of Learning Aptitude	(1)
Illinois Test of Psycholinguistic Abilities	(1)
Jesness	(1)
KeyMath Diagnostic Arithmetic Test	(4)
Leiter International Scale	(1)
McCall-Crabbs Standard Test Lessons in Reading	(1)
Metropolitan Achievement Tests (revised edition)	(1)
Minnesota Percepto-Diagnostic Test (revised edition)	(1)
Ohio Vocational Interest Survey	(1)
Peabody Individual Achievement Test	(5)
Peabody Picture Vocabulary Test	(5)
Perceptual Forms Test	(1)
Piers-Harris	(1)
Roswell-Chall Auditory Blending Test	(1)
Roswell-Chall Diagnostic Reading Test of Word Analysis Skills	(3)
Slosson Intelligence Test	(1)
Slosson Oral Reading Test	(1)
SRA Achievement Series	(1)
Stanford Achievement Test: Reading Tests	(3)
Stanford Diagnostic Tests	(3)
Stanford-Binet Intelligence Scale	(4)
Survey of Study Habits and Attitudes	(1)
Tennessee Self-Concept Scale	(1)
Test of Visual-Motor Integration	(1)
Wepman Auditory Discrimination Test	(1)
Wide Range Achievement Test	(4)
WISC-R	(7)
Woodcock Reading Mastery Tests	(2)

A total of 41 tests were used in the seven demonstration Centers for screening, pre and posttesting, diagnostic, and other purposes. A total of 22 different tests were used with a reported frequency of one (1). The only test that was used by all seven centers was the WISC-R. Thus, it can be seen that a standard battery of tests has not emerged for use at the secondary level. Also, it appears that the concerns of evaluators, as expressed by the types of tests that are used, are not directed at vocational considerations. Moreover, some of the tests listed above are not necessarily suited for older students because of the limitations imposed by restricted age norms. However, qualitative analyses can still be employed.

AN EXAMPLE OF A REQUIRED ASSESSMENT PROCEDURE

Scranton and Downs (1975) conducted a survey that revealed that secondary programming has developed at a much slower pace than elementary programs. Consequently there have been few organized efforts to develop a specific battery of tests for use in the secondary school. One exception is that of South Carolina. The following recommendations are adapted from the guidelines for evaluation of the State Department of Education of South Carolina.

Diagnosis of learning disabilities at the middle and secondary level

I. Criteria (when Wechsler scales are used)
 A. The candidate must be of legal school age.
 B. The candidate must have a health screening and there must be no deficits in vision, hearing, or physical areas.
 C. The candidate must not score below −1 standard deviation on the full-scale and/or performance or verbal scales of the WISC.
 D. The candidate must possess an identified learning disability based on profile analysis of the individually administered intelligence scale in addition to supportive evidence from at least *two* other supplemental sources of the "Observed psychological dysfunction."

 Atypical patterns of intratest scatter are considered significant if the candidate obtains an average scale score of 8 or lower on one or more of the following areas of dysfunction:
 1. *Visual*-Picture Completion, Picture Arrangement, Block Design, Object Assembly, Coding, Mazes.
 2. *Auditory/language*-Information, Simi-

larities, Digit Span, Comprehension, Vocabulary, Arithmetic.

3. *Haptic/sensory-motor*-Block Design, Coding, Object Assembly, Mazes.

A suspected visual dysfunction would entail examination with the following instruments:

1. Hiskey-Nebraska Test of Learning Aptitude
   a. Visual Attention Span
   b. Completion of Drawings
   c. Picture Analysis
   d. Spatial Reasoning
2. Bender-Gestalt
3. Benton Visual Retention Test
4. Graham-Kendall Memory for Designs
5. Detroit Tests of Learning Abilities

A suspected auditory/language dysfunction in an adolescent would require the use of the Hiskey-Nebraska and "other suitable" instruments in addition to the Wechsler scales.

A suspected haptic/sensory-motor dysfunction would be evaluated by the following tests:

1. Hiskey-Nebraska Test of Learning Aptitude
   a. Block Patterns
   b. Puzzle Blocks
2. Bender-Gestalt
3. Draw-A-Person
4. Oseretsky Tests of Motor Proficiency
5. Detroit Tests of Learning Abilities

TEST INTERPRETATION

A variety of tests have been used in the assessment of children with learning disabilities. However, there has been far less agreement about what instruments should be included in a battery for adolescents, but this should be dictated by the purposes for which assessments are made and the series of problems a particular student might present. The Wechsler scales hold a prominent place in assessment. Many investigators have attempted to discover characteristic patterns that can identify subgroups of students and offer direction in remediation. Profile or scatter analysis has been used in the interpretation of the Wechsler scales.

The WISC and the WAIS have been used with adolescents, depending on the age of the subjects, but most research about WISC profiles has been conducted with younger subjects. The recent revision of the WISC, the WISC-R, has not been in existence long enough for reports of research to become widely available. Until such time as such results are available, it would seem that caution should be used in the application of old conclusions to the new instrument.

Descriptions of the Wechsler scales appeared earlier in this chapter but the basic facts will be repeated. The raw scores of the tests are converted into scale scores, and three IQ scores are derived—the verbal, performance, and full-scale. The mean IQ for each scale is 100 with a standard deviation of 15.

Pattern or scatter analysis

A number of writers have suggested that specific WISC patterns exist that can be used to differentiate among children with various kinds of learning disabilities. One such system has been recognized by the South Carolina Department of Education (p. 76). Essentially, this approach is known as *scatter analysis* and was originally developed to differentially diagnose between various subpopulations of persons with a variety of mental disorders using patterns of the WAIS and the Wechsler Bellvue.* Investigators have repeated this approach with many test instruments by identifying a group of subjects who are classified as having some traits in common, for example, schizophrenia, and administering tests to the group to determine if there are patterns of response unique to the group.

A complete discussion of analysis for interpretation of the WISC has been provided by Sattler (1974). Generally, there are three major variations in conceptualization of scatter or pattern analysis with the WISC. These are:

1. Comparison of sets of individual scores.
2. Comparison between scales.
3. Comparison of the average of several subtest scale scores with subtest scale scores included in the average.

---

*The Wechsler Bellvue was a forerunner of the current Wechsler tests.

To compare sets of individual scores, it is necessary to determine the *standard error of measurement* (SE$_M$) for each of any two subtests in a set, square and sum each SE$_M$, extract the square root, and multiply this value by a Z value to determine whether or not these scores should be considered statistically different. Sattler explains this process in detail. It is a matter of analyzing values of actual scores obtained by the student (on the various subtests) through use of a given formula, which in turn will indicate whether or not score differences are sufficiently different to have potential meaning. Assessment personnel who wish to further investigate this application of pattern analysis should refer directly to Sattler (1974) for the appropriate procedure and the established formulae.

Comparison of the verbal and performance scales have been important to some examiners in the determination of learning disabilities. A great deal of attention has centered on this aspect of test interpretation. In practice, some reports include diagnostic impressions that attach great significance to relatively minor discrepancies between the verbal and performance scales. By referring to the tables in the Appendices of Sattler (1974), which report significant deviations for the scales and the subtests, exact values can be determined. Small deviations that are not statistically significant should not be regarded as important because deviations of this magnitude can occur by chance.

Sattler has noted that a pattern of subtest scores is not fortuitous and does not occur randomly. The examiner must make determinations about which factors might account for the performance. Many variables such as age, sex, race, and cultural background affect performance on the examination. Careful consideration of these factors should figure prominently in the interpretation of results.

Some writers assert that typical patterns may be found that can define diagnostic subgroups and, perhaps, direct remediation. Clements and co-workers (1964) have suggested that there are three typical patterns found on the WISC for subjects with minimal brain injury:

Pattern 1—Wide scatter in either or both scales with a higher frequency of lower scores in Arithmetic, Block Design, Object Assembly, Digit Span, Coding, and Mazes.

Pattern 2—A verbal scale IQ that is 15 to 40 points higher than the performance IQ even though the Arithmetic subtest may be quite low.

Pattern 3—A performance scale IQ score that is 10 to 30 points above the verbal scale.

Hartlage (1975) reports three types of children who show characteristics similar to the WISC patterns that are identified by Clements. The Hartlage patterns are:

Type 1—Children with lower verbal IQ scores show related inferiority of language dependent skills. This type of child tends to experience persistent problems throughout the educational career.

Type 2—Children with lower performance IQ scores and inferiority of perceptuomotor skills tend to be more impulsive, less self-critical, but have good prognosis for educational improvement.

Type 3—This type is characterized by erratic patterns with no superiority of either scale. This group tends to show signs of neurological disorders and are more hyperactive and irritable. This type shows a poor prognosis for school adjustment and educational success.

Bannatyne (1968, 1974) has suggested a method for analysis of WISC profiles that bears some similarity to the system used by the South Carolina State Department of Education. Whereas the South Carolina method is concerned with diagnostic categories, Bannatyne's method is used for the determination of ability patterns. Specifically, the method requires that the examiner sum the scale scores and determine average scores, according to the following specific groups of subtests:

A. Spatial ability
   1. Picture Completion
   2. Block Design
   3. Object Assembly
B. Sequencing ability
   1. Digit Span
   2. Arithmetic
   3. Coding
C. Verbal conceptualization ability
   1. Comprehension

2. Similarities
3. Vocabulary
D. Acquired knowledge
    1. Information
    2. Arithmetic
    3. Vocabulary

Comparison of the subject's scores in each of the four areas may reveal some wide patterns of differences between groups. Assuming the validity of this approach, it would seem advisable to determine statistical significance of scores to ensure that observed differences are not the result of chance variations.

Money (1962) has suggested a method that is similar to the technique used by Bannatyne. The categories are Perceptual Organization (Block Design and Object Assembly), Verbal Comprehension (Information, Comprehension, Similarities, and Vocabulary), and Freedom from Distractibility (Arithmetic, Digit Span). This method is based on the factor analytic study of Cohen (1959).

Research in the use of psychological tests to differentiate normal children from groups with frank neurological signs of brain damage have been conducted with good results (Boll, 1974). Children with brain damage, as a group, have deficits in vocabulary, concept formation, and perceptual-motor abilities that are similar to patterns in adults with brain damage with the exception that adults do not tend, as a group, to have severe deficits in vocabulary.

Reed and Reitan (1969), in an investigation of children with infantile hemiplegia, found a *general* depression of intellectual ability with below average WISC scores. There was no significant discrepancy between the scales, rather, the scores in each scale were about equal, whether or not the children had damage to the left or the right hemisphere. It would appear that damage to the left or the right hemisphere that occurs early in life may result in a general lowering of intellectual functioning.

Black (1974) found characteristic discrepancies between verbal and performance scales with children who experienced recent brain damage. Differences on WISC patterns may be attributed to acute damage, whereas chronicity tends to cause a general lowering of both scales. Boll (1972) and Reed et al. (1965) examined older brain-damaged children and found concept formation to be seriously impaired. Boll suggested that a more proper term to describe these children would be *conceptually handicapped*, rather than perceptually handicapped, because of these results.

Interestingly, when a similar approach was used in the investigation of younger brain-damaged children, concept formation was not found to be the most severely limited function but rather language and verbal ability (Reitan, 1974). Early brain damage may tend to depress all functions but may allow primitive development of conceptual formation because of compensatory ability related to the brain's plasticity (Reitan, 1974). Damage that occurs later in childhood affects verbal abilities, which may have a limiting effect on the expression of conceptual thinking. One factor that might relate to such results is that proposed by Luria (1973), who contended that higher-order functioning, or differentiation of hemispheric functions relating to language, does not appear in normally developing children until about 10 years of age.

Examinations and results of research with children who have frank neurological signs and known brain damage may not be relevant to theoretical views of minimal cerebral damage and "soft" signs. However, the contrast is most interesting when considering some recent findings of research with learning disabled children.

Rugel (1974) and Schwartz (1974), among others, have discussed behaviors of subjects related to language functions and characteristic patterns of behavior. One interesting pattern has been the ACID score, which is a variation of profile analysis on the WISC representing the Arithmetic, Coding, Information, and Digit Span subtests.

Dykman and Ackerman (1975) have concluded that learning disabled students in the elementary grades show depressed scores in these four subtests (ACID) and that the pattern persists into adolescence. This is interpreted to mean that students who show this pattern, or even a low score on any of the four subtests, will experience problems in scholastic achievement. The ACID factor apparently relates to the ability to sustain attention, to hold information, and to implement a plan of strategy in problem solving.

Although tests are the focus of a legal and social controversy, it is apparent that relevant information can be gained from their use. These tools may continue to yield information that will permit us to investigate the many aspects of learning disabilities as long as appropriate cautions are observed and safeguards are built into the assessment process.

The inability of a variety of tests to clearly identify subgroups of children in reading, arithmetic, psychomotor functioning, and many other deficit-areas does not mean that characteristic symptoms or syndromes do not exist nor that such syndromes have no meaning. Our present level of understanding about learning disabilities is limited and perhaps too much is expected of certain tests that were designed for different purposes. *Specific tests should be used with a variety of other measures and pragmatic educational strategies should be designed to use this body of information in addition to daily task analytic approaches.*

Diagnostic considerations

The examiner, or the recipient of assessment information, should be especially wary of validity assumptions about certain traits purportedly measured by tests. In recent years, tests that have been used with younger LD children have received close scrutiny. Belief in the existence of deficient processes in children may be determined by the faith one has in the acceptance of a hypothetical construct and in the ability of a test to measure it. If it can be demonstrated that children do not have visual perceptual problems, although a test indicates they do, then it becomes necessary to seriously consider the usefulness of the test as well as the importance of the "deviant trait" in explaining human differences. If an examiner cannot be held responsible for the validity of a test, the examiner can be held accountable for significant consequences that might befall the examinee if cautions are not noted in the evaluation summary.

Specific attention should be given to the *qualitative nature* rather than the numerical responses of students on test items. Hanck (1975) has demonstrated this procedure with the Illinois Test of Psycholinguistic Abilities. The examiner can gain a variety of information by noting the nature of the child's response to specific test items. For example, a student may earn raw score points equivalent to another subject who took the same test. It might be noticed that one student answers a *few* questions correctly while the other worked with much more speed, attempted to answer many more questions, and completed the examination with a high-error rate. The fact that these students have identical achievement scores can be misleading. One student may work very deliberately and have a high mastery level, but the actual ability level is disguised. The other student might be able to deal with factual information but be unable to respond to questions dealing with the depth of content.

The WISC might serve as an example for qualitative analysis. If a student has a high average for scaled scores, for example, 13, and one subscale deviates markedly from the average, yet is within the average range for most subjects who take the test, then it may be tempting to regard the lower, deviant score as indicative of a deficiency.

A subject's performance on a subtest, such as *Digit Span*, might be low but what does it tell us? Does it mean that the subject has poor auditory memory? Does it mean that the subject has difficulty concentrating or screening out irrelevant stimuli? Does it mean that the subject is prone to test anxiety? Did the examiner give the test more slowly than required by the manual? Merely reporting the low score in Digit Span and suggesting that the student's memory should be improved is a waste of time. Making the assumption that this is the sole cause of learning problems is ridiculous. The low score should induce the examiner, or interpreters, to organize and reorganize test elements and other bits of information to determine what factors are actually operating. If it is concluded that the subject actually has a problem with short-term memory, this information might be used in forming systems of behavior in the home and the school to reduce the consequences of the deficit. Chalfant and Scheffelin (1969) have concluded that there is no evidence that memory can be improved through outside intervention. In the face of such conclusions, it is difficult to understand why many students are induced to engage in rather meaningless activities (such as rehearsing digits) thought to improve memory. Other aspects of the child's problem, caused by poor memory, should be considered.

A low score on the Arithmetic subtest of the WISC might indicate that the student has difficulty with problem solving or that the basic skills for arithmetic are lacking. Moreover, administration of computational problems may indicate that the student can perform rather adequately when he is not required to organize the facts.

Qualitative analysis of formal tests can yield useful information that far exceeds the value of test scores. Nonetheless, this is only one source of information that should be used in making diagnostic and educational decisions.

AN ECOLOGICAL MODEL OF ASSESSMENT

One aspect of diagnosis has been the traditional assumption that something is inherently wrong with the learner and that discovery of the cause may lead to correction of a disorder. Diagnosis, a medical concept, is a process of classifying symptoms to discover an underlying condition. In medicine, the discovery of a disease or etiology of a disease is often tantamount to finding a cure. Application of this concept in education has been disappointing. Instead of finding a "cure" implicit in the presumed cause or etiology, we often find only a "label." Although formal diagnosis with standardized instruments is important and should be defended, even in a time when it is more social-

ly acceptable to criticize tests, standardized instruments cannot provide the information required for development of a meaningful daily lesson plan. Instead of blaming poor teaching on inadequate formal instruments because they do not give us direction in teaching, we must learn to analyze the instructional process.

Many highly important factors in learning are not known to the examiner who is not privy to the daily interaction of the student in the learning environment. An ecological model should be used to account for the interaction of the learner with the environment, with teachers and classmates, and with materials and instructional methods. Even the use of behavioral objectives ignores what the learner must *do* to meet outcome objectives.

Task analysis

To be cognizant of these important ecological factors, the task analytic approach has become increasingly popular as a method of concentrating on the tasks of the learner. *Task analysis* may be thought of as a dual process in that the behavior of the learner may be analyzed in the act of learning and the nature of the learning task or materials may also be analyzed and matched to the learner.

A brief explanation of the process can be presented by reviewing the approach of Gagné (1965) who uses task analysis to establish the criteria for a behavioral objective and to explore the process for accomplishing it. By examining the outcome or terminal behavioral objective, the teacher can work backwards from the objective to lower level tasks and define the exact sequence by which a student must approach the desired outcome. Once the teacher can identify all the mediating tasks, a probe of the learner's skills can be made to determine readiness. Each explicit task is presented at the lower levels and, as mastery is achieved, transfer is made to the next higher task. The teacher is able to determine the entry level for each learner (readiness), identify what skills the learner needs to have to succeed in an intermediary

task, and concentrate on the materials and instructional techniques leading to acquisition of a hierarchy of skills.

Criterion-referenced tests

In recent years the controversy over the use of norm-referenced tests has been a major concern of special educators. Historically, very specific eligibility criteria have been employed to determine which students may be identified (labeled) and placed in special education programs. These criteria have typically involved some use of standardized test scores. The newer trend is to eliminate reliance on single-test scores. As a result, criterion-referenced testing has gradually become favored as an alternative in measuring student achievement and progress as well as for supplemental testing to be used in program planning and evaluation.

The differences between these two types of assessment are quite clear. A *norm-referenced test* enables the examiner to compare and contrast the performance of an individual with that of many individuals. This is frequently an important objective of the place-

ment committee which must make a "diagnosis" to meet state requirements for eligibility. A *criterion-referenced test* measures the abilities of an individual against arbitrary criteria for performance in specific skill areas and is most useful in making daily instructional decisions. Obviously, the uses of either type of test are determined by the purposes for which a student is subjected to assessment. Neither type can adequately supplant the other. Neither type is inherently "good" nor "evil." A norm-referenced test may yield important information about a student that seems to be better suited for making certain decisions, such as evaluation, placement, and dismissal of students in special education programs. Criterion-referenced tests are more appropriate for determining *what* to teach and may offer some direction in *how* to teach.

A criterion-referenced test may be developed for use in special education programs as an intrinsic part of the daily instructional activities. The IEP incorporates specific behavioral objectives that are designated for each student. Instructional activities and assessment should be based on the objectives. Certain bodies of knowledge tend to be more easily organized into hierarchies (task analysis) that may be systematized for instructional purposes. Examples might be the low-level, teachable skills in reading and arithmetic that lead to more complex abilities. The specialist at the secondary level may be more concerned with content-referenced tests that measure individual growth in acquisition of knowledge in such disciplines as *history* and *science*. The specialist, in association with the regular classroom teachers, may utilize the terminal objectives for each course (American History, World History, and so forth) to organize and evaluate instructional activities.

The performance of a student on daily tests (outcomes) are used in the process of making decisions about instruction. This approach focuses on the important aspects of instruction and not the trappings that have come to be associated with instruction. In other words, if a student reaches a level of competence in a learning activity, instruction is ended because the learner exhibits evidence of meeting the criterion. If not, instruction is continued, the student is not moved to a new level with the passage of time (social promotion), and decisions are not made on the basis of group comparisons.

SUMMARY

In this chapter we have attempted to present the reader with an overview of the factors involved with assessment of secondary students for learning disabilities. It was noted that the lack of a restrictive definition and the lack of clarity about the characteristics of adolescents with learning disabilities complicates the matter of diagnosis. As a consequence, the federal government, although willing to support special education programs with funding of excess costs, has taken steps to ensure that the numbers of students who are classified as LD will be limited. In view of these factors, the development of assessment procedures at the secondary level should account for the specific purposes of assessment. These purposes must be guided

by the primary need to resolve important questions about the problems that led to the student being considered as a potential candidate for the learning disabilities program. Tests should be selected for their appropriateness, the statistical properties and limitations of standardized instruments must be appreciated, and information collected about students should be treated in a confidential and professional manner. Continued research with adolescents may improve the conceptualization of learning disabilities, identify specific characteristics, and lead to the development of better indices for diagnosis and educational intervention. Until that time, we must consider the use of a variety of assessment tools and techniques and utilize the results of any such assessment with care, keeping in mind that the primary purpose of the entire effort is greater success on the part of the student in both academic endeavors and personal/affective relationships.

DISCUSSION QUESTIONS

1. What are the reasons underlying a multifactored assessment? What dangers are there in this approach?
2. Discuss the major differences between norm-referenced and criterion-referenced tests.
3. Why are the results of standardized tests usually disappointing to many teachers?
4. Why is the mental age regarded to be of limited usefulness in describing older subjects?
5. What would be the implications for assessment of handicapped students if all standardized tests were banned?

REFERENCES AND READINGS

Bannatyne, A. Diagnosing learning disabilities and writing remedial prescriptions. *Journal of Learning Disabilities*, 1968, *4*, 242-249.

Bannatyne, A.: Diagnosis: A note on recategorization of the WISC Scaled Scores. *Journal of Learning Disabilities*, 1974, *7*, 272-274.

Black, F. W. WISC Verbal-Performance discrepancies as indicators of neurological dysfunction in pediatric patients. *Journal of Child Psychology*, 1974, *30*, 165-167.

Boll, T. J. Conceptual vs. perceptual vs. motor deficits in brain-damaged children. *Journal of Clinical Psychology*, 1972, *28*, 156-158.

Boll, T. J. Behavioral correlates of cerebral damage in children aged 9 through 14. In R. Reitan and L. Davison (Eds.), *Clinical neuropsychology: Current status and applications.* Washington, D.C.: V. H. Winston & Sons, 1974.

Busbee, C. B., and Black, R. S. Procedures for survey, screening evaluation, placement, and dismissal of children into/out of programs for the handicapped. South Carolina Department of Education.

Chalfant, J. C., and Scheffelin, M. A. *Central processing dysfunctions in children: A review of research* (NINDS Monograph No. 9). Washington, D.C. U.S. Government Printing Office, 1969.

Clements, S. D., Lehtinen, L. E., and Lukens, J. E. *Children with minimal brain injury.* Chicago: National Society for Crippled Children and Adults, 1964.

Cohen, J. The factorial structure of the WISC at ages 7-6, 10-6, and 13-6. *Journal of Consulting Psychology,* 1959, *23,* 285-299.

Dykman, R. A., and Ackerman, P. T. *Hyperactive boys as adolescents.* Unpublished paper, presented to the A.P.A., Chicago, 1975.

Gagné, R. M. *The conditions of learning.* New York: Holt, Reinhart & Winston, 1965.

Gallagher, J. J. Personal perspectives. In J. M. Kaufman and D. P. Hallahan (Eds.), *Teaching children with learning disabilities.* Columbus, Ohio: Charles E. Merrill Publishing Co., 1976.

Hanck, N. G. Tests and assessment: A second look. In B. Gearheart (Ed.), *Teaching the learning disabled: A combined task-process approach.* St. Louis: The C. V. Mosby, Co. 1976.

Hartlage, L. C. *Educational implications of three types of minimal brain syndrome.* Unpublished paper presented at the International Conference of the A.C.-L.D., 1975.

Kirk, S. A. Personal perspectives. In J. M. Kaufman and D. P. Hallahan (Eds.), *Teaching children with learning disabilities.* Columbus, Ohio: Charles E. Merrill Publishing Co., 1976.

Lerner, J. W. *Children with learning disabilities.* Boston: Houghton-Mifflin Co., 1976.

Luria, A. R. *The working brain: An introduction to neuropsychology.* New York: Basic Books, Inc., Publishers, 1973.

Money, J. (Ed.) *Reading disability: Progress and research needs in dyslexia.* Baltimore: The Johns Hopkins University Press, 1962.

Myklebust, H. (Ed.) *Progress in learning disabilities* (Vol. I). New York: Grune & Stratton, Inc., 1968.

National Learning Disabilities Assistance Project. *Catalogue of child service demonstration centers: 1975-76.* Merrimac, Mass., 1976.

Nazzaro, J. Comprehensive assessment for educational planning. In F. J. Weintraub, et al. (Eds.), *Public Policy and the Education of Exceptional Children.* Reston, Va.: Council for Exceptional Children, 1976.

Nunnally, J. C. Educational measurement and evaluation. New York: McGraw-Hill Book Co., 1964.

Reed, H. C., et al. The influence of cerebral lesions on psychological test performance of older children. *Journal of Consulting Psychology,* 1965, *29,* 247-251.

Reed, J. C. The deficits of retarded readers—fact or artifact? *Reading Teacher,* 1970, *23,* 347-352, 393.

Reed, J. C., and Reitan, R. Verbal performance differences among brain-injured children with lateralized motor deficits. *Perceptual and Motor Skills,* 1969, *29,* 747-752.

Reitan, R. Psychological effects of cerebral lesions in children of early school age. In R. Reitan and L. Davison (Eds.), *Clinical neuropsychology: A current status and application.* Washington, D.C.: Winston & Sons, 1974.

Rugel, R. WISC subtest scores of disabled readers: A review with respect to Bannatyne's recategorization. *Journal of Learning Disabilities,* 1974, *7,* 48-55.

Rutter, M., and Yule, W. The concept of specific reading retardation. Unpublished manuscript. (N.D.).

Sattler, J. M. *Assessment of children's intelligence.* Philadelphia, Pa.: W. B. Saunders Co., 1974.

Sax, G. *Principles of educational measurement and evaluation.* Belmont, Calif.: Wadsworth, Publishing Co., Inc., 1974.

Schwartz, G. A. *The language-learning system.* New York: Simon & Schuster, Inc., 1974.

Scranton, T. R., and Downs, M. C. Elementary and secondary learning disabilities programs in the U.S.: A survey. *Journal of Learning Disabilities,* 1975, *8,* 394-399.

Thorndike, R. L. *The concepts of over- and under-achievement.* New York: Teachers College Press, 1963.

Thorndike, R. L., and Hagen, E. *Measurement and evaluation in psychology and education* (3rd ed.). New York: John Wiley & Sons, Inc., 1969.

Walker, J. (Ed.). *Functions of the placement committee in special education.* Washington, D.C.: National Association of State Directors of Special Education, 1976.

CHAPTER 5

Accommodation and compensatory teaching

INTRODUCTION

This chapter discusses accommodation and compensatory teaching. This general approach to teaching is distinguished from the remedial approach by the following definitions. *Remediation or remedial teaching refers to those activities, techniques, and practices that are directed primarily at strengthening or eliminating the basic source(s) of a weakness or deficiency that interferes with learning. The focus is on changing the learner in some way so that he or she may more effectively relate to the educational program as it is provided and administered for all students.* The presumption is made that there is something wrong with the learner that can be identified and corrected. *Accommodation* *and compensatory teaching refer to a process whereby the learning environment of the student, either some of the elements or the total environment, is modified to promote learning. The focus is on changing the learning environment or the academic requirements so that the student may learn in spite of a fundamental weakness or deficiency.* This may involve the use of modified instructional techniques, more flexible administrative practices, modified academic requirements, or any compensatory activity that emphasizes the use of stronger, more intact capabilities or that provides modified or alternative educational processes and/or goals.

In both approaches, the goal is a positive change in academic performance and in most cases there will probably be a need to utilize some facets of both emphases. We have attempted to codify various aspects of accommodation and compensatory techniques to stress a different philosophy of teaching learning disabled adolescents in the sincere hope that it will not be overlooked in an educational atmosphere that tends to stress remediation of the learner. Actually, there may be sufficient overlap in our dichotomy to make this conceptualization questionable. In fact, we would hope that educators would eventually include the entire range of remedial and accommodation approaches as acceptable educational practices. Nevertheless, the distinction is made so that teachers may endorse a philosophy and suggest practices that the school may employ to enhance the chances of academic survival for a segment of the student population that is constrained by traditional academic requirements and procedures.

This chapter and the following one emphasize the major thrust of the planned educational effort not the preciseness with which we may say that we are "remediating" or "accommodating." *We are convinced that attention must be focused on the value of accommodation and compensatory teaching for two very important reasons: (1) because so much of the elementary school program emphasis has been on remediation, the potential effectiveness of accommodation and compensatory teaching may be overlooked, and (2) we believe that, in general, the older the student, the greater should be the emphasis on accommodation and compensatory teaching.* *

Since the preparation of this text was begun, another milestone in education has been reached with the implementation of guidelines to Section 504 of the Rehabilitation Act of 1973. Section 504, in tandem with P.L. 94-142, will serve as the foundation for a dramatic change in the lives of citizens who have emotional, mental, or physical handi-

---

*Note the *Guidelines for Use of Compensatory or Remedial Teaching* as followed at the Grove Learning Center, a private school in Minnetonka, Minnesota (Chapter 10). Their statement is quite consistent with this belief.

caps. The guidelines include persons with specific learning disabilities. Section 504 applies to employers, public and private schools, and universities. Among the provisions of the regulations are these points:

1. New facilities constructed must be accessible to handicapped students, and older facilities must be modified.
2. Colleges and other postsecondary institutions must provide programs and activities that are readily accessible to handicapped persons.
3. Institutions and employers must conduct an evaluation to determine what policies and practices will need to be changed to eliminate bias against students or employees with handicaps.
4. A "recipient to which this subpart applies" must undertake modifications in academic requirements so that otherwise qualified handicapped students are not excluded. This might include the substitution of courses or the change of the length of time required for completion of courses or adaptation of the manner in which courses are conducted.
5. Appropriate "educational auxiliary aids" are required for handicapped students.
6. Evaluation of a handicapped student's academic achievement in a course *shall be determined by methods that represent the student's achievement rather than "reflecting the student's impaired sensory, manual, or speaking skills."*

It is now clear that there is a legal basis for accommodation and compensatory teaching. Undoubtedly, there will be a great deal of confusion and debate among educators as the impact of this Act is felt in schools where traditions are challenged. Nevertheless, changes will occur that will be unsettling to many educators and patrons who fear that basic programs will be threatened and that standards will be lowered. We view these changes positively because, not only is the spirit of equality recognized in Section 504, but practical procedures will ensue that will make equality for students a reality in the instructional setting. Section 504 may prove to be the instrument that will ensure that handicapped students truly benefit from placement in the least restrictive environment, because it is clearly a civil rights issue.

Before we proceed with a discussion of accommodation, we will again emphasize that the goal is a positive change in academic performance that alters the methods of instruction or the techniques of evaluation without reducing the quality of performance. The procedure whereby this change will occur may often include a planned "mix" of accommodation and remediation. The specific combination would relate to specific goals and what we know or think we know about the student in question. It will vary from student to student, and any given plan of action for a student must be regularly reviewed and modified as necessary.

Remediation will be considered in another chapter, and it will be seen that it does have an important place in the total spectrum of educational provisions for the learning disabled student. There can be no argument with special education approaches that have assisted many students. The concern is that when they do not result in essentially normal functioning, accommodation must complement them so that the lives of capable students may not be artificially or unfairly limited.

GENERAL CONSIDERATIONS

Accommodation may be considered as any of a variety of methods of adapting the school organization, curriculum, or instructional methods to the learner. When we choose to meet the needs of LD students by stressing educational approaches other than (or in addition to) remediation, a number of possible techniques can be explored. Any approach should be conceptualized as being applied to a *specific student* rather than organizing an "adapted" secondary curriculum for LD students and expecting each student to go through the same steps. *Except in the most severe cases where a decision might be made to develop a self-contained program, most students should be expected to participate as much as possible in the regular curriculum of the school and should attend most classes with their non–learning disabled peers.*

As the individual characteristics of each student are evaluated from a broad educational perspective, a number of accommodating conditions might prevent failure. It should be noted that all of the following suggestions may not be acceptable in all schools, and careful planning should be made before attempting to introduce them. It will be interesting to see if such issues become legal considerations in future court cases.

A number of rather general administrative changes apply in most secondary settings that may be acceptable in even the most traditional school. The key to change in the secondary school is usually the principal. Any plans should be made in cooperation with the administration, and it would be best to select the most innocuous changes for the initial development of a program.

Communication with feeder schools

A junior high school usually receives new students from several elementary or middle schools. Similarly, the senior high school usually enrolls students from several junior high schools in the community. An essential consideration, particularly for the learning disabled student, is to ensure that the curriculum sequence at each level integrates with the next higher level. The student should be able to make the transition from one level to another without significant disparity in program content, scope, or expectations.

Communication should exist between the special education staff and diagnostic teams at each school level. The special education teachers should be (or become) acquainted with their counterparts in other schools. Students who are preparing to make a transition in the following year, should be given an opportunity to make several visits to the new school, spend some time in classes, and be warmly received by those staff members who will be assisting them in any special program planning in the new school. The receiving school should have student records well in advance of enrollment. Choosing classes should be discussed with the students and their parents (this usually requires more *special* planning than with non–learning disabled students). Special orientation should be provided for the families.

Enrollment assistance

The classes in which a student enrolls are of utmost importance to initial adjustment and ultimate success. Although the demands of the secondary schools are greater, careful planning can take into account learning and personality characteristics as well as educational pursuits and can make a smooth transition. Although many courses are required in the "standard" program, there are frequently a few options that may satisfy the credit requirements. A variety of electives offers flexibility in completing a schedule. We believe that enrollment is a particularly important aspect of each semester and are convinced that the student, the family, the counselor, and the specialist should be involved in making decisions. Some professionals might contend that the choice of classes is a personal matter that should be left to the discretion of the student, but when learning diabilities are identified care should be taken to ensure that the student makes wise decisions. There are many variables and the wrong courses, an overly heavy load, or an unsympathetic teacher can cause serious problems. Inappropriate enrollment can be a major cause of poor adjustment and failure.

Course equilibrium

A course load should reflect the needs of the student and should strike a balance between courses that are demanding and those that are not. A *demanding* course is a matter of interpretation. The learning abilities or disabilities of a particular student may make some courses easier or harder to cope with than others. We do not mean to suggest that some courses are "worth" more than others. However, some courses require much more reading and writing and the requirements of some are extremely difficult for certain students.

The special education staff should be aware of the curriculum options, the general content of each course, and the objectives. This is not an easy task at the secondary level because of the great variety of courses that are offered. Some special educators may have training or experience in secondary curricula and the counselor can certainly be expected to offer meaningful insights into the nature, degree of difficulty, and general content of most classes. It is suggested that each course in the school curriculum be identified with regard to such variables, catalogued, and arranged in a compendium. It should include all pertinent data, including the names of instructors.

Courses can be *clustered* for a student so that study in one class can be easily related to another that has a similar or related content. Courses should be *balanced* between "easy" and "difficult" ones. If a student has a schedule comprised of extremely difficult courses, failure may result.

Course substitution

If the school provides courses that are less demanding but that satisfy a required credit, the student may wish to enroll in them. Some high schools offer regular classes that are adapted and/or remedial in nature but that have the same objectives as other classes of the same content. Typically, these classes are in language arts or mathematics. Under certain arrangements, some classes may be substituted for the required course because of similar objectives but differing content. This is determined by state guidelines and local policy.

Course supplantation

This approach is similar to substitution. It means that the special education staff teaches certain content in the resource room that is counted as course credit and is listed on the student's transcript under the regular course name. Certification requirements in many states govern this approach, but some states currently allow this procedure in special education. Only in those cases where there is no other effective alternative would this seem to be justified. Teachers should only instruct students in course work for which they are prepared and certified. If this method (supplantation) is attempted it should be done with the full cooperation of staff members who teach in the specific content areas. Under such cooperative arrangements, the regular classroom teachers may be able to provide materials, guides, and specific ideas as to how to make such a course maximally meaningful. After doing this a few times, the regular classroom teachers may decide that *they* could make the necessary adjustments in their regular class setting. This is a type of spin-off benefit that is highly desirable.

Special texts

Many behavioral or outcome objectives are currently available for specific courses in the secondary curriculum. Many states and local school districts have developed their own. It is possible for the special educator to obtain a copy of the outcome objectives and determine the criteria that are necessary for mastery in specific courses of study. Alternative methods of reaching these objectives may be developed that would in many cases include special textbooks. Some companies have developed texts in history, science, and other content areas that cover the same material as other texts but that reduce the complexity of the reading matter by diminishing the difficulty of the reading level.

Alternative/modified curricula

A few special programs in the content areas are currently available for use with students who are not able to read efficiently. *Project MATH* is a comprehensive curriculum developed for preschool through senior high school. The system consists of lesson guides for the directed teaching of math operations and concepts in numbers, sets, patterns, fractions, geometry, and measurement. The system also includes a series of laboratory experiments and a method for teaching verbal problem solving. *Project MATH* is published by Educational Sciences, Inc.

Me Now and *Me And My Environment* are science curricula for use by junior high teachers who have no special training in this subject. These programs use the inquiry method of teaching and learning. The student does not see a book but actually carries out investigations of science principles directed by the teacher. The student uses work sheets, laboratory equipment, tapes, slides, filmstrips, booklets, games, and models, all of which are supplied as part of the program. Both programs were developed by Biological Sciences Curriculum Study (B.S.C.S.) of Boulder, Colorado and are available through Hubbard Publishing Company.

Some innovative teachers have modified the curriculum of various subjects at the secondary level to accomodate the learning needs of particular students. This is a time-consuming but rewarding activity that can greatly benefit students who are able to master a body of knowledge without the imposition of learning activities they cannot manage. This can be accomplished through simplifying and clarifying the reading content of texts and other materials of a course, the expressed development of criteria for mastery of the material that is known to the student and teachers, tapes with the simplified material or text transcribed for assistance to any student who wishes it, films, and other teaching aids. Some fine examples of this technique are reported by Weiss and Weiss (1974).

The Omega list

Just as LD specialists should be aware of required course offerings and course content, they should also be familiar with the teachers in their school. There are some teachers whose attitudes toward exceptional students are totally unsympathetic; others maintain a style of teaching that is rigid and unyielding. Many of these teachers are able to stimulate their nonhandicapped pupils into making remarkable gains in achievement. There are other teachers who are excellent practitioners of their profession, but who value some of the traditional trappings of academia that are actually barriers for the learning disabled student. These are teachers who by reputation, declaration, or demonstration are apparently highly structured in their approaches to education and who will not permit even minor variations in their instructional practices—variations that might benefit a student with special problems. Any teacher who is hostile to students with reading problems or other disabilities, who is unwilling to adapt the course work to the student's needs, or who is unfair and arbitrary should be avoided.

The LD specialist should maintain a mental *Omega list* that should include teachers in the school who would be the *last ones* selected for the placement of learning disabled students. It should not be in written form because this is unethical, would invite criticism, and could cause a serious breach in professional relationships.

FACULTY RELATIONS

An informal power structure exists in each school that operates outside the realm of official lines and staff relations. Some teachers are recognized as leaders and some are known as complainers. It is important to avoid the alienation of any faculty member, but especially those who might undermine the program. A clash with an important figure can be very damaging. Because the special educator may be called on to make a variety of contacts with many teachers in a school, there is ample opportunity for conflict. LD specialists may at times be younger or less experienced than others on the faculty. A revered, senior member of the faculty may resent suggestions from a new, inexperienced faculty member in special education. Many professionals resent being "told" to do anything but will cooperate if they can be convinced of the wisdom of the change.

Good public relations with regular classroom teachers may be the basic support needed for accomplishing special program goals. A young, eager, and aggressive LD specialist may alienate many teachers unless good public relations are established before attempts are made to alter the system. The special education teacher who wants (and needs) to "change the system" to accommodate learning disabled students will do the students no favors by attacking members of the staff, by complaining, spreading gossip, or remaining isolated. Good rapport with most staff members can serve as a foundation for many accommodation features that cannot be directed by the special education staff or imposed by the administration.

One means of establishing good public relations is to utilize principles of social psychology. Nearness, or propinquity, is an important factor that refutes the old adage that "familiarity breeds contempt." Investigations into what attracts people to one another have shown that popularity first of all depends on being seen. Frequent contacts with others does not ensure acceptance because other important variables are involved. However, the special educator who attempts to associate with other staff members in the faculty lounge, at school functions, and other social events will begin to build good personal relations.

Very similar social principles operate in the faculty lounge as in the adolescent peer culture, except that older persons are likely to have a wider range of experience and more opportunities to have similar interests. People tend to like those who give them some form of rewarding feedback. Association should not be based on flattery because the flatterer exposes insincere and ulterior motives. But, persons who are friendly, pleasant, entertaining, or even sincerely critical, tend to be appreciated by others.

Although the special education staff can make many arrangements for students, when these students attend regular classes they are under the direction and within the purview of regular classroom teachers. This is the most important reason for establishing good relations. Many useful instructional techniques can be implemented by regular classroom teachers to accommodate students. It is important that the faculty understand the nature of learning disabilities and the problems that these students have. Many LD students may be regarded as lazy, stupid, dull, or unmotivated. The attitudes and knowledge of regular classroom teachers are of paramount importance to successful programming.

One method of improving attitudes may be

through the in-service program of the school in which special education teachers organize meetings to be fitted into the school's schedule. Inducements are frequently used to get regular classroom teachers to attend these activities. It should not be surprising to find that many teachers are reluctant to attend such meetings even when pay increases might be involved. Therefore, the in-service program must be interesting, involve group participation, and should leave the teachers with something practical and useful to apply in the classroom. These events provide a means for bringing in consultants who can be very instrumental in changing the attitudes of teachers toward LD students. The major objective is to secure the support of teachers who will look favorably on special education and become actively involved with it.

ACCOMMODATION IN THE REGULAR CLASSROOM

The overall concept of special education at the secondary level should be reflected in a philosophy that recognizes that verbal ability, as measured by skill in reading, writing, or oral expression, is not necessarily indicative of intellectual or educational potential. Students who are inept in the skills of reading and writing are often capable of developing a fund of knowledge, an ability to reason, and an ability to perform competently in academic subjects if the methods of instruction and evaluation are adapted. Special and regular educators can work together to permit the student to demonstrate this capability. Current adaptations in regular class programs in nearly every subject area serve as testimony to the validity of this belief. The essential element in making this philosophy work is a regular classroom teacher who believes in the worth of individual students and who is secure enough that he or she can modify the manner in which both teaching and the evaluation of the effectiveness of this teaching occur. An effective learning disability specialist may assist or encourage such modification, but the teacher must believe that such modification is academically and professionally acceptable and that it can work.

Course objectives

One method of assistance by regular classroom teachers is that of providing a list of course objectives and requirements for each class in which a student is enrolled. This would include the major requirements of the course, specific dates for examinations, types of assignments, outside reading sources, and other pertinent information. This would be extremely helpful to the student, the parents, and the LD specialist—all of whom could use the information in planning study schedules. If a student has a disability in memory or organization, the LD specialist would be in a position to monitor and assist the student in planning activities rather than relying strictly on the student to seek assistance in preparation for important events of the regular class.

Course salvaging

Another important service that could be provided by the regular classroom teacher is informing the LD specialist if a student is beginning to fall significantly behind in course work. It may be possible to intercede before it is too late and implement corrective measures to ensure that the student will not fail the course. This should be done as early as possible. If a student is not known to be failing a course until late in the term, it is unlikely that much can be done to salvage the course. Failing a course causes the student to stay in school longer to earn sufficient credits to graduate, and this increases the possibility that the student will drop out.

Lecture outlines

Many classes in secondary schools are conducted in a traditional fashion with a lecture format. Even those with other significant components tend to include much lecture. Students are expected to read their textbooks and integrate their reading with class notes. Many students with learning disabilities experience problems in attempts to organize their thoughts and take notes during a lecture. They may not know what is important nor how to record meaningful notes. The teacher can provide a simple outline of the class lecture for each unit that can be used as a guide then for the flow of class discussions. The outline can also serve as a structure when preparing for tests. The resource teacher can use the outline for some information about the nature of the class content. The resource teacher can also use the outlines when considering the assignment of tutors to work with specific students. Non–learning disabled students also benefit from outlines of class lectures.

Technical vocabulary

Many college students have excellent reading and writing abilities but have significant problems in classes during the first year or two in college because they are unfamiliar with the technical words of different disciplines. The plight of the learning disabled student in high school may be quite similar. The specific language of biology, history, and other content subjects requires very selective reading. One effective way of assisting all students would be a handbook that includes the technical vocabulary for each subject as well as communication skills for each course. This handbook could be used to direct students in reading and writing. Special instruction might be given in how to read and interpret charts and graphs. If it can be demonstrated that even non–learning disabled college students experience such problems and can benefit from these considerations, it should certainly be important to LD students in the secondary school.

At the very least, a list of technical words and their meanings could be listed for each course and organized for use in the resource room. A list of specialized terminology would be useful as a basic core of target information that could be supportive in the content areas of specific classes.

Abstract concepts

Some courses, by nature or design, are very abstract. Any course that is based on abstract or subjective material, rather than primary factual information, can become most bewildering to many students. If the student is required to read, comprehend, analyze, and interpret a body of knowledge it is ap-

parent that a high degree of cognitive ability is required for success. Many high school students, even those with average or above average reading ability, simply do not have the ability, experience, or interest to manage abstract content. If one considers abstract reasoning ability to be that which requires the formal operational level of cognitive development as described by Piaget, then it is clear that large numbers of students in high school will have difficulty with such concepts. For example, Marxism and the theories of Adam Smith can be contrasted in only the most concrete way by many high school students. It would be beneficial to LD students if the teacher provided printed or taped summaries of key concepts and theories that would give order and meaning to a body of knowledge. This would be especially important in courses that use essay tests that are subjectively evaluated by teachers who may be looking for certain stereotyped responses that reflect their opinions or a particular point of view.

Oral and written reports

Some LD students are quite capable of expressing themselves orally but are incapable of preparing neat, orderly, and well-conceived written reports. Sentence structure and spelling may be grossly inadequate. To counteract this, such students may be allowed to record their reports or to have written reports edited and typed before submitting them to the teacher. Any tape should satisfy the written requirement if it is evaluated on its content. If tapes are not acceptable, written work should be evaluated for its content without regard to the mechanics. If it is absolutely necessary, two grades may be assigned, one for content and the other for mechanics with the former having more weight.

Motivation and reinforcement are important to students who continue to give up on language skills. Strict adherence to mechanics without regard to content can be disheartening to students who accumulate a collection of papers with numerous red marks and poor grades. An anecdote that was related by a resource room teacher in a junior high school might stress the importance of a dual system of grading. Steve, who had exerted very little effort in a language arts class, endeavored to complete a short story based on a trip he had taken with his grandfather who had died shortly afterward. The student composed a touching and sensitive story that clearly indicated that he had spent considerable time in preparing it. The language arts teacher's only remark was, "Next time, watch the margins."

Homework

Homework is a problem for many students, but may become the downfall of learning disabled students. The demands of homework create significant stress on inefficient learners. What might amount to 1 or 2 hours of hard work for a typical student may be impossible for an LD student. The tedious, rigorous, and time-consuming activity of reading, comprehending, and completing assignments is tiring. Before much of the school term has elapsed, a student may fall behind in assignments and become discouraged. Many grades are a composite of the various assignments during the term. If tests account for 50% or less of the final grade, an inordinate emphasis may be placed on the value of homework assignments.

Secondary teachers at times make assignments with little regard for other classes in which the student is enrolled. This can be a serious problem for LD students if tremendous amounts of work are expected by several teachers. It is difficult to coordinate the assignments among several teachers and, under most circumstances, it is probably not possible. Some teachers might be offended by any attempts to intervene in their classes. When one looks at the problem from the point of view of a regular classroom teacher, it can be seen that it would not be an easy task to independently coordinate such activities among several teachers and numerous students. However, if possible, it would be desirable to encourage teachers to reduce the amount of homework for certain students. This might be determined in cooperation with the LD specialist who could assist the teacher in estimating how much work to expect. In some instances it might be possible to substitute study time in the resource room for homework. Teachers could agree to accept *one* report or paper to satisfy the requirements of more than one class. For example, a student may complete a biographical report about an artist of the Renaissance period that could be accepted in both history and art courses.

Schedules

Teachers can assist students by supervising the development of study schedules that apportion time for the study of each subject. The resource teacher can be very helpful in planning these schedules because of an acquaintance with the entire class load of the student. With the assistance of the teacher and cooperation of the student and parents, a daily schedule can be developed to indicate the time that will be devoted to school work and to various other activities. Schedules should be arranged to allow for such reinforcing activities as breaks, snacks, and watching television. It is best to study for short rather than long periods to avoid fatigue.

Many LD students also have problems with self-discipline and attending to tasks for long periods. If a student can develop a reasonable schedule that produces results (feedback), then the tendency to remain at tasks will become more likely. There is nothing more frustrating to a student than to spend time "working at" homework without any clear direction in the activities. Charting daily accomplishments gives visible evidence of growth and accomplishment.

STUDY SKILLS

For many years, secondary schools and colleges have instructed students in alternate methods of approaching course work to assist them in learning and retaining essential facts and concepts for satisfactory performance in daily assignments and examinations. Some techniques have been more popular than others, but regardless of the approach, they all attempt to give the student a stylized

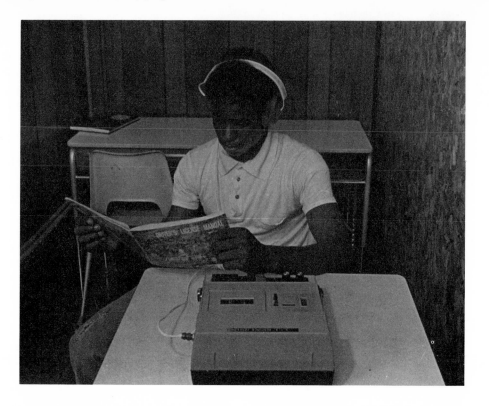

strategy for identifying, analyzing, storing, and recalling important information. Some methods are comprehensive with guided instruction in how to read content material and how to use reference materials and the library and its resources. Some techniques concentrate on the organization of information in preparation for specific assignments and tests. Some secondary schools have study skill centers where students may spend part of the school day learning to establish study habits. This type of instruction is a combination of teaching and accommodation techniques. As such, it would seem to be logically considered in an instructional category. It will be considered in this section of the text to differentiate it from remedial approaches.

The SQ3R method

This approach to study employs a specific technique in reading that conserves time and aids in the retention of information. It is probably well-known to most teachers but should be considered as a potentially effec-

tive study technique. The acronym stands for survey, *q*uestion, *r*ead, *r*eflect, and *r*eread.

When *surveying* any printed matter, the reader quickly scans the material noting chapter titles, major headings, charts and graphs, and other major components before actually reading it to gain information about the general content. The reader then poses *questions* about the material or uses ideas from a particular assignment that are to be kept in mind when actually reading the content. The questions are similar to prereading questions that some teachers give students in specific assignments to reduce the reading time and to make it more interesting. If students are told that they will be required to answer questions after reading a chapter, the reading time or pace will be slow because the students will attempt to "memorize" the entire content. It is much more efficient to give the student prereading questions that, when answered, will permit the student to terminate further reading. This accelerates the reading process, the student knows what to look for, and attention can be maintained.

The student then *reads* the material for specific answers to these questions. The student then *reflects* on the material that has been covered and attempts to identify the content that has been mastered and to seek out areas that may need more study. If necessary, the student then *rereads* portions of the material in an effort to find more information for questions that were not satisfied in the first reading.

Different reading rates for different material

Although learning disabled students may range in ability from nonreaders to those only slightly below grade level, all may encounter problems with reading in content areas. Reading materials at the lower elementary grade levels are generally designed to be attractive and interesting and to provide a certain degree of pleasure while reading skills are being developed. The body of the text is usually written in a narrative format with very few changes in the type of print. There is a certain predictability in such materials and students begin to develop insights into how to select the important points to remember for class discussion.

Content materials at the secondary level tend to be written in an expository format with less attention being given to the attractiveness or interest level of the material. The content may unfold as a succession of facts that are to be mastered by the student. The material is not predictable, there are frequent interruptions in the lines of the text such as parenthetical references to figures, tables, and diagrams, and the student must learn more difficult reading skills relating to critical analysis and inference. Many types of print are presented including bold face, capitalization, and italics. The material may not hold the attention of the reader and may be further complicated by the introduction of words and terms that are unknown to the reader. Reading rates must be adjusted to the content and the purpose for reading. Some students approach every reading task slowly and deliberately because they want to retain every bit of information for improved comprehension. Other students tend to subject each page to a swift attack and recall very little of what they read. Students must be taught to identify the purpose of reading in each instance and then read accordingly. The following general guidelines relate to reading speed for different purposes:

1. *Skim*—when locating references or new material.
2. *Rapid rate*—when reviewing or finding the main idea.
3. *Moderate rate*—when reading to solve problems, to isolate details, or to find specific answers to questions.
4. *Slow rate*—when reading critically, analyzing, evaluating, or finding very specific details.

The greatest problem in establishing an effective reading rate is related to differences that exist between narrative and expository material. Students who make excellent advances in reading achievement often accomplish this by succeeding in dealing with predictable variations that are so common in instructional materials. The sudden change from narrative to subject-centered factually oriented content material leads to a sense of frustration because of the different demands on reading comprehension. Lack of familiarity with content, technical words, and, sometimes, uninteresting style interfere with the application of reading achievement to content materials. These problems and the manner in which they apply to studying for tests seem to be the most significant factors that explain why advances in reading achievement are not always reflected in improved grades.

Introducing study skills

Some study skills are developed as students become accustomed to a study routine. It is probably best to introduce one skill at a time when it is actually needed in a situation. Unimaginative, boring study skill drills that seem to have no meaning will not be retained. For example, a student could be given a specific task that requires the use of a variety of reference materials in the library rather than subjecting the student to a tour of the library with parenthetical remarks such as, "This is the card file." It is much more relevant to give the student specific goals that require the use of an index, a card file, certain reference books, and other information sources. To learn by doing is as appropriate in the library as in any other activity.

The environment and study skills

The ability to dedicate oneself to the discipline of study is developed on an individual basis. The teacher can only train the student in techniques of study. The student must use these techniques at school and at home without continued monitoring to ensure that study time will be used productively. Independence in the secondary school is damaging to those students who cannot handle the freedom that comes with increasing age and assumed maturity. Self-discipline can be developed in students who can see a reason for learning, who have clear objectives, and who receive intermittent reinforcement and feedback for completing assignments. Simply outlining a study schedule does not ensure that the student will study.

The student should maintain a specific place for study in the home that meets personal demands. If these demands require extremely quiet surroundings, this should be arranged. The assistance of parents is important in this matter. The place of study should be maintained without moving from one location to another because a variety of materials such as pencils, books, references, and paper should be at hand.* Besides a specific place of study, a specific time each day usually aids in more efficient study skills.

The student should also have a complete and accurate record of all assignments that have been made with notations indicating when they are due. The teacher may be able

*We are well aware that some students are not fortunate enough to have the potential of a specific, quiet place to study at home. Others do not have parents who will reinforce or even cooperate in this recommended procedure. In such cases we must try to arrange the nearest possible approximation of these conditions and hope for the best. For some students, even a slight improvement in study conditions can be most beneficial.

to assist the student in planning for the completion of assignments especially if they seem to be too numerous at certain times. A specific part of the student's notebook should be reserved for this purpose.

Notebooks and notetaking

There is a tendency among secondary school students to keep very poor notebooks and to frequently lose them. Such carelessness may be attributed to the fact that notebooks are of limited value to the student because they contain useless information. Learning disabled students should be encouraged to keep a specific notebook or section in a loose-leaf binder for each course. Careful attention to the maintenance of a neat and orderly notebook and the development of good notetaking skills can contribute to improved learning.

Notetaking is a skill that takes time to develop. If an LD student has very poor ability in taking notes because of motor problems, encoding deficiencies, or poor memory, it will be necessary to make other arrangements. Tape recording may be an effective practice for some students, but many teachers are uncomfortable when a tape recorder is operating. The greatest problem for the student is that the use of a tape recorder requires either listening to an entire presentation again (which is like sitting through class again) or running the reel back and forth to try to find specific bits of information.

For students who cannot take adequate notes and cannot benefit from the use of tapes, it may be necessary to use an outline prepared by the teacher for the lecture that can be used as a guide for taking essential notes and for studying. In some instances, pairing of students who can share notes is practical but this requires the students to maintain a trusting relationship that is mutually beneficial. Such relationships are subject to the vagaries of fate as is any friendship. Some students may not like one another in a helping relationship arranged by teachers. Certain outstanding students may be selected to transcribe their notes for use by the resource room teacher.

If a student can take notes, he or she should be taught to pay particular attention to facts and ideas that the teacher stresses, any visual information presented, and key sections of the text that might be mentioned. Notes should be as brief as possible but should contain the essence of the instructor's remarks. It is risky to put the teacher's words into the student's vernacular because their meaning can be lost. It seems logical to train students to copy many concepts verbatim and to clarify them later or at the time of presentation if there is sufficient time in class. The best approach to notetaking seems to be the traditional outline. This method imposes order on the notes instead of culminating in a collection of fragmented information. It is most efficient if the outline can be used in its original form. There seems to be little reason to rewrite or type the notes once they have been completed in class except in instances where it facilitates learning. Some students are able to use certain personal forms of notation or shorthand to streamline notetaking. This practice can be taught and, if it works, can save a great deal of time. It is, however, less likely to work with students who have symbolic disorders.

Preparing for tests

Many tests developed by teachers are poorly constructed, lack validity, and are unreliable. Nevertheless, students must perform well on various examinations to receive credit for classes. It is, therefore, reasonable to assist each student in the skills necessary to prepare for tests and in the gamesmanship necessary to compete.

Tests may not truly reflect the knowledge that students have and may be rather arbitrarily graded by some instructors. It is sometimes important to have some information about the habits of a particular teacher as this information might be useful to students. It usually facilitates preparation for an examination if it is known that a teacher prefers a specific type of test or is interested in certain kinds of responses. In all fairness to students, it must be candidly stated that some teachers are unreasonable in their ex-

pectations. For example, Sax (1974) reports that an eminent German surgeon once failed six candidates for medical degrees because they were unable to answer this question: "Why does my dog wag its tail?" The correct answer, according to the professor was, "Because it is happy to see us" (p. 78). A teacher who is known for presenting unfair tests should be on the Omega list. But, any teacher can (and perhaps all teachers sometimes do) prepare tests that are ambiguous or otherwise poorly constructed and this can be especially problematic for LD students.

Resource teachers should have sufficient experience in *taking* tests to know how to assist students in *preparing* and *responding*. The objectives of a unit, the main concepts, key facts, and supporting information are used in preparing for any test. Objective tests are very demanding because they frequently require total recall of information, can be equivocal, invite guessing, and rely on memorization. Although a student may not have to make significant alterations in preparation for different kinds of tests, it is true that objective tests make use of more specific information and minutia. The student may want to commit more facts to memory especially if challenged with a completion test.

Essay tests present a different set of problems because they can tax the organizational, thinking, and writing abilities of a student who may have specific disabilities in encoding and expressive language. Essay tests have the added danger of subjective evaluation that can be affected by many factors not the least of which is the attitude the teacher has toward a particular student. In taking an essay examination, the resource teacher may assist the student by giving the student "trial runs" on some sample questions that might appear on the real test. This gives the student an opportunity to organize thoughts without the pressure of the actual test. Test responses can be evaluated and such evaluation may be provided to the student as feedback information. In an essay test, the student should adhere to specific rules. The following suggestions are helpful:

1. Each paragraph should use a structure with a beginning, middle, and end.
2. Definite facts and concepts must be clearly stated.
3. Straightforward, simple sentence structure should be used.
4. The response should be carefully worded to avoid wandering off the topic.
5. The student should be aware of the distinctions between certain key words in the question such as discuss, define, compare, contrast, attack, defend, describe, criticize, list, interpret, trace, and summarize.

Students who have *very* poor reading and writing skills should not be expected to take tests under traditional circumstances. It just does not show common sense. Alternative testing procedures must be allowed such as giving the student either a simplified form or the opportunity to give oral responses with the assistance of a monitor who can read and mark the test. Major national testing agencies currently provide for an extension of time and permit a reader/writer for handicapped students who take standardized tests. Student aides, selected by content area teachers, will be entrusted with testing matters for specific students under appropriate supervision. Most teachers understand that students do not perform well on tests because of the time limits and the difficulty of reading matter. This is especially true for LD students and one must seriously question the value of test results if the score is assumed to reflect an individual's knowledge of subject matter.

THE INSTRUCTIONAL INTERFACE

Fig. 4 shows a schematic representation of the interface between the secondary resource room and the regular class as they involve the student. When considering this relationship, it should be remembered that academic success or survival in the secondary school is determined by competition in the regular classes, meeting the evaluative criteria of each instructor, and accumulating an acceptable grade point average. Although the ability to compete for grades is in part determined by ability in reading, written and oral expression, and mathematics skills, grades are not specifically awarded for these skills.

The resource room is a supportive service *to the student* and not necessarily a service to the regular classroom instructors. The resource room is not a part of the mainstream at the secondary level, and, unlike the elementary school resource room, it is not a natural extension of the regular class because of the nature of the activities, the basic goals, and the orientation of the teachers.

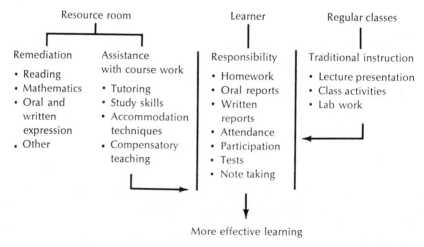

Fig. 4. Interface of instruction.

It should be obvious that if the resource room teacher neglects to assist the learning disabled student with course work or is denied the opportunity to fulfill this function, the student's academic survival is in serious danger. This is an extremely important function of the resource room for it has been demonstrated that many students with basic skill deficiencies *can* compete for grades and can demonstrate achievement in the regular classroom if sufficient accommodations are made. A student with serious deficiencies will find it very difficult to achieve without the intervention of the specialist. The student is likely to become just one more statistic on the school's list of dropouts.

SUMMARY

Accommodation and compensatory teaching should be a major emphasis of programs for the learning disabled adolescent. The use of positive reinforcement and reward systems (to be discussed in detail in Chapter 7) in conjunction with accommodation and compensatory teaching is also of considerable merit in many instances. Accommodation refers to a process whereby the learning environment is modified to promote more effective learning. This may include changing many elements of the environment, and in fact, in most instances successful accommodation is the cumulative effect of many small accommodative efforts. Accommodation includes such practices as course substitution, course supplantation, use of special texts and alternative curricula, and various other administrative techniques such as specialized assistance in enrollment and more careful "balancing" of the course load.

Good faculty relations are the key to effective provision of many if not all accommodative efforts. Because the learning disabled student in the secondary school is in many different classes with many different teachers, it is imperative that the LD specialist be on sufficiently good terms with these teachers to be able to obtain their active assistance. Without active interest and support, the secondary school learning disabilities program is doomed to failure.

The regular classroom teacher may assist the learning disabled student by providing a variety of types of information to the LD specialist and to the learning disabled student. Practices such as the provision of lecture outlines, advance information concerning the technical vocabulary, and modified homework assignments may benefit the student greatly. In some cases the LD specialist will provide regular ahead-of-time assistance directly to the student. In others, it is a matter of making certain that the student knows what to do with the extra provisions made by the regular classroom teacher, rather than specific "preping" on topics or terms that may cause difficulties.

Another type of accommodative assistance requires direct training and assistance for the learning disabled student that may be best provided by the LD specialist. This assistance is in the area of study skills, which include the ability to utilize different types and rates of reading for different material or different reading goals, notetaking and the maintenance of a class notebook that really assists in the learning process, and the establishment of the proper study environment.

Accommodation, as discussed in this chapter, is based on the idea that remediation as a total emphasis does not pay maximum dividends for the majority of learning disabled adolescents. We believe that to be true, although at this point in time, we cannot prove it to be the case. On the other hand, *some* remedial efforts apparently can pay dividends at the secondary school level, particularly if combined and coordinated carefully with accommodation and compensatory teaching. With this in mind, remedial efforts is the topic for consideration in the following chapter.

DISCUSSION QUESTIONS

1. What are the essential benefits of accommodation for a student?
2. Why are some teachers likely to resist or reject the concept of accommodation?
3. Distinguish between course substitution and course supplantation as techniques of accommodation.
4. Would accommodation, as proposed in this chapter, be more easily implemented in a school

that "tracks" students rather than "mainstreaming" them?
5. What are the essential differences in the demands on a student at the secondary level and those at the elementary level?
6. What competencies and qualities should a secondary specialist possess that would be different from a specialist at the elementary level?
7. Could the suggestions for accommodation and compensatory teaching be regarded as threatening to traditional standards of secondary education?

REFERENCES AND READINGS

Festinger, L., Schachter, S., and Back, K. *Social pressures in informal groups.* New York: Harper & Row, Publishers, Inc., 1950.

Inhelder, B., and Piaget, J. *The growth of logical thinking from childhood to adolescence.* New York: Basic Books, Inc., Publishers, 1958.

Sax, G. *Principles of educational measurement and evaluation.* Belmont, Calif.: Wadsworth Publishing Co., Inc., 1974.

Weiss, H., and Weiss, M. *A survival manual,* Great Barrington, Mass.: Treehouse Associates, 1974.

CHAPTER 6

Remediation of learning disabilities in the secondary school

INTRODUCTION

Remediation was the original approach to most public school learning disability programs and was most often implemented at the elementary level. Remediation is of value, but its value seems to vary inversely with the age of the child. This generalization, like all generalizations, may quickly be challenged by citing exceptions, but we will continue to believe it to be true—based on considerable observation of existing programs—until it is proved to be false. *Nevertheless, if used properly, with the right children, at the right times, and in the right proportion, it is of value*. If we accept the hypothesis of an inverse relationship between the age of the child and the value of remedial approaches, the suggestions made in this chapter may be more applicable, or may be applicable to greater parts of any individual educational program, at the junior high level as opposed to the senior high level.

There are various types of remediation, and there may be remedial effects to approaches or procedures that are not directly or obviously remedial. Perhaps the "purest" concept of remediation is that which relates to the medical model. In this interpretation of remediation, it is assumed that there is some cause for the deficit under consideration and that there is an attempt to help the student overcome the deficit by "curing" the cause of the deficit. When learning disabilities are conceptualized as the result of neurological dysfunction, it would seem logical to do something that will remedy the neurological dysfunction. We thus might be considered to be "curing" or "healing" the neurological dysfunction. Some learning disability theorists/practitioners have claimed that this is precisely what they can do. (Since much of the early research in the area of learning disabilities related to brain-injured children, there was, or was believed to be, specific causation for the symptoms observed.) However, only a few individuals actually claimed they were *healing* brain damage. Others indicated that brain functions had not developed properly and, through remedial/developmental efforts, the undeveloped or poorly developed areas of the brain could be assisted toward normal or more nearly normal development. Others who worked on the cerebral dysfunction hypothesis were more inclined to describe their success in terms of training the undamaged portions of the brain to take over some of the tasks of the damaged or dysfunctional portions.

In remedial reading and mathematics programs, *remedial* refers to the attempts to remedy problems that relate to the manner in which a child approaches the learning of reading or mathematics. Remedial reading experts assume different theories of underlying causation, and most have wisely concluded that it is a matter of multiple causation in many cases, with different factors appearing as the major cause in different children. The goal of most remedial reading or math programs is simple—the improvement of basic reading or math skills.

Two basic types of remedial programs are considered in this discussion:

1. Programs that focus on unusual lack of skill or competence in a basic skill area, such as reading or mathematics, and that utilize some specific approach to remediate (improve the functioning level) in this area.*

2. Programs based primarily on the remediation of some perceptual difficulty, some receptive, integrative, or expressive language difficulty, or some known or inferred organic dysfunction that is assumed to be the basic cause of the learning disability.

Many remedial programs have limited application at the secondary level, and it is likely that time will be better spent if the major activities of a secondary learning disabilities program are part of a program of accommodation and compensatory teaching (see the previous chapter). Time is of the essence, and by the time a student has reached the secondary level, the best approach may be to emphasize the learning of basic content and concepts through whatever intact or functional learning skills the student may possess. It may be noted that special educators in various private schools around the nation, educators who are quite free to use whatever approach is most practical, seem to have a similar belief (see Chapter 10). They use remedial programs to a limited extent and place their basic emphasis on content and concepts, especially as they relate to social and vocational skills.

---

*We are well aware of, but have chosen to omit, a discussion of a third basic type of remediation—medical remediation in cases where body chemistry, glandular abnormalities, and the like are involved. Educators can do little about such remedial needs since they do not possess training or the right credentials. However, they should be aware that such remediation may be needed in some cases.

This chapter discusses remedial efforts in some basic skill areas. Reading, spelling, handwriting, and mathematics are discussed as specific skill areas. A section on information-processing concludes the chapter. It should be noted in advance that the information-processing section is *not* an attempt to address the debate relating to the effectiveness of attempting to remediate processing disorders, but simply relates to the ability or inability of certain students to effectively utilize information that is presented to them in various forms. It is presented in an effort to encourage teachers to think through the relative complexity of the various ways in which they expect students to learn, to be sensitive to clues or indications that certain students are having unusual difficulties, and to adjust instructional techniques according to student needs.

Remediation in reading is discussed first, since this remains a major concern at both the elementary and secondary levels. The discussion relates primarily to the various issues involved in planning a reading program at the secondary level, rather than a comprehensive overview of various reading approaches.*

READING

Perhaps nothing is as important in school achievement as the ability to read, at least under typical circumstances in the school. More than any other problem in learning disabilities, reading has been the focus of much research and thought. It is also known that students with long-standing reading disabilities continue to experience significant achievement problems in the secondary school, which threatens to prevent them from succeeding in course work of the con-

---

*The reader who wants a more comprehensive review is referred to Chapter 6 of Gearheart, B.: *Teaching the learning disabled: A combined task-process approach*, St. Louis: The C. V. Mosby Co., 1976.

tent areas and may lead to failure to graduate. Not surprisingly, this has been a major area of concern to the emerging field of secondary learning disabilities but it is necessary to be cautious in the application of the same approaches that have been used with younger students.

The ability to read is a highly complex skill that apparently requires many individual and environmental prerequisites. Many kinds of problems can interfere with learning and cause reading failure, but these factors may occur in different combinations and are often not fully understood. Factors that may cause learning problems with younger children may tend to diminish in importance with age, but motivation, attitude, and self-concept increase in importance to adolescents. The problems that confront the secondary specialist in teaching reading are associated with the limited applicability to older students of research findings with younger children and the low level of research with older subjects that might give direction in planning and instruction. A number of approaches toward reading disabilities have been used with learning disabled children and other students with remedial needs. A brief summary of these methods follows.

Behavioral approaches

Various programmed machines, programmed materials, management systems, and behavior modification techniques have been used with LD students. The cost of some programs or equipment is so prohibitive that schools generally have not been able to afford them. (Other more economical hardware is becoming available, however.) The primary weakness with many programmed machines is that there is often no accompanying software making it necessary for the schools to develop the materials. This detracts from instructional responsibilities of teachers who are not usually prepared to develop programmed materials. Many types of token economies, programmed materials, and behavior modification techniques have been used in resource rooms. They all use the principles of operant conditioning to teach reading. (Additional information on the use of behavioral approaches in the secondary schools is presented in Chapter 7.)

Therapeutic techniques

In some private schools and clinics, severely disabled readers have been treated indirectly by using various counseling and therapeutic techniques, sometimes based on psychoanalytic theory, to affect the personality and emotional status of the individual in the belief that improvement of general functioning will serve as a basis for improved reading. Although this approach has not been widely used in public schools, it would seem that a program of simultaneous counseling and reading instruction might be most beneficial for many secondary students. Counseling may not actually improve any academic skill, per se, but it might augment teaching efforts as a consequence of improved motivation, self-concept, and adjustment.

The linguistic approach

There is some confusion about the nature of a linguistic approach because some programs of reading that are called linguistic seem to stress the syntactical and semantic aspects of language in the reading process while others tend to stress the sound–symbol association between language and the printed word. Perhaps a distinction should be made between beginning reading approaches and those used with children in developmental reading beyond the primary grades. The linguistic approach at the beginning level is concerned with the decoding process and attempts to establish a stable association between phonemes and graphemes. Actually, decoding techniques of this type are used in elements of many programs such as the Orton-Gillingham method, which emphasizes words in beginning reading instruction that have no uncommon or multiple relationships. Nonphonetic words are taught as special cases with mnemonic devices. Fries (1963) has written a widely accepted textbook about this subject and many commercial programs are based on the linguistic approach.

Multisensory systems

Teaching reading through specific modalities, or combinations of modalities, has generally been very popular in special education. This is typical of approaches that emphasize decoding or beginning reading. Children who have mastered the fundamental skills of reading are not likely to continue to make much progress in reading with the continued use of a multisensory approach. Fernald (1943), Blau and Blau (1969), and Gillingham and Stillman (1965) have developed techniques that have been used with many children who initially fail in reading with traditional developmental approaches. The visual, kinesthetic, auditory, tactile, and, occasionally, proprioceptive senses are emphasized to organize input and to use combinations of sensory modalities in the development of normal perception.

Phonics method

Another reading system that should be noted is the *phonics method,* the value of which has been central to arguments in the teaching profession for many years. Phonics has been introduced in various sequences with differing stress in many basic reading series. It is important to note that some writers seem to be indicating that a phonics approach is the best or only method to use with learning disabled adolescents. This is based on opinion rather than empirical evidence. The conclusions of Spache (1976) after reviewing the literature on phonics is pertinent to this discussion. Among other findings, he concludes that no system produces overall superiority, that there are strong negative correlations between the time spent in phonics instruction and comprehension, that no system succeeds in producing fluent reading with all pupils, that phonics may be contraindicated in teaching children with auditory deficiencies, that phonics is only one of several clues to word recognition, that letter-sound associations are an aid to reading and not a method of learning to read, and that the values of teaching phonics rules are dubious.

There is no evidence to support the belief that phonics is the best or only method of teaching reading to adolescents with learning disabilities. One problem with learning disabilities is that they are distinguished by the heterogeneity of the students who are so classified. Each case should be studied and evaluated individually, and the best professional decisions should be made in determination of teaching techniques.

Reading and vocational adjustment

Students who are poor readers in elementary school tend to remain poor readers at the secondary level (Muehl and Forell, 1973). Gillespie and Sitko (1975) maintain that LD adolescents have reading problems similar to those of younger children. Balow and Bomquist (1965) conducted a 15-year follow-up study of young adults who originally had learning disabilities in school. They concluded that males from a middle socioeconomic background who resided in urban areas tended to develop reading proficiency but assumed more unskilled and semiskilled jobs. When one considers the date of the study, it is apparent that the subjects had attended school prior to the LD movement and certainly before the trend toward secondary programming for learning disabilities and career education. With the development of exemplary programs it would seem that adolescents can anticipate many vocational options, among which might be college programs. In any event, with a new awareness and sensitivity to the needs of LD students, it should not be unreasonable to expect that their opportunities will be significantly improved and that they will not be trapped in low-status jobs.

Early (1973) supports basic literacy as the goal for students. If a student reaches this level, Early asserts that the student should no longer receive special instruction but should be taught reading in conjunction with the specific content of work–study classes. This view is based on the premise that learning disabled students should not pursue courses of study in academic areas. This is a narrow view when considering the intellectual ability of most students, the fact that many are highly motivated and interested in academic courses, and that a variety of alternative approaches can be employed to ensure success in such classes.

Process training

Reading disability has traditionally been associated with many factors such as cerebral dominance (Orton, 1937) and laterality. These were implicated as symptomatic of an underlying condition related to the inability to read or were specifically identified as directly contributing to failure. More recently, visual perception, auditory perception, and other processes have been singled out as important factors in reading. As a result, children have been subjected to various programs of ocular-motor, visual-perceptual, auditory-perceptual, and motor training to improve the bases for learning. Some writers have preferred perceptual training to specific academic teaching. Generally, these approaches are referred to as *process training*. Specialized tests and teaching techniques have been developed in these areas.

In recent years these approaches have come under close scrutiny of some writers who have attacked the concept of process training. Processes are not discrete and it is impossible to know how a child manages incoming stimuli, although assumptions are made about such processing. Tests that have been used to measure processing deficits have questionable validity and it is difficult to demonstrate a direct improvement of reading and other academic skills even if skills in the various perceptual modalities have improved with training. Certain factors must be considered in the understanding of process research. Notably, there is some question about the efficacy of deficits in some skills because many children with apparently normal development and good reading ability also show what might be called *abnormalities* according to some descriptions.*

Luria (1973) contends that specialization of the left hemisphere for language does not oc-

cur in a normal child until about 10 years of age. Laterality is not completely established until 11 years of age. Gilbert (1953) has shown that eye movements do not discriminate between good and poor readers so that ocular training as a factor in improving reading is hard to justify. Eye movements in disabled readers are normal when the words are familiar but variant when the reading matter becomes difficult. However, even good readers demonstrate this difference when the complexity of reading material increases.

Skills such as visual perception are apparently important in early reading but become less significant as children mature. Phonic skills do not augment comprehension and by the fourth grade students do not depend on them in reading (Spache, 1976).

Because of the equivocal and controversial research in process training with younger children and the paucity of research with adolescents, it is difficult to justify the use of process training in the secondary program. Although secondary students may show deficiencies in specific processes as determined in the course of evaluation and accepting the fact that it may be desirable and necessary to include such measures in the original diagnosis, there is simply not enough information to clarify the status or importance of process characteristics in adolescents. The earlier review of characteristics (Chapter 1) clearly reveals that we are not in a good position to know if students gradually compensate for early deficits or if they diminish in importance. There is evidence that early reading skills fall into disuse after the basic foundation of reading skills is established.

Although process training has been criticized, evidence remains that some students tend to respond to presentation of reading instruction in preferred modalities. Students may demonstrate different learning aptitudes and these may change in preference at different times in development (Morency, 1968). Preferred modalities can be identified but this is a highly individual situation and any conclusions about teaching through modalities should be applied cautiously to adolescents.

---

*The reader is referred to Hammill, Goodman, and Wiederholt (1974), Hammill and Larsen (1974), and Cohen (1967) for further discussion of this controversy.

The decision to select one instructional method over another should be determined by the specific characteristics of the learner because there is *no one* method for such a heterogeneous group of persons. Another consideration in choosing an instructional method relates to the degree of disability and the age of the student. If the teacher is working with pupils who are nonreaders, it may be necessary to choose an approach that emphasizes basic decoding, is highly individual, and is considerably different than approaches that have been previously used. For students who are performing above a third or fourth-grade level and who have some of the basic skills mastered, a much different approach that will attempt to increase the rate, proficiency, and level of reading achievement should be selected.

Reading skills

Occasionally, there is reference in the literature to the improvement of oral reading skills with older, poor readers. In fact, the traditional belief has been that oral reading is actually a reflection of silent reading or at least is a mechanism for the instructor to investigate silent reading. It is now known that the demands on the nervous system are so great during oral reading that the subject has little opportunity to process all the information fluently and still attend to the meaning of the content. Even rather skilled and proficient readers show poor comprehension when required to read extremely difficult and unfamiliar passages.

Oral reading behavior is unique in that very young readers use it exclusively because they do not have the ability or experience to read silently. Gradually, the obvious manifestations of reading orally begin to disappear, although a number of children in the middle grades continue to subvocalize and even experienced readers resort to vocalization with extremely complicated material.

However, oral and silent reading behaviors are distinct and divergent processes. Spache (1976) indicates that the accuracy of oral reading does not necessarily indicate silent reading competence nor does it indicate reading comprehension. Many students can flawlessly read a passage orally but not be able to comprehend any of it. Poor oral readers can demonstrate very good comprehension after silent reading.

In the process of silent reading, an individual may ignore irrelevant information, grasp information from a few important clues, use the context or cloze procedures to obtain meaning, and glide over parts that are too difficult and that can be inferred from the rest of the passage. This process offers much promise for the improvement of reading in hesitant, slow readers who have some mastery of rudimentary reading skills.

The rate of reading among some students is so slow that they cannot use reading to attack large bodies of knowledge. It is important to ensure such readers that the rate of reading can be increased without seriously affecting comprehension. The facility of some very fast readers is that they know what information to seek, how to analyze the importance of reading matter, how to adjust speed to the nature of the content or the purpose of reading, and how to recall the essential facts. Very slow readers are frequently simply reluctant to read faster for fear of risking the loss of comprehension. The familiarity that a student has with specific words or technical vocabularies, the general level of ability to engage in critical thinking, and the level of intelligence are important in comprehension.

One practice that has been used in some schools to determine expectations of readers is to use alternate forms (correlated) of tests of reading in assessment of actual reading performance and auditory comprehension. One form of the test can be administered to the student according to the standardized procedures and the other form can be read to the student and responses to questions recorded. If the student earns a much higher score (as determined by Z scores) on the second administration, it must be concluded that the student may have the ability to comprehend much higher levels of information than is apparent through the normal (reading) approach. This may be an excellent way to determine which students have the greatest need to attend classes in which reading is eliminated or reduced through accommodation. If the student can comprehend material without reading it, there is no reason why the student should not be subjected to the most complex courses of study with modifications.

On the other hand, if students demonstrate very low levels of comprehension and are easily perplexed by most bodies of knowledge, it may be necessary to make very different decisions about the placement of the student and the nature of the expected educational outcomes. Each case must be decided individually and with the cooperation of the parents and the student when such important decisions are involved.

Depending on the severity of the reading disability, the motivation of the student, and other factors, it may be possible to stimulate improved reading in the actual content areas of the courses in which the student is enrolled. Landis and co-workers (1973) have reported such an approach with apparently good results. They stress that it is important to avoid the presentation of "elementary school techniques," which can "turn kids off," and they contend that drills should be kept to a minimum. Brown (1972) asserts that excessive attention to reading, writing, and other verbal skills may cause students and their families to think of LD students as defective thinkers. Brown believes that alternative methods should be used in accomplishing educational goals with adolescents.

Lane and Miller (1972) have reported that listening can improve the reader's level of achievement (similar to the neurological impress method*). The teacher reads aloud to the student who follows the written text and simply listens. This seems to be highly related to comprehension levels.

Efficient reading in most good readers is a skill that develops gradually over many years and improves with practice. Students who do

---

*The *neurological impress method* of reading instruction involves guided imitation of the teacher by the student, who engages in choral reading with the teacher. The teacher gradually permits the student to assume the major role in reading until no further support is provided.

not read very much or very often are not likely to continue to develop in reading achievement, so that motivation to read plays an important role in the process. The ability to read an article or passage critically demands a high level of reading skill. The reader must be able to conduct all the processing behaviors necessary to cover the content— grasp the meaning during the act of reading, simultaneously evaluate the passage and formulate questions, and generate conclusions.

If LD programs are limited to admitting students with levels of achievement below some arbitrary level (for example, sixth-grade level), it is likely that two general groups of students will make up the learning disabled group. One group will be essentially nonreaders or have marginal skills, and the other group will have assumed some mastery over the basic skills of reading but will be unable to cope with most reading assignments. Although special programming must be individually determined, it should be quite possible to make general plans based on these two major groups.

In any event, the teacher should realize that the number of *nonreaders* among the general LD population will probably be relatively small. The incidence of nonreaders will be highly variable between school districts and may tend to be correlated with the socioeconomic status of the community. Although students may reveal low scores in an achievement profile, individual inspection of the reading behavior of most students will reveal that they can decode. As we have noted earlier, the important variables in teaching reading to intelligent adolescents may not be inherent in the methodology that is used but in the attitudes of the students. The fact that students can actually decode is evidence of some success and may promise future growth.

Motivation and reading

The problems of many adolescents may be explained partly by learning theory. It must be remembered that students have experienced 6 years or more of being subjected to reading methodology. In some respects, they become quite proficient in learning not to learn. By the time the primary grades are completed, they clearly understand that they do not perform well in reading and that their peers are excelling. In the face of continuous failure, disappointment, and inability to live up to the expectations of their teachers and parents, they learn to avoid reading because it is such an unpleasant activity. For them, reading never builds self-confidence, reaps no rewards, and causes them to be set apart, to be stigmatized, and to fail.

By the time the student has been subjected to a variety of remedial approaches, quite often with materials that are suitable for much younger children, the entire gamut of reading activities becomes totally aversive. Many poor readers are thoroughly convinced they cannot read by the time they enter junior high school. After being mocked by fellow students, receiving poor grades, being scolded by teachers, and disappointing their parents and themselves, LD students are not likely to enthusiastically embrace the teaching objectives of the resource teacher who may use some of the old inducements and materials to try to teach these "veterans" to read.

The adolescent will not learn to read unless he or she wants to. However, the added maturity of the student in the secondary school and the widening cognitive abilities can be enlisted in the attempt to continue reading instruction. The adolescent is less egocentric, can view the world from different vantage points, begins to recognize the importance of long-range planning, and may be convinced that opportunities are curtailed in this culture unless one can achieve a basic level of academic proficiency.

Reading instruction should be based on the revival of motivation and should judiciously avoid any stereotyped format that employs elements of approaches that have been attempted previously. The methodology may not be as important as the style.

Summary

There are no miracles in the field of reading. No one method is superior to another in all applications, and there is no single, appropriate approach for all secondary LD students because they are not all alike in their abilities, disabilities, motivations, and environmental characteristics. In general, the secondary specialist should have thorough training in a variety of diagnostic and instructional methods in reading and should be able to develop, modify, and match elements of materials to particular students. The specialist should also be able to assist regular classroom teachers in methods of teaching reading along with content at the secondary level.

General practices in reading instruction may be summarized as follows:

1. Students should receive training that relies on contextual skills because a heavy reliance on structural components and memorization of rules can be counterproductive.

2. Initial reading instruction for nonreaders must be very different from methods that have been used with a particular student, and every effort should be made to avoid using elementary level books that give the students the impression they are working with "baby stuff."

3. Students should be encouraged to see a reason for continuing to improve reading. Older students may appreciate the importance more so than younger ones.

4. Any system of reading instruction should employ a feedback mechanism that aids in self-correction and that is reinforcing.

5. If students have a grasp of reading fundamentals, they should be guided in techniques that get at the meaning of reading content. Prereading questions, scanning, and other study skills are important to reduce a reading risk to a manageable and useful activity.

6. Remediation of reading should be part of an entire program and should not detract from survival in content areas because of preoccupation of the student's time in the resource room.

As indicated previously, there is no single method or approach that is generally effective with all learning disabled students. This, of course, applies to the area of reading as to all other skills and subject matter areas because LD students have a variety of different learning characteristics. However, we know that teachers, at least, want a "place to start." We feel the obligation to share some observations about certain reading approaches. Therefore, we have elected to take the risk that, by emphasizing a certain method, some readers will believe that we are recommending a panacea for the reading problems of learning disabled adolescents. We are only presenting the results of observations of what has taken place. The final verdict on any method or approach should await extensive empirical evidence.

With all of these cautions, we will proceed to say that we have seen and/or heard about a number of instances in which teachers have agreed that various Gillingham-related approaches are effective in teaching reading skills at the secondary level, particularly with students at the junior high level. These may be called Orton-Gillingham, Stillman-Gillingham, or simply Gillingham approaches. Gillingham-related approaches have been used more than anything else in secondary programs.

Although the Orton-Gillingham approach is a multisensory method, it is also very systematic and structured. There are very specific exercises and activities that gradually build on emerging skills on a daily basis. The greatest asset may be that it is methodical and that it relies on routines without moving too quickly into newer skills before the student is prepared and not until more fundamental skills are automatic. Because of the structure that requires the teacher to follow a certain order, it may not be possible to utilize the technique with more than one or two students at a time because the students must have similar reading skills for a teacher-directed activity to be appropriate. For maximum benefit, students with highly divergent reading skills should be grouped according to their characteristics. Because of the heavy reliance on simultaneous stimulation of input channels, it is important to avoid using this technique with students who react adversely to sensory bombardment or overstimulation.

Moreover, students who have some mastery of initial reading skills would find the method of diminishing value. Essentially, this technique forstalls independent reading until a large number of sound–symbol associations are made. Completion of the program may take as long as 2 years. Consequently, the application of this approach with older students in a typical secondary setting must be weighed heavily against other activities and classes the student may be participating in if the teacher is interested in providing direct assistance with these activities and classes.

Another approach that has been used, but not as much as the Gillingham approach, is the multisensory approach that developed out of the work of Fernald (1943). Whereas the Gillingham approach is concerned with phonics and stress on individual letters and sequences of letters, the Fernald approach, although multisensory, emphasizes whole words that are usually presented in a cursive form. In many ways, the Fernald approach has been imitated by many "modern" approaches in learning disabilities. The Fernald approach is not available in a packaged form, but depends more on the individual innovation and motivation of the teacher. This may be one reason why it is not as widely used as it once was when commercial programs were not generally available.

SPELLING

Correct spelling requires total recall of a specific sequence of letters that have been retained by a process of memorization. Some writers believe that spelling is simply a matter of practice and the more contact (frequency) a student has with reading matter (practice), the more the store of correct spellings will accrue. The high correlation between poor spelling and poor reading should not be surprising although there are some students who seem to be able to spell better than they can read. However, spelling and reading processes are different. Reading employs a variety of skills that have general applicability in recognizing words. Contextual clues or a minimum of visual clues are all that is necessary for decoding; it is not necessary to know the exact spelling of words to read them. A person can, therefore, read with good facility and, at the same time, have great difficulty in spelling. Reading is a decoding task and spelling is an encoding task.

Speculation about what occurs in the process of spelling leads to the conclusion that a number of separate skills are involved. Disabilities in spelling have been related to problems or combinations of problems in visual memory, auditory memory, auditory and visual discrimination, and motor skills. Ultimately, these skills must be integrated for proper execution in correct spelling. It is extremely difficult to determine with any precision just where the problem might originate and, ultimately, what can be done about it. Consequently, many teachers depend on considerable practice for remediation. The Fernald technique is very popular among teachers because it incorporates multisensory stimulation with practice sessions.

Spelling research has followed three tracks: examination of the speller, investigation of instructional methods, and analysis of spelling words. An excellent review has been completed by Cahen and co-workers (1971) who revealed certain interesting conclusions. They were more interested in what makes a word difficult to spell rather than in instructional methods. In general, they support the presumption that exposure is very important.

Word frequency is associated with spelling difficulty. Misspelled words that are apparently common in the speech of children may not occur with great frequency in the books they read. A distinction must be made between words that students commonly use, but may not often see, and words they see in print, but may not often use in conversation. Certain words seem to invite misspelling more than others because of low-frequency, diphthongs, confusing vowel sounds (discrimination), and the length and order of letters. Phoneme–grapheme correspondences appear with consistency in the English language, and spelling difficulty may be related to the magnitude of correspondences with a certain word.

Apparently phonics training can be helpful in the improvement of spelling but there are a variety of peculiar misspellings found among children (who may be good or poor readers). If a child is familiar with English orthographic patterns, a variety of substitutions and additions that can make orthographic sense may occur. Reliance on phonics will be satisfactory only so long as spelling can make uniform application of sensible phoneme–grapheme matches. When the word violates its "sound," an error can occur. If a student is unable to reproduce the sequence because of an inability to revisualize, an entirely different problem is operating. Other students may have trouble in transferring into motor responses in the act of writing. Some students can spell quite well orally but are unable to write the same words. The teacher must manipulate the variables until a satisfactory approach for diagnosis emerges from observation of the student. For example, an LD specialist brought about dramatic improvement in one student by teaching the manual alphabet, which was used as an intermediary step before the act of writing.

At the secondary level, with the time constraints and the need for students to perform in academic classes, it becomes necessary to consider priorities and trade-offs. If the specialist spends an inordinate amount of time in drilling students on spelling, several likely outcomes will occur. One, students will probably not be motivated by such a boring and tedious activity. Secondly, the time that is used for explicit coverage of spelling is going to consume part of the class time that might be used in other more important learning activities. Thirdly, there is little evidence that direct training in spelling has benefits in reading comprehension, a much more important area for students. Depending on the circumstances with individual students, it might seem advisable to teach spelling incidentally with other activities. Aside from the many problems believed to cause disorders of spelling, it seems reasonable to believe that frequency of contact will help in the development of correct spelling, which might be approached in the process of reading and other learning activities with appropriate planning.

HANDWRITING

The first consideration in a handwriting problem is the determination of the condition as a manifestation of a more general language deficit or as a specific deficit unrelated to other disorders. If a student does not read much and spends little time writing, it is reasonable to expect that the diminished frequency of writing activity will not foster written expression. Handwriting is another encoding activity and as a form of expressive ability in communication, it should be anticipated that a student will not necessarily demonstrate skill here that is comparable to such decoding tasks as reading. As Johnson and Myklebust (1967) have shown, expressive language takes much longer to develop and follows the tedious development of other aspects of language. Students who can read and comprehend their own language with great facility are frequently incapable of exhibiting similar skill in oral or written expression. This pattern of development is most easily exemplified in the process of learning a foreign language. The novice may find that after much exposure to the new language he or she is able to understand what others say but has great difficulty composing sentences in the other language. Very gradually, the ability to speak fluently develops.

From a broad perspective, there are four general problems in handwriting:

1. General expressive disorders of language
2. Problems with syntax and grammar and impoverished vocabulary
3. Problems of written mechanics
4. Motor problems (dysgraphia)

Some students have serious disorders of verbal skills that prevent them from using written expression because the subskills of receptive and integrative processing are inadequate. Many students have difficulty with parts of speech, tenses, and a variety of grammatical rules. Many written passages evidence problems of word order, additions, substitutions, and distortions. Many students are defeated by the need to use commas, capitalization, and other forms of punctuation correctly. Some students are able to express themselves orally but are incapable of forming letters, words, and sentences with a pencil.

Much secondary classroom activity requires that students take copious notes to be used for preparation for tests. They must use handwriting in homework and may be required to prepare written reports or book reviews. Ackerman and co-workers (in press) have revealed that many secondary LD students have extremely slow writing rates, for example, take significantly longer to write their names than other students. As in the case of spelling, by the time a student has reached the secondary level trade-offs with respect to writing must be considered. How much time should be spent in directly teaching handwriting? Like other questions, this is difficult to answer and should be applied to individual cases. It is certain that students with extremely slow handwriting rates will simply not be able to keep pace with the typical classroom requirements. Accommodations must be made to reduce the demand on the student and still maintain the quality of education.

A typewriter may be the salvation for some students. Typing may increase the student's ability to manage course work along with the added benefit of improving reading and spelling. It will not work for all students, however, and considerable opportunity in school with good machines and specific instructional systems should be used before parents are encouraged to purchase an expensive typewriter in the hope that it will be beneficial.

ARITHMETIC AND MATHEMATICS

Perhaps no other area in learning disabilities has been as neglected as arithmetic and mathematics. The distinction between the two is emphasized by Chalfant and Schefflin (1969). Arithmetic refers to the rudimentary operations of computation, and mathematics refers to the more advanced branches of applied sciences. The ability to perform basic

computational operations is sufficient for most types of jobs and professions, and the training received at the secondary level often surpasses the student's need for vocational purposes. As a result, many students enroll for the minimum requirements in mathematics and fully intend to avoid such course work after meeting the obligations for graduation.

As was noted earlier, there may be a tendency for professionals to expect too much of students in arithmetic and mathematics because of the unique relationship to the curriculum. Students can learn to read after the primary grades by self-directed activities. They are unlikely to make such growth in arithmetic without direct instruction. Therefore, the achievement scores that a student earns will often show a trough in arithmetic abilities. The student must take specific classes in geometry, algebra, and other courses to be exposed to more advanced

work. The conceptual development of many, perhaps most, students does not increase much in mathematics beyond the junior high school level because only a few students tend to take advanced classes. The ability of students to avoid further classes in mathematics may be one reason why there has been little interest in conducting research in learning disabilities and mathematics at the secondary level.

In fact, there has been very little interest at any level. The overriding concern has been with reading. It is true that students who have reading problems will show achievement problems in arithmetic as soon as reading is the primary skill used for learning about arithmetic and mathematics. Many of these students are able to perform computations and solve problems that are presented orally, but typically they are prevented from excelling in an area where they may have talent because of teaching methods that inexorably insist on textbook instruction. It may be apparent that improved reading will augment achievement in mathematics, but it would seem that a flexible and liberal approach to the instruction of mathematics without the imposition of the reading requirement would lead to growth in various dimensions of mathematics.

It is indeed unfortunate that reading deficiencies eventually interfere with achievement in mathematics. Deficits in symbolic association that interfere with learning to read do not seem to affect the emergence of basic arithmetic concepts in the same children except incidentally because of teaching methodologies that emphasize reading (an unneccessary approach for the most part). Rutter and Yule (1973) reported that young children with specific reading disabilities demonstrated no particular problems in arithmetic. Hemispheric specialization, or assymetry of the brain, permits the individual to develop divergent skills that are verbal and nonverbal. Except as the processes are interrelated for cognition or as they are forced to be merged in the classroom by instructional demands of the teacher, the skills associated with each hemisphere can be quite independent. Because of the lack of interest in this aspect of learning by professionals our knowledge of specific learning disabilities in arithmetic and mathematics is limited.

From the broad perspective, the problems of secondary students with learning disabilities in mathematics should be considered from two viewpoints. If students have severe discrepancies in achievement, a basic mathematics program should be stressed in the curriculum. Students should be expected to develop (at least) functional abilities in arithmetic that would ensure competencies for application in most occupations and in consumer needs. This should be a high priority responsibility of the learning disabilities specialist. Otherwise, there are certainly many learning disabled students who demonstrate verbal deficiencies but who could use training in mathematics to good advantage. Certain professions, for example, engineering,

might be suitable for such students if appropriate training and accommodations can be made.

Cawley (1975) has considered the special problems of remediation of mathematics disabilities. He identifies a number of reasons why it is usually difficult for a student to receive specific remediation in a secondary setting. Most importantly he asserts that it is necessary to staff the school with a team that would include remedial and instructional specialists, mathematics instructors, and a diagnostician. Although this approach is easy to support, it seems reasonable to relate such planning in program development to the incidence of specific learning disabilities in mathematics. This cannot be determined at the present time. For students who evidently have great ability in mathematics, it is imperative that learning disabilities specialists attempt to assist mathematics teachers to change their attitudes toward acceptance of accommodation techniques. The learning disabilities specialist would not ordinarily be sufficiently trained or capable of providing instruction in such courses. Research and curriculum development in this area are needed greatly.

A general review of learning disabilities and mathematics is presented by Marsh (1976). This review makes the point that Piagetian theory can be successfully employed in understanding child development and is particularly appropriate in the investigation of mathematical concepts because many Piagetian tasks deal with quantification. Also, skills in mathematics lend themselves to easy identification as compared with reading. Therefore, a teacher can use a task-analytic approach in systematic teaching of arithmetic and mathematics.

SELECTION OF MATERIALS

It is not surprising to discover that there are very few commercial materials available for LD students at the secondary level. Lerner (1976) has made some suggestions that should be of interest to secondary teachers. Because of the wide range of differences and needs of students and the number of courses in the content areas of the curriculum, very specific choices must be made that can only be determined by systematic analysis of a student's needs and an examination of the purposes of instruction.

Wiederholt and McNutt (1977) have reviewed methods of evaluating materials for handicapped adolescents and conclude that most of the existing methods are more appropriate for much younger students. They recommend the use of two types of evaluation, *static* and *dynamic*.

Static evaluation refers to the obtainment of information that is necessary to decide what to buy or use. By contrast, a dynamic evaluation relates to the process of making decisions about the alteration of materials or discontinuance of their use. In general, a static evaluation of materials requires the inspection of materials to determine if they can meet the objectives of educating a student. Preparation time of the teacher, the nature of teaching strategies, cost, and durability are among the factors involved. Obviously, important aspects such as readability, language, motivation, and prerequisite skills of the student are critical in making determinations for use.

Dynamic evaluation might involve pretesting and posttesting, analytic teaching or applied behavioral analysis, observation, and interviewing. Mastery or criterion-referenced tests are well-suited to evaluation of students in content areas of the curriculum. For example, the interest of the teacher in a subject, such as history, is to get the student to assimilate information, retain factual concepts, and utilize critical thinking. Mastery of the body of information is the objective. Materials may be selected because they are readable, but the evaluation of the student's progress is determined by criterion- or content-references rather than by measures of reading ability.

It is certain that sufficient commercial materials will not be available for a number of years. Selection of materials will be a challenging activity. Until more specific recommendations are forthcoming it will be necessary for teachers to develop particular skill

in evaluation of *specific materials* for *specific students*. The first step in the process would be to use the IEP for each student and initiate a search for relevant and appropriate materials. Additionally, teachers may have to modify many materials and integrate certain segments from several sources. Teachers who engage in this very important activity will eventually develop skills that will shorten the time required for evaluation of new materials. Teachers should be cautious in selecting materials until evaluations are conducted.

INFORMATION-PROCESSING

In various sections of this book, we have made reference to the "verbal bias" of our culture and of our schools. *What we must recognize and understand is the difference between intelligence or intelligent behavior and verbal skills (for example, reading, writing, and oral expression).* Although our culture tends to be impressed by individuals who can express themselves verbally and articulately in a speech or letter, persons who are not able to do this must not be considered unintelligent. Rules and regulations have been established that equate intelligent behavior with such skills. A person must have a demonstrable reading level and earn certain achievement scores to be graduated from some high schools or to be accepted into college or graduate school. Scores from the Graduate Record Examination (GRE) are considered first in many graduate schools and students may be summarily dismissed from further consideration unless they have certain minimum scores. This may be defensible if it can be demonstrated that certain types of verbal skills are absolutely essential for the performance of roles associated with certain professions. It is quite certain that many jobs do not require such ability and the demonstration of verbal ability as denoted by a certificate or diploma serves a gatekeeping function by reducing the number of applicants. However, the fact remains—*low-level verbal skills do not necessarily mean low-level intelligence.*

Although the use of linguistic symbols may

be facilitating in reasoning during the act of thinking in mature and intelligent adults, it has been clearly demonstrated in Piagetian research that the ability to reason or to engage in abstract logical thinking does not require the use of a verbal language (Furth, 1970, pp. 66-67). In other words, people can, in the absence of language, develop the ability to perform logical operations. This has been demonstrated in studies of deaf students who do not have a linguistic system but who can engage in problem-solving activities and derive solutions that are extremely complex and that can apparently be solved by hearing people who are facilitated by language. Language may serve a symbolic function in abstract reasoning, but it is not absolutely essential.

Without delving into the complexities of Piagetian research, suffice it to say that these conclusions have tremendous significance for adolescents with learning disabilities who, by definition, have disorders of a verbal nature. Just because an LD student cannot read well, write prose, or deliver an emotional address in speech class does *not* mean that the stu‐ dent is unintelligent or incapable of engaging in processes of reasoning that use a symbolic system of logic.

Krauss and Glucksberg (1977) have engaged in a line of ingenious research and have formulated some interesting conclusions about the information-processing capability of children. In a study of the communication performance of children, they determined that effective communication is prevented when children engage in tasks that are overly demanding cognitively. If the communication task is simplified and the cognitive load is reduced, the performance of very young children in specific communication tasks approaches adult level competence.

This is reminiscent of the theoretical discussion of Johnson and Myklebust (1967) who attribute the cause of some learning disabilities to overloading of the brain in certain tasks. Chalfant and Schefflin (1969) have presented a similar rationale related to central processing functions. There should be no confusion between what we are proposing and what has been debated in the field of learning disabilities under the term *processing disorders*. Rather than identifying specific perceptual modalities or cognitive processing as embraced by many theorists, we are proposing a much less theoretical and more pragmatic approach to the instruction of adolescents that simply regards any form of linguistic input to the learner as central to learning in most activities of the curriculum in the secondary school.

Sitko and Gillespie (1975) stress the importance of teachers being able to effectively organize instruction so that students can efficiently use information-processing abilities. Learning may be thought of as a process of the interaction between the learner's ability to assimilate informational input and the complexity or organization of information presented in a learning task. Whether or not one views this process from a very theoretical approach, such as cognitive processing, or from a very practical point of view, such as abstract teaching, it is obvious that learning can be enhanced by simplifying the tasks of organization and learning to ensure that students reach desired outcomes of teaching. Different levels in the mastery of subject matter by various students may not be as much a matter of the innate intellectual or motivational disparity between students as it is a function of the complexity of teaching that is not sensitive to individual input variables.

The linguistic basis for differences in learning may be supported by research as in the finding of Wiig and Semel (1974) who have demonstrated that adolescents with learning disabilities show quantitative reductions in comprehension of logico-grammatical sentences.

If linguistic input cannot be decoded by the learner, as in reading, or if the input cannot be comprehended by the learner, as in listening to a teacher who uses complex language, the learner will not be able to assimilate the information and profit from instruction. Prawat and Gaines (1974) have indicated that LD adolescents are as capable as normal college students in using elaborative strategies in a paired-associate task. Although successful performance on such tasks has been related to performance on school achievement tests and it would be anticipated that the LD students would not do well in the task because of poor achievement scores, it was found that the learning disabled students were able to perform as well as a normal, older group. *Therefore, some differences in the learning of LD adolescents may be directly attributed to the complexities of input that they cannot understand.* The inability to read causes a diminished level of acquaintance with the vocabulary and linguistic structures of the language that may not ordinarily occur in the conversation of adolescents but that will likely appear in the lectures of teachers.

The abstract nature of a lecture for students who are deficient in processing complex information because of a lack of experience or opportunity to acquire comprehension leads to confusion in the interpretation of information. In the vernacular of the computer programmer, "Garbage in, garbage out."

Although numerous additional research studies concerning the conceptual styles of teaching, variables of instructional techniques, and qualities of comprehension in LD students must be conducted to verify or refute the assumptions thus far made, it seems plausible that conditions in the learning environment that do not account for information-processing abilities of students may be major factors contributing to failure.

Working from this premise, it is suggested that LD specialists endeavor to reduce the *complexity* of learning situations without diminishing the quality of instruction. This might be incorporated in any instructional activity of the resource room as well as in a variety of techniques that might be used to compensate for learning differences such as modified or alternative classes, accommodation in the regular classroom, and other approaches to reduction of the sheer complexity of teaching styles.

Instructionally, the learner should be aware of the exact objectives of learning activities, should be led into a logical sequence from simple to complex, should receive constant feedback information, and should be evaluated on a regular basis to determine if growth is occuring and if the student appears to comprehend. Every effort should be made to avoid ambiguous directions and unnecessary confusion and abstraction in teaching activities.

SUMMARY

Remedial efforts in the secondary school have limited value unless they are very carefully planned in coordination with accommodation and compensatory teaching. In general we may hypothesize that the effectiveness of remediation varies inversely with the age of the child and directly with the degree of coordination with accommodation and compensatory teaching. The type of remediation reviewed in this chapter is that which focuses on the *direct* improvement of the functional level of reading, handwriting, spelling, and mathematics; remediation directed toward perceptual or processing abilities was dismissed as a practical approach for any significant number of learning disabled adolescents. In addition to skill and subject-oriented remedial efforts, consideration was given to variations in information-processing abilities as pragmatically related to the inability of some students to effectively utilize information when presented in certain forms. The debate over the effectiveness of attempts to remediate processing disorders was deliberately avoided, but *the need for teachers to learn to think in terms of how they expect students to learn and how some may learn most effectively remains a need of highest priority.*

DISCUSSION QUESTIONS

1. The question of the value of phonics has been a matter of debate for many years. What is the position of this text relating to this issue?
2. What are your opinions about the position of a school board or policy that maintains that basic literacy should be the primary goal for all students?
3. What is meant by the term *process training?* Why is there a controversy over this issue?
4. How can social learning theory be used to explain

the reactions of students who have reading disabilities?
5. Is it feasible to think that there may be "new and different" methods of teaching reading to secondary students? If so, how do such methods differ from approaches used with younger students?
6. List the many reasons that might be used to justify the exclusion of a learning disabled student from college. Are any of them truly valid or are they based on traditional values?

REFERENCES AND READINGS

Ackerman, P. T., Dykman, R. A., and Peters, J. E. Learning disabled boys as adolescents: Cognitive factors and achievement. *Journal of the American Academy of Child Psychiatry*, (in press).

Balow, B., and Bomquist, M. Young adults ten to fifteen years after severe reading disability. *Elementary School Journal*, 1965, 66, 44-48.

Barsch, R. *Movigenic curriculum* (Bulletin No. 25). Madison, Wis.: State Department of Public Instruction, 1965.

Blau, H., and Blau, H. A theory of learning to read by "modality blocking." In J. Arena (Ed.), *Successful programming: Many points of view*. Pittsburg: Association for Children with Learning Disabilities, 1969.

Bloom, B. S., et al. (Eds.), *Taxonomy of educational objectives. Handbook I: Cognitive domain*. New York: David McKay Co., Inc., 1956.

Brown, G. Words and things. *Journal of Learning Disabilities*, 1972, 5, 572-575.

Bruner, J. S. *Toward a theory of instruction*. New York: W. W. Norton & Co., Inc., 1966.

Bursuk, L. Z. *Sensory mode of lesson presentation as a factor in the reading comprehension improvement of adolescent retarded readers*. New York: New York, University Press, 1971.

Cahen, L. S., Craun, M. J., and Johnson, S. D. Spelling difficulty—A survey of research, *Review of Educational Research*. 1971, 41(4), 281-301.

Cawley, J. F. *Math curricula for secondary learning disabled students*. A paper presented at Learning Disabilities in the Secondary School, a Symposium sponsored by the Montgomery County Intermediate Unit, Morristown, Pa.: March, 1975.

Chalfant, J., and Schefflin, M. *Central processing dysfunctions in children* (NINDS Monograph No. 9). Washington, D.C.: U.S. Government Printing Office, 1969.

Cohen, S. A. Studies in visual perception and reading in disadvantaged children. *Journal of Learning Disabilities*. 1967, 2, 8-13.

Coleman, J. S. The adolescent subculture and academic achievement. In M. Powell and A. H. Frerichs (Eds.), *Readings in adolescent psychology*. Minneapolis, Minn.: Burgess Publishing Co., 1971.

Copeland, R. W. *How children learn mathematics* (2nd ed.). New York: The Macmillan Co., 1974.

Cratty, B. *Perceptual-motor behavior and educational*

processes. Springfield, Ill.: Charles C Thomas, Publisher, 1969.

Cruickshank, W. A. *A teaching method for brain injured and hyperactive children* (Special Education and Rehabilitation Monograph Series, No. 6). Syracuse N.Y.: Syracuse University Press, 1961.

Delacato, C. *The diagnosis and treatment of speech and reading problems*, Springfield, Ill.: Charles C Thomas, Publisher, 1963.

Early, M. Taking stock: Secondary school reading in the 70's. *Journal of Reading*, 1973, 16, 364-373.

Fernald, G. *Remedial techniques in basic school subjects*. New York: McGraw-Hill Book Co., 1943.

Fries, C. *Linguistics and reading*. New York: Holt, Rinehart & Winston, 1963.

Frostig, M., and Horne, D. *The Frostig program for the development of visual perception: Teacher's guide*. Chicago: Follett Publishing Co., 1964.

Fry, E. A readability formula that saves time. *Journal of Reading*, April 1968, 513-515, 575-577.

Furth, H. G. *Piaget for teachers*. Englewood Cliffs, N.J.: Prentice-Hall, Inc., 1970.

Gagne, R. M. *The conditions of learning*, New York: Holt, Rinehart & Winston, 1965.

Gearheart, B. R. *Teaching the learning disabled: A combined task-process approach*. St. Louis: The C. V. Mosby Co., 1976.

Gearheart, B. R. *Learning disabilities: educational strategies*. St. Louis: The C. V. Mosby Co., 1977.

Getman, G., Kane, E., Halgren, M., and McKee, G. *Developing learning readiness*. New York: McGraw-Hill Book Co., 1968.

Gilbert, L. C. Functional motor efficiency of the eyes and its relation to reading. *University of California Publications in Education*, 1953, 11, 159-232.

Gillespie, P., and Sitko, M. *Conclusions from reading difficulties of the learning disabled adolescent*. A paper presented at Learning Disabilities in the Secondary School, a Symposium by the Montgomery County Intermediate Unit, Morristown, Pa., March, 1975.

Gillingham, A., and Stillman, B. *Remedial training for children with specific disability in reading, spelling, and penmanship* (7th ed.). Cambridge, Mass.: Educators Publishing Service, 1965.

Gleason, G., and Haring, N. Learning disabilities. In N. G. Haring (Ed.), *Behavior of exceptional children*. Columbus, Ohio: Charles E. Merrill Publishing Co., 1974.

Griffiths, D. E. The nature and meaning of theory. In D. E. Griffiths (Ed.), *Behavioral science and educational administration* (63rd yearbook, Part II). Chicago: National Society for the Study of Education, 1964.

Hammill, D., Goodman, L., and Wiederholt, Visual-motor processes—Can we train them? *Reading Teacher*, 1974, 27, 469-480.

Hammill, D., and Larsen, S. The effectiveness of psycholinguistic training. *Exceptional Children*, 1974, 41, 3-15.

Hewett, F. A hierarchy of educational tasks for children

with learning disabilities. In E. Frierson and W. Barbe (Eds.), *Educating children with learning disabilities.* New York: Appleton-Century-Crofts, 1967.

Johnson, D., and Myklebust, H. *Learning disabilities: Educational principles and practices.* New York: Gunre & Stratton, Inc., 1967.

Johnson, S. W., and Morasky, R. L. *Learning disabilities.* Boston: Allyn & Bacon, Inc., 1977.

Kephart, N. C. *The slow learner in the classroom* (2nd ed.). Columbus, Ohio: Charles E. Merrill Publishing Co., 1971.

Kirk, S. *Educating exceptional children* (2nd ed.). Boston: Houghton Mifflin Co., 1972.

Kline, C. L. The adolescent with learning problems: How long must they wait? *Journal of Learning Disabilities,* 1972, 5, 262-284.

Krauss, R. M., and Glucksberg, S. Social and nonsocial speech. *Scientific American,* 1977, 236(2), 100-105.

Landis, J., Jones, R. W., and Kennedy, L. D. Curricular modification for secondary school reading. *Journal of Reading,* 1973, 16, 374-378.

Lane, P., and Miller, M. Listening: Learning for underachieving adolescents. *Journal of Reading,* 1972, 15, 488-491.

Lerner, J. *Children with learning disabilities.* Boston: Houghton Mifflin Co., 1976.

Lovitt, T. C., and Hurlburt, M. Using behavior-analysis techniques to assess the relationship between phonics instruction and oral reading, *Journal of Special Education,* 1974, 8, 57-72.

Luria, A. R. *The working brain: An introduction to neuropsychology.* New York: Basic Books, Inc., Publishers, 1973.

Marsh, G. E., II. Teaching arithmetic and mathematics to children with learning disabilities. In B. R. Gearheart (Ed.), *Teaching the learning disabled: A combination task-process approach.* St. Louis: The C. V. Mosby Co., 1976.

Meyers, P., and Hammill, D. *Methods for learning disorders.* New York: John Wiley & Sons, Inc., 1969.

Morency, A. Auditory modality, research, and practice. In H. K. Smith (Ed.), *Perception and reading.* Proceedings of the International Reading Association, 1968, 12(4), 17-21.

Muehl, S., and Forell, E. R. A follow-up study of disabled readers: Variables related to high school reading performance. *Reading Research Quarterly,* 1973, 9, 110-123.

Myklebust, H. (Ed.). *Progress in learning disabilities* (Vol. I). New York: Grune & Stratton, Inc., 1968.

Orton, S. T. *Reading, writing, and speech problems in children.* New York: W. W. Norton & Co., Inc., 1937.

Prawat, R. S., and Gaines, P. Paired-associate performance in normal and learning disabled youngsters. *Psychology in the Schools,* 1974, 149-152.

Rutter, M., and Yule, W. The concept of specific reading retardation. Unpublished manuscript, 1973.

Sitko, M., and Gillespie, P. *Conclusions for speech and language difficulties of the learning disabled adolescent.* A paper presented at Learning Disabilities in the Secondary School, a Symposium sponsored by the Montgomery County Intermediate Unit, Morristown, Pa.: March, 1975.

Skinner, B. F. Why we need teaching machines. Harvard Educational Review, 1961, 31, 377-398.

Spache, G. D. *Diagnosing and correcting reading disabilities.* Boston: Allyn & Bacon, Inc., 1976.

Wiederholt, J. L., and McNutt, G. Evaluating materials for handicapped adolescents. *Journal of Learning Disabilities,* 1977, 10, 132-140.

Wiig, E. H., and Semel, E. M. Logico-grammatical sentence comprehension by adolescents with learning disabilities. *Perceptual and Motor Skills,* 1974, 38, 1331-1334.

CHAPTER 7

Maximizing motivation at the secondary level

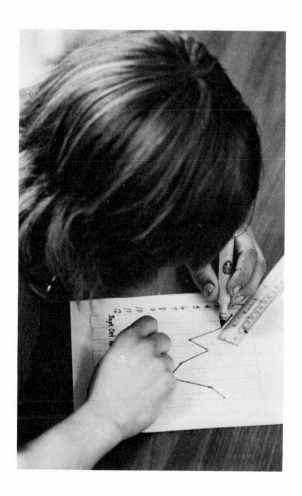

INTRODUCTION

It is difficult to find a text that reviews the field of learning disabilities without delving deeply into the behavioral scientist's frame of reference for part of its significant content. A review of demonstration programs funded by the Office of Education, Bureau of Education for the Handicapped, indicates that a considerable number of these programs include strong behavior modification components (Gearheart, 1977). Several well-accepted basic texts by recognized authorities that deal with educational procedures for *all* handicapped children are strongly behaviorally oriented (Hewett and Farness, 1974; Haring and Schiefelbusch, 1976). Some that were written as learning disabilities methods texts are essentially behavior modification manuals oriented toward learning disabilities. In a review of university programs designed to train teachers of the learning disabled conducted in 1975 by staff members of the Department of Special Learning Problems of the University of Northern Colorado, it came as no sur-

120

prise that a majority of the training programs surveyed included a required component in behavior modification techniques, applied behavior analysis, or some similar behaviorally oriented training component. Many states require a course in behavior modification for certification as a teacher of the learning disabled. We may therefore conclude that, for a variety of reasons, behavior modification techniques, applied behavior analysis, or some other closely related technique or approach with some slightly different formal label are a part of many learning disability programs, are recognized in the written content of a majority of texts on learning disabilities, and are supported by the federal government as a part of viable learning disabilities programs and/or efforts.

In addition to the general, overall acceptance of the work of behavioral engineers in dealing with learning disabled pupils, we find an even more compelling reason to consider such efforts with relation to the special segment of the learning disabled to which this book is addressed. As noted previously, there has been limited attention directed toward secondary pupils as compared with elementary students. Much of this lack of attention may be because of disappointing results of attempts to use methods with older children that have been successful with younger children. This has, at least for the present, led educators to an even greater tendency to utilize behaviorally oriented techniques with older children. We will, therefore, consider in some detail how behavior management applies to secondary learning disabled pupils. We will briefly review the history of this movement, indicate the major terminology and basic theory required to understand behavioral efforts, and emphasize practical applications in this chapter. Our major concern will be reward and contracting systems that are illustrated with selected case studies. The reader should remember throughout that this is not being promoted as the *only* or the *best* technique. It is merely presented as one *viable* technique that if used with appropriate content or skill building efforts, may be of great value.

HISTORY OF THE MOVEMENT

A number of summaries, varying in length, of the history of behaviorism are available. The purpose of these accounts may be quite different and the orientation (psychology, education, and so forth) is often varied. The reader should be sufficiently conversant in the topic to be able to fully understand and appreciate its applicability in efforts with learning disabled students. Behavior modification has taken on negative connotations with some teachers—as one teacher once told us, "Behavior modification is just an extra long four-letter word as far as I'm concerned." This may be caused by misunderstanding, and, hopefully, teachers may learn to appreciate the potential value of this approach or at least *parts* of it.

Some aspects of what is now called behavior management have been used for centuries. Good teachers have used planned reward systems for as long as recorded history permits us to determine such things with any real accuracy, and some of the teachers who have said they could not accept behaviorist principles were actually using them with great success. *Total acceptance* of all that has been said by any authority who has ever been called a behaviorist is not a prerequisite to using *some* behavioral principles to good effect. With this in mind, we will proceed with our brief historical account.

Skinner is often considered the father of the behavioral movement (Skinner, 1938). However, works by Watson (1913) and Mowrer and Mowrer (1938) are also part of the beginning of behaviorism.

Although Skinner began his writings in the 1930s, he did not reconceptualize his learning principles with implications for human problems until later (Skinner, 1953). In an effort to test this reconceptualization, Azrin and Lindsley (1956) attempted to teach 7- to 12-year-old children cooperative behavior. They placed two children on either side of a table and demonstrated that cooperative behavior, defined as simultaneous placement of two metal pins in matching stimulus holes, could be taught, extinguished, and retaught without the use of specific instructions.

In 1958, Gewirtz and Baer (1958) attempted to determine how the satiation and deprivation of adult attention toward a child would affect the adult's reinforcing power. Their results indicated that a child deprived of adult attention (being left alone in a room for a short time) was more responsive to that adult afterwards than a child who had continuously interacted with an adult in a friendly manner. The responsiveness of the child was determined by the extent to which the adult could effect the frequency with which the child dropped marbles into specified holes.

Williams (1959) described the tantrum behavior of a 21-month-old child. After a long illness the child would scream for a considerable length of time after being put to bed. Williams assumed that the parents were reinforcing the tantrum behavior by remaining in the room with the child. He suggested they simply put the child to bed, close the door, and not return to the room. The first night, the child cried for 45 minutes, but by the tenth night the child remained quiet when the parents left the room. The tantrum behavior had been extinguished by eliminating the reinforcement. A later examination of the child revealed no obvious side effects from this procedure, and the examiner reported the child to be a happy, outgoing 3 year old.

Any book on behavior modification or behavior management will indicate that the 1960s was *the* decade of behaviorism. It was the period that demonstrated "a meteoric rise in the use of the principles of learning to alter a wide range of human behaviors, from initial efforts that focused upon more deviant aspects of human behavior to the more recent emphasis upon normal behavior in the natural environment" (Bradfield, 1971, p. 1). From initial studies of abnormal behavior, usually in institutions for disturbed children or in clinics for children with severe behavior problems, researchers moved to attempts to change the behavior of mentally retarded individuals.

During the same decade, educators, viewing the results obtained with exceptional children, began to investigate the applicability of these principles to normal children

(Clarizio, 1971; Brown, 1971; Sulzer and Mayer, 1971). All reported a high degree of success and some believed that a panacea had been found for regular classroom teachers to use with children who exhibited talking-out or out-of-seat behavior. (Since we were teaching in regular classrooms during this time, we can personally attest to the eager acceptance, diligent study, and, oftentimes, indiscriminate application of behavior modification, as it was then always called.)

Although studies indicating the usefulness of positive reinforcement and positive reconditioning principles had been conducted with children having learning difficulties as early as the 1920s and 1930s, it was not until the mid 1960s that behavior modification principles became applied to what we now call learning disabilities. For a time it was believed by some that a determined application of behavior modification principles could and would "cure" almost any type of learning disability (Bradfield, 1971).

Because of the significant number of books and articles that indicate inappropriate or indiscriminate use of behavior modification, it may be helpful to consider some common misconceptions about behavioral approaches. In addition to the value of clarifying certain specific misconceptions, this may also be one of the more effective ways to amplify the nature and scope of behavioral approaches. It is with these two goals in mind that an adaptation of Worell and Nelson's (1974) enumeration of misconceptions of behavioral approaches is included here.

MISCONCEPTIONS ABOUT BEHAVIORAL APPROACHES*

MISCONCEPTION NO. 1. *Teachers should teach, not play psychologist or provide therapy.*

This statement may be true. However, involvement with behavioral approaches is not "playing psychologist" or "providing therapy." Research indicates that behavior is *learned*. This includes responses to environ-

---

*Modified from Worell, J., and Nelson, M. *Managing instructional problems: A case study workbook.* New York: McGraw-Hill Book Co., 1974.

mental factors, such as those in the classroom and the academic setting, and these *are* under the control of the teacher.

Considerable research in recent years has centered on many problems that teachers typically encounter in their classes. Lindsley (1965) surveyed regular classroom and special education teachers to specify these problems. Contrary to his own expectations, he found 60.5% of the teachers wanted a decrease in inappropriate behaviors, while only 33% indicated as their major concern an increase in academic performance. Six percent of the teachers expressed concern for increasing academic behaviors and decreasing inappropriate behaviors. One half of one percent reported no classroom problems. This study is representative of many others with similar findings. The indications are that most teachers wish to maximize academic success, but they feel that a reduction in a variety of inappropriate behaviors is a prerequisite to such success.

We are well aware that a teacher's task is to teach. The sad fact is that many students are not learning effectively. The improvement of certain skills, such as attention, will enable some of them to achieve in academic areas.

MISCONCEPTION NO. 2. *Inappropriate behavior indicates an underlying cause, and you cannot really change the behavior until you find the cause.*

This misconception is based on a misapplication of the medical model. Some educators have difficulty operating within any other framework but this. It should not be assumed that behaviorists believe that behavior does not have causes. Certainly behavior is caused; but, at times it is very difficult to discover the cause, and knowledge of the cause may provide little worthwhile guidance in correcting the problem. A further problem is that of multiple causes. At times it would be beneficial to know the origin(s) of a given behavior, but this information is often of little value.

The behaviorist asserts that if we can make it sufficiently important to the individual for

him to change his behavior, he will do so. When dealing with learning disabilities in adolescents, it is possible, perhaps even likely, that the academic retardation was caused by an earlier process disability. In many such cases, the original cause of present academic problems has disappeared. Even if we could discover precisely what was wrong 6 years ago, it would have little importance in providing direction for remediation. The residual effect is likely to be a combination of a failure syndrome (as regards academic tasks) and some sort of substitute coping mechanism (perhaps resulting in antisocial behavior). A tendency to be suspicious of anything relating to formal learning tasks is common. *These are the behaviors with which we must work, not the earlier problem that no longer exists.*

MISCONCEPTION NO. 3. *If a child has an unusually poor home environment, there is no point in trying to change the child unless we can change the home.*

In dealing with adolescents, this seems to be no more than a convenient cop-out. Students of junior or senior high school age usually have about 5 remaining years to live at home. When the student leaves the home, he must be ready to function in an adult world. A home in which there is little consistency, or one that is very punitive, compounds problems a teacher may encounter in school; however, research has indicated that behavior is correlated with the situation in which it occurs (Patterson and Harris, 1968; Cobb, 1970). For example, John may have great difficulty attending in his history class, yet he may have no difficulty attending to a basketball game. Students may demonstrate great variability in behavior from one setting to another that may reflect positive changes as a result of planned intervention. It is not likely that these changes will be carried over to the home situation, but, particularly with secondary school students, there may be good reason to ignore a poor home environment. Understanding that the role of education is much more difficult in such cases is only realistic, but to equate difficulty with certain failure is not tenable.

MISCONCEPTION NO. 4. *Some children cannot be changed.*

This misconception, emphasized separately by Worell and Nelson (1974), is an extension of No. 3. However, instead of using parental and environmental influence as a reason for giving up on a particular child, teachers may use a label as an explanation. Labels such as "hyperactive," "dyslexic," and "mentally retarded" are commonly used to *explain* behavior rather than to *describe* it.

Even the most severely mentally retarded persons have been assisted to accomplish such tasks as toilet training after years of previous effort has led to failure. Limitations (when in fact they do exist) have great importance in relation to what and how much can be learned, but they do not indicate that the child cannot learn. A good example is the blind child. His blindness dictates that he cannot be effectively taught to read the printed word in its normal form. But through Braille, the blind child can be taught to read. In learning disabilities we must be particularly careful when we deal with medical labels and syndromes; the word of the physician tends to become absolute and final. Physicians may speak of brain injury and not have in mind what others think of when they see that the brain-injured child cannot read. The ramifications are many, but the principle is simple: children's behavior can be changed and it is the educator's task to change it as a part of the learning process.

MISCONCEPTION NO. 5. *It is not ethical to change a person's behavior without his knowledge and consent.*

This idea sounds very humanistic and democratic. But there are many reasons for *requiring* a student's active participation in his own learning experiences. It is not realistic to expect a child to have sufficient perspective to appreciate the long-term consequences (either good or bad) of his behavior. On the contrary, he needs more immediate reinforcement for his efforts. For example, most 16-year-old boys are probably more interested in members of the opposite sex than they are in learning the intricacies of balancing a checkbook or the skills of addition and subtraction that are prerequisite to that task. In the case of many educational goals and the behavior required to reach these goals, the teacher must assert meaningful leadership.

If a teacher is concerned about securing the student's consent, it is possible to enlist the student's cooperation in setting up the contingencies, counting his own behavior, recording his own progress, and/or administering his own reinforcement. Any procedures that include mutually established, open policies will increase the self-esteem and self-discipline of each student. For further suggestions, see pp. 130-138 on contracting.

MISCONCEPTION NO. 6. *Students should do schoolwork because they enjoy it; we cannot accept a system that involves bribery.*

This idea seems to be fairly common among teachers. However, after giving some thought to the motivations that seem evident in adults, it does seem that we are all involved in bribery as it is often used in reference to behavior management. An acquaintance of ours was motivated, at one time, to learn to knit. She took classes; she tried and tried. Regardless of how much she practiced, the stitches were never even. Eventually, after much failure, she decided knitting was not for her. This is not unlike what happens to some learning disabled students. Perhaps, upon entering first grade they were motivated to read or add and subtract. After years of failure, they may decide that reading or math proficiency is not attainable. Just as it will take some unusual reward to motivate our friend to take up knitting again, it will take some unusual reward to get learning disabled students to willingly try reading or math. If knitting were a skill needed to function well in our society (therefore making it necessary for her to learn it), the promise of a 1-week vacation in the Bahamas or a $500 check might bribe her to attempt the task once again.

The belief that all reward systems are forms of bribery is unfortunate and is based on narrow and emotional thinking. Bribery denotes something immoral or illegal; thus, when we use the word the whole idea takes on negative connotations, and rational thinking becomes difficult. Perhaps it is the suggestion that we might use money in a reward system that causes the most problems, but let us examine the educational system as it now works. If a child is really good in athletics, we spend additional money to help him become even more proficient. We spend money for travel for him to go to athletic events; then we buy a trophy to present to him if he is unusually successful. We may not directly pay him for establishing a new record, but we provide things that only money cay buy. We are not suggesting that we change our policy of supporting athletic competition. We are pointing out that we do use money to promote better performance and that it is effective. We are also suggesting that it is *not* immoral.

The use of positive rewards, whether they are extra field trips, free time, primary rewards, or whatever is effective, is designed to get the student *started*. The goal is the same in all cases. It is to help the child with learning problems to experience success in learning and to eventually find enough motivation in successful learning (something he has not experienced) to make him want to learn for the sake of learning.

MISCONCEPTION NO. 7. *I tried behavior modification once and it didn't work—that's proof enough for me.*

If this principle were valid, anything that fails the first time would be abandoned forever. The fact is that nearly all teachers use some behavioral approaches, find success in some, and thus repeat them. Often, a teacher who tries to change a child's acting-out behavior may be taking on a relatively involved case. Without guidance in both planning and implementation it is easy to make errors, and the result is not what was expected. This does not mean that behavioral approaches will not work. When behavioral approaches do not work it often means that the techniques and procedures were not well planned or were not well implemented. *The*

principles are sound. The implementation may be difficult.

BASIC TERMINOLOGY IN BEHAVIOR MANAGEMENT

An understanding of the basic terminology used in behavior management is necessary for a complete understanding of the remainder of this chapter. Because each book written about behavior management uses somewhat different terms and may indicate slightly different meanings (even for the *same* terms), the more commonly used terms and the definitions that apply more specifically to secondary school students are included here. We are not attempting to provide a manual describing all the complexities of behavior management. Any of the books listed at the end of this chapter that deal directly with behavior modification are good sources for further explanation. Our concern here is to provide the teacher with a summary of the information required for application of certain of the behavior modification principles with an emphasis on *application*.

reinforcement—Any event that tends to change subsequent behavior when it follows that behavior.

positive reinforcement—Any event that increases the likelihood of the desired response. Another term commonly used is reward.

social reinforcer—A reinforcing stimulus mediated by another individual within a social context. The teacher watches for John to attend to his task and, when he does, makes an appropriate comment in the presence of other students. On occasion, unplanned social reinforcers occur between the students when John looks over at Kevin and says, "Hey, man, you're doin' good on those!"

token or tangible reinforcers—Any reinforcer that can be touched, smelled, eaten, played with, and so forth. Token reinforcers usually derive their potency from being paired with other reinforcers such as money, because of what money can buy; awards, because of the accomplishment they represent, and so forth.

intrinsic reinforcers—Those reinforcers available from performing the task itself. Knowledge, curiosity, and pride in achievement are assumed to be operating in students when they consistently function well in school.

time-out—The procedure for the removal of various forms of reinforcement. The student may be removed physically or all reinforcement may be removed. The procedure may include ignoring a student or asking him to go into a room adjacent to the classroom.

modeling—Behavior elicited after the same or similar behavior has been observed. John observes that Jim has completed his work and is now listening to records. Therefore John applies himself diligently to completion of his task.

target behavior—The behavioral goal or the end goal. By the end of the semester, the teacher wants John to be able to get 25 out of 30 multiplication facts correct.

self-management—The process by which the subject is able to monitor and change his or her own behavior. A student may record each task completed. This process of recording serves as the reinforcer to ensure that all required tasks are being accomplished.

contracts—A joint agreement between student and teacher concerning the accomplishment of specific objectives.

self-recording—The recording of various behaviors on the part of the subject, such as a + or − each time the student thinks about whether he or she has been attending to the task for the last few minutes.

BEHAVIOR MANAGEMENT (MODIFICATION)—THEORY AND PRACTICE
Operant behavior and operant conditioning

It is best to describe and define *respondent behavior* and *classical conditioning before* defining operant behavior and operant conditioning because they are often confused. The contrast between them may make the definition and explanation of operant behavior and operant conditioning more meaningful. The methods discussed in this chapter apply to *operant conditioning*, not to classical conditioning. *Respondent behavior* is largely involuntary, and certain behaviors may be acquired through classical conditioning. For example, if a neutral stimulus, such as a school building, is repeatedly paired with an unconditioned stimulus, such as failure or criticism from an adult, the neutral stimulus will be conditioned to elicit the same response as the unconditioned stimulus. The response will take the form of fear, avoid-

ance, or some other type of negative behavior. The response remains the same throughout the learning process, even though it is elicited by a new stimulus. If the school building had been paired with success or praise, the response would have been more positive. *This respondent behavior is sometimes called* reflex *behavior and must be differentiated from operant behavior.*

Operant behavior is primarily voluntary behavior, and it may be considered as operating on the environment and the environment operating on it in return. *Operant conditioning* means that operant behavior is controlled by the consequences that immediately follow it; that is, consequences help to determine the future probability of the behavior's occurrence. Thus, by manipulating what happens *after* certain behaviors (whatever the target behavior may be), it is possible to increase the chances that it will recur or diminish. A smile, *after* the occurrence of desired behavior, may increase the likelihood that the same behavior will recur, *if the student likes receiving the smile.* Applying the same principle, a reprimand, after the occurrence of certain behavior, may increase the likelihood that the same undesirable behavior will recur, *if the student is gaining desired attention by the reprimand.* Thus, the use of operant conditioning theory requires not only understanding the principle, but also *sufficient sensitivity to recognize what is rewarding to each student.* The emphasis in this chapter will be on the use of positive reinforcement, a practice that we have observed in a number of secondary school settings. Positive attention and praise, the arrangement of situations so that positive attention and praise may occur, and other closely related behavior modification techniques are of value, but some teachers know just enough about operant conditioning to get into difficulty when the situation becomes complex. Some teachers act and react in a manner that is designed more to take care of their own needs and feelings rather than the needs and feelings of their students. With the learning disabled student, this can be disastrous. The result is that

we may often reinforce those very behaviors we would like to change but do not know what to do to alter the cycle of action and reaction. It is with this belief in mind that we advocate *positive reinforcement* and *maximizing motivation* as the focal points of operant conditioning efforts with learning disabled adolescents.

Reinforcement

For purposes of this discussion, various types of reinforcement will be arbitrarily divided into the following categories: tangible reinforcement or rewards, social rewards, rewarding activities, and feedback and success experiences. Although they will be discussed separately, this does not imply that they must be used separately. Actually, the use of rewards should be varied to provide the utmost in reinforcement. The choice of rewards must depend on what is actually rewarding to the student. For example, most people respond to and are rewarded by praise; however, for some students praise is not rewarding. They hold a negative opinion of themselves (for whatever reasons) and will distrust the teacher because they believe the compliment is undeserved. Praise can have negative effects if the student has values different from the teacher as demonstrated by the student who thinks reading is socially unacceptable but the teacher compliments him for reading. By the same token, scolding a student, while not rewarding to most, may be a reward for the student who is eager for any kind of attention.

Tangible rewards include things such as candy, gum, money, and points. Behavior modification has been rejected by some teachers because of this emphasis on tangible rewards by some authorities. While tangible rewards can and often do provide the incentive a student initially needs, the wise teacher will soon pair them with social rewards.

Social rewards are rooted in interpersonal relationships and include things such as a smile, verbal and/or written praise, encouragement, interest, or attention. Because of the unpleasant nature of earlier associations the student may have experienced with authority figures, the attraction of the teacher as a social reinforcer is diminished. Because of past association with nagging, yelling, and threatening experiences, any comment from a teacher may be aversive. In these cases the teacher *must* begin with tangible rewards. These should be paired with social rewards so that the latter, through recurrent pleasant association with tangible rewards, become powerful shapers of behavior in and of themselves. To illustrate, the teacher may say something like, "Here is a coke (tangible reward). I am so pleased with the number of algebra problems you completed during this period" (social reinforcer). Many students will not need tangible rewards but respond immediately to verbal and social rewards. Students usually do not become dependent on tangible rewards unless the teacher fails to utilize social reinforcers and/or incorporate feedback systems and ensure success experiences.

It is important that the student recognize his progress, however small a step that might be. He might require specific instruction to learn to recognize his success. Contracts (pp. 130-138) are an effective way of providing the student with an awareness of his progress since they clearly delineate the task the student is to accomplish. Other objectives and motivating records of progress that might be used are:

1. Race track competition (move assigned car for each assignment completed)
2. Variations of football yardage (sample contract on p. 135)
3. Bank accounts (each student has an "account" from which he can have deposits or withdrawals according to behavior)*

When using social reinforcers, the teacher may need to pair them with a statement regarding the student's progress. ("John, you did very well. In only 20 minutes you completed six problems. Do you realize that is 50% more than yesterday?")

---

*Because of the wide age range (grade 7 through grade 12) some of the examples and/or ideas presented will be applicable at one end of the age range but not at the other. Teachers must innovate, based on the principle involved.

Success experiences also provide a very important source of reward. Although extrinsic (tangible and social) rewards are often relied on rather heavily in the beginning of a behavior modification program, they should gradually be replaced by rewards that are intrinsic (satisfaction in accomplishment or realization of success). A disabled reader may become competent (not the best or a speed reader—just competent) and find immense satisfaction in that. The potential dropout may find that small, daily accomplishments are rewarding enough to keep him coming to school. Teachers can rely on mastery and curiosity motives to assist in modifying behavior. Some suggestions to assist the student to realize some satisfaction in accomplishment might be:

1. If all daily assignments are handed in for a specified period, dismissing the student from the last test and giving him a 100
2. The unrestricted use of a tape recorder
3. The use of slides in an area of the student's interest
4. The use of a microscope (the student can prepare slides or use those already prepared)
5. Time to put models together
6. Work with a geology kit
7. Time to work in any area of special interest

Reinforcement schedules

The *schedule* of reinforcement is of paramount importance in operant conditioning. One type of schedule is *continuing reinforcement*. In continuing reinforcement, if a teacher asks a student 10 questions, the student will be reinforced 10 times if he correctly answers each question. This schedule may be the fastest way to establish new behavior, but it may also be considered a weak procedure because it is very susceptible to extinction. If a student becomes accustomed to reinforcement for each positive response, the positive behavior might be immediately extinguished if the reinforcement is terminated. However, it may be essential for the teacher to begin at this level and then proceed to another reinforcement schedule as soon as possible.

Another type of schedule is *ratio reinforcement*. If reinforcement is on a one-to-three ratio, every third response is reinforced. A one-to-ten ratio schedule would reinforce every tenth response. Some students may benefit from this type of reinforcement. Again, the teacher will want to change the schedule as soon as the student indicates a readiness to proceed with less reinforcement. Another version of ratio reinforcement is *variable ratio reinforcement*. This type uses reinforcement after different (variable) numbers of responses, that is, every third response, every eleventh response, every sixth response, and so forth.

In *interval reinforcement*, a student is reinforced according to elapsed time. If the teacher reinforces the student every minute, every 10 minutes, or every 25 minutes, it is called *fixed interval reinforcement*. This schedule of reinforcement can cause problems because the student may be emitting negative behavior when the time limit expires. If he is rewarded while emitting negative behavior, there is a good chance that the negative behavior will recur. The student may also begin to associate reinforcement with a certain number of problems or a certain interval of time. In this situation the student may hurry to complete his problems with little concern for accuracy or display positive behavior only when the time interval is about to expire. Because of these problems, a *variable interval reinforcement* schedule is suggested. This type of schedule provides reinforcement at varying periods of time. The student does not know for sure when or how he will be reinforced. *Generally, variable (or intermittent) reinforcement is most resistant to extinction.* Most of us are aware of how reinforcing an unexpected word of praise from a colleague can be and how this spurs us on. Adolescents appear to respond in a very similar manner.

Successive approximation

The process of successive approximation, or shaping, is almost always necessary in teaching new skills. When using successive approximation, the teacher must reward responses that indicate movement in the direction of the desired behavior. It is important that the teacher know which type of reinforcer will work best with the student before beginning. If the goal for the student is to work at his desk for 15 minutes, the teacher will liberally reward the student for sitting at his desk. The teacher will then reward any attempts made by the student to begin to work (opening his book, taking out his notebook). The teacher may gradually withhold rewards until the student works for a specified period. The time is gradually lengthened. Any positive behavior is rewarded liberally at first and, as the student's behavior approximates the goal, reinforcement is provided less frequently. Ultimately, reinforcement is given on a variable interval schedule since this is most resistant to extinction.

Admittedly, the above example is an oversimplification. The case studies on pp. 138-144 illustrate some of the problems a teacher may encounter on a daily basis.

At this point the similarities of successive approximation and task analysis might be discussed although task analysis is not, strictly speaking, a component of behavior modification. This will illustrate an alternative method of assisting the student to realize his successes. The goal for the student may be that he be able to maintain a checkbook. The successive tasks would include:

1. Addition and subtraction of single digits
2. Addition and subtraction of double digits
3. Addition involving carrying
4. Subtraction involving borrowing
5. Writing a check including: writing of dates, writing amounts of money using decimals, and writing amounts of money using words
6. Deposits and withdrawals

Some of these tasks may need to be subdivided into even smaller tasks for certain students.

The teacher must provide the student with a task on which he would reasonably expect the student to succeed. The teacher might begin by rewarding the student for attendance to the task and then gradually require attendance for a longer length of time or begin immediately to reward more work. As mentioned earlier, the teacher's goal is to eliminate the need for extrinsic rewards. Tangible rewards are paired with social rewards, which, in turn, are used to assist the student in developing intrinsic rewards. As the student masters one skill, he moves on to the next in the task analysis list. When new and/or difficult tasks are presented to students, it may be necessary to go back to some tangible rewards for a short period of time. As each skill is mastered, the student is made aware by the teacher that it is, in fact, accomplished. As we stated earlier, some students must be taught to recognize their success.

Contracts

Contracts are joint agreements between a student and a teacher to accomplish an objective. This can be a contract for a specific academic task or to have the student attempt a task. Contracts involve the student and the teacher in a commitment to one another in a realistic and responsible manner. Perhaps the most important feature of contracting is the involvement of the student in deciding what the task will entail (objective) and what the reward will be (reinforcement). The following guidelines are adapted from guidelines developed by Homme (1970). They provide a useful description of the characteristics of proper contracting.

GUIDELINE 1. *The contingency (reward) should be immediate.*

This guideline is particularly important in the beginning stages of contracting. Initial contracts should demand a small amount of behavior (completion of three written sentences or 10 math problems) and an immediate check to determine whether the behavior has been completed. Later, the task can become more lengthy or complicated. It is important to remember that most secondary students must overcome the effects of many years of failure. The reward should be contingent on the adequate performance of the task, not merely on the passage of time. Contracting will succeed to the extent that the precision of the performance-reward relationship is detailed and respected.

GUIDELINE 2. *Initial contracts should call for and reward small approximations.*

Although alluded to in Guideline 1, this principle is of such importance that is must be stressed as a specific guideline. It is one of the most misunderstood principles of contracting. The initial performance required of a student must be small, simple-to-perform approximations of the final goal. If the required performance is too precise or too difficult, no reward will be enough. After the student has completed several contracts, more lengthy or more exacting tasks can be assigned. After some success the student is generally encouraged to attempt something more challenging.

GUIDELINE 3. *Reward frequently with small amounts.*

Research and experience have shown the effectiveness of small, frequent reinforcements rather than infrequent, large ones. For example, Bob may respond far more willingly to the demand of completing the first half of a business letter if he knows that he will be able to listen to 3 minutes of a record at that point rather than waiting until the entire letter is completed. This is particularly important in the early stages.

GUIDELINE 4. *The contract should call for and reward accomplishment rather than obedience.*

Contracts should be stated in terms with this tone: "If you can spell (orally) the first three words on the spelling list, you may work on your film," rather than, "If you do the assignment, I will let you. . . ." Rewards for accomplishment lead to independence. The teacher's long-term goal should be to eliminate the contracts. However, it must be recognized that this may not be accomplished quickly, perhaps not even within 1 academic year.

GUIDELINE 5. *Reward the performance after it occurs.*

This may seem so obvious that it need not be mentioned, yet many teachers fail in this regard. Often, teachers say something like: "Okay, you can play one more game of cards (reinforcing activity), then you must complete your math (object of contract)." The concept of contracting is that tasks and reinforcing events be broken down into small units so that the task/reinforcement sequence will occur many times during a class period or a day. The *correct sequence* is to be arranged by the teacher and carefully followed on a planned, regular basis.

GUIDELINE 6. *The contract must be fair.*

This simply means that the two major aspects of the contract should be reasonable and balanced. "If you work for 48 of the 50 minutes in the period, you get 2 minutes free" does not provide reasonable, proportional reward; but neither does "If you do five math problems, you can have the rest of the period to listen to a record." The reward must be related to the length, difficulty, or magnitude of the task.

GUIDELINE 7. *The terms of the contract must be clear.*

It is important to indicate exactly what is to be performed and what the reinforcer will be. In the example, "If you work hard during this period, you can read a magazine the last 5 minutes," the conditions are not clear. The teacher and the student may have very different ideas on the meaning of "work hard." This could be clarified by indicating a specific time (work for 30 minutes) or the task to be accomplished (finish the outline of Chapter 6 in your social studies book). The student must always know exactly what is expected and what the reward will be. It is surprising how quickly students adapt to this and soon set goals either of longer duration or greater difficulty than the teacher.

GUIDELINE 8. *The contract must be honest.*

The contract must be adhered to in terms of specifications and carried out immediately. At times, the teacher cannot fulfill the contingencies of the contract because of some unavoidable circumstance. For example, the teacher may say, "You can shoot baskets in the gym after you complete your page of math," and then find the drama class is practicing a play in the gym. This is an honest error and can be made up by allowing the student to choose another activity or to begin the next period with the time earned for shooting baskets.

GUIDELINE 9. *The contract must be positive.*

Contracts should be stated positively because a negative tone is aversive and may incite some students who have experienced conflict with authority figures in the past. The terms of a contract should contribute to a positive educational experience rather than detracting from it. By using positive terms, the teacher avoids the threat of punishment.

GUIDELINE 10. *Contracting as a method must be used systematically.*

The question a teacher might well ask each time a behavior is required of the student is, "What is the payoff?" That is, when John is asked to complete some problems on percentages, what is his payoff? Does he get satisfaction from completing the page correctly? Does he feel satisfied because he can work percentage problems? Or, does he need some other reward such as reading a comic book? For most learning disabled students, repeated failure has reduced or eliminated the feeling of satisfaction that can be gained from correctly completing a task because of failure expectations. Another reward must be provided when such conditions are operating.

Teachers sometimes feel very uncomfortable when rewarding students "for doing what they should do anyway." This feeling, and the philosophy in implies, does have some merit. However, many students, because of learning disabilities, have missed the normal developmental experiences that would permit them to achieve satisfactorily. The principle of successive approximation can also apply here. If the student begins to complete some tasks because of the reward, that is a step forward. He may soon begin to gain some intrinsic reward, then the external rewards can be fewer and received only after longer periods of work. Ultimately, external rewards may be discontinued. All of us receive rewards. Our monthly paycheck is one reward, the sudden look of understanding on a student's face can be very rewarding, or the principal's favorable written evaluation can be the reward that carries teachers through months of preparations, checking papers, and so forth. Rewards are an integral part of most areas of our lives. Therefore, it does not seem inconsistent to plan reinforcement for students who are experiencing failure in school.

Developing a contract

Negotiating contracts can be time consuming and very complex. The teacher who has not previously used contracts might want to begin with a simple minicontract. It would include only one task, specify the reward, and be completed within one class period or less. (See the example below.)

MINICONTRACT—SHOP

I will listen to and follow directions, leave others' materials alone.

Then the last 15 minutes of the period I can read *Mad* magazine.

Student _____

Teacher _____

It will take just a few minutes to determine what tasks the student must perform and what the reward will be. As the teacher and student become familiar with the minicontracts and feel at ease with them, it will be easier to negotiate more complicated forms.

Some teachers may feel more secure if they have a detailed outline that they may follow in negotiating a contract. The contract checklist may serve this purpose. Although the contract checklist may appear lengthy or complicated, the procedure is not. Several

---

A CONTRACT CHECKLIST

1. Explain a contract.
2. Show an example of a contract.
3. Discuss possible tasks.
    Student-suggested tasks: _____
    _____
    _____
    _____
    Teacher-suggested tasks: _____
    _____
    _____
    _____
4. Agree on the task.
5. Student and/or teacher suggest reinforcers.
6. Negotiate the ratio of the task to the reinforcer.
7. Identify the time allotted for the task.
8. Identify the criterion or achievement level.
9. Agree on the method of evaluation.
10. Negotiate the delivery of the reinforcer.
11. Set the time or date for renegotiation.
12. Teacher and student both sign contract.

---

of the steps may be eliminated after the first contract has been negotiated.

Sample contracts

The six contracts that follow (Fig. 5, A-F), along with the preceding guidelines and checklist, should provide the basis for the development of meaningful, effective contracts. Contracting depends on two factors: *simplicity* and *specificity*. Fig. 5, A and B are rather formal contracts. Some students respond to the "businesslike" appearance of such a contract. Contracts that use any motif to which the student responds can be very effective. Fig. 5, C may be most effective with seventh and eighth grade students. For others it will be too "childish." As students become more adept at responding to contracts, an entire week's work may be contracted with tasks, rewards, and consequences all negotiated. Fig. 5, D involves several academic areas. With slight modification, it can be applied to any area. When students are assigned to an LD teacher for only certain academic areas, the entire week's work can be negotiated

Contract

This is an agreement between _____

STUDENT'S NAME

and _____. The contract will be

TEACHER'S NAME

binding from _____ to _____. It will

DATE   DATE

be discussed on _____.

DATE

The terms of agreement are:

I will (student) _____

_____

_____

_____

I will (teacher) _____

_____

_____

_____

The terms of this contract include the completion of the student's task and the delivery, by the teacher, of the contingencies agreed upon. If the student fails to fulfill his/her part of the contract, the rewards will be withheld. If the teacher fails to provide the rewards, the student has the right to take the matter to the principal.

DATE: _____ STUDENT: _____

TEACHER: _____

Continued.

Fig. 5. A, Sample contract. **B,** Responsibility contract. **C,** Math football contract. **D,** Daily academic contract. **E,** Weekly academic contract. **F,** Contracted goals and objectives. (**A** modified from Walker, J., and Shea, T. Behavior modification: A practical approach for educators. St. Louis: The C. V. Mosby Co., 1976. **B** to **E** from Gearheart, B., and Weishahn, M. *The handicapped child in the regular classroom.* St. Louis: The C. V. Mosby Co., 1976.)

Responsibility contract

The undersigned _____ hereby agrees to undertake the following *responsibility*:

_____

_____

_____

_____

for which he shall receive upon successful completion of his responsibility certain *privileges*, stated below:

1. _____

_____

_____

_____

B

2. _____

_____

_____

_____

3. _____

_____

_____

_____

This contract shall be binding for the week of _____

DATE SIGNED: _____ STUDENT: _____

RENEGOTIATION DATE: _____ TEACHER: _____

Fig. 5, cont'd. For legend see p. 133.

Math football

TO REACH YOUR GOAL COMPLETE THE FOLLOWING TASKS:

50 Yd. _____ 50 Yd.

40 Yd. _____ 40 Yd.

30 Yd. _____ 30 Yd.

20 Yd. _____ 20 Yd.

10 Yd. _____ 10 Yd.

GOAL _____ GOAL

TOUCHDOWN!

AFTER EACH 10 YARD GAIN I WILL _____

_____

AS A VICTORY CELEBRATION I WILL _____

_____

DATE: _____ PLAYER: _____

COACH: _____

Continued.

Fig. 5, cont'd. For legend see p. 133.

Contract

Subject	MONDAY	TUESDAY	WEDNESDAY	THURSDAY	FRIDAY
MATH					
READING					
SPELLING					
P. E.					

IF ALL ASSIGNMENTS ARE COMPLETED EACH DAY I MAY

IF ALL ASSIGNMENTS FOR THE WEEK ARE COMPLETED I MAY

IF I DO NOT COMPLETE AN ASSIGNMENT DURING THE ALLOTTED TIME I WILL

STUDENT: _____

TEACHER: _____

DATE: _____

COMPLETED ASSIGNMENTS:

D

Fig. 5, cont'd. For legend see p. 133.

WEEKLY ACADEMIC CONTRACT

Contract

	DATE	ASSIGNMENT	COMMENTS
MATH	MONDAY		
	TUESDAY		
	WEDNESDAY		
	THURSDAY		
	FRIDAY		

CONSEQUENCES:_____

_____

_____

_____

_____

STUDENT: _____

TEACHER: _____

ADDITIONAL COMMENTS:

DATES: _____

Continued.

Fig. 5, cont'd. For legend see p. 133.

GOALS AND OBJECTIVES
Contract

In what academic areas and/or in which basic skills do you need assistance? _____

_____

What do you want to accomplish this year in the learning assistance room?

A. Goals:

   1. _____

   2. _____

   3. _____

   4. _____

F

B. Objectives:

   1. _____

   2. _____

   3. _____

   4. _____

   5. _____

   6. _____

   7. _____

DATE: _____ STUDENT: _____

TEACHER: _____

Fig. 5, cont'd. For legend see p. 133.

with rewards and consequences for performance and nonperformance (Fig. 5, *E*). This eliminates the need for many contracts. Students develop a contract similar to the one shown in Fig. 5, *F* at the start of the year. The teacher and the student then discuss what has been decided. At times much discussion must take place before the student can complete this form in an affirmative and positive manner. This form can also be modified so that the student may establish his or her goals and objectives for each week. This procedure is most effective when students are relatively self-directed. (When students are first introduced to this form, there may be a tendency toward facetious comments. In this case, the teacher does not sign and attempts to promote a more serious approach. Usually, this works quite well after a few tries.)

Maximizing motivation—case studies

Maximizing motivation (whether it be accomplished through what the implementers choose to call behavior modification, behavior management, operant conditioning techniques, or simply maximizing motivation) can work with secondary school students. It is most effective when used in conjunction with other approaches and techniques and when it is based on knowledge about the students to be assisted. The three case studies that follow were chosen to illustrate how maximizing motivation may work in a variety of cases, in coordination with other approaches or techniques, and with individuals and groups. One case study was selected to demonstrate how behavior modification may be effective, even in cases where the teacher does not believe in behavior modification. We hope you will read these studies carefully and consider the various lessons to be learned from each. We trust you will see how these cases, with variations dictated by circumstances in individual situations, may be applicable and valuable to you.

John's contract

John was referred to the LD resource room because of severe academic and behavior problems. John was 14 years of age and the oldest of three boys in his family. On occasion his behavior was so unacceptable that he was in danger of being expelled from school. John's parents were concerned about his poor academic performance but more concerned about his acting-out behavior. The school personnel were concerned about both and considered the problem behavior to be more serious than the parents believed.

In school, John needed constant prodding to complete anything. He was suspected of a variety of antisocial acts even though he was rarely seen in the actual execution of them. He was regularly observed writing on his desk and throwing rocks and fighting on the school grounds. He was a constant source of classroom disruption and was frequently reprimanded for his noncooperative behavior. When frustrated, his usual reaction was to either behave aggressively or become very sullen and refuse to discuss his problems.

The resource teacher discussed various activities with John that he found rewarding and/or reinforcing. Together they identified the following potential reinforcers: bike riding, photography, art, assisting the physical education teacher, and playing checkers.

As a result of a staffing (which made John the part-time responsibility of the learning disabilities teacher), the following factors regarding John's academic work and behavior problems emerged:

1. Insufficient studying and noncompletion of school assignments
2. Difficulty in attending and listening to the teacher, obeying classroom rules, staying in seat, and completing assigned work
3. Arguing, yelling, or walking away when an instructional activity is interrupted or when a request is not granted
4. Reacting to failure by hitting, cursing, or refusing to talk to anyone
5. Throwing rocks at people and windows
6. Writing on own desk or property of others

It is important to note that the problems indicated were stated in behavioral terms. When this is accomplished, nothing is left to individual interpretation. The statements describe the actual behavior that is inappropriate and this provides the student and teacher with a basis for initiating change.

After identifying inappropriate behaviors, they should be listed according to priority since experience indicates it is unrealistic to expect a student to change all the behaviors at the same time. The first three behaviors listed were selected as the areas of initial concern. It was believed that if these could be eliminated, a more meaningful effort could be directed at the others. It was also reasoned that the last three behaviors *might* be eliminated since they could be reactions based on frustration resulting from the first three.

As a result of further discussion with John, the LD teacher believed that a contract approach might be effective. The teacher believed that John would need some material rewards, possibly points and some reinforcing events. The teacher also believed that because of the seriousness of John's problems,

---

CONTRACT

  This contract has been drawn up to assist John in learning more desirable student behavior. The following procedures will be used:

I. When John exhibits appropriate behavior by:
1. Staying in his seat during the entire class period (15 points)
2. Completing at least the first third of his assignment (15 points)
3. Observing the classroom rules as posted (20 points)
   he will be given points that can be exchanged for time with the Physical Education teacher (50 points earns 30 minutes).

II. When John earns 50 points for 3 consecutive days, he will have earned one class period in which to draw or use his camera.

III. If John does not comply with appropriate behavior as described in (I) and (II) above, he will be asked to go to the counselor's office and must remain there until the end of the class period.

  Changes can be made in this contract when all parties deem it advisable.

_____	_____
Student	LD Teacher
_____	_____
Date	Counselor

---

an arrangement of aversive consequences would be mandatory if John failed to complete his portion of the contract. The school counselor agreed to have John sit in his office if he failed to comply with the contract. Points were paired with verbal reinforcers and reinforcing events to make them conditioned reinforcers. It was planned to use some tangible reinforcers in the early stages but to phase them out as soon as possible.

The above contract was developed.

When the contract was put into effect, John exhibited model behavior for 3 days. He was able to draw on the fourth day. The fifth day he was so disruptive in class that he had to go to the counselor's office. He completed no assignments. The LD teacher reassessed the contract and requirements and indicated a need for change. It appeared that the requirements for the contract were too difficult. The academic requirements were altered so that John could more easily perform them and thus obtain more reinforcement. A kitchen timer was used to administer bonus reinforcement. The timer was set for various, short durations. When it sounded, if John

was exhibiting appropriate behavior, he was awarded points. If he had received points each time the timer sounded, he was allowed time to draw toward the end of the period.

Three difficult weeks followed the initiation of the contract. Some days John was so uncooperative, aggressive, and disruptive that he needed to be sent to the counselor. On other days he earned the time to draw and earned some free days during which he could use his camera. Although exact records were not kept, the LD teacher observed overall progress. John completed more assignments and was involved in fewer confrontations with other teachers.

By the fifth and sixth weeks, a pronounced if not dramatic change was observed. John worked for points (which were paired with social reinforcers) and for the free day to use his camera or to assist the physical education teacher. He no longer needed the timer.

After 10 weeks, John was able to work for the entire class period while receiving points only at the end of the class. The free day was awarded only after 5 consecutive days of receiving the maximum points.

The reader may logically ask, "Did all of John's problems go away?" The answer is "No." Much of John's inappropriate behavior was reduced in the resource room. However, he was still experiencing academic problems. The LD teacher was able to assist him with reading and math skills in the resource room but was just beginning to work with other teachers in attempting to eliminate some of his inappropriate behaviors in their classes. (This was the situation at this writing.)

Perhaps if John continues to receive some positive reinforcement for his appropriate behaviors, a self-reinforcement system will be internalized that will assist him in demonstrating these behaviors without the use of planned rewards. It is also possible that since John now attends to instructions and will complete tasks, he *may* be able to complete more of the assignments given by other teachers.

What John will do depends on too many factors to be reliably predictable. We can say that some students, after making the type of progress John has made, do return to the mainstream of education and of society and behave "normally" for the remainder of their formal educational careers. Usually we have no way of measuring with any degree of accuracy what happens after they leave school. Some are later lawbreakers, but many are not. And we should note that many "good students" also run afoul of societal standards in later years.

Wheat, the great motivator

Bob was assigned to the learning disabilities assistance center for the last period of the day. He was a freshman reading on a 3.2 (GE) level. The LD teacher tried various reading methods, but none seemed to interest him. Bob would look at any assignment and half-heartedly attempt to complete it if the teacher sat next to him and continually urged him to work. After several conversations with Bob, the teacher determined that among Bob's favorite foods were potato chips and Coke. He also enjoyed going to the student lounge to visit with friends.

The LD teacher told Bob that he could earn money to buy potato chips and Coke or to buy time to go to the lounge if he completed his work. Bob had to earn $8.00 (in dollar vouchers) to "buy" a small bag of potato chips and $10 to "buy" a Coke. Fifteen minutes in the lounge cost $20.00. To earn the "money," Bob had to complete each assignment within the allotted time. (The time varied, based on the difficulty of the assignment. However, for the first 2 weeks no time limit was longer than 15 minutes.) For each assignment the amount of allotted time and "money" earned were negotiated by the teacher and Bob. At the end of 6 weeks, Bob was working for 45 minutes for the $20.00 for a 15-minute visit to the lounge. Coke and potato chips were phased out in favor of time in the media center viewing films concerned with growing wheat. (The teacher had learned that Bob's father had obtained national recognition for his work in developing new strains of wheat and that Bob was eager to learn more about his father's work.)

At the close of the school year, Bob no longer needed "money" but continued to receive reinforcers such as free time in which he could choose activities such as reading about wheat, using the headphones to listen to music, or time to go to the lounge.

Bob had first come to the LD center in January. By June, he was reading on a 4.6 grade level. The resource teacher said that the strongest motivator was learning about wheat. She scoured the library for books, films, and articles to foster that interest. When Bob began to gain more skills in reading and could read some sections of social studies books that concerned wheat, he was further motivated to gain more reading skills so he could read more. According to Bob's LD teacher, the Coke and potato chips were simply "immediate" rewards to assist him on a day-to-day basis. As soon as he recognized his own growing abilities, they were no longer needed. The other rewards used were for variety and were supplemental while the LD teacher found more material concerning wheat.

The reader may ask, "Was Bob 'cured' or was the disability remediated?" Obviously, if he is going into his sophomore year and is reading at a 4.6 grade level, he is not "out of

the woods." He has areas of severe deficiency in most academic subjects. Perhaps all that can be said is that a motivating factor has been found. It remains to be seen whether that remains a meaningful motivator. It also remains to be seen whether or not Bob will be sufficiently motivated to attempt more in other academic areas and whether or not the LD teacher can persuade Bob's other teachers to attempt similar techniques or to modify his curriculum. Accommodative techniques and practices must be used even if he does continue to improve in reading skill. At any rate, for Bob, wheat (or rather knowledge about wheat) was the great motivator.

The teacher who did not believe in behavior modification

Mrs. Smith, a learning disabilities teacher, had one group of five boys, ages 14 and 15, who were extremely perplexing. They simply didn't care about anything except cars. She tried to emphasize the importance of reading, pointing out both present and future importance. The boys were not particularly hostile; they did listen to her but really didn't do much class work. On occasion they would complete some assignments, but more often they just idled away the class period. Oh, yes, Mrs. Smith repeatedly told her educator friends that she did *not* believe in the use of behavior modification.

Mrs. Smith discussed her concern for the boys with her husband. She told him the boys seemed unconcerned about their future and that no matter how interesting she tried to make their assignments, they simply didn't do the work. In the process of discussing this problem, she mentioned the fact that they were always discussing cars—how an engine works, what made a car really "hot," and similar topics.

Mrs. Smith's husband owned and operated a small auto repair business. He suggested that since the boys were so interested in auto mechanics, she might tell them that he would be glad to try to teach them some of the basics of auto repair "so they'll at least know something when they get out of school."

After giving that some thought, Mrs. Smith decided she would talk to the boys about it and see what they thought. At first they were doubtful and suspicious. She told them that she had made arrangements for them to visit her husband's garage for 1 hour the next day after school if they obtained parental permission. They apparently made a group decision to go and all appeared the next day with the required permissions. The day after their first visit to the garage, the students were excited about their experiences. They had been allowed to discuss their knowledge concerning cars and had demonstrated to themselves that they did know many things regarding mechanics. But the most exciting factor seemed to be that they had been allowed to "work" on some of the engines Mr. Smith had in the shop. During the first class period after their first visit to the garage, Mrs. Smith enjoyed a new relationship with the boys. *She* was the wife of their new-found friend (and teacher).

That evening Mrs. Smith began to think of ways to capitalize on the boys' interest. She spoke to her husband about her problem and they agreed that the school shop teacher was an excellent source for books on auto repair. Mrs. Smith spoke to the shop teacher and obtained the books. But she was depressed when she realized how far above the boys' reading level they were. According to Mrs. Smith, her only alternative was to simplify the reading material so the boys could cope with it. That evening she started to rewrite the introductory chapter of a basic auto repair book. In the process, she incorporated the word attack skills the boys would need to be able to read more of the material independently.

The next day she brought the material to class. The boys were, as usual, discussing cars. Mrs. Smith began the period by telling them that if they wanted to go to her husband's garage after school, they would have to earn the time. If she didn't need to remind them to do their work more than four times, they could go. However, if she had to remind them more frequently, she would call her husband and tell him who was allowed to

work on cars that afternoon. The boys accepted the idea enthusiastically.

Then Mrs. Smith provided them with the reading material for the day. The boys' comments ranged from "This isn't reading, it's about cars," to "Hey, I can read this stuff." That day the boys worked diligently, attempting to read their assignments. All five were allowed to go to Mr. Smith's garage. Each evening Mrs. Smith was kept busy rewriting material and incorporating word attack skills.

After a few weeks, the boys expressed an interest in some of the more popular auto-related magazines. After securing her principal's permission, Mrs. Smith and the boys ordered various magazines that the boys wanted to read. During the interim between ordering the magazines and their arrival, Mrs. Smith had a visit with the boys' math teacher. They were failing miserably in basic arithmetic computation. Mrs. Smith decided to divide the class period between math and reading. This was met with considerable opposition by the boys. After enduring three days of their complaints about math, Mrs. Smith told them that they would have to earn time to go to the garage by diligently attempting the math problems without complaining. Again, if they did not need to be reminded to apply themselves to the math tasks and did not complain about the task more than four times, they could go to the garage. The first day all went well. The second day two of the boys were not allowed to go to the garage because of excessive complaining. None of the boys ever missed going to the garage again.

The automotive magazines finally arrived and the boys eagerly read them. Since the boys were so interested in them, Mrs. Smith concentrated on whatever word attack skills the boys still needed to be able to read the magazines independently. All of the boys made great progress. Their arithmetic computation skills advanced steadily in both speed and accuracy.

One day the boys had a conversation with the shop teacher at school. That day he visited Mrs. Smith and discussed his impressions. He felt that the boys had exceptional knowledge in the area of auto mechanics and had learned a great deal from her husband. He suggested that they speak to the counselor and make arrangements for the boys to take shop for credit. He also asked Mrs. Smith if she would share the materials she had rewritten with him since he had some other students who found the reading difficult.

The schedules were adjusted, and the boys began to take shop at the school. They continued to visit Mr. Smith's garage simply because they enjoyed working with him. By the end of the year, the boys had gained an average of slightly more than 2 years in reading and 1 year in arithmetic computation.

It is interesting to note the principles in operation here since Mrs. Smith was "not interested in behavior modification." Mrs. Smith first listened enough to find out the boys' major interest: car repair. She capitalized on this motivating factor by using materials in which the boys were interested. Secondly, she adapted the materials so that they could succeed. By utilizing the adapted material she could demonstrate to the boys the need for independent reading. Word attack skills suddenly had a purpose.

She set up a very informal contract or reward system. The boys had to earn the time at Mr. Smith's garage. When she attempted this in relation to the reading, there was no problem. Perhaps the boys were so motivated they didn't need any further reinforcement. However, when she had them earn time by completing math problems, the terms of the contract took on new meaning. The boys were not motivated and two had to be prevented from going to the garage. By enforcing the terms ("no more than four complaints or you can't go"), Mrs. Smith taught all of the boys that their portion of the contract had to be fulfilled.

By allowing the boys to choose some of their reading material (auto mechanics magazines), she was ensuring their continued interest. This provided her with the freedom to concentrate on word attack skills. It also provided the boys with a reason to learn to read independently.

The boys' visit with the shop teacher at school proved to be extremely beneficial. Since Mrs. Smith had obtained the books from him, he was aware of what she was attempting to do. The boys' obvious interest and knowledge impressed him enough that he took steps to assist the boys in adjusting their schedules and to try using the simpler reading materials with other students. Although she did not realize it, Mrs. Smith was modeling (for the shop teacher) techniques for motivation and accommodation. She certainly was using contracting, in the best sense of the word, but without a written instrument. One can only wonder how effective she might have been if she *had* believed in behavior modification techniques!

SUMMARY

Although certainly not the only type of program emphasis in existing secondary learning disabilities programs, behavior management systems, and those that may be definitely identified as behavioral in orientation, are among the most popular today. Some degree of behavioral orientation is common in learning disability teacher training programs, and most of the secondary programs outlined in Chapters 10 and 11 have a definite behavioral component. On the other hand, behavioral emphasis must be considered as having limited application in some settings and with some students. Without adequate information as to appropriate educational goals for each student, behavioral approaches may, in fact, lead in some relatively meaningless direction. We may thus conclude that behavioral approaches have value and may be successfully applied in a number of varied instances and settings, but must be carefully planned and directed.

Reward systems and a variety of contracting techniques seem to be of greatest practical use in secondary schools. Maximizing motivation, with the hope that some motivational efforts may lead to continued momentum and meaningful self-direction is the emphasis that seems to be the most worthwhile. Specific guidelines for the development of effective contracting were presented in this chapter, along with six sample contracts that may serve as models. These models should be modified in most cases, so as to be applicable to the individual student and his unique needs. Three case studies were presented to illustrate how behavioral principles have been applied to learning disabled adolescents. Like the sample contracts, these should be viewed as examples, not as the "only way" to apply behavioral principles.

Many teachers who say they do not believe in "behavior modification" actually use some behavioral components quite effectively, without realizing that they are following behavioral guidelines. It would be interesting to discover how effective these teachers might become if they "believed" in behavioral approaches.

DISCUSSION QUESTIONS

1. Which of the seven misconceptions relating to behavior management would most likely be accepted by elementary teachers? Secondary teachers? Parents?
2. What are the problems that might be encountered in setting up a management system at the secondary level?
3. Given a hypothetical situation in which a student is expected to complete basic mathematics assignments, develop an outline of the course of events that might occur in successive approximation.
4. What provisions would need to be made with the school administration and with parents before developing a management system?
5. Propose a behavioral view of learning disabilities.

REFERENCES AND READINGS

Azrin, N. H., and Lindsley, O. R. The reinforcement of cooperation between children. *Journal of Abnormal and Social Psychology,* 1956, 52, 100-102.

Bailey, E. J. *Academic activities for adolescents with learning disabilities.* Evergreen, Colo.: Learning Pathways, Inc., 1975.

Blackham, G. J., and Silberman, A. *Modification of child and adolescent behavior.* Belmont, Calif.: Wadsworth Publishing Co., Inc., 1975.

Bradfield, R. H. (Ed.). *Behavior modification of learning disabilities.* San Rafael, Calif.: Academic Therapy Publications, 1971.

Brown, D. *Changing student behavior: A new approach to discipline.* Dubuque, Iowa: William C. Brown Co., Publishers, 1971.

Buckley, N. K., and Walker, H. M. *Modifying classroom behavior.* Champaign, Ill.: Research Press, 1970.

Cobb, J. A. *Survival skills and first grade academic achievement* (Report No. 1). Center for Research and Demonstration in the Early Education of Handicapped Children. Eugene, Ore.: University of Oregon, 1970.

Clarizio, H. E. *Toward positive classroom discipline.* New York: John Wiley & Sons, Inc., 1971.

Coloroso, B. Strategies for working with troubled students. In B. Gearheart and M. Weishahn (Eds.), *The handicapped child in the regular classroom.* St. Louis: The C. V. Mosby Co., 1976.

Gearheart, B. R. *Teaching the learning disabled: A combined task/process approach.* St. Louis: The C. V. Mosby Co., 1976.

Gearheart, B. R. *Learning disabilities.* St. Louis: The C. V. Mosby Co., 1977.

Gewirtz, J. L., and Baer, D. M. Deprivation and satiation of social reinforcers as drive conditioners. *Journal of Abnormal and Social Psychology,* 1958, 57, 165-172.

Gnagey, W. J. *The psychology of discipline in the classroom.* New York: The Macmillan Co., 1968.

Hamacheck, D. E. (Ed.). *Human dynamics in psychology and education.* Boston: Allyn & Bacon, Inc., 1968.

Haring, N. G., and Schiefelbusch, R. L. *Teaching special children.* New York: McGraw-Hill Book Co., 1976.

Hewett, F. M., and Farness, S. R. *Education of exceptional learners.* Boston: Allyn & Bacon, Inc., 1974.

Homme, L. *How to use contingency contracting in the classroom.* Champaign, Ill.: Research Press, 1970.

Jessup, M. H., and Kiley, M. A. *Discipline: Positive attitudes for learning.* Englewood Cliffs, N. J.: Prentice-Hall, Inc., 1971.

Karlin, M. S., and Berger, R. *Discipline and the disruptive child: A practical guide for elementary teachers.* Englewood Cliffs, N.J.: Parker Publishing Co., 1972.

Lindsley, O. R. *Classroom application of operant techniques in managing children.* Paper read at Yeshiva University, New York, October, 1965.

MacDonald, W. S., and Tanahe, G. (Eds.). *Focus on classroom behavior.* Springfield, Ill.: Charles C Thomas, Publisher, 1973.

Mowrer, O. H., and Mowrer, W. A. Enuresis: A method for its study and treatment. *American Journal of Orthopsychiatry,* 1938, 8, 436-447.

O'Leary, K. D., and O'Leary, S. G. *Classroom management: The successful use of behavior modification.* New York: Pergamon Press, Inc., 1972.

Patterson, G. R., and Harris, A. Some methodological considerations for observation procedures. Paper presented at the American Psychological Association, San Francisco, 1968.

Schloss, E., Strother, C., Hagin, R., Griffin, M., and Lehtinen-Rogan, L. (Eds.). *The educator's enigma: The adolescent with learning disabilities.* San Rafael, Calif.: Academic Therapy Publications, 1971.

Skinner, B. F. *The behavior of organisms.* New York: Appleton-Century-Crofts, 1938.

Skinner, B. F. *Science and human behavior.* New York: The Macmillan Co., 1953.

Stellern, J., Vasa, S., and Little, J. *Introduction to diagnostic-prescriptive teaching and programming.* Glen Ridge, N.J.: Exceptional Press, 1976.

Stephens, T. M. *Directive teaching of children with learning and behavioral handicaps.* Columbus, Ohio: Charles E. Merrill Publishing Co., 1970.

Sulzer, B., and Mayer, G. R. *Behavior modification procedures for school personnel.* Hinsdale, Ill.: Dryden Press, 1972.

Walker, J. E., and Shea, T. M. *Behavior modification: A practical approach for educators.* St. Louis: The C. V. Mosby Co., 1976.

Watson, J. B. Psychology as a behaviorist views it. *Psychological Review*, 1913, *20*, 158-177.

Wiener, D. N. *Classroom management and discipline.* Itasco, Ill.: F. E. Peacock Publishers, Inc., 1972.

Williams, C. D. The elimination of tantrum behavior by extinction procedures: Case report. *Journal of Abnormal and Social Psychology*, 1959, *59*, 269.

Worell, J., and Nelson, C. M. *Managing instructional problems: A case study workbook.* New York: McGraw-Hill Book Co., 1974.

CHAPTER 8

Career education and vocational preparation

INTRODUCTION

Vocational success seems to be an implied promise of American education. Students are encouraged to remain in school with the expectation that upon entering the work force their potential for earned income will have a direct positive relationship to the number of years spent in school. It is true that in most cases the ability to obtain and hold a job is directly related to specific vocational preparation and indirectly related to the possession of a high school diploma. However, many variables influence vocational adjustment and education must attempt to relate to as many of them as possible. The obvious importance of vocational adjustment to each individual demands that the school significantly improve vocational programming.

The traditional purpose of high school has been to prepare students for college. The college preparatory emphasis continues despite the fact that many members of the student body do not plan to attend college. The growth and acceptance of vocational education has been restrained and a pecking order has been established with prestige accorded the "basic academic program." Many educators view vocational education, career education, and alternative learning procedures as threatening to traditional standards.

Most teachers are interested in attracting the "best" students to their classes and vocational educators have been no more willing or better prepared to accept students who have poor academic abilities than liberal arts teachers. Nevertheless, such students have been directed into vocational tracks primarily because they are not able to excel in classes that reward traditional academic talent. To a learning disabled student, the difficulties with these two programs are similar. In both there are reading assignments and the need to apply a variety of academic skills in practical situations. Students with minimal academic proficiency will not necessarily fare any better in vocational education than in traditional college preparatory programs without strong support.

Modified vocational education programs have been provided for certain groups of handicapped students, for example, mentally handicapped, blind, deaf. Such programs, have been developed as an alternative for seriously handicapped students who may reasonably be expected to fail in general education and vocational education. The purpose of these modified programs is the development of specific vocational competencies, interests, attitudes, and knowledge necessary for performance in a narrow span of occupational choices. Such programs are not commonly provided for learning disabled students, although there have been some encouraging exceptions in the past few years (see Chapter 11).

LD students have been excluded from many modified programs in the past because guidelines generally restrict participation to only the most severely handicapped. Also, very few attempts have been made to develop vocational programs for the learning disabled because of the emphasis on younger children, process remediation, and remediation of basic skills.

Perhaps the most powerful vocational skill is the ability to read, although the ability to reason may be the key to advancement. If a student is unable to read efficiently or is oth-

erwise limited by the imposition of a serious handicap, attempts must be made to either strengthen the deficit or capitalize on other abilities. This must be individually determined by assessment of a student's aptitudes, attitudes, abilities, interests, and past achievement. A particular handicap may not deter a specific individual from the attainment of vocational adjustment, but the scope of opportunities may be more limited than if the individual were not handicapped. The reason for this circumstance, in many instances, may be more a function of an employer's attitude than the actual requirements of the job.

Many issues must be considered when vocational programs for LD students are being developed. The history of vocational education for other groups must be examined to avoid their mistakes and take advantage of their successes. For example, special educators have been content to place mentally handicapped persons into low-status, low-paying jobs because it has seemed reasonable to expect that persons with limited intellectual ability will be better suited for such occupations. Many of these handicapped persons are "underemployed" because our expectations have been too low. The issue of underemployment becomes even more perplexing when planning for LD students. Functionally, many LD students have academic characteristics similar to those of mentally handicapped persons. However, by definition, they are more capable in many ways and are intellectually equivalent to the majority of their nonhandicapped peers. So, if mentally retarded persons experience underemployment, what are the implications for LD students who would have little or no difficulty performing most jobs if they only had greater academic proficiency? Can we justify their exclusion from many occupations because of academic inadequacy? Can we support training objectives aimed at preparing them for unskilled and semiskilled employment? Should the learning disabled and the mentally retarded be trained for the same jobs with the ultimate likelihood that educable mentally retarded applicants would not be selected by employers in preference to more capable students? The moment we open this line of inquiry, a great many other problems arise. One of the more important is the role of vocational education in the curriculum. This topic has been debated for many years and is not likely to be easily resolved in the near future.

Part of the difficulty many persons have in conceptualizing the role of vocational education is a result of the value system of the predominant culture. The typical American view of any occupation equates what a person *does* for a living with what the person *is*. Prestige is associated with jobs that pay very well, that enjoy professional status, or that are stereotyped as glamorous. Most unskilled, semiskilled, and skilled occupations are not viewed as prestigious although skilled occupations may pay well.

Green (1973) observes that we tend to ask children, "What do you want to *be* when you grow up?" We do not ordinarily ask, "How do you intend to make your living when you grow up?" The job one performs becomes a part of one's identity and people are characterized by their occupations. A person *is* a garbage collector, *is* a custodian, *is* a teacher, *is* a doctor, *is* a lawyer. If a job is not very prestigious, or even considered by some to be degrading, we may excuse the individual if the job pays well because he "can laugh all the way to the bank."

These perceptions are pervasive and tend to determine the worth of individuals by judging the status of their jobs. This idea has been operating in the public secondary schools where more worth is attached to the intention to attend college than to "vocational" objectives. Some special educators should be chastized for their approach to students in work–study programs. We have, in essence, approached students with the attitude that, "We know that the jobs you will likely be able to hold are not very important or prestigious, but it's the best you can do and, anyway, there is dignity in work."

Ironically, many people, including those in the coveted professions, are not provided with a true sense of identity or any satisfactory life interest through their employment (Green, 1973). It is becoming increasingly apparent that people must either change jobs until they are satisfied or must cultivate interests and derive self-esteem and satisfaction from activities totally separate from their employment.

Regardless of potential occupational avenues for the learning disabled student, the school must consider the complex of factors associated with adjustment following school and not only gainful employment. When possible, students should be placed in jobs where they can derive satisfaction from their work. But we must also encourage and teach students that they can find fulfillment, reward, and self-esteem apart from their jobs. If we cannot honestly convince a student that dignity is associated with the collection of garbage, we should recognize that this activity may, at least, be a satisfactory way to make a living.

A person's major source of identity and satisfaction can be quite separate from his or her job. We need to stress the quality of life *apart* from jobs and the significance of interpersonal relationships. If we cannot improve a tedious and unrewarding job or change jobs, then we must be able to enrich our lives away from our jobs. This is part of the hope of career education.

CAREER EDUCATION

As was stated in Chapter 3, the secondary school has been under attack from various directions for several years. Among the many criticisms are claims that many students lack academic proficiency, the curriculum is not relevant to the needs of students, there is an unnecessary emphasis on college preparation, students are not partners in the educational process, students do not have the attitudes and skills necessary for survival in the technological society, and schools only meet the needs of an elite minority.

A new innovation in education, *career education*, has been proposed as a means of changing the curriculum, improving the schools, and improving the lives of students who may more meaningfully relate themselves to the world. Hoyt (1976) has been a major force in developing and promoting the career education concept. He defines career education as:

. . . the totality of experiences through which one learns about and prepares to engage in work as part of her or his way of living. (p. 4)

A career is the culmination or totality of work that is accomplished in a lifetime. Education is not restricted to formal instruction in a classroom but to the total impact of experiences one may have in a lifetime. Career education addresses the work of individuals that may be paid or unpaid activities as well as those activities that occupy leisure or recreational time. It should be clear that career education is a philosophy and that it is not synonymous with vocational education.

Hoyt (1976) states that the societal objectives of career education are to help all individuals to:

1. Want to work
2. Acquire skills necessary for work in these times
3. Engage in work that is satisfying to the individual as well as being of benefit to society (p. 5)

Society and the school must share the responsibility for encouraging the desire to work, for training people to work, for making work available, for making work meaningful, and for ensuring a sense of satisfaction in the endeavors and accomplishments of work.

The individuality of each student must be respected, thus mandating the alteration of school programs to really meet the needs of each student rather than forcing conformity to arbitrary or traditional curricular patterns. Alternative learning procedures must become as acceptable as traditional learning experiences. If a student can meet the outcome objectives of the curriculum through *any* means, no distinction should be made between students who follow different paths to those goals.

We are a long way from infusing career education concepts into our schools as evidenced by the continuation of customary approaches to learning, the emphasis on basic academic courses, and the stress on the purity of the high school diploma.

Each student should be able to realize maximum, practical potential in the tool subjects. Career education does *not* advocate a lessening emphasis on basic academic skills. In fact, it proposes that they are very important in our modern society. However, the school and society should not discriminate against those students who *cannot* achieve commensurate with their presumed abilities or with arbitrary standards.

Career education should be introduced early in the elementary curriculum and should extend through and beyond the school years. Teachers, parents, administrators, people in the business community, and patrons of the school should share in the process of injecting career education concepts into the lives of all students. The emphasis is on the total individual and the total environment. Such concepts would connect the fragmented curriculum. Not only would jobs be stressed, as would competencies in a range of occupational options, but careers, vocations, and avocations would be of equal importance.

Career education would be a continuous process intermingled with all elements of the school and community. It would not be a separate curriculum but rather an element of those already in existence. It would promote maturity and a sense of worth and purpose. It would not lower academic standards but would complement them. Vocational education is not career education. It stands by itself as a part of the curriculum that is no less significant, nor more important, than any other part.

REHABILITATION AND VOCATIONAL EDUCATION

Vocational rehabilitation services for handicapped citizens having nonmilitary service–connected disorders were first provided through the Civilian Vocational Rehabilitation Act of 1920. Since that time, the Act has remained in effect with major revisions in 1943 and 1954. The most significant legislation to date is the Rehabilitation Act of 1973, especially because of Section 504, which specifically prohibits discrimination in employment and educational opportunities because an individual may have an emotional, physical, or mental handicap.

Under the provisions of rehabilitation guidelines, the government has provided assistance to individuals who require extraordinary help for vocational placement, training, and adjustment. Students with substantial handicaps (mental retardation, deafness, and so forth) have been eligible for services as they near the completion of high school. In many states, schools have been permitted to enter into cooperative agreements with state agencies to provide direct services to handicapped students under the provisions of the Rehabilitation Act. Typically, work–study programs (modified vocational education) have been the main avenues for delivery of such services. Special education personnel have been trained to staff such cooperative programs in many states. Because of the eligibility criteria that restrict services to the more severely handicapped, LD students have not ordinarily been able to avail themselves of these programs.

The federal government has also demonstrated clear leadership in vocational education with a series of laws dating back to the Smith-Hughes Act of 1917. The most important legislation in this line was the Vocational Education Act of 1963 and amendments to it in 1968 that included specific provisions for handicapped students.

This recent legislation has led to the construction of many area vocational schools, increased occupational training, the preparation of more vocational teachers, and an increased acceptance of vocational education. The Vocational Education Amendments of 1976 have authorized higher levels of funding and established national priorities. In the 1968 amendments, 10% of state funds were set aside for the handicapped and this provision is included in the 1976 amendments. A total of 15% is earmarked for postsecondary vocational education. Moreover, funds are available for research, curriculum development, and counseling among many other outstanding provisions. The same categories of handicapped persons seem to be recognized in vocational education laws as in rehabilitation legislation. Under current guidelines in most states, it appears that the learning disabled will have difficulty securing services under the handicapped provisions although they would be eligible under other portions of the Act.

A number of problems confront planners who wish to serve LD students with vocational programming. How should vocational programs be conceived and where will funds come from? Should LD students be placed in regular vocational programs or should attempts be made to channel them into modified programs with other students who are called handicapped? The trend toward noncategorical placement, the de-emphasis of labels, and the general requirements of P.L. 94-142 are, in some respects, inconsistent with existing federal legislation in rehabilitation and vocational education.

Appropriations for the handicapped are based on a stable estimate of the numbers of students who will be expected to fall into traditional categories of severely handicapped students. The addition of another 2%, or more, of students classified as learning disabled would put a burden on existing delivery systems and would deplete budgets based on a much lower estimate.

Some would argue that the learning disabled student is not a seriously handicapped person and is, therefore, not really entitled to services under special program categories that are reserved for the most severely handicapped. Others would contend that even though an LD student may not have obvious manifestations of a serious handicap, he or she is just as handicapped and yet as capable as such students as the blind.

Following this latter line of reasoning, the LD student might as well be blind when confronted with traditional academic expectations. Accommodations are made for the blind student, but they are not generally implemented for the learning disabled. Therefore, how can exclusion policies be justified if it can be shown that a segment of the student population in secondary schools is prevented from entering particular occupations because of specific disabilities?

Beyond this, a host of other complicated problems emerge that have implications for postsecondary programs and universities. For example, if a blind student may receive a degree in law, medicine, or education, then why not an LD student? Would a university be willing to provide the same accommodations and compensatory teaching for the LD student as it does for the blind student? Would a college faculty approve of a degree candidate in education who has a reading level lower than the grade he or she proposes to teach? These and related issues are likely to become problems in the near future as universities (and secondary schools) are confronted by parents and students who wish to test the parameters of federal guidelines pertaining to Section 504 of the Rehabilitation Act of 1973. It seems reasonable to expect that a student with sufficient abilities and motivation will not be content to be limited to training that leads to a low-paying, low-status job simply because of the inability to perform in academic work as prescribed by traditional authority. It is probable that litigation will occur as the result of constitutional or legal issues arising from a situation in which a student believes that his opportunities are artificially restricted by school admission policies or professions that discriminate against persons because of learning disabilities.

Perhaps this discussion seems far afield, but these issues are pertinent to professionals who want to develop reasonable academic and vocational programs for learning disabled students. It would be a disservice to students to design simplistic programs that lead to underemployment. It would also be unfortunate to automatically cut off students from college pursuits. Circumscribing all these issues and concerns are societal attitudes and occupational prerequisites relating to demonstrable academic achievement. Nevertheless, in the midst of all these problems, special educators, vocational educators, rehabilitation counselors, and administrators

must make decisions. To better serve the secondary LD student, it will be necessary to provide compensatory teaching and accommodation, offer remediation that is appropriate, infuse career education concepts into the curriculum, and give students a series of options that may lead to vocational placement and/or postsecondary training. Innovative programming will be necessary to develop a comprehensive, exemplary program of this type. Present limitations of resources and trained personnel and the lack of appropriate models are temporary obstacles that will eventually yield to planning efforts.

TYPES OF VOCATIONAL PROGRAMS

Career education concepts should be introduced into the curriculum at the elementary level. Specific training in vocational education may begin at the junior high school level. The typical work–study programs in special education have been preceded by a *prevocational* component. Nonhandicapped students who wish to enter a vocational preparation curriculum are able to take courses at the junior high school level in many districts, which leads to more advanced training at the high school level. In planning for the development of vocational training for the LD student, a variety of circumstances must be considered. For example, a decision must be made about the nature and scope of the vocational program. So little work has been accomplished in this area that it is difficult to make general recommendations that might be of widespread applicability. One approach is to review the types of vocational programs that have been or that might be employed in the education and training of secondary LD students. The information presented in this section is, therefore, an attempt to provide the reader with a general overview of the range of types of programs that might be adopted by a school. Variations or innovations will undoubtedly emerge in the future as interested professionals turn their attention to this neglected area.

The professionals responsible for planning vocational training of LD students may wish to explore the possibilities of arranging for vocational training in the existing vocational education course work available to nonhandicapped students. If sufficient preparation can be made and cooperation ensured, students can be placed in regular vocational course work with support services offered by the resource room teacher. Operating under the concept of the "least restrictive environment" and from the basis of a cost-efficient system, this approach has a great deal of merit. New personnel are not required, no expenditures are necessary for materials and equipment, and a mechanism is available for meeting the objectives of the vocational program. The key to the successful utilization of existing vocational programs is careful evaluation of individual student needs and available support systems. The outstanding feature of this approach, a factor that must be considered, is the low cost of skill training. However, the needs of students must not be sacrificed in the interest of cost-efficiency if existing vocational education courses are not satisfactory.

It is probable that a sizable number of LD students can benefit from regular vocational education. Special education personnel should support students in these classes in much the same manner as for other classes as described earlier in this text. If it is decided that some students require modified vocational education programming, a variety of options are possible.

The U.S. Office of Education, Bureau of Education for the Handicapped, has prepared a technical manual, *Improving Occupational Programs for the Handicapped*, that lists types of vocational programs for the handicapped and reviews some exemplary programs in several states. Prevocational programs (exploration of work possibilities) are not described. The major types of vocational training programs described in this manual are:

I. *Low-cost skill training*
    A. Work experience
    B. Work–study
    C. On-the-job training (OJT)
    D. Off-campus work stations
    E. Cooperative programs

II. *High-cost skill training*
    Any program directed at a particular group that leads to very specific skill training and that is inordinately expensive

Following is a more detailed description of each type.

Work experience. This type of training is a little more advanced than prevocational programming. The objective is to guide the students toward a general employment orientation. Simulated work experiences are presented to give students the tasks and responsibilities associated with a working situation.

Work–study. This approach utilizes on-campus and off-campus work stations. In on-campus programs, the student, over a 3-year period, may work with custodians, cooks, or in the library. In support of the work activities, classroom training may be offered that deals with specific topics such as work conditions, completing application blanks, and keeping records. In off-campus work stations, the student may work in a number of job situations under the supervision of actual employers. Part of the school day or week involves return to the classroom for training that is related to the experiences of the student in the job stations. Although off-campus job stations may be specifically for training (in many instances employers are paid to participate), some employers may retain a student as an employee after graduation. The number and variety of such stations is proportionate to the size of the community.

On-the-job training (OJT). This type of program is based on the concept that specific skills may be directly taught to trainees at the job site rather than having a student exposed to a variety of job stations or to limited or general work experiences. The approach has been used with more severely handicapped students because the training assistant may learn the job, bring back samples to the school, initiate basic training of the student, take the student to the job and work alongside the student, and eventually withdraw and provide less frequent supervision. If the student is able to meet the demands of the job, and otherwise adjust, the student may be formally employed.

Off-campus work station. This approach is also used with more severely handicapped students, as a rule. An industry or business in the community provides a work location in the plant or office building where students are brought to work under the supervision of a coordinator employed by the school. Depending on the nature of the work required by the host employer, students may work there indefinitely and draw a wage. In the case of retarded persons, this is an intermediate arrangement between a sheltered workshop placement and actual competitive employment. Whether or not this arrangement would be appropriate for LD students, depends on many variables.

Cooperative programs. This type of program is generally best suited for institutions that may need to secure services for their residential students because of prohibitive costs in establishing a program on the institutional grounds. In this instance, the institution would enter into an agreement with a neighboring school or vocational-technical school so that students could be transported to the cooperating school for services. This would probably not be very useful for the majority of public school programs, although rural areas and private schools would benefit.

Higher-cost skill training. A high-cost program may be very similar in most respects to other types of vocational training, but costs are increased by a number of factors. Typically, a low pupil–teacher ratio (many professionals—teachers, counselors, aides, psychologists, work evaluators, and so forth), expensive equipment, and construction costs contribute to the higher cost. It is unlikely that most public schools would be able to justify a high-cost program.

For the most part, it seems likely that some type or combination of low-cost approaches would be desirable if it is determined that a modified vocational program is needed. School personnel should very carefully study the target population and decide which students could be better served in the regular vocational education classes. In some cases such study might be used as a needs-assessment to encourage the school to broaden and strengthen the total vocational education program. If a sizable number of students do not seem to be candidates for the existing vocational education program, it may be necessary to choose a modified program. Undoubtedly, one controlling factor would be the budget available for such an endeavor. A low-cost approach would be more acceptable to the administration of the school for obvious reasons.

ESTABLISHING A PROGRAM

According to the Bureau of Education for the Handicapped (Technical Manual), program planners who have implemented vocational training programs for handicapped students have made a variety of mistakes. Some major errors or weaknesses are:

1. Training based on a low achievement expectation
2. Lack of funds, good facilities, equipment, and materials
3. Too few effective instructors
4. Poor supervision and monitoring of progress
5. Employment opportunities are sexually stereotyped

Furthermore, it has been concluded that programs fail their students in three important ways.

1. They fail to prepare the environment for the student and the student for the environment.
2. They fail to seek assistance from services or groups outside the program.
3. They fail to make programs relevant to the job market and environment where students must live.

Beginning a new program is not an easy task. There are few uniform suggestions that can be applied. Handicapped students are heterogeneous in spite of their commonalities. The curriculum must not be rigid, and individual needs must be met. Program planners interested in establishing vocational education for LD students should observe the cautions listed above while initiating new services. One additional caution should be observed—the program must not preclude college and other postsecondary options for some students.

The following outline is provided as an aid in the development of a modified vocational education program.

I. Establish advisory committee
   A. Organize a representative body with members having a variety of expertise, if possible
   B. Select a chairperson
   C. Select a recorder

D. Charge the committee with the task of studying the problem

E. Organize meetings, study and research sessions, and subcommittees

II. Define target population

A. Use the state definition of learning disabilities

B. Estimate the number and location of students in the target group

C. List students by age, sex, and grade

D. Estimate the incidence of any superimposed medical conditions

E. Estimate the number of target students who would be capable of meeting admission criteria for postsecondary programs

F. Identify the number and types of jobs that might be performed by students in the target group

G. Identify the jobs available in the community or in nearby communities

H. Other

III. Review laws and regulations

A. Review state laws and guidelines pertaining to special education, vocational education, rehabilitation, and references to eligibility

B. Review laws pertaining to child labor, child abuse, peonage, minimum wage and working conditions, and general school laws

C. Summarize laws for target population as they relate to:

1. Diagnosis
2. Evaluation
3. Treatment
4. Training
5. Education
6. Sheltered employment
7. Transportation
8. Restrictions on placement and training activities
9. Other

IV. Determine demographic characteristics

A. Use a map of the community and indicate population density

B. Superimpose location of unit of interest (school, district)

C. Locate junior and senior high schools on map

D. Locate and identify business and industrial job sites proposed for target population

E. Determine rate of unemployment by job category

F. Contact employers (survey instrument) and determine employer needs (specialized training and so forth)

G. Other

V. Review resources

A. Local sources

1. School budget
2. Possible private or nonprofit organizations

B. State sources

1. Rate of reimbursement for special education, vocational education, and support services
2. Other

C. Federal sources

1. Vocational education acts
2. Rehabilitation acts
3. Titles of Elementary and Secondary Education Act
4. Developmental Disabilities Act
5. Other

D. Grants

1. Bureau of Education for the Handicapped
2. Bureau of Occupational and Adult Education
3. Social and Rehabilitation Services
4. Rehabilitation Services Administration
5. State grants
6. Private
7. Other

VI. Space and equipment

A. Estimate equipment needs

B. Determine space needs and explore the possibility of finding low-cost or rent-free space in community

VII. Community services

A. Determine scope and extent of community services

B. Determine possible input of labor and trade unions

C. Determine possible relationship with vocational-technical schools

D. Assess the nature and extent of existing vocational services in the schools and community colleges

E. Estimate possibility of cooperative programs

F. Other

VIII. Determine tentative program type

A. Utilizing the available data, propose program types that might be implemented (high-cost, low-cost, and so forth)
B. Project staff needs, budgets, space needs, and other significant costs
C. Estimate equipment needs and operating budget
IX. Final report
A. Finalize report
B. Report to convening body

Professionals should be selected to plan and implement the program based on their expertise in education and rehabilitation. A new program would benefit from the services of consultants from the state department of education, universities, and community agencies. If existing models for vocational education of other handicapped groups can be imitated, planners should determine how elements of the models can be most effectively utilized. The general program model should include a prevocational sequence for the junior high school and a vocational sequence for the senior high school. Specific job clusters would be used at the vocational level. The objectives and the curriculum components should be developed with the job clusters serving as the foundation. An additional consideration is work assessment. Many standardized techniques of work evaluation are available for use in school programs. Evaluation of students should occur in each phase of the program and be an early concern of the program planners, so it would be advisable to secure the services of experts in developing this area. Work evaluation is specialized and generally beyond the capabilities or experience of most school personnel. The program sequence should be:

1. Prevocational program (junior high level)
2. Vocational program (senior high level)
3. Job try-out or placement
4. Evaluation of adjustment
5. Follow-up

PROGRAM CONSIDERATIONS

A number of considerations should be considered prior to implementation of a voca-tional sequence. Many of these were discussed briefly in the preceding section. Specifically, these relate to the nature of the program and its sequence, organization, and personnel.

Sequence

With the advent of career education, a new emphasis has been placed on vocational education with early exposure of children to work-related concepts. During the junior high school years, work should be explored in greater detail. This has traditionally been referred to as the *prevocational* program. Heretofore, only modified programs for handicapped students have stressed a prevocational component although it would certainly be desirable to introduce such elements into the curriculum for all students. Depending on the resources of the school, some prevocational programs have primarily been the responsibility of special education teachers in special classes or prevocational teachers employed for the express purpose of providing work-related training.

Students at this level of development usually receive instruction in vocational information, prevocational work evaluation (simulated work experiences), societal relationships, homemaking, and specific math and reading concepts related to work. Students are taken on field trips, have sessions with speakers invited from the community, view films and filmstrips, and engage in other activities to develop an awareness of work. There are a number of commercial programs being designed (stimulated by increased funding in career education) that will permit schools to develop comprehensive units of instruction. Relationships between people, interactions between employers and employees, the importance of personal hygiene, health, and appearance, the completion of occupational applications and related forms, and conduct in job interviews are studied.

Some prevocational programs have developed simulated work experiences in the classroom or have had students participate in on-campus work stations. Students may "work" in a number of such stations throughout the year with the purpose of exposing students to the nature of work, interrelationships with others, supervision, and demands of a routine. The student is not ordinarily paid for such activities because they are considered instructional in nature. On-campus work stations might include work in the cafeteria, the library, the office, or any of a variety of other locations important to the daily functioning of the school.

The *vocational* program is directly concerned with developing work skills. This typically begins in high school when students develop the maturity for coping with such instruction and with the awareness that such activities may be related to employment in the near future. This level of training is the most diverse because of the number of variables that might influence it. Whatever the nature, it should be sequentially related to the prevocational program at the entry level and also to postsecondary programs or employment after high school graduation.

Students may enter vocational education courses of the regular curriculum or they may be trained in any of a variety of low-cost or high-cost programs that were described earlier in this chapter. This level of training may also be the most difficult to conceptualize because it is very difficult to develop programs that may lead to general and specific work skills and an adequate background to allow students to enter college or other postsecondary programs. In other words, specific training objectives can be established but it is difficult to do this if the school attempts to keep various options open to students after the completion of secondary school.

Organization

Although special education has customarily assumed direct responsibility for vocational programming for eligible students, it is evident that new organizational patterns will need to emerge so that all teachers can *share* the responsibility. The concepts of the least restrictive environment and noncategorical classification must be accounted for at the secondary level. Presently, there are few models to imitate. General educators, voca-

tional education teachers, rehabilitation specialists, and special educators will have to experiment with different approaches in an effort to incorporate the principles of shared responsibility and cooperation.

Personnel

If it can be determined that modified vocational programs should be offered to LD students, state departments of education and university teacher-training programs will have to rethink personnel preparation standards. This area needs immediate attention. Until recently, very few teachers have been prepared to work with secondary students in learning disabilities. A few states have required different competencies for secondary special educators who have worked with the mentally retarded in work–study programs. Two general types of special educators must be prepared: (1) a teacher who has primary responsibility for dealing with academic training in resource rooms or in self-contained classes (a situation that will probably be of limited demand), and (2) a teacher who has a firm background in occupational information and training. Both of these teachers would be trained special educators with a secondary emphasis. However, one would specialize in remediation of basic academic skills, delivery of accommodation and compensatory teaching, and services to the other teachers in the school. The other would be trained to deal effectively with vocational education and to relate to the business and industrial community. The more specialized the vocational component of a school, the greater the need for both types of special educators. We cannot predict the future, but it is apparent that teachers whose basic training is in elementary special education programming are not equipped to work with adolescents who have needs of a different type and magnitude.

SAMPLE PROGRAMS

A few programs have been reported, although the general level of activity in this aspect of programming is very limited. There are currently a few demonstration centers

funded under Title VI-G through the Bureau of Education for the Handicapped that focus on vocational needs of LD students. (See Chapter 11 for descriptions of some of these programs.)

Colella (1973) has reported on the accomplishments of a modified high school program in career development of Nassau County, New York. According to the description, it can be surmised that the school is not typical of most public school settings because its exclusive purpose is to serve handicapped students. The school employs a work experience counselor who integrates programs in the school with employers and work locations in the community. The curriculum for the students involves forty periods of class instruction each week. Twelve periods are devoted to academic skill development, and eighteen periods are reserved for instruction in occupational education. The remaining ten periods are divided among electives. Colella reports that the modified program has been

successful as demonstrated by a marked increase in attendance.

Schweich (1975) has discussed the results of a program that uses a very different approach. The program was begun in the Archway School in Brooklyn, New York. The specific target population of the staff was the group of LD students who were evaluated and believed to not have college ability. A work–study program was designed to operate on a four-semester cycle. The first semester was restricted to academic training. The remaining three semesters were divided between academic work and job placement on a half-day basis. The job clusters selected for the program were clerical and semiprofessional occupations, and program results indicate considerable promise in this program model.

A well-developed program is conducted through the Occupational Training Center of Mesa County Valley School District of Grand Junction, Colorado. After a complete evaluation and determination of eligibility, a student may enter the Center for basic training in technical skills, attitudes toward work and supervisors, relationships with employees, and general work orientation. If the student makes adequate progress, he may be moved to a more advanced level of training with work simulation and consistent work evaluation. Eventually the student may enter one of nine job clusters for vocational training: child care, upholstery, graphic arts, building trades, clerical, service station, electronics, domestic and custodial, and nurse's aide. Students attend the Center for half a day and return to their home schools for the other half. Special education teachers are assigned to the Center to assist the students and work with vocational educators. Eventually, students may branch into either work–study programs or regular or modified vocational education classes leading to job placement. A total of 180 students are served each day. This number includes students with a variety of handicapping conditions.

Another exemplary program has been developed at the Bryant High School in Bryant, Arkansas. This project, known as Pre-Career and Occupational Training (Pre-COT), is specifically designed for secondary learning disabled students. The purpose of the project is to increase academic achievement, to encourage students to remain in school, and to provide occupational training. The program involves students in nine occupational areas by simulating work activities that are product oriented: photography and film development, electronics, woodworking, pottery, horticulture, needlecrafts/textiles, production control, sales, and management. A unique aspect of the program is that non-handicapped student aides are selected by the staff to conduct activities in the occupational areas. Personal observation of this program led to the conclusion that the relationship between the student aides and the participants was most effective. It was apparent that the involvement of other students in the program led to a general acceptance of the program among peers in the school. The quality of work completed by students was typically excellent. It should be noted that the illustrations in this book were provided by students in this program. The program also provides direct compensatory teaching activities, remedial teaching, and assistance to regular classroom teachers. The cooperative relationship between the two learning disabilities teachers and the remainder of the staff clearly demonstrates the feasibility of approaches recommended in this book.

SUMMARY

It is not surprising that little attention has been given to the vocational education of secondary LD students for this neglect is only part of the larger issue—a general lack of meaningful secondary programming. In any event, this area may become one of great importance in the future as we begin to emphasize and plan for the long-range needs of LD students and cease to attend only to more immediate educational concerns.

We have attempted to demonstrate a need for the reconceptualization of the status of vocational education, for the infusion of career education into the schools, and for the serious study of the problems and answering of the many questions relating to the school's role in the vocational education of LD students. It would be desirable to provide the reader with significant findings of longitudinal research, but there are none. It would be tempting to suggest the rudiments of a curriculum that would have general utility, but this would be premature. There are a number of books, monographs, and curricula directed toward career education for handicapped populations, but we are not certain how appropriate they may be for the learning disabled. In fact, it may very well be that a majority of learning disabled students can be satisfactorily served by inclusion in existing vocational education programs. The greatest need may be to concentrate our efforts on developing awareness in society to relax barriers and eliminate prejudice that relegates LD adults to unsatisfying jobs or underemployment. This can be a challenging, exciting, and rewarding area for professionals who truly wish to serve students with learning disabilities.

DISCUSSION QUESTIONS

1. Most public school educators tend to adopt middle class values. How does this affect the goals and purposes of the secondary school?
2. Informally survey ten people, from varying backgrounds, with the following questions: What is career education? How many careers have you had to date? Should everyone have job skills or be trained in a profession? Summarize your results. Is there any consensus on these questions? Is there a pattern in the responses reflecting effects of certain experiences?
3. Find five job listings in the paper. Cut them out. Show them to ten other people and ask them to arrange them in order of "status" or "prestige" as they see them.
4. The Council for Exceptional Children has a new division, Division of Career Education, organized in 1976, reflecting the renewed (or new) interest in the area of career education for learning disabled students. Some professionals view this as a result of political and socioeconomic pressures and changes. Identify some of these political and social pressures.

REFERENCES AND READINGS

Colella, H. V. Career development center: A modified high school for the handicapped. *Teaching Exceptional Children*, 1973, *5*, 110-118.

Conner, J., and McAllister, E. Pre-career and occupational training: A program description of a project in the public schools of Bryant, Arkansas, funded by Title IV-C, ESEA, 1977.

Green, T. F. Career education and the pathologies of work. In L. McClure and C. Buan (Eds.), *Essays on career education*. Portland, Ore.: Northwest Regional Education Laboratory, 1973.

Hoyt, K. B. *An introduction to career education* (DHEW Publication No. [OE] 75-00504). A policy paper of the U.S. Office of Education, 1976.

Mesa County Valley School District. *Occupational Training Center*, A program description. Grand Junction, Colo.

Schweich, P. D. The development of choices—An educational approach to employment. *Academic Therapy*, 1975, *10*, 277-283.

U.S. Office of Education. *Improving occupational programs for the handicapped*. A technical manual prepared by the Management Analysis Center, Inc. of Washington, D.C. for the Bureau of Education for the Handicapped.

CHAPTER 9

Counseling

INTRODUCTION

The counseling program augments other services of the school through assistance in personal adjustment and individual academic and social growth. It supports the social, academic, and vocational objectives of the school. Modern counseling is an amalgamation of concepts and approaches that have developed since the early 1900s. The scope of services has gradually broadened, particularly during the last 30 years as counselors have responded to the needs of students in an increasingly complex society. Today, a systematic approach to counseling requires highly trained professionals who can deliver a variety of services that assist students in achieving both short-term and long-term goals.

The development of counseling may be better understood through examination of its major historical periods. The following outline of the history of the counseling movement is adapted from a description provided by Hansen, Stevic, and Warner (1977, pp. 9-12).

Vocational guidance. Frank Parsons encouraged the development of a system that would make it possible to match a particular individual with appropriate occupations by determining the interests and abilities of the individual. He created a vocational bureau in 1908 for that purpose, and his efforts have earned him recognition as founder of the counseling movement. The process of examining the characteristics of the individual and the occupations to determine a logical match stimulated the development of contemporary systems of vocational assessment that use

161

psychological instruments and other methods for data collection. While the early period of the counseling movement was firmly rooted in vocational concerns, it gave way to later developments that focused on the educational system, per se, so that vocational aspirations might be more fully realized.

Educational guidance. Gradually, counseling was broadened to encompass the total life of the individual because it became obvious that isolated concerns, such as vocational guidance, and neglect of other aspects of the individual's development would be fruitless. The educational guidance of the individual became a prominent consideration of school personnel who attempted to broaden the scope of guidance services to include methods of teaching young persons to develop a sense of identity, to establish personal goals, and to develop educational pursuits that would serve individual purposes.

Adjustment. A disagreement among guidance professionals occurred as a result of differing views about the degree of emphasis that should be placed on educational guidance versus an emphasis on mental health. The developing fields of psychiatry and clinical psychology had a profound influence on counselors who became concerned with the personality adjustment of students, a concern that culminated in a deemphasis on educational and vocational guidance. Assistance in personal adjustment and crisis intervention began to surpass other considerations of the counselor. This was viewed either as a contribution to the emerging field because of the emphasis on mental health or as a detriment because it focused on situational adjustment problems rather than developmental adjustment patterns. Nevertheless, the emphasis on adjustment caused a significant change in direction.

Development counseling. Advocates of a movement opposed to crisis intervention as the single consideration of the counselor ultimately triumphed. From the 1950s, the counseling movement emphasized assistance in normal developmental patterns. The counselor's role was expanded to provide important services to students at any point in the maturational process when information or intervention might be useful to the individual in making important decisions. However, counseling services were still restricted to specific problems at important junctures in the life of the individual.

The modern view. The 1960s brought a new emphasis with passage of federal legislation, including financial assistance for the primary purpose of preparing students for the sciences. With this federal legislation came increased demands for the counselor to assist in this effort. The subsequent forces of social change relating to the Vietnam conflict and the expansion of civil rights created new pressures on the school, a changing view of the opportunities for minority groups including women, and a significant new responsibility for the counselor. In this new responsibility, the counselor was asked to become a partner in the process of reordering society and erecting new priorities. The relatively new trend of career education has also caused the counselor of the 1970s to reemphasize vocational guidance in addition to the goals of assisting students with adjustment and normal development.

The involvement of counselors in programs for handicapped youngsters reflects growing professional concern for a variety of students who experience developmental problems that interfere with normal adjustment and growth. Counselors have assumed important roles in the advisement of students and parents at the secondary level. For example, they have contributed significantly to the success of work–study programs for mentally handicapped students.

However, guidance services specifically designed for LD students have been slow to develop. This might be explained by the fact that LD programming has been directed at preschool and elementary children while most counselors have been employed in secondary schools where relatively few recognized LD programs have existed. It can be argued that unique counseling programs for the learning disabled need not be established. However, the needs of LD students are considerably different from those of normally developing students because of the strong impact of academic failure on self-esteem and social relations. For these reasons, it is desirable to expand and extend the counseling program for LD students and their parents. This can be accomplished by using LD specialists, other teachers, and certain responsible, sensitive students to supplement the limited time and resources of the counseling staff.

ROLE OF THE COUNSELOR

The American School Counselor Association has established policies for the functions of the secondary school counselor. The following list from their policy publication of 1964 designates the major functions of the counselor:

1. Planning and development of the guidance program
2. Counseling
3. Pupil appraisal
4. Educational and occupational planning
5. Referral work
6. Placement
7. Parent help
8. Staff consulting
9. Local research
10. Public relations

It can be seen that the counselor is not directly involved with the student in a teaching relationship nor as an authority figure. Relationships between the counselor and the student are deliberately planned to be different from interactions with other adults employed by the school. A unique degree of trust is essential if the counselor is to successfully accomplish assigned responsibilities.

Counselors are trained to work with students on an individual basis or in small groups. Underlying all counseling activities is the intention of directing students into ways of thinking and behaving that will lead them to an appreciation of their abilities and interests. The counselor attempts to stimulate self-direction and initiative so that each student will realize that social, educational, and intellectual achievements are largely determined by each individual.

Counseling theories

Various theories and models have been used by counselors in their work with students. University training programs tend to expose counseling students to a variety of established approaches. Most counselors eventually adopt a personal style that draws upon many sources, but there are a number of generally recognized theories that provide the basis for development of personal counseling theories. Shertzer and Stone (1976) have identified the basic counseling orientations as:

1. Psychoanalytic adaptations
2. Trait-and-factor theory
3. Self-theory
4. Behavioral theories (pp. 168-172)

It is not surprising that psychoanalytical approaches were readily adopted by counselors because the counseling movement began to emerge at about the same time as the theories of Freud and his followers. Freud's original concepts are still present in some contemporary approaches to counseling and psychology, and most theories of personality development incorporate some aspects of the psychoanalytical view. However, the varied demands placed on the counselor and the constraints imposed by time tend to reduce the extent to which therapeutic techniques based on this theory are used in the schools. The counselor cannot possibly serve large numbers of students through the use of practices that are based on classical psychoanalytical theory. Consequently, more practical approaches have evolved.

The trait-and-factor approach to counseling grew out of the influence of the psychological testing movement in the belief that the counselor could *direct* change in the client more effectively and efficiently by assessing personality traits through the use of standardized instruments. The data were used to identify strengths and weaknesses, to select a course of study, to guide personality development, to intervene in personality maladjustment, and to identify career interests and potential. Tests became the mainstay of many counseling approaches because of ready access to objective measures with which to plan and organize a multicomponent program for individual students. Tests are still widely used by many counselors who feel that the results can be used to make direct decisions about the counselee. The trait-and-factor approach bases counseling strategies on diagnosis and the use of standardized tests. Current theorists in education and psychology seriously question this approach.

A popular theory that exemplifies an alternate counseling approach is the *nondirective* technique of Carl Rogers. The emphasis is switched from counselor-centered, or directed, to client-centered therapy. Individuals are given the responsibility of determining problems and issues and generating solutions for themselves rather than relying on the authority of the counselor. The counselor develops rapport with the client and permits a free and open environment to support the client who feels nonthreatened and able to interact. However, the counselor assumes no responsibility for directing the session nor solving the problems of the counselee. The acceptance by the counselor is believed to allow the client to engage in a process of self-evaluation, of inner-directed, self-initiated planning that leads to growth. According to this theory, once the individual assumes responsibility for himself and his actions he will assume a healthy attitude toward himself and the world, will interact responsibly with others, and will establish appropriate life plans.

A number of references to behavioral approaches have been made in various sections of this book (see Chapter 7 for considerable detail). The principles of learning, as espoused by behaviorists, have been applied to classroom techniques of instruction and to counseling. The premise that all behavior is learned serves as the cornerstone of behavioral counseling. The counselor makes no assumptions about internal mediators but considers personality characteristics to be merely products of the experiences of the individual. The counselor shapes the behavior of the client to create the desired changes. The learning environment is the focus of counseling so that social modeling and operant conditioning, among other variations, are utilized by the counselor in therapy.

Important services for learning disabled students

The students and the resource teacher must be able to rely on the many services of the secondary school counselor to assist at important junctures in the students' school career. Some of the most important of these services include:

1. Assistance with transition to secondary programs
2. Appraisal
3. Providing information: educational, vocational, psychosexual
4. Career planning
5. Referral to community services
6. Individual counseling
7. Group counseling
8. Consulting with regular classroom teachers about LD students
9. Parent counseling
10. Assistance with entrance to postsecondary schools

HUMANISTIC DIMENSIONS OF COUNSELING

The field of learning disabilities has been preoccupied with delivery of educational services with a primary emphasis on young children. The field is still young, and it is understandable that some areas of related services would be neglected in the midst of the desire to reorient the educational system to remedial approaches and systems of management to ameliorate learning disabilities. Many of our attempts in education have not provided consistently good results and have often been based on hopeful anticipation rather than sound empirical evidence. It is necessary to sharpen our skills and focus on more concentrated, longitudinal research; this should be a fundamental goal. However, it is also necessary that we widen our scope to include the human concerns of learning disabled students and their families. Our search for instructional techniques must not blind us to the tragic effects that a disability may have on the family unit and the individual. Guidance and support in a therapeutic milieu may be more beneficial than a specific remedial approach. This is especially true of adolescents who have confronted failure for years. In fact, the first step might be to use counseling techniques that bring the student to a more complete conceptualization of the nature of his educational/academic problems and an understanding of what he must do to correct or compensate for them. In this case, a specific compensatory or remedial approach may be more effective because the student becomes a partner in the teaching process rather than simply submitting to a program that seems to have no apparent significance. This would indicate a need for less rigidity in the lines that separate professionals in their roles. The resource teacher and the counselor should interact in such a manner that counseling functions are shared. The LD specialist will have more personal, individual contact with students than many teachers in the school because of the limited class size and small group instruction. The counselor and the regular classroom teacher are not likely to be able to interact on a one-to-one basis with the students in a daily routine as effectively as the LD specialist.

An improved guidance program would attend to several features that must be considered in the complex structure of the secondary school. We must search for new and innovative ways to circumvent the problems that seem to be inherent in the system of the secondary school. The limitations of time, money, and other resources must not be used as excuses for maintaining the *status quo.*

AN EXTENDED COUNSELING PROGRAM

The counseling staff may select candidates from persons in the school who would be trained to perform some specific counseling activities for students and parents. Specific criteria should be used in the selection of each individual. Learning disability specialists should obviously be included as well as regular classroom teachers and students. The duties and responsibilities would be different for professional and nonprofessional members of the extended counseling program. For example, student-counselors should be restricted to peer counseling interactions. The selection criteria should be very explicit. Only the most mature, sensitive, and responsible students should be utilized.

Prior to the development of an extended program a plan should be developed and approved by the appropriate administrative authorities. The approved plan would serve two purposes—to secure administrative permission and to give shape and direction to the effort.

Any person who is selected and who agrees to participate in the extended counseling program should be subjected to the same expectations as regularly employed personnel. Services cannot be provided unless participants are punctual, maintain a schedule, and keep appointments. The fact that volunteers are not paid does not excuse them from meeting professional standards and ethics.

The guidance program has the potential of significantly improving the daily adjustment and opportunities of LD students and their families. These objectives could be accomplished by the extension of services from the counselor throughout the teaching staff and student body. The counselor should select and train personnel and students to conduct counseling-related activities that would be closely supervised, monitored, and evaluated. Many programs in psychology, education, social work, and speech therapy have expanded services beyond the limitations imposed by a small staff, restricted time, and finite resources. The counselor, the LD resource room teacher, and selected students could form the core of an extended guidance program. Careful planning, efficient administration and supervision, and systematic evaluation could maintain the workings of an exemplary program.

Key points of structure in the extended counseling program

The following general statements may be used as points of focus that may serve to direct the organization and build the structure of a local counseling program. Each school is unique. Resources are variable, and the abilities of personnel or their willingness to cooperate are certainly not the same in each setting. Nevertheless, any school that genuinely attempts to extend the counseling services for LD students can succeed. The following points are related to that objective.

1. We must not think of guidance as *"telling a student or a parent what to do."* The

counseling process involves sharing of information and feelings that will develop into an awareness of problems, needs, and alternative solutions. Any agent of the counselor should be trained in this ability to share. The counselor or counseling agent might offer suggestions or make recommendations, but parents and students have the right to make final decisions.

2. *Counselors and counseling agents should be aware of their own biases, should state them, and should avoid the temptation to interject them into the counseling process.* Prejudice or rigid attitudes create inflexibility in the counseling process. This inflexibility then becomes part of the problem rather than the solution. Because we are all subject to some bias, individuals in certain situations should avoid some encounters in deference to another who is better equipped to deal with a particular student or problem.

3. *Members of the counseling team should be prepared to deal with frustration and hostility of students and parents that may be directed at the counselor as a representative of the school.* A counselor may want to encourage the expression of negative attitudes as a means of exploring and identifying problems. But the counselor must have the maturity to interact with counselees without becoming

personally embroiled with expressed anger. The ability to separate personal emotions from issues is an absolute prerequisite to effective counseling.

4. *Counselors should know their limitations, should recognize areas in which they may uncover sensitive information that should be dealt with by different professionals, and should be able to make referrals.* Each person in the counseling process, including the counselor, has limitations in the ability to manage certain problems. Each counseling agent should be fully apprised of the areas that are taboo, and referral must be made to agencies or professionals outside the school in such instances. This is especially true for student-counselors who must not attempt to cope with problems they are not prepared to handle, ethically or legally.

5. *Confidentiality is mandatory.* Each client should enter the counseling process with the full expectation that any statements will be fully confidential. Any breach of confidence is a serious matter that has many adverse consequences.

6. *The counselor should accept responsibility for his own actions.* Any action of the counselor should be initiated for a purpose and evaluated in terms of its effect. The counselor must be ready to assume full re-

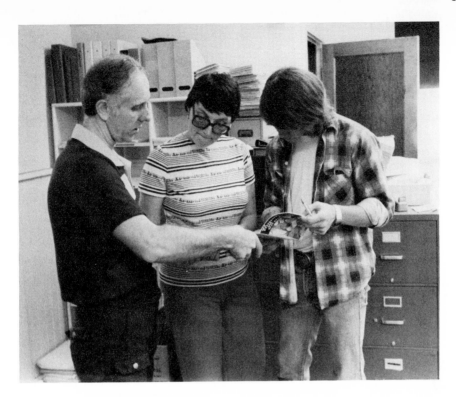

sponsibility for any results that evolve from professional intervention. The counselor *must not* assume responsibility for the client. Parents and students should be guided toward acceptance of responsibility for their own lives, for planning, for identifying problems, and for generating possible solutions. The role of the counselor is supportive, not directive.

Student-counselors and other volunteer or nonprofessional counselor assistants must be carefully instructed about their limitations of responsibility and authority. They must be fully aware of when to ask professional staff members for assistance.

Services of the extended program

The following points do not represent a model for the delivery of counseling services to LD students. Rather, they are intended to serve as a basis for generating discussion and thinking in this most important endeavor.

Student services

The present level of services in counseling should be vastly expanded and altered to provide direct and continuous support to students. LD students require more involved counseling than other students because they experience unique adjustment problems that are superimposed on those that occur as a natural consequence of maturation. To secure this support, current service patterns must be reconceptualized. A form of shared responsibility should supplant the traditional model. This will likely involve the skills of teams of counselors and regular and special educators in the process. Collapsing the traditional lines of authority and responsibility for certain functions in the counseling program would extend services beyond the present limitations without necessarily increasing the staff or the budget. The counselor has sufficient training to serve in the capacity as a leader who can organize, supervise, and monitor activities related to counseling that are conducted by other professionals.

Many functions of teaching and counseling overlap. It is difficult to neatly separate them into discrete categories that can be identified as purely "education" or purely "counseling." Therefore, some of the following suggestions might logically be included in a comprehensive educational program as well as in an exemplary counseling program. They relate to areas of service needs in delivering counseling services to secondary LD students. They might be shared by teachers, counselors, and students.

Service areas for LD students

I. Implications of the diagnosis
   A. Placement in any special program typically involves many proceedings that are directed by rules and regulations (for example, due process) prior to and during evaluation. This is undoubtedly a period of stress for the student and the family. Support services should be provided. The student should know why tests are being given, should be informed of the need for information, and should be provided with samples of tests. Other students who have previously experienced the process of evaluation could be selected for "rap" sessions that might ease the adjustment of the student.
   B. The student should understand why special education programs have been developed, should know about the objectives of such programs, and should be given some general information about the development and direction of the field.
   C. Educational jargon used in reference to tests should be explained. Wherever possible, such jargon should be avoided.

II. Support in academic functioning
   A. The pervasive objective in counseling is to guide the student to a level of development in which responsibility for academic adjustment is internalized. Whether or not the counselors (or agents) are operating under a specific theory, it is clear that many students make great strides in achievement when they assume responsibility for self-direction and growth.
   B. Students must understand how special education activities relate to regular classroom activities. The relationship should be obvious and directly related to daily activities of the regular curriculum.
   C. The counselor (or agents) can offer a valuable service by participating in monitoring procedures to ascertain student progress, by providing feedback for students, and by permitting necessary intervention at the earliest possible moment.
   D. The counseling program can also be of service in support of academic functioning by organizing regular periods of discussion or group sessions to reaffirm academic goals, to relate academic goals to future life goals, and to reinforce success-striving behavior and study habits.

III. Support in social development
   A. Specific problems of social development, such as crime and drug abuse, would be a central concern of the curriculum for all students. However, because of the growing belief that LD students are more likely to adopt deviant behaviors, specific attention to these issues might be justified in the counseling program.
   B. Achieving social maturity may be a difficult process for any adolescent. The complications of a learning disability may introduce other obstacles to social maturity. A variety of techniques may be used to emphasize the importance of social maturity, adeptness in social skills, and the ability to interact with young adults and older adults, both men and women. Social skills may be useful in improving the opportunities of students who have deficits that may be offset by self-confidence and the ability to interact with others.
   C. Students need to know how to cope with the realities of daily living. Much of the social growth of adolescents is left to chance and the natural settling of interactions between members of the peer group in the "pecking order." The counseling program can elevate the status of a student by teaching coping skills or, if you will, *how to function as an adolescent*. Transactional analysis groups have been used in some schools for this purpose. The LD specialist may be more aware of daily problems that affect each student and is certainly aware of how conflict, dis-

couragement, and depression impede academic growth. Students may be taught about the subtleties of relating to others, how to date, how to conduct friendships, and how to deal with conflicts that occur with parents, teachers, and friends.

D. Students should also be prepared to know what it means to be an adult. Especially during the senior year it seems to be of critical importance to discuss such important issues as employment, marriage, child rearing, and so forth from a very practical point of view. We do not directly teach people how to be partners in a marriage or how to be parents. Although these may be concerns of the curriculum for all students in some less specific way, it is essential to stress these points in the social education of LD students.

Parent services

Perhaps, the weakest link in the total service program of the typical school is in planned, scheduled contact with parents. There are special problems connected with counseling of parents and most notably with parents of adolescents. Part of the process of growing up involves breaking the ties that bind the individual to the family. A child cannot become an adult without independence and self-reliance. An adolescent may believe that the process of emancipation from the family is too long and unendurable. Parents may feel that certain restrictions must be imposed on the behavior, alliances, and freedoms of adolescents for "their own good" until such time that they demonstrate maturity and good judgment.

It is only natural that the interests of the parents and those of the adolescent will collide. At least in our culture, the conflict and turmoil that exists between parents and adolescents is a natural consequence of development and change. In fact, they are, for the most part, healthy signs of normal growth. However, for parents and adolescents who do not understand this phenomenon such conflict can cause a great deal of unhappiness and, in extreme cases, may result in serious abnormal adjustment reactions.

The teacher, or any other school authority, who enters into the same arena with parents and teenagers must proceed with caution. Any dealings with parents may be viewed with suspicion by students. Any teacher who "takes the side" of parents may be thought of as a traitor who has entered the enemy camp. Needless to say, any professional encounters with parents and students should be carefully planned and handled tactfully to avoid any appearance of partiality.

Unfortunately, some parents tend to regard the secondary school with contempt while others completely disregard it. Secondary school personnel often violate a behavioral principle by neglecting to give parents and students positive feedback. The school is quick to complain about a problem but tends to be "too busy" to make the effort to transmit complimentary information to parents when things are running smoothly.

Another factor influencing the relationship of parents with schools is associated with the tendency for the interests of parents in school activities to wane over time. Parents who pin their hopes and dreams on young children may be found in great numbers in attendance at elementary school P.T.A. meetings. Parents of students in the intermediate grades are scarce at such school functions. Most secondary schools do not have active P.T.A. groups. Perhaps the years of participation in such activities as scouting, church socials, organized athletic events, and the many school-related events take their toll on parental interest. With parents of handicapped students, it is not unusual to find a certain acceptance or resolution (if not resignation) that reduces their enthusiasm.

Research concerning parents of severely handicapped children generally indicates that there is a certain process of adjustment for these parents. Various, rather vague stages have been identified and are characterized by denial, rejection, blame, guilt, and finally acceptance or some similar order of events (Wolfensberger, 1967). This subject has not been thoroughly investigated with parents of learning disabled children. Unlike parents of severely handicapped children who recognize obvious signs of a handicap early in the child's life, parents of learning disabled children are not likely to have been informed of a "diagnosis" until an apparently normal child has experienced a few years of failure in school. Therefore, the reactions of the parents may be quite different. It is also possible that the reactions and attitudes of parents who have adolescents with long histories of academic difficulty will be different from those of parents with younger children who have the same school-related problems. There will be many individual differences, but it may be generalized that the interest and cooperation of parents of LD adolescents may be much more difficult to capture and maintain.

Legally, the school has no inherent right to suggest techniques of child rearing to parents. The teacher is responsible for teaching the child, and the parents are responsible for raising the child. However, these domains obviously overlap and the school that can successfully influence the home may benefit the adjustment of the student as well as enhance the learning environment of the school.

Service areas for parents

I. Information
   A. Although many different individuals will be involved in activities such as assessment, the need of parents for information can be facilitated by the use of one or two designated contact persons in the school who can function as coordinators. The scheduling of parent conferences and other contacts for each family should be the assigned responsibility of one individual who can maintain appropriate records and document minimum-to-maximum involvement. At least one conference should be held each semester. A professional who is responsible for monitoring parent contacts can make certain that information is updated and can encourage the involvement of even the most reluctant parents. At the very least, telephone calls can be made with some frequency. Parents may show more interest if the school is interested.
   B. Information may be disseminated to parents by telephone calls, home vis-

its, school conferences, and the mail. Specific policies of the school should be known to the parents.
   C. Areas of information might include the following
      1. Due process procedures
      2. Student discipline and codes of conduct
      3. Placement in special education
      4. Nature and objectives of courses
      5. Objectives of special education
      6. News of interest—new laws, medical information, and so forth
   D. An essential ingredient of providing information to parents relates to an awareness of timing. Parents are justifiably disturbed when they are informed, after the fact, that a student has been engaging in misconduct for a long time or that a student has failed a course. Even if parents do not cooperate in effecting changes, they should be notified of any problem at the earliest possible moment. Positive information should also be transmitted.

II. Parenting
   A. As noted, the school has no legal responsibility to assist parents with child rearing practices. Certainly, no parents should be "forced" by the school to submit to any form of instruction or therapy. If it is clear that a family is in need of intervention, the *counselor* may intercede to encourage the family to seek assistance and submit to therapy. Various approaches have been described by Abrams and Kaslow (1977).
   B. At any point in the process of special education, it would be desirable to interest parents in such active groups as the *Association for Children with Learning Disabilities.* The school can provide more direct assistance by inviting parents to visit the school individually or in group sessions to participate in information-training programs concerned with learning disabilities as well as parenting practices.
   C. For parents who have extreme difficulties in coping with normal adolescent development or with such deviances as drug abuse and delinquency, special school programs might be offered that

would utilize local school personnel and professionals from the community and from university staffs in a series of training sessions to improve relationships between adolescents and their parents.

III. Schooling and parent involvement

A. The school should train each teacher in the methods of conducting parent conferences. This should include the limitations of teachers in providing information and advice.

B. A policy about the involvement of parents in the instruction of children at home should be made. It takes at least 4 years to train teachers to teach. Parents should not assume instructional responsibility, especially for learning disabled students, without proper guidance, support, and evaluation by teachers. A specific course of home study may be developed that could assist in the development of competency on the part of parents.

C. Frequent conferences should be held.

D. In addition to legally prescribed information that parents have a right to by law, the parents should be involved in continuous reorientation to facts about the child's present functioning and future goals. Parents should not expect too much too fast and should gradually develop realistic goals for the child's ultimate development in accordance with individual abilities and disabilities.

SUMMARY

In this chapter we have briefly described the history of counseling, discussed its objectives, and described the major theoretical approaches. We have also proposed an extended counseling program that would be directed at provision of improved services for learning disabled students and their parents. Such a program would be of value for any target group of students, however, the needs of LD students exceed those of their peers because of the special problems associated with their learning disabilities. Many services are "built into" the curriculum, but LD students often require additional counseling in learning to cope with the realities of daily living. The support of professionals and peers in a dedicated effort to facilitate daily adjustment in encounters with parents, teachers, and peers may prove to be of real assistance in meeting academic objectives. The adolescent who is frustrated, depressed, or angry, and who has no outlet for emotions or sources of support will not be an agreeable companion nor a motivated student. Further investigation is needed to more accurately determine the relative effectiveness of a variety of counseling approaches, but in the meantime we should apply what has been proved to be effective. When more precise information is available, it should be applied immediately.

DISCUSSION QUESTIONS

1. After reading the review of the historical development of counseling, how much different is modern counseling from its original purpose?
2. List the various areas or types of problems experienced by an LD student that might require the intervention of a counselor.
3. What would be the responsibility or appropriate action of a resource room specialist who is privy to information about an LD student that indicates violation of school regulations?
4. What is meant by the term *student advocacy*?
5. Discuss the issue implied by the statement, "A teacher should keep a student's confidence at all costs."

REFERENCES AND READINGS

Abrams, J. C., and Kaslow, F. Family systems and the learning disabled child: Intervention and treatment. *Journal of Learning Disabilities*, 1977, 10, 86-94.

American School Counselor Association. *Policy for secondary school counselors*, Washington, D.C.: American Personnel and Guidance Association, 1964.

Hanson, J. C., Stevic, R. R., and Warner, R. W., Jr. *Counseling: Theory and process* (2nd ed.). Boston: Allyn & Bacon, Inc., 1977.

Shertzer, B., and Stone, S. C. *Fundamentals of guidance* (3rd ed.). Boston: Houghton Mifflin, Co., 1976.

Wolfensberger, W. Counseling the parents of the retarded. In A. A. Baumeister (Ed.), *Mental retardation*. Chicago: Aldine Publishing Co., 1967.

Existing programs for learning disabled youth

One of the more effective ways of considering any type of educational programming is to take a close look at some programs that are in actual operation. If these can be selected to reflect a variety of approaches and if they are representative of some of the better programs available for such consideration, they will do much to expand and clarify theoretical or hypothetical discussions and considerations.

Therefore, information regarding ongoing programs for learning disabled youth is provided in Chapters 10, 11, and 12. Chapter 10 presents an overview of private school programs for the learning disabled. These were first in chronological development and continue despite federal laws that would seem to dictate that these students should be served in the public school. Chapter 11 reviews a number of model programs for learning disabled adolescents that are supported primarily through federal funds. These programs are designed for possible replication, and most are deliberately experimental in nature. They may, therefore, have several different components, with no accurate way to tell at this point which components are most generally effective and/or which are best for specific types of learning problems. Nevertheless, they indicate the variety of approaches presently under active consideration.

Chapter 12 might be best described as a minichapter. It is concerned with postsecondary programs for the learning disabled, a topic of real significance. When we launched initial efforts to prepare this book, we believed we would find sufficient information about postsecondary programs to justify a full-length chapter on this topic. References in journal articles and in general texts on learning disabilities seemed to indicate the existence of a variety of provisions for the learning disabled at the postsecondary level. When we followed through the various "leads" regarding such programs, we were disappointed to find that not very much of an organized nature was taking place. Because we feel that the topic (postsecondary programs) is important, we elected to report to the reader just what is really available. We sincerely hope that the situation will improve in the very near future.

CHAPTER 10

Private schools and programs for learning disabled adolescents in the secondary school

INTRODUCTION

While public schools were responding to the needs of elementary level learning disabled children, they tended to overlook programs at the secondary level. This resulted because of several factors, including: (1) the concept of perceptual disorders, especially as related to visual perception, is not as applicable to adolescents as to younger children (many adolescents who *did* have visual perceptual problems at an earlier age have, for the most part, adjusted to them), (2) adolescents often develop ways to accommodate for, or at least "cover up" their learning difficulties, and (3) some learning disabled adolescents develop behavior difficulties that cause so much attention that this becomes the focus of school authorities, thus they are thought of as "students with behavior disorders," not "learning disabled." In addition, many learning disabled students simply drop out of school, a convenient path (for secondary schools) not open at the elementary level. Another factor that helped make it possible for the public schools to procrastinate was the establishment of private schools for learning disabled secondary school students. Thus, in many cases, private schools had a head start on the public schools in programming for learning disabled adolescents. For this reason, it is highly advantageous to review a number of existing private secondary schools that serve the learning disabled.

GENERALIZATIONS ABOUT PRIVATE SCHOOL PROGRAMS FOR THE HANDICAPPED AND LEARNING DISABLED

A number of generalizations may be made about private schools and programs for handicapped children (children with any of a variety of handicapping conditions). Additionally, more specific statements may be made about private schools and programs for the learning disabled. As with all generalizations, there are schools and programs to which these may not apply, except perhaps to indicate that they do not "fit" the general mold. However, these generalizations are valuable in providing a perspective within which to consider the specific program descriptions later in the chapter.

1. Private schools for the handicapped are not always highly regarded by professionals in the field of education and particularly by some public school special educators. Reasons for these feelings are varied, but often include one or more of the following.

(a). Historically, private schools have served children with more severe problems and public school officials have at times experienced some pressure generated by the fact that such children *should* be helped in the public school with the application of more time, effort, and money. Yet they (the public schools) had, in effect, said that they could not help. With the passage of P. L. 94-142 (p. 238) and with various state laws mandating public school assistance to *all* handicapped children and youth, the efforts of such schools have underscored the possibility of concrete results.

(b). Because of their private status, private

schools can, and some do, use policies and procedures that the public schools cannot use, particularly in management of behavioral problems. This leaves public school special educators in a position in which they are condemned if they do not provide services but cannot use procedures available to private schools.

(c). Private schools obviously must charge tuition and, in the case of boarding schools, must charge for room, board, medical assistance, and so forth. Public educators have sometimes felt that they were charging too much, were in business primarily to make a profit, and were, in general, taking advantage of parents who were already heavily burdened by their handicapped child. (See a further discussion of this charge of profit motivation on the part of private facilities on p. 178.)

(d). Regarding this belief, private facilities, which must have at least a minimum student load to exist, are often charged with accepting students who obviously do not "fit" the basic orientation and purposes of the school just to keep the funds coming in and the school in operation. In some cases, concern about this perceived problem is heightened because the local district is under pressure to pay for much of this high-cost education and treatment because of a tuition payment policy that is a part of local and state reimbursement structure.

2. Private schools for the handicapped are often organized around the personal philosophy of a leadership individual (the director or some noted or not-so-noted authority in the field). They may, therefore, adhere rather rigidly to a specific methodological philosophy. (This is viewed by some as a definite strength and by others as a serious weakness.)

3. Many private schools for the handicapped, particularly smaller schools, have been started by parents of handicapped chil-

dren who have children in the school and who are very active members of the board of directors. In some cases, it is very difficult for such a board member to remain totally objective when making policy decisions.

4. The title *school for the handicapped* tends to be used very loosely. An entity organized to work with handicapped children may be called a *school* and take any one of several functional variations. It may be little more than a diagnostic facility or it may serve a diagnostic function plus provision of limited tutorial type assistance. It may be a day school with little real diagnostic capability or may be a day school with complete diagnostic facilities and various types of specialized medical supervision. It may be a boarding school with complete educational facilities or it may be a boarding facility that is primarily a "holding facility" for very severely handicapped children. It may include only young children, may enroll children and youths through 20 or 21 years of age, or may include adults of all ages. A school may have a title that seems to indicate (for example) that it is only for learning disabled children, when in fact it includes many types of handicapping conditions. (These observations are not made in a spirit of negative criticism but rather are provided as needed information. In our experience we have found so many teachers and parents of handicapped children who were unaware of this nonspecific use of the word school we felt it necessary to include it as part of the general information about private schools for the handicapped.)

5. There has been a tendency for a significant number of small private programs (schools) to be organized, apparently flourish for a few years, and then be suddenly discontinued. This can be a serious problem if parents or public officials assume that a given private program will take care of certain specialized needs and thus relieve the public sector from providing such services. (This also seems to cast some doubt on the unusual profit making ability of such programs, for few enterprises in our nation that are making unusual profits are discontinued in such a manner.)

6. Private schools are more often organized in areas of the nation where there are large population concentrations and in states where there are a greater than average number of private schools for nonhandicapped children and youths. In other words, where it is common to think of private college preparatory schools or private boys' schools or girls' schools (often organized around some specific theme in addition to general educational goals), it is also common to find private schools for the handicapped. When these schools are located in an area where there are unusually good outdoor recreation possibilities, this may become part of the theme of the school. Swimming, horseback riding, and outdoorsmanship all become important elements in this type of school.

The preceding generalizations are among the major ones that may apply to a variety of private schools for the handicapped. In addition, there are certain more specific statements that may be made about programs organized primarily to serve the learning disabled. Those that may be of value in developing a meaningful perspective include the following.

1. Private programs for the learning disabled are relatively newer on the private school scene than private school programs for other handicapping conditions.

2. Some private school programs for the learning disabled are part of a more general program that also serves other handicapping conditions. When they are a part of such "combined" programming, they are most likely to be combined with programs for children with behavior disorders.

3. There appear to be more private programs for the learning disabled that are part-time, tutorial-remedial type programs than there are for other handicapping conditions. This relates to a considerable extent to the fact that, with other handicapping conditions, parents do not tend to utilize private facilities unless the condition is relatively severe. With the learning disabled, parents seem to turn to private facilities or programs in the case of less severe disabilities. This may *not* continue to be the case as public

schools develop more effective programs for the learning disabled.

4. Based on listings of private facilities in operation at this time, it appears that a majority of private programs and facilities for the learning disabled are primarily for elementary age children. This tendency is even more pronounced when we consider the part-time, tutorial-remedial type programs. (Note that this emphasis on elementary age children closely parallels the situation that exists within the public schools.)

5. Although many private programs for the learning disabled are programs in which other handicapping conditions are also served, most programs specifically exclude children with certain handicaps. This will be illustrated to some extent later in the chapter by the descriptions of private programs that serve learning disabled pupils in secondary schools. However, since the descriptions relate only to programs that serve secondary level pupils, it may be of interest to consider the range of limitations that are in effect in other programs. The following restrictions and limitations are representative of those which may be found in the guidelines of various schools.

Types of problems not accepted by various private schools*

Below average intelligence, psychotics, delinquents, or severely physically disabled

Physically handicapped and retarded children

Mentally retarded and children having severe emotional problems

Severe behavior problems; problems basically emotional or psychiatric in nature rather than a psychological overlay caused by a learning disability

Severely mentally retarded, blind, deaf, primary emotionally disturbed

Blind, deaf, nonambulatory, drug addicted

Drug abusers, frankly psychotic

Although difficult to summarize precisely, the limitations indicated by schools for the

---

*From the *National Association of Private Schools for Exceptional Children: 1975 Directory*, Lake Wales, Fla., 1975. This is a composite sample of restrictions from many schools.

learning disabled that are listed in the 1975 Directory of the *National Association of Private Schools for Exceptional Children* tend to exclude the mentally retarded (except in a few cases for the very mildly retarded), the severely emotionally disturbed, the nonambulatory, and drug users. A few, however not many, mention the blind and the deaf. In *practice* it appears that most do not attempt to serve the blind or the deaf, but do not specifically mention this fact in their guidelines because they assume that parents of blind or deaf children would not tend to approach their schools. All reputable private schools require considerable basic information about children who are potential enrollees, and, because they are private, they are free to accept only those they believe they may serve effectively.

One factor related to private schools for handicapped children that was mentioned in the enumeration of generalizations in the preceding section deserves further examination before proceeding with the description of specific private schools. This is the fact that private school programs "are often viewed with suspicion by legislators and public school personnel who perceive them as being more interested in profit than in children's welfare" (Marver, p. 659, 1976). Along with a variety of other conclusions, Marver concluded that for the most part, profit levels of those private schools that are organized for profit are low and the negative allegations regarding the motives and behaviors of nonpublic school educators are largely unfounded. He suggests that private schools for the handicapped have been established largely as alternatives to other nonpublic or public schools, and in many cases simply because *no* programs were in existence that could, or would, serve the children in question. His study and the conclusions generated did *not* address the question of quality or effectiveness of such private schools, but did provide data that seem to indicate that most private schools operate on a *very* slim profit margin. Our own experience with this question is that many private programs (many are nonprofit), like many small private, liberal arts colleges, are operating barely above the level of bankruptcy. Also, personal experience with a number of private programs for the learning disabled indicates that most were established to serve a definite need with no "high profit" motive involved. This, like Marver's study, does not address the question of program quality, and it must be recognized that "rip-off artists" operate within the professions of medicine, law, education, and undoubtedly many others.

All school programs, public or private, have strengths and shortcomings. Having spent many years in the public schools, we can recall how we were certain that *we*, in our school, had a better reading readiness program, junior high social studies program, or some other specific program than a number of surrounding schools. And we could readily explain exactly why. Interestingly enough, most of those other schools felt the same way about their programs. The same situation exists with private schools and for some of the same reasons. It is maintained by some public school educators that the private schools overpromote their programs and make claims that simply cannot be substantiated. The motivation is believed to be profit—something that public schools do not have to worry about. We believe that such overpromotion does exist in some cases, but for consideration in this chapter we tried to select private schools with established reputations and found that most had waiting lists that seemed to indicate that they were not continually hurting for lack of students. Most of these schools seem to do what the public schools do, that is, promote or publicize the accomplishments of their more successful students. This is part of a game that all educators have tended to play since education became an organized entity.

The schools outlined here represent various parts of the country, with more from areas where more private schools exist. This determination has not been accomplished on a strict ratio basis, but as noted earlier, more private schools for the handicapped exist in areas where there are greater population concentrations and where there are more private schools for nonhandicapped children. The information provided in these discussions was derived from published brochures, from personal communication with the directors, headmasters, or educational directors of these schools, and, in some cases, from personal visits to the school. The personal communications were in response to specific questions about the school, and school officials understood our motivation and interest. In a number of these communications, in addition to information requested, directors recommended that those interested in private school programs should not believe all the published claims made by the private schools, but rather should personally visit the facility. As one director said, "Many programs look very complete and excellent in writing but fall short when under close scrutiny. Additionally, many programs cannot be shown in their best light on paper. . . ."

When information was requested from these schools, we asked for tuition costs and room and board costs where applicable, but indicated that we did *not* plan to enumerate such costs on a school-by-school basis. Instead, Fig. 6 (p. 205) indicates cost ranges by type of service or program provided. This approach has been taken to avoid the appearance of advertising for these schools and to prevent readers from attempting to "add up" the strengths of various schools as a basis for some sort of cost versus value-received comparison. Such comparisons are not valid when made on the basis of the type of information presented here. To make such comparisons we would have to analyze each separate cost factor for each school, which we believe would detract from the value of the educational description. In addition, it would not be in keeping with the purposes of our presentation in this text.

With the above information (how descriptions were obtained, the matter of costs, and so forth) in mind, we will proceed to describe seven schools that serve students at the secondary school level. These are schools that were in operation at the time of publication of this book, and most appear to be programs that are here to stay. They may be considered representative programs; that is, representative of a much larger number of schools in operation throughout the United States and Canada. Following these descriptions is a hypothetical, *minimal* program that is intended to typify a number of *other* programs that were established to serve the learning disabled during the period when public schools appeared to be either unwilling or unable to provide any type of concrete assistance. We believe that programs represented by this hypothetical example may be on their way to extinction as public schools are in the process of expanding and improving secondary programming.

EIGHT SCHOOLS—A VARIETY OF APPROACHES

The eight school programs described in this chapter represent the major variations that may be found in private educational programming for the learning disabled adolescent in the United States today. Seven of these programs are actual programs, described on the basis of information received from school officials; the other one is a composite, hypothetical program. These programs were selected because they represent most of the variables that may be found in such schools as they actually exist. Some are large schools, while others are small and operate on the basis of an absolute maximum enrollment. Some tend to be more "exclusive" in student clientele, although none are in the category of the exclusive private preparatory schools that cater only to children of the very wealthy. Some are located in areas of unusual or unique beauty (mountains, ranch setting, and the like); others are located in the midst of urban areas. Some are day schools, some are boarding facilities, and several provide for both day and boarding students. One school is actually a "chain" of schools, located in four different states, but most are single campus facilities. Several of the schools were started for the learning disabled, after learning disabilities became a recognized subcategory of special education. Others were started for children who were having "difficulty in school" (and at the beginning included a wide variety of primary

handicapping conditions) but have evolved in the direction of serving children identified as learning disabled. Of the seven actual schools, all but one totally or primarily focus on students with learning disabilities. One school serves the emotionally disturbed and the learning disabled (with the former as the primary focus) but was included in this chapter because of a unique contracting feature that deserves special attention and consideration. These schools, in composite, provide a picture of private programs for the adolescent learning disabled student.

Public schools tended to be inordinately slow in developing meaningful programs for the learning disabled at the secondary school level, and the development of these, and other similar schools, are in part a result of that inertia. As many of the directors of these schools told us, they are simply doing what the public schools have not seen fit to do. Because many of these schools have been "in the business" of teaching the learning disabled adolescent for much longer than many public schools, their programs should offer guidance for public school programming.

PLEASE NOTE: The seven actual school programs described in this chapter are all of value; no attempt has been made to evaluate which is best or most effective. All are members of the NAPSEC (The National Association of Private Schools for Exceptional Children). Some are discussed in more detail, but this does not indicate relative value. In general, boarding schools require more description because of their 24-hour, 7-day-per-week program. Also, some of the first programs are described more extensively. Because there are many similarities between various programs, similar programs are not described in such great detail. Finally, although these descriptions were developed on the basis of information received directly from the schools, we assume full responsibility for any inaccuracies that may exist.

Pine Ridge School, Williston, Vermont
Introduction

Pine Ridge School was founded in 1968 specifically for the purpose of serving learning disabled adolescents. It is primarily a residential school, and current plans are to maintain this focus; however, some programming is provided for local students on a day-school basis. The vast majority of students come from other parts of the United States with some coming from Canada.* The school population is predominantly male; at this writing there is an approximate three to one ratio; however, this may be caused in part by the nature of the recreation program at Pine Ridge, not necessarily the actual ratio of learning disabled adolescents. (We should note that because private schools are not responsible for serving all learning disabled students within a specific geographic area, as is the case of the public schools, we cannot necessarily infer percentage or ratio data for the population as a whole on the basis of private school enrollment data.)

Age range at Pine Ridge may vary slightly from year to year, but includes those ages generally associated with junior high and senior high programs in the public schools. At the time of our last contact with the education director, the actual age range of students then enrolled was from 13 to 19 years of age. Since the objective for students at Pine Ridge is successful graduation from high school—and many stay at Pine Ridge until completion of the high school program—the upper age range is generally considered to be 20. Students are admitted when there appears to be considerable likelihood that they can attain maximum benefit from the program, which is usually no younger than 12 years of age. Admittance to Pine Ridge is based more on the results of evaluations completed after a potential student applies for admission than on any single rigid criterion. This topic is more

*One Canadian student who attended Pine Ridge School at age 17, after years of difficulties in Ontario, made such unusual progress in reading and other academic areas in just 1 year, that his case became the center of attention in a highly publicized controversy regarding the responsibility of the provincial government in the education of children with learning disabilities. A Supreme Court ruling recently established the responsibility of the public schools in education of the learning disabled, which now may leave the schools with the alternative of providing an appropriate education within the province, or paying for enrollment in private school programs. This ruling is parallel to decisions in the United States.

fully explored in the following discussion of admissions procedures and requirements.

Admissions procedures and requirements

The admissions review committee at Pine Ridge School carefully screens each applicant to determine whether or not he or she meets the school's requirements for admission. It is of particular concern that every student benefit from the Pine Ridge program to the greatest extent possible. Experience has indicated that since the program is not designed to meet the special needs of truly retarded or severely acting-out youngsters, they do not achieve sufficiently. Inappropriately placed students often deter from the educational growth and the building of strong, positive self-image in the rest of the student body.

The admissions procedure, then, is of considerable importance to the school, to the parents, and to the agencies placing students at Pine Ridge.

Basis of acceptance. Suitability for admission is based on an evaluation of all previous educational and psychological testing (also neurological and psychiatric reports if available), the on-campus interview, and the Pine Ridge assessment. No student is ever refused admission on the basis of race, creed, sex, or national origin. Before a decision can be made, all available data (reports, test results, and so forth) must be received by the school, each candidate must visit the campus for an interview, and the Pine Ridge School assessment must be completed.

Procedure. The following steps must be followed by all applicants.

Information seeking. Parents or agencies may either write or phone for specific information. The Admissions Director is usually available during the regular business hours (9:00 A.M. to 4:00 P.M., Monday through Friday) to discuss any matters pertaining to the school. The school brochure along with information and release forms will be mailed immediately upon the receipt of an inquiry. Parents or agency representatives are welcome to visit the campus prior to any formal interview involving a prospective candidate.

Test data. If, upon receipt of information,

the parents or agency wishes to pursue the matter further, the parents (agency) should arrange to have all previous test data forwarded to Pine Ridge School. Of particular importance are the results of a recent (within 1 year) Wechsler Intelligence Scale, *including the subtest scores*. Release forms are included with the brochure and should be sent by the parents to the appropriate institutions or persons from whom the data may be obtained.

Interview. All applicants must come to the school for an admissions interview. During the 5- to 6-hour session, the candidate will normally meet with the Headmaster, the Educational Director, the Assistant Headmaster (who is head resident counselor), and the Guidance Counselor. The parents (agency representative) also meet with the Headmaster and the Educational Director. At this time a student (or students) will take the candidate and parents on a tour of the campus. This gives visitors an opportunity to discuss the school with the student guide and other available students.

On-campus assessment. An on-campus educational assessment is required at the time of the interview. Upon completion of this assessment, an oral interpretation of the results is given to the parents (agency). If specifically requested, a written evaluation outlining findings and specifying the plan of remediation will be made available at a later data. This evaluation is particularly useful to parents seeking financial assistance from public agencies or school districts.

Decision. Upon completion of the interview and assessment (and if the test data described above have been received by the school), the parents (or agency representative) are advised as to the candidate's suitability for Pine Ridge School. If both the school and the parents (agency) feel that enrollment at Pine Ridge School is advisable, the complete application should then be submitted.

Reservation of space. Parents wishing to reserve space for the candidate must submit a required deposit as soon as possible. No reservation is considered to be firm until the deposit has been received. The deposit is applied to the tuition charge.

Fees. The following fees are related to the admission procedure. There is no fee for an informal visit during which no interview and assessment takes place. There is a fee for the assessment made at the time of the interview. If the student attends Pine Ridge School, the amount of this fee is applied to tuition. If the school does not accept a candidate, the fee is returned. There is a small additional fee for a written assessment and educational plan if one is requested by the parents (agency).

Staff and student population

An eight-member administrative staff includes the Headmaster, Executive Director, Educational Director, Director of Summer Program, Tutorial Supervisor, Assistant Headmaster, Director of Public Relations, and Guidance Counselor. A 25-member instructional staff includes classroom teachers and remedial language tutors. There is a ten-member residential counseling staff. A ten-member physical education and activities staff includes a full-time Director of Activities. An 11-member support staff includes the kitchen, office, maintenance, and housekeeping personnel. In addition, Pine Ridge School has a Medical Director and an Optometric Consultant.

The primary student population includes 72 residential students, 54 boys and 18 girls, ages 13 to 19. A limited number of local students are at times served on a day-school basis if they share the general learning characteristics of the total residential school enrollment and if there is available time and space. A description of general learning characteristics of Pine Ridge School students follows.

Learning characteristics of Pine Ridge School students

Measures of intelligence place students at Pine Ridge in the low average to superior range, with the majority falling in the average to high average range. For purposes of description, this population demonstrates three distinct patterns of learning behaviors and learning disabilities.

Students in the first group demonstrate receptive deficits at the perceptual, lexical, and syntactic levels. Perceptually, they demonstrate poor visual as well as auditory sequencing and memory deficits and have generally short attention spans and low tolerance for frustration. They lack adequate word recognition, word attack, and spelling skills but are able to comprehend what they are able to decode and to use context clues to achieve meaning when reading. They generally achieve at a slightly higher grade level in mathematics than in reading and spelling.

The students in the second group demonstrate integrative deficits that are largely associative and conceptual in nature. They demonstrate a cluster of perceptual and sensory-motor deficits that include poor body concept and laterality, confused directionality, poor visual spatial perception, poor visual discrimination, and poor visual or auditory sequential memory. They characteristically have difficulty in making proper judgments, comparisons, and generalizations. Particular difficulty is noted when dealing with the concepts of size, distance, direction, weight, or volume, and with temporal and numerical concepts. They also demonstrate difficulty projecting into the future and show marked social disperceptions. In skill areas, they achieve high scores in tests of oral reading and word recognition, but low scores in reading comprehension and mathematics.

The third clearly defined group consists of students who demonstrate deficits in written or oral expression. They show perceptual deficits in visual and/or auditory sequencing and memory, visual-motor expression, or oral-motor expression. They lack the organizational skills that are basic to effective written composition and can often verbalize what they intend to write although they are unable to write it. The students in this group achieve high test scores in reading comprehension and mathematics, but low scores in oral reading and spelling.

Although variations do exist and some students may exhibit learning characteristics that are found in more than one of the three general patterns described above, all are students who are capable of learning (as indicated by Wechsler test scores and other informal measures) and whose primary educational difficulties may be most accurately described as learning disabilities.

The Pine Ridge School educational program

Although "education" is viewed in its broadest sense by the staff at Pine Ridge and the total program at Pine Ridge is an integrated program, for purposes of this description, the program will be divided into: (1) the initial learning assessment, (2) the academic-tutorial program, (3) the guidance and counseling program, (4) the recreation program, and (5) the residential program. The initial learning assessment must obviously precede the other four components, but after the program is planned, the other components become the totality that is the Pine Ridge School program. Regular assessment of learning needs is relatively simple because of the amount of one-to-one contact between staff and students.

The initial learning assessment. Goals of this component include:

1. To identify the student's preferred modality for learning
2. To identify weak or deficient processing abilities
3. To determine the student's functional level of language and mathematical skills
4. To identify the student's educational needs and help plan a habilitative program

Several instruments are used in the assessment. Prior to admission, the student is requested to submit to a WISC or WAIS, a thorough vision examination, and a thorough audiometric examination. In cases where the vision examination is incomplete or where poor convergence may be indicated, a local specialist provides a thorough visual screening, prescribing glasses when necessary and recommending visual training for students demonstrating poor convergence. These recommendations are implemented by the school nurse.

At the admissions screening, the following are administered.

1. The Peabody Picture Vocabulary Test as a measure of receptive vocabulary
2. The Wepman Test of Auditory Discrimination
3. The Detroit Tests of Learning Aptitude, Test 12, Memory for Designs, as an example of visual-motor coordination and perception of spatial relationships and as a measure of visual-motor memory
4. The Woodcock Reading Mastery Tests, which yield a functional reading level and skill levels in letter identification, word recognition, word attack, passage comprehension, and word meanings through the completion of analogies
5. A standardized spelling test, analyzed for dysphonetic or dyseidetic spelling
6. An informal exercise requesting the student to record in writing the events of that day, which provides an example of handwriting, syntactic ability, and composition skills and information about temporal orientation and ability to recount events in sequence
7. The KeyMath Diagnostic Arithmetic Test

Upon admission the following are administered:

1. Gates-McKillop Reading Diagnostic Tests
2. Detroit Tests of Learning Aptitude, Test 18, Oral Directions
3. Illinois Test of Psycholinguistic Abilities, Grammatic Closure Subtest

The academic-tutorial program. Pine Ridge School offers an individualized, skill-oriented academic program during six class periods per day (5 days per week). Included are one period of each of the following: one-to-one tutoring, a skills laboratory that augments the tutorial work, mathematics (from basic perceptual math through trigonometry and precalculus), English literature including training in basic communication skills, social studies, and a workshop to develop perceptual and cognitive abilities. The curriculum is designed to satisfy the student's individual needs for training in perceptual-motor, fundamental language, cognitive, and psychosocial skills.

Each Pine Ridge student meets daily with a tutor trained in remedial language techniques and diagnostic-prescriptive teaching to work to improve basic language skills. Each tutorial program is completely individualized with goals and instructional approaches prescribed on the basis of strengths and weaknesses identified on standard and informal educational and perceptual tests. Progress in the prescribed skill areas is monitored weekly by a tutorial supervisor, who works with the tutor to effect any modification in emphasis or approach necessary for consistent progress.

For most students, tutorial work is extended by the daily skills lab, in which the student works independently to build those language skills identified in the prescription. The tutor works with the student to determine the learning activities to be undertaken in this time, monitors performance, and notes adjustments in the program based on that performance. The student is responsible for maintaining a record of his training activities and for evaluating his progress in weekly and quarterly reports.

The objectives of the total program are conceptualized as behavior or abilities to be developed in and with each student. These abilities are classified into 18 categories under four major headings as follows:

A. Perceptual-motor abilities
   1. Sensory-motor abilities
   2. Visual perceptual abilities
   3. Auditory perceptual abilities
B. Fundamental language abilities
   4. Listening abilities
   5. Reading abilities
   6. Integrative abilities
   7. Speaking abilities
   8. Writing abilities
   9. Quantitative abilities
C. Cognitive abilities
   10. Critical thinking abilities
   11. Communication abilities

12. Information-processing abilities
13. Knowledge and meaning abilities
14. Problem-solving abilities
D. Psychosocial abilities
15. Societal abilities
16. Group action abilities
17. Individual action abilities
18. Personal abilities

A specific set of behavioral objectives has been established for each of the 18 preceding items. The following set of objectives for visual perceptual abilities provides an example of one such set of objectives.

Visual perceptual abilities*

The student is able to:
1. Demonstrate visual acuity or corrected visual acuity
2. Demonstrate consistent left-to-right orientation and function including ocular-motor sequencing (PRSPP)
3. Match spatial forms
4. Interpret perspective
5. Visualize orientation of objects in space
6. Discriminate similarities and differences in objects, pictures, letters, words (PRSPP)
7. Identify letters (Woodcock, GMcK)
8. Isolate figure from ground(PRSPP)
9. Identify part-whole relationships
10. Perform visual closure
11. Utilize external configurations in identification of stimuli
12. Perform visual tracking tasks (PRSPP)
13. Perform visual sequencing tasks
14. Perform fine motor tasks requiring visual-motor integration; that is, paper folding, braiding, beading, coloring, and so forth
15. Reproduce spatial forms or designs by copying (Det. 12, PRSPP)
16. Reproduce spatial forms or designs from memory (Det. 12)
17. Write the alphabet (PRSPP)
18. Write legible cursive handwriting (Peterson scale)

The guidance and counseling program. The guidance and counseling program at

---

*The information found in parenthesis to the right of certain of these objectives indicates the instrument(s) used to determine the need. PRSPP is the Pine Ridge School Perceptual Profile; Det 12 is the Detroit Tests of Learning Aptitude, Part 12; GMcK is the Gates-McKillop Test.

Pine Ridge School is designed to help students develop improved self-concept and interpersonal relationships. Through small, weekly group meetings with the Guidance Supervisor, students learn to participate in a group in which personal thoughts and feelings are shared in a nonthreatening environment. Through this group process, students develop responsibility to themselves and others, gain respect for individual differences, and become more aware of their personal values and goals.

The Guidance Supervisor also works as a counselor in solving personal and interpersonal problems, seeing students on an individual basis, and working with the residential and teaching staff to encourage each student's personal growth. When appropriate, the Guidance Supervisor may arrange long-term counseling for certain students with a qualified outside source.

Additionally, specific guidance is provided for students who are nearing graduation to help them make the adjustment from school to the world of work or college. This is accomplished in weekly meetings with seniors where an awareness of values, goals, and career possibilities are incorporated into students' decisions about their futures.

The recreation program. A creative and varied recreation program provides each student ample opportunity to experience new activities and develop recreational skills. This program is a vital part of the Pine Ridge experience, expanding each student's knowledge, skills, and horizons and providing new areas for success and improved self-esteem. Pine Ridge School has a full-time program director with a large staff, which enables students to have a wide range of choices in activities. Weekend activities are emphasized as strongly as weekday ones, but they vary each week. Weekday activities change with each quarter to take advantage of seasonal opportunities and to allow students to indicate preferences several times during the school year.

One of Pine Ridge's greatest assets is its rural location, less than 10 miles from the center of the Green Mountains. The school owns a large tract of land that is utilized by the outdoor program as its workshop. A marked trail system has been developed, suitable for hiking, cross-country skiing, and cross-country running. Other outdoor offerings include forestry, hiking, rock climbing, campcraft, campfire cooking, basic wilderness survival, use of map and compass for route finding and simple surveying, first aid, fishing, and canoeing and kayaking. Overnight camping trips of varying degrees of difficulty and for different purposes leave the campus almost every weekend.

Team sports run the gamut from small scrimmages and intramural games to organized teams that practice daily and play against other local schools, particularly in soccer and basketball. Other sports offered are informal hockey, touch football, volleyball, baseball, softball, and kickball.

Traditional individual sports include tennis, swimming, skating, weight training, bowling, yoga, bicycling, downhill and cross-country skiing, horseback riding, and others. The variety of nonathletic activities ranges from hobbies to arts and crafts and piano. Darkroom facilities are provided for photographers. A number of continuing projects such as the newspaper, yearbook, radio station WPRS, and drama activities are also available.

On Friday evenings, Saturdays, and Sundays there are opportunities to go on trips with the outdoor program, do laundry, attend church services, go to museums, concerts, and other special events, or participate in sports or other activities on campus. For 4 days in October and May all students and staff leave campus for a variety of camping trips, ranging from bicycling to backpacking. Groups cook out and sleep in tents. A typical list of trips would include easy camping, fishing, bicycling, horseback riding, canoeing, backpacking, and rock climbing. The recreation program is varied, individualized as required, and, in total, adds much to the development and social adjustment of students enrolled at Pine Ridge.

The residential program. The residential program at Pine Ridge School is committed to two primary goals. The first is to foster and

encourage the development of positive psychosocial skills. The development of psychosocial skills is accomplished through a strong balance of positive reinforcement from all of the staff and a consistent approach to discipline. Each student is helped to understand that one must be responsible for one's own actions.

The second objective is to provide each student with a comfortable and supportive family environment within the community. Residential staff members, assuming the role of surrogate parents, attempt to provide each student with realistic and obtainable goals for personal behavior. They encourage involvement in constructive leisure activities. Students having difficulty with interpersonal relationships are provided with personal direction and assistance. The values of respect, integrity, tolerance, and kindness are reinforced in all aspects of the school's program.

The achievement of these objectives is fostered through daily dorm life activities and participation in the recreational program. Dormitory daily schedules include encouragement of a high level of personal hygiene and a development of pride in one's own surroundings. Students clean their dormitories and help keep the campus free of litter. At various times during the year each student performs the duties of waiter, serving the dinner meal and clearing the table. Through these activities, the student's sense of identity with and responsibility to the school community is strengthened.

In addition to the job program, with responsibility shared equally by all students, the school offers a number of custodial and supervisory work assignments for which each student thus "employed" receives a small honorarium. Students may make application for these positions on arrival at school. If their work is satisfactory, they may hold the position throughout the year. These positions are usually assigned on a first come–first served basis, although a certain number are reserved for those students who do not have sufficient financial resources to maintain a student bank fund. This program provides valuable work experience for the students. In total, the residential program attempts to "tie together" the various other components of the program, strengthen the student's sense of self, foster meaningful relationships, and develop a stronger, deeper sense of community.

Other information of interest

In reviewing the basic information that should be presented about the various private school programs in this chapter, it became obvious that there was information that might be of value in painting a meaningful picture of the program that did not "fit" conveniently into the established descriptive categories. These odds and ends items are briefly outlined here. Although some of this information is logically interrelated, most may be best presented through a simple listing with no attempt to establish relationships or meaningful flow from item to item.

Pine Ridge School is approved by the state of Vermont to grant a high school diploma to students who fulfill the requirements for graduation.

The physical location of Pine Ridge School—close to outdoor recreation areas in Vermont's Green Mountains, New Hampshire's White Mountains, and New York's Adirondack Mountains—has considerable effect on the physical education and outdoor recreation programs. This, in turn, likely has an effect on student interest in attendance at Pine Ridge.

There is an emphasis on multisensory learning approaches at Pine Ridge, particularly applications of what is known as the *Gillingham* approach. (See p. 110 for further discussion of this approach.)

Pine Ridge School is most appropriately characterized as a basic skill-oriented, academic emphasis program, as contrasted to a prevocational or vocationally oriented program.

Pine Ridge School has a separate, well-attended summer program for students that provides a unique opportunity for a graduate level summer practicum for training practitioners in the various techniques and methods of diagnostic-prescriptive teaching. This program includes a week-long intensive theoretical introduction to the field of learning disabilities (for teachers-in-training) followed by 6 weeks of practical experience in tutoring learning disabled children.

Summary

Pine Ridge School, located in Williston, Vermont, was originally established as a school for learning disabled adolescents in 1968. It is a residential school with students coming from the United States and Canada. Its basic orientation is toward basic skills and academic achievement. Many students complete their entire high school program at Pine Ridge. There is a strong recreation/outdoor activities program at Pine Ridge. The male-female ratio of the student body is approximately three to one. Only students who, in the view of the staff, can be diagnosed as truly learning disabled and who possess average or above average mental ability are admitted to the Pine Ridge program. In addition to the regular academic year program, there is a 6-week summer program (a 24-hour, 7-day-per-week program) and a related educational program designed to train graduate level learning disabilities practitioners.

Brush Ranch School, Tererro, New Mexico
Introduction

Brush Ranch School is a private, nonprofit boarding school for girls and boys with learning disabilities. Located in the Rocky Mountains, close to Santa Fe, New Mexico, Brush Ranch is the largest (in terms of physical size of school property) of the schools reviewed in this chapter. It is relatively small in school population, with a maximum enrollment of 60 students. Brush Ranch School maintains a substantial waiting list of students already screened and ready for admittance, limiting its enrollment to students 10 through 18 years of age.* It features and takes full advantage of the unusual physical characteristics of the area (283 acres of school property

---

*Because of the heavy demand and large waiting list (approximately half of the present maximum enrollment), Brush Ranch School officials are exploring the possibility of a second campus.

in the Sangre de Cristo Range of the Rockies, the Pecos River flowing through the ranch grounds, and surrounded by the Santa Fe National Forest) in offering comprehensive recreational programs including fishing, riding, tobogganing, hiking, skiing, and backpacking in addition to the more traditional soccer, softball, boxing, and tennis. Brush Ranch School officials very carefully consider each applicant and admit only those whose needs are most consistent with the ability of the school to deliver a maximally effective program.

Admissions procedures and requirements

To determine if Brush Ranch School is appropriate for any given applicant, the directors request the results of all clinical, medical, and educational evaluations that are already completed and available. Based on the initial review of these evaluations, additional testing may be requested. Permissions to gain additional information from former schools, physicians, and agencies are standard to Brush Ranch School admission procedures (as they are to all other private schools reviewed here), and a visit to the school by parents and candidates is required. Brush Ranch School is specifically a school for the learning disabled and does not accept students who are mentally retarded or who are emotionally disturbed to the extent that they require psychiatric care.

During the school visit, the parents and child meet the directors and other staff members, tour ranch property, and are assisted in obtaining complete, first-hand knowledge of the program. It is believed that it is highly important for all concerned to be convinced that Brush Ranch School is the right school for the child. If the decision is made to enroll the child, an enrollment contract for the following school year is arranged. Agreements regarding visits (by parents), reporting procedures and other necessary communications, and the necessary financial arrangements are made in the final conference that is normally held at the ranch. As with many other schools, a deposit is required to hold a space for the upcoming school year. (In some

instances, vacancies occur midyear. Usually, there are students waiting for admittance whose parents have indicated that they are interested in midterm placement if it becomes available.)

Staff and student population

The student population of Brush Ranch School is limited to 60 students between the ages of 10 and 18. The large majority of the student body consists of students aged 14 through 18. These 60 students are taught by seven certified teachers (most of whom hold master's degrees) and nine teacher aides (all of whom hold bachelor's degrees, but have not completed all of New Mexico's requirements for certification). An additional seven supervisors and/or directors live on the school property and work with both teachers and students. The teacher-pupil ratio (computed in a similar manner to those quoted in other program descriptions in this chapter) thus becomes approximately one to three. Consultive services are provided by an educational consultant and a clinical psychologist, both holding doctorate degrees, and two medical doctors, one the school physician and the other a child psychiatrist. One of the teacher aides who holds a degree in nursing serves as school nurse.

Although Brush Ranch School does not accept students who are emotionally disturbed, it is expected that students with learning disabilities, particularly those with long-standing learning problems, may have significant emotional overlays. Thus the school population does include students who require assistance with behavior problems.

Learning characteristics of Brush Ranch School students

The focus of Brush Ranch School is learning disabilities, therefore, children who have been diagnosed as having "mild neurological dysfunctions," "minimal brain damage," or dyslexia, are included in the school population. The majority are more simply viewed as learning disabled students, and school directors are more interested in whether it appears that the Brush Ranch program can assist the child to grow socially and academically than in clinical diagnostic labels. There is the specific admission requirement that the potential student appear to have the intellectual ability to learn, which, in turn, means that all students do have potentially normal range learning ability. Most of the classic learning disability characteristics can be found in at least some of the students, but there is no attempt to group or classify students according to such characteristics. The most common characteristic of all students is probably that characteristic that brought them to Brush Ranch School—academic difficulties, particularly in reading, other basic communication skills, and mathematics.

Brush Ranch School educational program

Brush Ranch School emphasizes a four-fold program in much of their literature and in actual program planning. Officials there told us that they believe they may best accomplish their goals for each student through a planned program of (1) academic instruction, (2) vocational programs, (3) recreational activities, and (4) social development activities. Even though these areas of emphasis are most effectively planned and implemented as an integrated program (and that is how it is accomplished at Brush Ranch School), the academic and vocational program will be discussed in this section and recreational activities and opportunities for social development in the next section to be consistent with the rest of this chapter.*

Brush Ranch School staff members have many priorities in mind as they plan for and work with students at the school. However, certain objectives are viewed as basic or primary. These are:

---

*It should be noted that although recreational activities and opportunity for maximum social development are important in all school programs, they take on greatly added significance in *boarding* programs where the school must provide a substitute for the home/neighborhood environment. Thus the reader will see much more emphasis on these components in those programs that are primarily boarding school programs.

1. To increase achievement in basic skill areas
2. To assist the student to become an *active* learner. (This requires that the school provide an educational setting where active learning, as opposed to passive learning, is stressed.) This active learning emphasis should then assist the student to develop as an independent learner, develop academic and social confidence, and develop goal setting and attainment techniques
3. To demonstrate to students that academic competency can be relevant in their lives
4. To develop academic and creative potential while preserving individuality
5. To assist in the development of positive attitudes toward self and others. (This objective is nurtured through the deliberate, planned creation of an atmosphere of mutual respect and trust toward and between all members of Brush Ranch School.)

In addition to records of academic achievement and external evaluation by educational evaluators, Brush Ranch School personnel maintain detailed notes on observed behavior of students. This includes such factors as independence, responsibility, enthusiasm, and types of social behavior. School personnel are reminded to note both *positive and negative* behavior, and planned sharing and evaluation of these anecdotal records provide an opportunity for program modifications as required by the development of individual students.

In that the student enrollment represents many age and grade levels, a *vertical grouping* plan has been implemented. At Brush Ranch School, *vertical grouping* simply means that although different age groups are in the program, one's age does not determine the skills, projects, and activities on which he or she concentrates. The student's individual needs determine his or her activities.

The academic program at Brush Ranch School is based on knowledge of individual student strengths, regular academic assessment, and the implication of behavioral records. Individual programs are regularly re-examined to be certain that maximum achievement is maintained. The very low teacher-pupil ratio permits a great deal of one-to-one interaction in the teaching-learning setting. (Class schedules, specifying which students were in which classes or activities throughout the day indicate that class size tends to be four to five students per class.) Flexibility of scheduling, given the Brush Ranch School teacher-student ratio, is excellent.

The vocational program at Brush Ranch School has all of the same class size characteristics of the academic program. Classes include such areas as photography, drafting, woodworking, commercial art, typing, shorthand, and others. School authorities view the vocational program as a very important facet of the total school effort and find that activities in these courses can be correlated with more purely academic activities, thus giving added relevance to the academics. The high degree of individual attention makes it possible for each instructor to be aware of and utilize all such information in a manner that would be virtually impossible in the typical, large public high school. *Success* on the part of students is a major goal, and this correlated program maximizes the potential for success.

The recreation program

As with all boarding school programs, the Brush Ranch School must plan for a 24-hour day, 7 days per week. The ranch proper includes several riding rings, two major game areas, two trout ponds, a swimming pool, a tennis court, several picnic areas, and the Pecos River running through the grounds. Marked trails extend into the nearby mountains. In addition to the activities readily suggested by the preceding list of facilities, tobogganing, ice skating, kickball, boxing, soccer, volleyball, riflery, tumbling, skiing, fencing, and weight lifting are part of the recreational program. Teachers and teacher aides are selected with some consideration given to their interests and abilities in these

recreational areas. Actually, a sort of self-sorting procedure takes place in schools of this nature in that teachers who are drawn to such schools tend to be those who are interested in outdoor activities. Although not necessarily recreational, some of the vocationally related interests are carried through into nonacademic time and become recreational in nature. Special activities such as stamp and chess clubs, yoga, planned campfire activities, and movies help to fill the day. A study hall is open 3 nights a week and at times receives considerable use. Dances are held on a scheduled basis, and, in general, there is plenty to do. The opportunity for staff members to observe students in these less formal settings provides additional information that is highly valuable in planning for the academic and vocational areas.

Other information of interest

All students are full-time boarders. Many other boarding schools have become involved in part-time or after-school services, but the location and the nature of this program do not lend themselves to other than boarding students.

A large majority of the Brush Ranch School referrals are through professional sources.

The Brush Ranch School has a relatively long school day, typically extending from 8:30 A.M. until 5:00 P.M.; however, the 3:30 to 5:00 P.M. segment of the day is devoted to physical education and/or recreational activities.

Summary

The Brush Ranch School is a boarding school organized specifically for students with learning disabilities. Brush Ranch School does not admit students who are mentally retarded or whose primary difficulty is an emotional problem. However, the most often observed handicap or difficulty in addition to the basic learning disabilities is lack of adequate social adjustment, particularly in relations with the peer group. Brush Ranch School is located 36 miles from Santa Fe, New Mexico, on the edge of the Sangre de Cristo range of the Rocky Mountains. It is large (283 acres), is surrounded by a national forest, and is organized to take full recreational and motivational advantage of its ideal location. Presently limited to 60 students, but with a large waiting list, school officials are considering the possibility of opening another campus. The educational approach is based on a balanced academic, vocational, and recreational emphasis. A fourth consideration, social development, completes the four cornerstones of the Brush Ranch School emphasis.

Maplebrook School, Inc., Amenia, New York
Introduction

Maplebrook School is a small school (enrollment is limited to 55 students) located on a 30-acre campus in the foothills of the Berkshires. Founded in 1945, Maplebrook is the oldest of the schools reviewed in this chapter and was obviously opened long before the advent of present-day interest in the learning disabled. It is a nonprofit, coeducational boarding school, and unlike most other boarding schools for the learning disabled, provides a 12-month academic program. The Maplebrook program serves boys and girls who exhibit learning problems, who have difficulties in interpersonal interaction, and who have an IQ score greater than 75. Maplebrook adheres to a more humanistic orientation leading to differences in program implementation that are described in the following section.

Admissions procedures and requirements

Initial admissions criteria are: (1) 11 through 15 years of age (students over age 15 *may* be accepted in some unusual circumstances, but enrollment after age 15 is not consistent with the most desirable program planning), (2) an I.Q. of 75 or above, and (3) presence of a learning problem that Maplebrook staff members believe the program will substantially benefit. Although it is recognized that children with learning problems will often have resultant behavior and/or emotional problems, if these problems are such that they appear likely to require resi-

dent psychological counseling, the student may not be accepted.

If it appears to the parents or guardian that initial criteria may be met, the following steps must be completed:

1. All appropriate academic, psychological, medical, and social history reports must be sent to Maplebrook for evaluation.
2. If enrollment at Maplebrook remains a serious consideration, the prospective student must remain on campus for a 1-week trial enrollment. During this week, the student is evaluated (through planned observation, academic and basic skills assessment) by the educational staff and is seen by the clinical psychologist. If staff recommendations are positive, if the prospective student and/or his or her parents still desire enrollment, and if space permits, the student is enrolled immediately. If space does *not* exist immediately, the student's name is placed on the waiting list. A nominal fee is required for this 1-week stay.

Staff and student population

Maplebrook School staff includes the administration, nine faculty members working directly in the educational program, six house parents, two part-time psychologists, a part-time riding instructor, a part-time guitar instructor, and a part-time piano instructor. The nine faculty members working full-time, directly with students, include five classroom teachers (all certified in special education), a certified physical education teacher, as ASHA certified speech and language pathologist, a home economics teacher, and a principal whose primary responsibility is the total educational viability of the program.

The student population totals 55, with a present age range from 11 to 19. Slightly more than 70% of the present student population is between the ages of 15 and 18. Teacher-pupil ratio, considering only educational staff and making equivalency adjustments for part-time staff, is approximately one to five. If total staff is considered, the staff-pupil ratio is between one to three and one to four.

Learning characteristics of Maplebrook School students

The student population at Maplebrook may be described as exhibiting learning disabilities, with many of the symptoms usually associated with minimal brain damage. Many indicate perceptual impairments and most have some type of secondary emotional symptoms, though these are, in most cases, not very severe. Maplebrook School officials do not accept students who are mentally retarded, primarily emotionally disturbed, known delinquents, or those with uncontrolled epilepsy. According to school officials, the most often observed disability (or difficulty) in addition to learning disabilities is that of poor social development and poor social interaction skills. Maplebrook School does admit children with borderline mental ability, and thus admits students with a slightly lower level of mental ability than do many other learning disability schools.

Maplebrook School educational program

The Maplebrook educational program is based on an individualized, diagnostic-prescriptive teaching approach, but the total school atmosphere is deliberately homelike, nonclinical, and humanistic. *The social environment at Maplebrook is considered to be of prime importance*, and is intended to be both reassuring and motivating in terms of self-motivated desire to achieve. Maplebrook literature indicates that the Maplebrook approach "has its roots in the loving, benevolent yet structured pedagogy found in most good schools earlier in the twentieth century. . . . This approach treats the needs of the individual with respect to affection, recognition, tutoring, and discipline without withdrawing him from the peer structure."*

Students are based in self-contained homeroom situations but rotate into specialty areas such as physical education, health, sex education, home economics, prevocational training, and language therapy. Diagnostic

---

*From *The Maplebrook approach: A guide for parents and professionals*, undated brochure.

testing is completed by classroom teachers, the language therapist, the psychologist, and the principal. Individual plans are established, emphasizing specific goals and objectives. These goals are regularly evaluated and reestablished if necessary. Although humanistic in emphasis, the program is structured and discipline is based on positive reinforcement. In a program called the *Independent Thinking Program*, students can earn an increasing number of campus privileges by demonstrating the ability to take responsibility for their own actions.

Emphasis with younger students tends to be on remedial, academic, and social skills. Older students, those nearing the time they will leave Maplebrook, will have specific emphasis placed on prevocational skills and social interactions required for success in living. This upper level program includes practical application through the "senior house" project, which is explained further in the description of the residential program.

The recreation program

Outdoor sports, including swimming, tennis, and golf, complement a full physical education program. Horseback riding, planned field days, and involvement with other various sports are planned in season. Game areas for indoor games (particularly valuable in winter) are provided within the dormitories. The Maplebrook staff believes that the dormitory plan (as opposed to smaller cottages) lends itself to recreation and socialization and has many spin-off benefits. A planned program of concerts, plays, and other group activities provides a worthwhile break in the schedule and permits further opportunity for students to exercise increased levels of social skills. In cases where such skills are not being adequately developed, this planned program provides a means of "evaluation in practice."

The residential program

Maplebrook School, like other boarding schools, is "home" for the students enrolled for long periods. As indicated earlier, the role of peer group dynamics at Maplebrook appears to be part of the core of the program and from our vantage point seems to receive more relative emphasis at Maplebrook than at any other program reviewed in this chapter. Acceptance of the spirit of Maplebrook (the therapeutic environment in which students become part of a family and in effect create their own milieu or environment) is discussed in the initial conference with both child and parents. Then, during the 1-week trial enrollment, the child has an opportunity to determine whether this setting and this point of view appeal to him or her personally. In most cases, if the child does not want to try Maplebrook, he will not be accepted. After a student is accepted, it is assumed that the entire family unit is a part of Maplebrook. When nearby, parents take an active part in many activities and most participate in the Maplebrook Parents' Association.

Unlike many boarding schools, Maplebrook subscribes to the full dormitory plan. Rather than cottages, separate rooms that hold two to three students are clustered in the boys' and the girls' buildings. Four house parents rotate in each building. Houseparents frequently experiment with roommate changes (after students have developed some feeling of stability) to relieve conflict, match disabilities, or introduce variety. Maplebrook staff members feel that the practice of roommate changes (planned, not arbitrary) has contributed significantly to the socialization of students at Maplebrook.

The "senior house" at Maplebrook is a home on campus consisting of four bedrooms, two baths, a living room, dining room, study, kitchen, and full basement. Students completing their final year at Maplebrook spend part of that year at senior house and do their own shopping, cooking, laundry, housecleaning, and general planning and organizing of spare time activities. Houseparents live in to provide guidance as needed and for general supervision; but, within practical limits, the house and its management belong to the students living there. Senior house will house six students at one time, and two groups of students (six boys in one group, six girls in the other) rotate in the house each 12 weeks. As they go back to the dorm, their attitudes, the concerns with which they had to deal, and the general picture of what is involved in "living on your own" is communicated to younger children in the dorm far better than any discussion or lecture session led by adults could ever do. Younger students look forward to this program, which includes both freedom and responsibility.

Other information of interest

Students from three local preparatory schools visit the Maplebrook School campus weekly for small group or individual interaction with Maplebrook students. This program has proved to be of value to all concerned.

Maplebrook has a student work program in which almost half of the student body typically participates. This permits the development of additional individual responsibility for specific tasks, and the money earned is important both as a source of spending money and as a forerunner of gainful employment in the future. Students must go through a regular hiring process to obtain such jobs—again an important experience in preparation for life.

A recent survey of former Maplebrook students indicates that the majority have returned to their local schools or have entered vocational training programs. A vocational training program at New Haven, Connecticut, was recently established by the Maplebrook Parents' Association in conjunction with several organized rehabilitation agencies and appears to fulfill an important need.

Summary

The Maplebrook School is a boarding school for learning disabled adolescents located in Amenia, New York, in the foothills of the Berkshires. The oldest of the schools discussed in this chapter (established in 1945), Maplebrook limits its enrollment to 55 students, aged 11 to 19. It is unique in that its program is year-round, rather than the more typical 9-month academic year program. The total approach at Maplebrook is

described as humanistic and nonclinical, but those more familiar with the school choose to describe it simply as "the Maplebrook approach." A 1-week trial enrollment is required before a student is admitted to Maplebrook, because the entire school (staff and student body) must be relatively compatible for the therapeutic environment to be effective. This is not to say that prospective students must be "well adjusted" before entering. On the contrary, the most common problem or disability other than the basic learning disability is poor social interaction skills. However, in practice it appears that the 1-week trial enrollment is highly effective in determining which students will eventually succeed at Maplebrook.

Consistent with the philosophy of acceptance that pervades the school, parents of students are asked to participate in various planned aspects of the program to a greater extent than in most boarding school programs. The Maplebrook School emphasis is perhaps more "different" from the composite emphasis of schools reviewed here than any other school. This does not refer to physical setting, as in the unusual ranch setting of Brush Ranch School, but rather to the unusually strong overall emphasis on the humanistic approach and the value of a therapeutic environment.

The Groves Learning Center, Minnetonka, Minnesota
Introduction

The Groves Learning Center was established in 1972 as the first private school in Minnesota for children with learning disabilities. It was founded as a nonprofit, coeducational day school by a group of 15 concerned parents, educators, and a physician to provide a facility for capable children in the Minneapolis–St. Paul area who were unable to learn in conventional classrooms. The center began with 21 students and at the time of this writing enrolled 65. The Groves Learning Center utilizes an eclectic program of individualized instruction, including both remediation and compensatory components, with more emphasis in subject matter content (compensatory emphasis) provided for older children. The program has been well received in the Twin Cities area and tends to operate at capacity; however, because of a program of planned return to the public school program, vacancies do regularly occur. The Groves Learning Center has initiated a number of community service efforts (in addition to the regular program) that are outlined in the final section of this discussion.

Admissions procedures and requirements

The Groves Learning Center is a day school, thus students live within commuting distance of the Center and most initial requests for information about the school come from the Minneapolis–St. Paul metropolitan area or nearby communities. This being the case, a considerable amount of personal interaction between parents of prospective students and Center staff can take place before formal acceptance is made. (The preceding does *not* mean that students from other geographic areas will not be accepted, but rather that if they are, they must make arrangements to live in the immediate area.) With most students coming from nearby school districts, information may be obtained from these districts. Additional diagnostic data is obtained through an evaluation center that is a part of the Groves Learning Center, but also provides valuable service to local school districts, to parents who come on a private basis, and to other professionals.

The Groves Learning Center accepts learning disabled children between the ages of 6 and 16, who exhibit and/or meet the following characteristics and enrollment criteria:

1. At least normal intellectual capacity
2. Serious academic underachievement
3. Evidence of underlying psychological processing deficits that can reasonably be expected to contribute to the academic underachievement
4. Absence of serious psychopathology
5. Indication that special education is the appropriate method of treatment.

The Groves Learning Center does not accept mentally retarded, emotionally disturbed,

deaf, or blind students. Like other private school programs, the Groves Center is not obligated to attempt to serve *all* children, and officials there do not accept students whom they feel they cannot serve effectively.

Staff and student population

The Groves Learning Center has 16 staff members, all holding state certification. Two staff members hold doctoral degrees and eight hold master's degrees. A licensed Consulting Psychologist, a School Psychologist, and a Speech Therapist provide specialized skills as required. Two teacher aides are also employed. The overall student-staff ratio is approximately four to one, a level that the Center expects to maintain. The present enrollment at Groves Learning Center is 65 students: 54 boys and 11 girls. The majority of the present enrollment is of secondary school age. (Forty-six of the 65 students are between the ages of 12 and 16.)

Learning characteristics of Groves Learning Center students

School officials report that "students present a spectrum of moderate to severe disorders such as perceptual handicap, brain injury, minimal brain dysfunction, dyslexia, hyperactivity, and others. As a result, they have difficulty in listening, thinking, talking, reading, writing, spelling, or arithmetic skills."* In addition to more specific academic difficulties, many students at the Groves Learning Center have poor self-esteem and weak ego strength, which is considered by the staff as providing a significant, additional handicap. As noted in the listing of disorders above, students at the Groves Learning Center exhibit characteristics that fit the full range usually attributed to children and youth who are experiencing learning disabilities.

The Groves Learning Center educational program

The Groves Learning Center educational program is based on the philosophical con-

---

*Personal communication with Dr. Raleigh J. Huizinga, February 14, 1977.

viction that there is no single method or procedure that will work with all learning disabled children. Instruction is geared to a number of variables, including age, length of time the disability has existed, type(s) of disability, and individual social, psychological, physical, and intellectual abilities and capacities. Programs are updated weekly in accordance with the manner and rate at which each student is progressing both socially and academically. The program approach might be best described as an individualized, eclectic approach utilizing a diagnostic-prescriptive teaching model. The ultimate goal is return of the student to the regular public school program, and educational planning is pursued with this in mind.

The Groves Learning Center is organized into several academic modules or clusters, each with a cluster leader. Within each cluster the needs of the student determine the nature of the instruction (one-to-one, small group, tutorial, or lecture) as well as the amount of instruction provided. This permits the flexibility and precision necessary to meet the educational needs of the student without sacrifice of the necessary scope and sequence of educational objectives. Faculty members within each cluster are responsible for the daily planning for each child, and cluster leaders along with the head teacher are responsible for the coordinated program of education. Thus, all faculty—whether they teach science, social studies, shop, physical education, art, reading, or math— develop and reinforce each student's acquired learning skills so that the child experiences a totally integrated learning environment. Each child, therefore, experiences reinforcement on a coordinated basis in the appropriate skills throughout the full school day. This structure permits the grouping of all academic activities around related student needs and abilities in the belief that learning is built on many integrated skills and that an individual who can express his ideas through many media in different situations is being educated in the broadest sense of that term.

Groves Learning Center officials believe that much of their success relates to the close contact that is maintained with students (one-to-one in many cases, very small groups in others), and the manner in which they have learned to use continuous monitoring and management of academic progress as a guide for weekly program updating. The Groves Learning Center has also developed a specific set of guidelines for the application of compensatory and remedial teaching. This is not a matter of "either-or," but of "how much of each, when, and why."

Guidelines for use of compensatory or remedial teaching. Appropriate educational services for the learning disabled require the provision of *both* remedial and compensatory teaching. These two forms of instruction serve different purposes that may be planned to be complementary in the total educational program. Remedial teaching is directed toward a child's learning disability for the purpose of developing the psychological process or processes that may be deficient. With compensatory teaching the child's learning disability is circumvented, while his abilities are used to aid his mastery of subject matter content.

Remedial and compensatory teaching are differentiated on the basis of the following factors.

Teaching goal. The goal of remedial teaching is to develop the central psychological processes in which a child is disabled (for example, mental maps to represent spatial directions). On the other hand, the goal of compensatory teaching is the mastery of specific subject matter content (for example, the geography of the United States).

Role of disability and ability areas. With remedial teaching, the child's disability areas are given direct attention so that the severity of the disability can be lessened and a basic level of competence can be achieved. For example, if a child has an auditory channel disability, remediation in the form of total verbal bombardment may be given. With remedial teaching, the child's abilities are used temporarily until appropriate competency is developed in the child's area or areas of disability and are then gradually phased out. For the child with an auditory channel disability and a visual channel ability, visual aids are used until the child can decode auditory stimuli and are then eliminated.

On the other hand, with compensatory teaching, there is an intentional avoidance of the child's disability areas so that they do not hinder his mastery of the subject matter being presented. For the child with an auditory channel disability, as much information as possible is presented in visual form.

Instructional content. There should be a complementary relationship between remedial and compensatory teaching in terms of the content used in each. The content of compensatory teaching is that of the school subjects as conventionally given to the child in his grade level placement.

The content of remedial teaching should be related to social and academic tasks that the child is having difficulty mastering. Therefore, a child having difficulty with the content of social studies would have this material presented on both a remedial and a compensatory basis. For example, a fifth grader with a visual problem may be receiving instruction in map reading in social studies. In compensatory teaching, the classroom teacher presents a modification of map reading activities so that the child can lean heavily on his strengths, for example, auditory and kinesthetic modalities. In remedial teaching, the visual aspects of map reading would be developed.

Age factors. The amount of remedial teaching given to a child depends on the age factor. For young children as much remedial teaching as possible is given because the younger the child, the greater the probability of ameliorating the disability. As a child becomes older, the likelihood of ameliorating his disability is decreased because he has a greater deficiency to overcome and because repeated failure to perform in a disability area results in a negative emotional reaction to remediation.

Compensatory teaching is used more for older children than for younger ones. The older child has much subject matter content to acquire before leaving school, and, if this content is not acquired in some alternative

manner, he will not master it and may always be deficient in some important area of academic and social knowledge.

The Groves Learning Center educational program is another program originally developed specifically for learning disabled children and youth. Organized as a day school with a full-day program, a part-day program for children who remain enrolled in their regular schools for approximately half of the school day is presently under experimental implementation. School officials are attempting to utilize as much of the basic content and emphasis of the full-day program as possible in this half-time program, and only long-term experience will indicate how effective this program will be and to which children it will be most applicable.

Other information of interest

As is the case with many other private learning disabilities programs, the Groves Learning Center has developed a number of related programs and services of interest. These include the following.

An evaluation center that, in addition to serving students enrolled in the Center, provides educational and psychological evaluations and develops educational programming recommendations for students with special learning needs. This includes students referred by physicians, school district officials, other professionals, or parents. These students primarily include those who could be called learning disabled and thus might be candidates for the Groves Learning Center but may also include children who have other unique learning problems and would not be eligible for enrollment at the Center.

An instructional materials center has been established that develops and evaluates new materials and procedures. Consultation services are available to school districts or agencies in the area regarding such topics as teaching methodology or behavior management systems in addition to the major instructional materials concern of the center.

Workshops for teachers, principals, and other administrators are regularly scheduled by the Groves Learning Center staff. The major concern of these workshops is teaching and programming for children with special needs.

A summer tutorial program called *the 100-minute hour* is open to all students who may require intensive academic remediation. A full-day program SMILE (Summer Means Individual Learning Experiences) was begun in 1977.

The Groves Learning Center engages in basic and applied research and provides the results of such research to interested professionals.

The Center provides a practicum site for master's level learning disabilities teachers-in-training.

The Center sponsors parent-education seminars and other special projects that serve to increase public awareness and support within the community.

Summary

The Groves Learning Center, Minnetonka, Minnesota, is a private, nonprofit day school organized in 1972 to serve learning disabled students from ages 6 to 16. A majority of the Groves students are of secondary school age, and the student body male-female ratio is approximately five to one. With an avowed eclectic orientation, the Groves Learning Center implements a planned balance of remedial and compensatory program components. In addition to direct services to students, the Center provides a number of community service programs including a diagnostic-evaluative function, workshops and public information activities, an instructional materials center, and a variety of research efforts.

Gables Academies, Miami, Florida*
Introduction

Gables Academies differ from other programs reviewed in this chapter in a number of respects. Gables Academies exist in eight

---

*Gables Academies are located in Miami, Ft. Lauderdale, Melbourne, and St. Petersburg, Florida; Baton Rouge and New Orleans, Louisiana; Atlanta, Georgia; and Charlotte, North Carolina. The national administrative center for the Academies is in Miami.

locations in four states. The original Gables program was established in 1961, before the term *learning disabilities* was in common use, but the thrust has always been that of assistance to children with learning difficulties. The original emphasis was more specifically related to reading and, as is true in the case of other learning disabilities schools, reading remains an area of priority emphasis. Gables Academies offer a day school program and a residential program at all eight facilities; current plans are to continue this pattern. Gables Academies offer academic programs for grades 1 through 12. Like other private learning disabilities schools the population is predominantly male, and at this writing, the largest enrollments were at ages 12 through 15.

Admissions procedures and requirements

The Gables Academies letterhead indicates that the Academies specialize in reading and learning problems, but school brochures, publicity releases, and the like all emphasize "learning disabilities." Admission requirements at Gables are similar to those of other learning disabilities schools reviewed in this chapter—normal range of intelligence, no primary or severe emotional disability, and some indication of educational needs sufficient to predict that Gables Academies can assist the student toward more effective learning. Before admission, certain basic assessment takes place and all available educational data are evaluated. Medical records and developmental history are also carefully considered. Then, the parents, the child, and the Director of the Academy meet informally, discuss the results of the total evaluation and a decision is made based on the educational recommendations of the Director and the feelings of the parent and the child regarding these recommendations. The Gable's staff refers to this procedure as *admission by evaluation.*

Staff and student population

The total faculty for all Academies is 80, of which 10 are teacher aides with temporary certification. These 80 faculty members teach 430 students, with the maximum possible enrollment (given present facilities) considered to be approximately 500 students. The overall teacher-pupil ratio is therefore between one to five and one to six. Approximately half of the total staff of 80 hold graduate degrees in education, with specializations in learning disabilities, reading, speech and hearing, elementary education, or secondary education areas such as English, mathematics, or science.

At this writing, there were 55 students aged 6 through 8, 110 students aged 9 through 11, 145 students aged 12 through 14, and 120 students aged 15 through 18. Of this total of 430 students, approximately 350 were males, 80 were females.

Learning characteristics of Gables Academies students

More children attending the Gables Academies have more difficulties in the communication skills (especially in reading) than in any other area, and in the age 12 and above population, the second most often observed disability is that of emotional problems that accompany (and in most cases are assumed to be directly related to) the basic learning disabilities. Gables Academies include children who are academically retarded in reading, mathematics, and other subject areas. Also included are children with specific problems in handwriting and children with unusually short attention span. There are children at the Academies who exhibit all of the major characteristics typically associated with learning disabilities.

The Gables Academies educational program

The Gables Academies educational program is best described as "diagnostic-prescriptive" in nature. School officials believe that, in the absence of a careful diagnostic workup, a learning disabilities program may be little more than a copy of past educational content and methods—content and methods that have already proved to be ineffective. Therefore, based on diagnostic results, a prescriptive profile is developed that emphasizes individual strengths, abilities, and learning style. Lesson plans emphasize instruction that utilizes the preferred learning styles and most effective learning modalities. Positive reinforcement and strong attention to the value of success in the learning setting underlie much of the instruction at the Gables Academies. Instruction is provided through nongraded, small skill-needs groups, or an individual basis. In reading, no specific method or approach is endorsed. "An eclectic approach embracing both analytic and synthetic methodologies is used. The entire curriculum has as a focal point a concentrated emphasis upon reading and the communication skills."* Counseling services and the services of a speech pathologist and/or psychologist are provided as needed.

The Gables Academies make every effort to provide special programming, yet make the school day as similar to the regular school environment as possible. Gables' vacation schedules parallel those of the local public schools, the school days are organized around class periods, and classes are organized by grades, that is, grade 1, 2, 3, and so forth, even though instruction is individualized and nongraded. To a considerable extent, the services of independent, outside professionals are utilized in testing and the total Gables program benefits from the experience of eight different school staffs (the eight Academies) for planning and evaluation purposes. Although it is difficult to establish certain facts without long-term, comparative, on-site evaluation, it appears that the Gables Academies are less remedial and more "strengths" oriented than many other private schools.

Summary

There are eight Gables Academies in four states that serve learning disabled students from ages 6 through 18. A majority of the Gables Academies students are of secondary school age, and the student body male-female ratio is approximately four to one. The Gables program is diagnostic-prescriptive in

*Personal communication from James D. Meffen, President, Gables Academies.

nature, with educational prescriptions based on learning strengths and unique learning styles of each student. The educational program is eclectic and more strength oriented than remedial in nature; the major emphasis is on reading and communication skills. The Gables Academies offer both boarding school and day school programs and are among the longest established programs of those reviewed in this chapter.

Charles River Academy, Cambridge, Massachusetts
Introduction

Charles River Academy was founded in 1965 as a private, remedial day school for boys. The only school program reviewed in this text that is located in the heart of an urban area, Charles River Academy is sometimes referred to as an alternative school for adolescents with special needs. Coeducational since 1974, it also may be appropriately described as providing a program for learning disabled secondary school age students. At full capacity Charles River Academy enrolls 60 day students and recently initiated a 5-day boarding program for a limited number of these students. With some very few exceptions, students at Charles River Academy come from the greater Boston area.

Admissions procedures and requirements

Admission requirements at Charles River Academy are flexible, the major concerns being that the applicant have demonstrable learning problems, that he can be helped by the school, and that he have normal intellectual ability. Reports from previous schools, from other professionals, and the results of testing and personal interviews at the Academy provide the basis for admission decisions. The mentally retarded and severely emotionally disturbed are not admitted.

Staff and student population

A staff of 12 teachers and 10 tutors instruct the 60 students of Charles River Academy. (The 10 tutors are assigned to Charles River Academy as a part of graduate practicum programs in conjunction with Lesley College,

Northeastern University, Boston University, and Harvard University). Students may enter after age 12, but not after age 17; the student body is composed of students of ages 12 through 19.

Learning characteristics of Charles River Academy students

Students exhibit most of the characteristics usually associated with learning disabilities, but at Charles River Academy the major characteristic is long-term academic failure. A characteristic usually associated with this record of failure is difficulty in establishing meaningful relationships. This is the second most common characteristic. Staff members have both undergraduate and graduate level training in a variety of subject areas, and many have extensive training in special education. A strong emphasis on vocational preparation and career education is supported by staff members with in-depth educational training and experience in these areas.

On the whole, Charles River Academy students have seriously underdeveloped academic skills, but have average or above average intellectual ability. If enrolled in a traditional academic program, most would be called academic failures and many would be regularly cited for various behavioral difficulties. Students with serious primary emotional problems are not accepted, thus there is no provision for such difficulties. Students who had been called *lazy* or *highly unmotivated* in the regular school setting often become motivated learners in the environment of Charles River Academy. Of the Academy's enrollment, 33% come from the inner city. Many of the students might be called *underexposed* to education; some would definitely be called *underprivileged*.

The Charles River Academy educational program

The educational program is individualized as much as possible, particularly in math and language arts. Average class size ranges from three to eight. Class offerings include the traditional areas that might be expected in a small high school; vocational areas are much more complete and reflect the overriding concern for effective vocational training.

The goals of Charles River Academy are:

1. To bring a student's academic skills up to his or her potential
2. To help the student acquire vocational and avocational skills that will be useful in further education and later life
3. To encourage the student to develop a sense of joy and self-awareness that will be of benefit in the family, community, and work environment

The 5-day boarding program, started in 1971, is an important component in fully meeting the needs—consistent with the above goals—of certain of the Academy's students. This is similar to many of the live-in projects in which students plan, cook, and serve meals, clean and care for the dormitory and grounds, and learn to work cooperatively with others toward common goals. As a part of this program, students have an opportunity to participate in many social, sporting, and cultural events in greater Boston.

Academy officials believe that the small class size, the personal contact, and the specialized training and experience of the staff all combine to produce the results that have gained the school considerable recognition.

The recreation and activities program

Charles River Academy has many clubs—literary, electronics, photography, and audiovisual to name a few. They have several musical ensembles and dramatic activities and produce a yearbook, literary magazine, and school newspaper. Through an arrangement with the nearby YMCA (a 2-minute walk from the school) and the YWCA (a 6-minute walk away), all students have scheduled gym and pool activities and an opportunity to participate in a wide variety of sports. Many field trips are taken during the year and, through what is called the *Challenge Program*, students are involved in woodlore, tracking, camping, and survival skills. The Charles River Academy Sailing Club uses the facilities of the Boston Community Sailboat Association, and many students have mastered the fundamentals of sailing. This cooperative arrangement and those with the YMCA and YWCA are characteristic of the way in which a school in an urban area can utilize the various resources around it to the advantage of students who are so desperately in need of assistance. As with other learning disability schools, the Charles River Academy uses success in recreational and activity areas as a bridge to success in academics.

Other information of interest

A summary of what former Charles River Academy students are presently doing indicates a significant number in specialized, technical, or vocational schools and/or in college or university programs. Others hold well-paid, responsible jobs.

In addition to outdoor facilities that belong to other agencies, but can be used by the Academy, the Academy owns and maintains a 300-acre wilderness camp in New Hampshire.

At one point, in 1973, the Charles River Academy was seriously underenrolled, and there was some consideration of the question of the continued usefulness and need for such a school. After a survey of the greater Boston area, it was felt that the need for a school for learning disabled adolescents did exist but that many who needed the school did not know of its existence. After some additional public relations efforts and the move to make the Academy coeducational, it became necessary to turn down some applicants who truly needed the program because there were too many applications for existing vacancies.

Summary

Charles River Academy is an urban, remedially oriented school, originally established for boys, but currently coeducational. With a balanced academic and vocational emphasis, the Academy is able to overcome what some might view as a disadvantageous location and benefits from the facilities of nearby agencies or organizations (YMCA, YWCA, Boston Sailboat Association, and others). The Charles River Academy exercises very flexible requirements for admission, but, like most other programs, does not admit the mentally retarded or the emotionally disturbed. If the activities in which former Charles River Academy students are presently engaged can be used as an indication, the program has been quite effective for many students.

Leary School, Inc., Falls Church, Virginia
Introduction

Leary School was founded in 1964 and opened in 1965 as a school "dedicated to raising the achievement level of normal children in line with their ability and potential."* It retains this original purpose, although its methods have changed and its degree of sophistication in approaching such children has increased in line with existing knowledge through the years. The Leary School philosophy is stated in one simple sentence in various school publications as follows: "Our goal is to maximize our children's self-esteem while developing their academic productivity to the full extent of their potential."

Leary School does not actually "fit" the framework established for this chapter because it is not primarily for students whose major problems are learning disabilities. Students who attend Leary School do have learning problems, and, for a minority of these students, learning disabilities are the primary difficulty; but the majority are children with emotional and/or behavioral problems, with learning disabilities as the secondary area of concern. Leary School will not be reviewed in the same manner as the other schools included in this chapter, for it would not be consistent with our stated purposes. On the other hand, Leary School does serve some learning disabled children and it is unique in one particular aspect that led us to include it so that we might outline this aspect of its operation.

The private school/public school contract

Leary School is a private day school, but of the approximately 180 student capacity of

Leary School, 120 "places" are reserved and under contract with the Fairfax County Public Schools. Fairfax County Schools publicized a request for private facilities to submit proposals to provide certain highly specialized educational services for the Fairfax County Schools. (This is not too different from the situation when a public school corporation submits requests for proposals for private contractors to sod and landscape several schools, for specified custodial/janitorial services, or for building remodeling.) This type of contracting is not authorized by state legislation in many states, but is a legal alternative in Virginia. Leary School submitted a *Proposal for provision of services to handicapped children*, which was accepted by the governing board of the Fairfax County Public Schools. As a result, the school district is guaranteed 120 places at the Leary School for handicapped children and youth who need the type of services provided by the contract.* It would seem that the Fairfax County Schools indicated good judgment in contracting with an established private facility to provide services that they were obviously not "tooled up" to provide. This would *not* be good judgment unless there were good evidence that the private facility could deliver the required services. In this case there was such evidence.

In personal communications with Mr. Leary, we were told that Leary School had never tried to *compete* with the public schools, but rather had tried to respond to needs that were not being met by the public schools. Other private school directors indicated somewhat similar rules of practice and operation. H. Rutherford Turnbull, III (1976), an Assistant Professor of Law at the University of North Carolina, and one who has been heavily involved on behalf of handicapped persons has said: "The public schools are not able, and should not be expected, to have overnight capacity to educate all handicapped children. For this reason, they will

---

*From the original statement of purpose of Leary School, 1964.

*Our thanks to Albert D. Leary, Jr., for sharing with us the proposal and a great deal of detailed data on this unusual arrangement.

have to seek help from private sector groups such as developmental day care centers and other private schools for the handicapped." We believe this may be true, at least for the immediate future, but believe it will vary in relation to geographical area and degree of disability.

Summary

Leary School, a private day school for children with a wide variety of learning problems, is not truly similar to other schools reviewed in this chapter in that it serves a population of students who might be best described as exhibiting emotional or behavioral disorders. Many of these children could be called learning disabled, except for these more primary emotional problems, and a significant minority of the student body is primarily learning disabled with emotional problems as a secondary disability. Leary School was included in this chapter because it has an unusual contracting arrangement with the Fairfax County Public Schools that leads to a situation in which the public schools are the major source of fiscal support for a private school. We are not proposing this as a model that is universally desirable or recommending that it be duplicated under any specific set of circumstances, but we do believe it has merit in some situations. It is unique, it is working well in Fairfax County, and we believe it deserves further investigation for possible application in other areas of the nation.

Smallsville School for the Learning Disabled, Smallsville, USA*

Smallsville School for the Learning Disabled was started in Smallsville in 1974, following a 3-year effort by Mr. and Mrs. John

---

*A hypothetical example that contains elements of many small, private programs for the learning disabled that we have actually observed. Most such programs were conceived in good faith, based on real need, but implemented with very limited understanding, insufficient staff, and almost no chance for significant success. It must be noted, however, that this situation would not have developed had the public schools been assuming their proper function.

Edwards to get the local board of education to initiate classes and programs for the learning disabled. In 1973 they were joined in their planning efforts by three other sets of parents who also had children who were experiencing significant learning difficulties and whose needs were not being met by the schools. Because many teachers in the district were aware that there was considerable unmet need (though many did not really understand the nature of the need), the Edwards and other members of the small but vocal local Association for Children with Learning Disabilities (ACLD) were able to obtain information from school records that indicated that there might be as many as 70 to 80 children in Smallsville who needed special help of the type they envisioned. Because of the limited population base, they believed they would be able to support only a part-time school effort but did receive assurances from parents in two nearby towns that they would support the school (if it became a reality) by sending their children for 2 or 3 days per week for late afternoon sessions.

The total cost estimates looked almost impossible until, in the spring of 1973, they discovered that there was a school psychologist who was retiring in nearby Big City, who was considering coming back to Smallsville to live. He was making inquiries about the possible need for private psychological services when he and the Edwards got together. He had been a school psychologist for the past 25 years, was conversant with the assessment tools often used to indicate the possible existence of learning disabilities, and, although he was far from a learning disabilities specialist (as far as basic knowledge and specific educational expertise in the area of *educational* practices for the learning disabled were concerned), he seemed to Mr. and Mrs. Edwards and their friends to have appeared almost as if by miracle. He was hopeful that the very limited proposal they had in mind would develop into at least part-time employment or that he could develop other contacts as a result of this opportunity. Had the concerned parents taken the time and effort to check carefully, they might have discovered that Dr. Ready (the psychologist) had in fact been "coasting" professionally during the last few years prior to his retirement, and had not really kept up on the rapidly developing area of learning disabilities. However, since he knew so much more than the others involved, this never came to light.

Another bit of "good fortune" came the way of the proposed Smallsville School for the Learning Disabled. A speech and language clinician, who had also taught second grade for 2 years, wanted part-time employment. She was in many ways better informed than Dr. Ready, with major competence in the more purely language related learning problems. In conversations with the Edwards and other concerned parents, she expressed hope that one-fourth time employment would evolve but agreed to start out on an hourly basis. The possibility of employing another educator on a part-time basis was discussed but was postponed until a more clear picture of need could be established. It was agreed that parents would provide volunteer help, that they would *not* attempt to assist with their own child, that they would follow the instructions of the professionals, and that they would respect confidentiality.

One final concern before advertising for clients for the school was a physical facility in which to conduct the program. As is often the case with such part-time educational enterprises, a portion of a church facility was rented. Details such as liability insurance, cost of extra custodial services, storage facilities, and actual rental fees had to be worked out and finally approved by the church board of directors. Smallsville School for the Learning Disabled was then incorporated as a nonprofit educational corporation. At the outset it had two part-time professional employees and five volunteers who received some training under the direction of the professionals. Smallsville School grew to the extent that another part-time professional employee (a former special education teacher who had taught the educable mentally retarded) was added and the role of Dr. Ready became less important, though it seemed desirable to some parents to keep one person with a doc-

tor's degree on the staff. A professor from the Special Education Department of Biggsville State University conducted some in-service training for both the professional staff and for parent volunteers and agreed to serve as a consultant for special problems.

Smallsville School for the Learning Disabled was primarily a diagnostic-tutorial effort and eventually served a variety of cases. The majority were children with mild learning disabilities, about half of whom received concrete assistance through the efforts of the School staff because their difficulties were accurately pinpointed and appropriate educational efforts were initiated. Another fourth of the children were helped primarily because they were receiving individual attention, and they were thus motivated to try harder. It was primarily a matter of caring that made the difference with this group. The remaining fourth of the learning disabled children did not improve. In addition to those children already mentioned, there were a few children who were primarily mentally retarded who became part of the school. They were left in the school program as long as there were no serious behavior difficulties, but parents were told not to expect too much. Though their parents were not actually misled by school personnel, the fact that they were *retained* in the school was a questionable practice. One child who was a definite Down's syndrome youngster was not admitted, even though the parents offered to pay extra fees.

Smallsville School for the Learning Disabled was a school—or was it? Smallsville School did actually serve to benefit children—or did it? Please understand that such programs, schools, or whatever they may be called, have existed and continue to exist. They are a phenomenon of the present decade. Because they do exist they deserve careful consideration. The following discussion relates to a variety of "Smallsville Schools," wherever they may be.

A school or program like that at Smallsville may provide a worthwhile program for at least some of the children enrolled, but such programs are usually dependent on the availability of individuals who are already in the community, who are interested in part-time work (this usually means another family member is the major breadwinner), and who are competent in the skills required for the position. Since a team of professionals is required, this means that there must be several such individuals who "just happen to be available." This may happen, but it is the exception to the rule when it does. In a number of cases, we have seen a working team established through much effort and the good fortune that made such individuals available and then, because one key member moved out of town, the program ended. Without that key person the program usually falters. In a number of cases a poor substitute was found "for the good of the children," and the program became just a holding facility.

Another variation on this situation is when community size and private program needs are sufficient to support one full-time professional, but requires a superdedicated, evangelistic type leader to keep things going. When this individual leaves, there often is no way to attract another such person and the program dies. An additional problem with any program that gets started, serves some of the needs, and then vanishes overnight is the effect it may have on children who are just beginning to find success. Sometimes this may be more detrimental to children than if the program had not started at all. *It is possible to have a good* Smallsville *program, one* *that is well staffed and that can provide continuity, but more often the opposite happens.*

THE COST OF PRIVATE SCHOOL EDUCATION

As indicated earlier in this chapter, we do not believe that most private schools are organized for the purpose of making money. In fact, the majority are nonprofit and, in most cases, the directors and teachers in such schools are not making fabulous wages. We have reviewed seven schools in this chapter, six of which were serving learning disabled adolescents as their primary target group. Fig. 6 indicates the range of cost for attendance at these six schools.

We would caution readers to heed the advice we received from several directors of private schools. Do *not* rely on information you may receive in letters or brochures or read in books, journal articles, or advertisements to tell you whether a given school is appropriate for a specific child. A personal visit, providing a first-hand look at the program, a visit with staff members, and a chance to observe other students is the only way to make any such important decision. Brochures and advertisements can suggest *where* to look; only a personal visit can lead to a satisfactory decision. We would add an additional observation of our own— do not assume that cost is necessarily in direct proportion to the services that *you* might want for some student in whom you are interested.

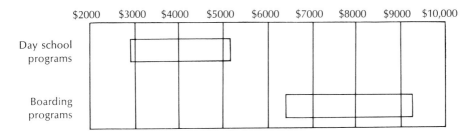

Fig. 6. Annual cost of private school attendance based on the six schools reviewed that primarily serve the learning disabled. This reflects all costs except weekly spending money, cost for clothing, and the like. Boarding costs include the cost of a private educational program plus the cost of housing and meals, 7 days a week, during regular school sessions.

SUMMARY

A number of viable, growing, effective private school programs for the learning disabled adolescent exist in the United States today. (Other, less viable programs also exist, but many of these are rapidly disappearing.) These programs were initiated because of a void that existed in public school programs for the learning disabled at the secondary level. With the passage of laws that would seem to dictate that the public schools provide appropriate programs for these students, it may well be that the private school programs will slowly disappear; however, it is more likely that they will simply change in the direction of serving students with more severe disabilities. In the meantime, they provide examples of what can be accomplished with the adolescent with learning disabilities.

School programs reviewed in this chapter may be grouped into two major classifications, boarding and day schools. However, it appears that some day schools are beginning to provide boarding opportunities for at least some students, and some boarding schools are beginning to provide at least limited day school type programs for some students. Each type school has its fairly obvious advantages and disadvantages.

As for generalizations about these programs, at least these few can be made:
1. Most schools tend to exclude the mentally retarded and those with severe emotional problems.
2. There are many more boys than girls in most schools.
3. An emphasis toward compensatory teaching, rather than remedial teaching, seems to be the trend as students become older.
4. A strong vocational emphasis (as opposed to academic emphasis) is common.
5. A student role in the decision regarding admission and attendance is apparently considered desirable.
6. Nonacceptance of students whose needs are not fairly consistent with the emphasis of the school is common.
7. Difficulties in social relationships with peers is almost universally recognized as the most common "second" disability of children enrolled in private schools for the learning disabled.
8. Directors of private schools for the learning disabled generally agree that the only acceptable way to make a meaningful decision about the appropriateness of a given school for a specific child is to visit that school while the school is in session.

DISCUSSION QUESTIONS

1. Contrast remedial and compensatory teaching, as implemented at The Groves Learning Center.
2. This chapter states that private schools for the handicapped are not always highly regarded by professionals in the field of education, especially by public school special educators. Explain why this is the case.
3. How do you expect P.L. 94-142 to affect the role of the private school, if at all?
4. Based on the information given in this chapter, prepare an evaluation check sheet or list of questions one might use for evaluating or comparing private schools (that is, pupil-teacher ratio, cost, and so forth) that parents or agencies could use to make inquiries or secure appropriate information.
5. Find out if there are any private schools for learning disabled students in your state. If so, secure brochures and information about the services provided.
6. Briefly list the five generalizations about private schools for learning disabled students in this chapter.

REFERENCES AND READINGS

Basic references for this chapter were program description materials and personal correspondence from the directors (headmasters, educational directors, presidents, and so forth) of the following schools:

Brush Ranch School, Tererro, N.M.
Charles River Academy, Cambridge, Mass.
Gables Academies, Miami, Fla.
The Groves Learning Center, Minnetonka, Minn.
Leary School, Inc., Falls Church, Va.
Maplebrook School, Inc., Amenia, N.Y.
Pine Ridge School, Williston, Vt.

In addition to printed material, all respondents provided answers to a series of questions. Several schools provided data on specific students (with names deleted); some were visited and/or contacted by telephone for clarifying data.

Other references

Marver, J. D. The cost of special education in nonpublic schools. *Journal of Learning Disabilities*, 1976, 9, (10), 651-660.

National Association of Private Schools, 1975 Directory, Lake Wales, Fla.

Turnbull, H. R., III. *Special education and the law: Implications for the schools.* Keynote address delivered to the Council of Administrators of Special Education (C.A.S.E.), International Convention, Chicago, Ill., April 5, 1976.

CHAPTER 11

Secondary school programs for the learning disabled in the public schools

INTRODUCTION

The traditional organization and structure of the secondary schools was outlined in Chapter 3. It was also stated that this organization and structure, plus the time-honored college preparatory goal of the schools, tend to inhibit the development of meaningful programs for secondary school learning disabled students. A study by Scranton and Downs (1975) has been cited in earlier chapters to indicate that secondary school programs for the learning disabled have not been particularly common. The fact that children who are not doing well in school can drop out of school in many states after completion of the eighth grade or at age 16 has

made it possible for some secondary schools, particularly the senior high schools, to avoid dealing with many learning disabled students. A partial accommodation to the needs of some learning disabled students through certain vocationally oriented programs that require less than normal reading ability and the efforts of some very good secondary teachers who have helped the learning disabled in spite of the system have provided meaningful programs for some students in some locations. But overall, the current situation is not an encouraging picture.

We should remember that private schools for the learning disabled have certain advantages over the public schools. They can, and do, admit *only* those students whose needs appear to be consistent with their approach(es). Boarding schools commonly have students 24 hours per day and can plan many activities during nonclass hours that directly supplement the school program. They do *not* have the problem faced by public school secondary level learning disability specialists of an administration that may not be sympathetic or supportive and teachers (who actually provide much of the learning disabled student's academic program) who are uninterested and in some cases openly hostile. They do not face varying interpretations of mainstreaming, which may cause programs to change rapidly almost overnight. They do not have to worry about "selling" parents on the need for individual assessment procedures that must precede program placement or about due process in the manner in which it must be observed in the public schools.*

As we prepare to enter the decade of the 1980s, two facts seem to be clear as they pertain to the secondary schools and learning disabled students. *First, there are not many exemplary, broad-scope secondary school programs for learning disabled students available in the public schools.* Some schools have at least one good program component and a few may have more than one, but many have "programs" that are not worthy of being called programs. Unfortunately, some schools may be able to employ an LD specialist who is poorly trained and/or equipped to deal effectively with the adolescents' needs and with the secondary school structure curriculum (because of an orientation to elementary programming), and who is unable to orchestrate the components of a program relevant to secondary LD students; yet this program may be considered to be acceptable by the local school district and may meet state regulations. The quality may be poor but legally appropriate. The situation, taken on a national scale, is discouraging, but certainly not hopeless. *Second, with the implementation of P.L. 94-142, if parents really demand good programs, something must change.* Some school districts are trying to improve, but many will wait until forced to do so. Those factors mentioned at the very start of this chapter will continue to militate against rapid development of programs, and if we add the high cost of education and the current dollar crunch being felt by school boards, it becomes clear that it will take much pressure, perhaps in the form of specific litigative efforts, to get some school boards on the move.

Fortunately, there are some schools that are making commendable efforts to develop viable secondary level programs for the learning disabled. In this chapter we will review six of these programs, which are funded by the Office of Education, Bureau of Education for the Handicapped as *Child Service Demonstration Centers* (CSDCs). We will then summarize the components that should be available to provide an effective broad-scope, secondary school program for the learning disabled. This summary will be based, for the most part, on existing programs or those we know to be in the developmental stage at this time. This summary and these descriptions, in combination with the private school descriptions presented in the preceding chapter, should provide a good idea as to what an acceptable secondary school program for the learning disabled should include.*

The Illinois Child Service Demonstration Center
Background

Evanston Township High School, Evanston, Illinois, has served some learning disabled students (enrolled in regular classes) since 1968. From 1968 to 1973, individual-

---

*This brief statement of some of the factors that add up to advantages for the private secondary school programs is provided for perspective and not to excuse the public schools for their tardiness in providing good programming for learning disabled adolescents.

*Descriptions of the following six programs are adapted from the *Catalogue of Child Service Demonstration Centers: 1975-1976*, a description of 29 Learning Disabilities Model Centers, federally funded by the Bureau of Education for the Handicapped. This catalogue was developed and published by the National Learning Disabilities Assistance Project, Merrimac, Mass.

ized programs were developed for learning disabled students on a selective basis. In 1973, in response to a school directive that specified that *all* students identified as learning disabled must be included in some type of organized program (that is, that waiting lists must be eliminated), a program reorganization was initiated. In this reorganization certain major problems were identified: (1) faculty and student schedule problems were evident, (2) age and motivational differences were apparent, and (3) personality conflicts that interfered with learning were a continuing problem. It appeared that some type of selective grouping (related to areas of deficit, level of functioning, and the first and last problems indicated above) might be the best initial approach to the problem. Although many secondary programs in Illinois are patterned after existing elementary programs, the Evanston project was initiated as an attempt to discover and/or develop definitive remedial programs and curricula that would meet the unique needs of learning disabled adolescents.

Identification/diagnosis

A screening questionnaire was sent to ninth and tenth grade English, Social Studies, and Combined Studies teachers. As a result of this screening, 120 referrals were received. Further investigation reduced this number to 100, as students were eliminated whose learning problems appeared to relate primarily to emotional problems or to poor use of the English language because of non-English speaking backgrounds. A series of staff conferences and completion of a multidisciplinary evaluation resulted in a final target group of 40 students. Evaluation included the use of standardized intelligence, reading, math, personality, and motor skill tests. Social, developmental, academic, and medical histories were also obtained. Four general diagnostic areas—intellectual potential, cognitive processing abilities, academic achievement, and personality characteristics—were considered the most important factors for establishing homogeneous instructional groupings.

Educational programming

In the Evanston program, individual educational plans, including both short-term and long-term objectives based on diagnostic data, are developed for each student. Because this federally sponsored project has research implications that dictate certain types of groupings for comparative purposes, a number of different approaches and intervention procedures are used. These include groupings with different variations in program emphasis (that is, oral receptive language, oral expressive language, word attack skills, reading comprehension, and written composition), different types of group counseling, vocational experience programs, and work with trained volunteer tutors. A curriculum committee consisting of four learning disabilities specialists has developed a variety of materials and instructional sequences. These include sequences for phonics, reading comprehension, and written expression. Difficulty levels within tasks are carefully controlled and sequenced. One goal of the program is to determine differences that might exist between three different student groups in terms of response to the various types of instruction. Criteria for these groups are discrepancy between verbal and performance scores on the WISC, ability level as determined by the WISC, and areas of language deficit.

Among other goals of this project is that of finding better ways to determine when students should be enrolled in such a program and when they should be taken out of such a program. For those with borderline disabilities, the questions "How much is enough?" and "When do special efforts reach the point of diminishing returns?" are most important. The question of termination is quite important in any multifaceted program; many times a student may be ready for termination from one program component, but requires much more effort in another. In this program, a formative evaluator instructs teachers in methods of evaluation that relate to various learning areas, as well as to the entire instructional sequence.

Other program features

Students from Northwestern University serve as tutorial volunteers and receive valuable experience in working with the learning disabled. Learning disabilities specialists carefully direct such efforts to make certain that Evanston High School students are receiving the best possible instructional/remedial program. Parents are highly involved with the project (even though typical high schools often do not have active parent participation except perhaps in competitive sports) and regular parent and parent-student conferences, are held. An advisory council has been appointed consisting of local personnel, resource personnel from the state office of education, the state legislature, the University of Illinois, and parent groups. This council meets every 2 months to review project progress, make suggestions regarding existing problems, and recommend procedures for the ongoing program.

Summary

The learning disabilities demonstration center at Evanston Township High School, Evanston, Illinois, features selective grouping practices and the development of a curriculum based on the diagnosed needs of learning disabled students at the school. This model serves grades 10 and 11, but may be expanded in the near future. As a federally funded model center, the expectation is that the model will be replicated elsewhere in Illinois. The program emphasizes selective grouping of learning disabled adolescents for remediation, the use of locally developed (or modified) materials, and a curriculum designed to be more appealing to the students than the standard curriculum and related materials. Special emphasis is given to phonics, visual memory and perceptual skills, auditory/intrasensory processing, spelling, and written expression.

The Iowa Child Service Demonstration Center

Background

Des Moines, Iowa has had learning disabilities programs for some time, but it was determined that the resource room/mainstreaming approach that was successful for many learning disabled adolescents was not significantly beneficial to some of the more severely disabled students. As a result, the *Career Laboratories Utilizing Experience* (CLUE) program was conceptualized.

Identification/diagnosis

All students that are in the CLUE model program have been in the regular learning disabilities program and thus have gone through extensive screening and diagnostic procedures. Thus, only when the "regular" learning disabilities program is not effective, may the student be considered as a candidate for the CLUE program. Referral may come from either regular classroom teachers or from the resource room learning disabilities specialist. Adjustment, communication, or social problems, which are believed to have resulted from the basic learning problem, are a part of the total description of the CLUE student. A multidisciplinary team reviews all available records and information and determines whether the CLUE program is needed by the student. If the decision is affirmative, the normal, due process procedures are completed and the student becomes a part of the career-oriented CLUE program.

Educational programming

After admission to the CLUE program, the student is given additional diagnostic tests and an appropriate placement level is determined for the various academic and skills areas. Then, in cooperative planning with the laboratory teacher, students choose electives from the regular school program that they believe will be most interesting and consistent with their skills. The laboratory teacher may play both a consultative and a directive role in assisting the student to make realistic mainstream program choices. After the teacher and the student have arrived at what appears to them to be a meaningful (tentative) educational plan, this plan is discussed with parents and prospective employer(s). Specific curriculum guides have been developed to assist in curriculum/program planning, and a series of 20 project-developed minicourses are available as needed. These courses include a range of topics in language, mathematics, and social studies and were developed with the needs and skill levels of the more severely learning disabled in mind. Also included in the guides (primarily for regular classroom teachers who work with these students part-time) is a description of deficit areas commonly encountered and various approaches that may be effective in given situations.

After an individual curriculum plan has been established for each student, progress at the most rapid "comfortable" rate is encouraged. In addition to the career laboratory curriculum, the teacher plans an actual work experience for each student. Seventh and eighth grade students are placed in community service settings with a minimum of two different experiences each academic year. Ninth grade students are given job exposure experiences in the form of interviews, field trips, and internship placements. Senior high students are placed in at least two actual jobs each year. The emphasis in these varied placements is on retraining procedures and the ability to adapt to change. The goal of this program is placement, at the senior level, into occupational settings that provide opportunity for horizontal or vertical movement and advancement.

Continual student evaluation takes place in reading, mathematics, behavior, and actual job performance. Standardized tests and established checklists provide much of the evaluative data, the latter being made quite meaningful through excellent cooperation with local employers. Social and emotional coping skills are evaluated by the laboratory teacher based on his or her observations and a composite of observations from employers and regular classroom teachers.

Many students remain in the CLUE program through the senior high level and complete school with assured initial employment. Others may gradually return to the regular learning disabilities resource room and to more mainstream class programs; however, support services are provided during the transition.

Other program features

A parent advisory council was organized at the request of the Des Moines School Board. Composed of parents of both elementary and secondary level learning disabled youngsters, it provides wide and valuable representation and grass roots level input. Expansion of the CLUE program, based on observed growth in students, particularly in behavioral and school participation areas, is underway. A board of consultants from the business community and from social service agencies provides regular assistance to CLUE. Their efforts in suggesting and facilitating the provision of work experience have been a key factor in program success.

Summary

The Iowa CLUE project, located in Des Moines, is an interesting example of a program established for students with severe learning disabilities—those who were "failing" in the regular school program and in the regular learning disabilities resource room program. Students in this program have all the usual characteristics of the learning disabled plus one more—they have been unsuccessful in the learning disabilities program that has apparently been effective with many other learning disabled students. Program goals include improvement in basic academic skills, increased knowledge of occupation-related information, and improvement in social and emotional coping ability. These goals are pursued through carefully designed instructionally and occupationally related experience. Instructional activities center around a group of locally designed minicourses and are supplemented by selected mainstream courses and work experience in the community. A variety of supplementary services and excellent cooperation with the local business community are essential components of the CLUE program. Some students remain in the program through high school graduation, and many of them leave school with assured initial employment. Other students show marked improvement after 1 or 2 years of the CLUE program and are slowly moved back toward a more traditional secondary program with supportive help as needed. In a manner similar to that in which one state has special programs for the gifted and programs for "the highly gifted," Des Moines has learning disabilities programs for the "learning disabled" and for the "severely learning disabled." As more school systems attempt to comply with the requirements of P.L. 94-142, it seems likely that they too will need to provide at least two variations of a learning disabilities program in secondary schools.

The Kansas Child Service Demonstration Center
Background

The state plan in Kansas in the area of specific learning disabilities indicates that direct services should be provided for learning disabled students who, it is estimated, comprise 3% of the school age population. A need for unique educational programming provisions for the secondary age learning disabilities population is noted in the state plan. A proposal for a model demonstration center was submitted by the Kansas City Schools, and the program was approved to begin during the 1975-1976 school year. Adequate state and local funds are available to guarantee continuation of the program after the termination of federal funding. Staff members from the special education department at the University of Kansas are interested in the program and have been of assistance from the beginning. Their interest relates to a general concern with programs for children with learning disabilities and a specific interest in secondary level learning disabilities programs because of their special sequence of study to prepare teachers to teach the adolescent learning disabled student.

Identification/diagnosis

Students are initially brought to the attention of the project staff through teacher referral or self-referral. This *student request for enrollment* feature is an important component of the Kansas City program. The referral form requests information about hyperactivity, distractibility, poor self-concept, and other similar factors usually associated with learning disabilities. Skill levels in lan-

guage and math must also be indicated. The CSDC staff reviews the form, gathers some additional information if required, and then determines whether further evaluation is justified. Regardless of the source of referral, student participation in the program is voluntary and parents must give permission for the extensive evaluation that precedes actual program entry.

Standardized tests are used to establish basic skill levels; any student who scores at the grade 5 level or below may be considered as exhibiting a severe learning disability, if otherwise eligible. The other basic requisite for program admission is a score of 85 or above on an appropriate, standardized test of intelligence.

Educational programming

The educational program for each student is individual, based on diagnosis and evaluation, and aided by another unique group, the Advocate Committee, which permits and encourages interaction between school administrators, regular classroom teachers, and learning disabilities staff. The Committee makes suggestions regarding management of classroom adjustment problems, student placement, and program alternatives. It consists of regular faculty members who have expressed an interest in the learning disabilities program and have agreed to act as faculty representatives of various subject areas, the school nurse, and a school counselor. Learning disabilities staff members regularly meet with this group. Educational intervention includes a prescription containing three components: deficits determined through diagnostic efforts, materials and programming suggestions for each deficit area listed, and objectives for each area. Each student's contract is established on a weekly basis and lists assignments and objectives for that week. Once the weekly prescription is established and discussed with the student, he may work on his assignment on an independent basis except as he requires individual help. The total program includes this prescription, which is related to academic and skills areas, modification of mainstream classes in most cases, and an exploration of career opportunities, which is not a part of the basic, regular secondary school program. Functional reading and math, attention to social and emotional development, and careful weekly monitoring are important parts of the program. Services of this program continue as long as the student appears to need them, and are terminated when the student's level of achievement permits successful, total reintegration in the regular school program.

Other program features

An Advisory Council composed of four parents, one business person, two educators, and a representative of the State Department of Education meets formally three times each year, and individual members provide regular input through periodic consultation with project staff. Job experiences for the students are obtained with assistance from the Advisory Council and other school staff members. Such experience is planned on an individual basis with each student, as is consistent with his level of readiness and personal need. A multifaceted information dissemination program includes efforts of University of Kansas Special Education staff members who act as consultants and present program descriptions throughout the state, the Community Information coordinator, and members of the Advisory Council.

Summary

The Kansas Child Service Demonstration Center is located in Harmon High School in Kansas City, Kansas and serves learning disabled adolescents, ages 12 to 17. The basic strategy of the Kansas CSDC model is to develop a balanced program of individualized instruction and modification of mainstream classes and curriculum. Emphasis on study skills, work habits, and social and emotional adjustment is combined with concern for basic skill acquisition, functional reading skills, and functional math skills. A diagnostic-prescriptive model is used to identify and assess needs, and a weekly contract relating to deficits and specific objectives is utilized. Appropriate materials and programming are

an integral part of the remedial program that is developed individually for each child. The Kansas City CSDC is presently being replicated in a number of areas of the state.

The Louisiana Child Service Demonstration Center
Background

The Louisiana CSDC grew out of the need to develop more effective services for learning disabled students in isolated areas of Louisiana, Arkansas, and Mississippi. School systems in this tri-state area identified the need for more learning disabilities programming, especially at the secondary school level, and project HOLD (Helping Operation in Learning Disabilities) was developed under the leadership of staff members at the Special Education Center at Northeast Louisiana University and the administration of the Ouachita Parish schools. Four school systems in the area were involved in the original planning and implementation of this project, which includes providing services for learning disabled adolescents at four different levels of intensity of service. The four project sites are in the Ouachita Parish School System—Calhoun High School, Riser Junior High School, Richwood High School, and West Monroe High School. The Northeast Louisiana University Reading Laboratory provides the setting for remedial service to the most severely disabled.

Identification/diagnosis

Students who appear to their teachers to be having learning difficulties are screened as a basis for further investigation. Those who show evidence of average, above average, or potentially average intelligence, combined with a 2-year or greater discrepancy between the apparent level of mental maturity and the level of achievement, are referred for further individual diagnostic evaluation. This evaluation is provided by NLU diagnosticians. Another source of referral is the existing files at the NLU center, which identify students in the target schools who have been previously diagnosed as learning disabled. (It is not assumed that these students are *still* learning disabled, but their names are included for further diagnosis.) All state guidelines regarding parent permission, due process, and the like are strictly adhered to.

Diagnosis includes information provided by a social worker, a psychologist, a speech and hearing clinician, and an educational consultant. The *social worker* interviews parents and other significant adults in the student's environment to determine developmental information, level of adaptive behavior, and any indication of pathology within the primary environment. The *psychologist* assesses intellectual and perceptual motor abilities, adaptive behavior, and personality. The *speech and hearing clinician* conducts a puretone threshold hearing evaluation, speech reception threshold tests, and tests for auditory discrimination. Additional evaluation of communication disorders, as appropriate in individual cases, is also accomplished. Articulation, vocal quality, fluency, and receptive and expressive language levels are investigated. The *educational consultant* administers diagnostic and achievement instruments appropriate for the determination of specific difficulties and levels of achievement in basic skills and basic academic areas. The information gained from diagnostic efforts of this interdisciplinary team become the basis for educational planning. After integration of these various findings, and the development of specific program recommendations, they are reviewed and interpreted for parents.

Educational programming

The educational program is actually a series of four programs ranging from one that provides no special setting instruction to one in which half the day is spent in a special, clinical setting, with much of the instruction on a one-to-one basis. There may be some overlap from program to program. The outline below indicates the essential differences between the four levels of instructional assistance. In essence, each school provides for one of these program alternatives.

A system of objectives in reading presented at the World Congress on Dyslexia in

Program alternatives—Louisiana CSDC

Level I	Regular classroom instruction (with no special class or resource room instruction) utilizing specific suggestions and materials as provided by/through the project.	Students less than 2 years behind academic expectations.
Level II	Resource room 1 hour per day. Academic skills taught in a group of 16 to 18 students. Focus on remediation of specific skills. Remainder of day in regular classroom.	Students who are 3 years behind academic expectations.
Level III	Part-day remediation in small groups (five or less) and much individualized instruction. Emphasis on skill subjects. Remainder of the day (half-day) spent in regular class, but in subjects that require a minimum of written work.	Students who are 3 years behind academic expectations.
Level IV	Clinical instruction at the Northeast Louisiana University Reading Laboratory for half of the school day. The other half-day is spent in the regular school setting with very careful selection of classes. All clinic instruction is on a one-to-one basis.	Students who are the most severely disabled— 4 or more years behind academic expectations.

1974 and the IRIS Reading System are used as the basis for modules that have been developed by project staff. Various commercially prepared materials are used as they seem appropriate to the defined needs of individuals. A project developed system is used in the area of mathematics, and a staff artist, under the direction of staff specialists and with suggestions from teachers, assists in the production of modified materials that supplement commercial materials.

Other program features

One major function of HOLD is to retrain teachers who already hold Master of Education degrees to serve as resource persons in schools or educational consultants in clinical settings. The advisory council of project HOLD meets monthly to plan workshops, provide suggestions to the project staff, and assist in promotion of the project as a replicable model. This council includes the president of the local Association for Children with Learning Disabilities (ACLD), a pediatrician, a psychologist, dentists, an optometrist, a judge, ministers, and university professors. Expansion plans are ambitious and appear to be materializing satisfactorily.

Summary

HOLD, a model project designed to provide insight into the most effective way to serve the needs of learning disabled adolescents in isolated areas of Louisiana, Arkansas, and Mississippi, is in fact a four-level project. Located in the Ouachita Parish school system, and working in conjunction with Northeast Louisiana University, HOLD provides program components ranging from one in which the students are placed full-time in the regular classroom (with suggestions and materials from project staff) to one in which the most severely disabled are served through a half-day, one-to-one clinic setting. With what appears to be very strong local support and very active participation from Northeast Louisiana University, this project also involves more direct teacher training efforts than many of the other CSDC projects. Although not regularly called diagnostic-prescriptive in nature, HOLD has most of the components that usually lead to such a designation.

The Oklahoma Child Service Demonstration Centers
Background

Programs for the learning disabled were first started in Tulsa, Oklahoma in the early 1960s, through funds provided by the Tulsa Education Foundation. This early programming was a direct result of strong parent interest, which was also the major factor in the provision of learning disabilities programs in Oklahoma City a few years later. The Oklahoma State Association for Children with Learning Disabilities (ACLD) has been very active since the mid 1960s and was a major factor in the passage of mandatory services in 1970 for the learning disabled. As in most other states, the first programming was in larger population areas and was primarily for elementary aged children. Thus the major need (in addition to improvement of existing programs) is now recognized to be in secondary programs and in provision of viable programs in rural areas. The Oklahoma Child Service Demonstration Centers are designed to serve this latter need—secondary programming in rural areas—and are currently located in Cushing, Drumright, Perkins, Ripley, Stroud, and Yale, Oklahoma.

Identification/diagnosis

Prospective students for these programs are identified through referral by teachers, counselors, administrators, parents, or, in some cases, self-referral. A careful review of the results of standardized achievement tests is a major procedural approach, but serves primarily as the "triggering" device for further investigation. If a student is four or more grade levels below his present grade placement in reading, spelling, arithmetic, or social studies, further diagnosis may be initiated. Such students are given a psychoeducational evaluation and specialized perceptual or personality tests. Classroom teachers complete a pupil behavior rating scale and the student is interviewed by the school psychologist. A multidisciplinary team reviews the composite results of these various evaluative tools and techniques in a case conference setting. Participants in this conference are the project director, school psychologist, counselor, reading specialist, learning disabilities specialist, prescriptive teachers, and resource room teachers. Physicians and optometrists are called in as appropriate in specific cases.

Educational programming

The Oklahoma model is a diagnostic-prescriptive, intervention model. It is individualized, with the content of the curriculum different for each student. Both cognitive and affective functioning are considered, and prescriptions are evaluated biweekly with program alterations as necessary. Major use is made of programmed, multisensory reinforcement, and considerable media equipment and materials are available. The Regional Special Education Instructional Materials Center (SEIMC) provides specialized materials in addition to those regularly available in the resource room, one of which is located in each of the six small secondary schools in the project. Each resource room has such basic teaching aids as tape recorders and overhead projectors, and various media units are used extensively.

The six-system CSDC includes full-time resource room teachers in the resource rooms located in each of the schools, a diagnostic prescriptive team composed of a psychoeducational evaluator and two teachers with master's degrees in learning disabilities (who serve all six schools), a full-time project director, several part-time consultants, and several volunteer tutors who work under the direction of the resource room teachers and the two learning disabilities teachers. Advanced practicum students from Oklahoma State University provide a variety of services as prescribed and supervised by project staff.

The individual program for any given student may relate to visual or auditory dysfunctions, to difficulties with recall and memory, or to other specific areas or types of disability. The main strength of the program is its individualization—individualization in remedial efforts, compensatory efforts, regular class program in which the student is involved, percentage of day he is served in the resource room, length of program, amount of one-to-one tutorial service, and type and amount of personal counseling provided. The biweekly prescription evaluation and redirection (as needed) makes this individualization unusually effective. Each student is considered separately as regards program termination. As soon as an individual student appears to be able to function without outside help and after careful consideration of all related factors—consideration that includes explanation of the situation to both students and parents, the program may be terminated. For some students, such termination may occur after several months' service; for others the special educational service must be continued throughout their entire secondary school careers.

Other program features

In addition to positive benefits to students served, one project of the Oklahoma CSDC, a comprehensive catalogue of materials that is available and appropriate for use by secondary level learning disabled students has been utilized in many school districts in many states. Research with biofeedback training and a group counseling program have produced apparently beneficial results (in terms of academic gains) in efforts that undoubtedly will be replicated by other projects in forms that are consistent with their approach(es).

Summary

In Oklahoma, six centers have been established in small school districts in an attempt to develop effective programming for small secondary schools in rural or semirural areas of the state. Participation in the project depends on the student being four or more grade levels below expected grade placement in reading, spelling, arithmetic, or social studies. A diagnostic-prescriptive model, this program is based on both cognitive and affective functioning and prescriptions are reviewed biweekly and modified and/or continued as appropriate. A full-time resource room teacher serves in each of the six districts, assisted by a director, two full-time teachers with master's degrees in learning disabilities, a psychoeducational evaluator, and part-time consultants from nearby universities. Advanced practicum students also work in the project under the direction of the classroom teachers and with the advice and assistance of the learning disabilities teachers. The program is highly individualized with both remedial and compensatory components applied as dictated in individual cases.

The Texas Child Service Demonstration Centers
Background

Learning disabilities was officially recognized as part of special education in Texas in 1970. Two years after the initiation of learning disabilities programs in the state, there were over 100 school districts with learning disabilities programs but only three had programs especially designed for the secondary level. Based on this information, the Texas Education Agency established a development, demonstration, and service program in Corsicana, Texas. (This program was established in cooperation with four other agencies and with funds provided by the Bureau of Education for the Handicapped of the U.S. Office of Education.) This original program involved in-depth individual appraisal of students and transportable instructional materials for language arts, mathematics, and science. *Project Echo* was established in 1974 to replicate the Corsicana model in five other sites, ranging from urban to rural and representative of a cross section of the Texas school population. Plano and Greenville are suburbs of Dallas, Galveston is a coastal city, Laredo is a border town with a large Mexican-American population, and the West Central Texas Education Cooperative includes three small towns on the Texas Great Plains.

Identification/diagnosis

Initial screening includes standardized intelligence and achievement tests, grade records, absentee records, and other pertinent school records. Sensory screening is accomplished to determine which students may have sensory deficits as the primary disability. Some students are identified through the time-tested procedure of teacher referral.

Over 100 students are identified at each site who are significantly underachieving and who have no sensory deficits. With parental permission (as required by state regulations), in-depth appraisal takes place. Those students who best meet the eligibility requirements are recommended to the Admission Review and Dismissal Committee at each school. This committee is typically composed of the principal, a diagnostician, a resource teacher, a regular classroom teacher, and the local project (site) coordinator. This group meets with the parents of each student considered for admission and often meets with the student. When all agree, the student is placed in Project Echo.

Educational programming

Each of the sites is staffed by a coordinator, three instructional personnel, two teacher aides, and a secretary. The teachers are learning disabilities specialists with specialties in language arts, mathematics, and science. The learning disabilities teachers work directly with Echo students within the regular class setting. In addition, assistance is provided in resource rooms located at each site. Thirty minimodules—10 each in language arts, mathematics, and science—are included in the program. In addition to these three academic areas, the multimedia materials are directed at auditory or visual learning abilities and at multisensory learning abilities. These minimodules are used in addition to commercial materials selected as required to meet the needs of individual students.

Each minimodule, during its development, was systematically reviewed and evaluated regarding cultural fairness, appropriateness as a learning disabilities teaching tool, and general pedagogical soundness. Each has been revised as necessary. The Southwest Educational Development Laboratory in Austin has worked with both the original Corsicana project and Project Echo in the development and evaluation of materials. Each minimodule includes pretests and posttests to indicate student progress and sequenced mastery tests that permit self-pacing on the part of the students. Students normally proceed through all of the modules, but may spend varying amounts of time per day or week in this specific facet of the program. The Project is best described as diagnostic-prescriptive, and it utilizes task analysis and contingency contracting in attempting to provide maximum success for students. For most students, the program is primarily a mainstream program with resource room support. For some, particularly those with severe learning disabilities, the program uses total resource room intervention as long as necessary.

Other program features

One of the more important outcomes of this program has been the minimodules mentioned in the preceding section. Additionally, there are two orientation and training modules for staff and teacher development. To the greatest extent possible, these minimodules are used by the regular classroom teacher within the regular class setting. In addition to training at the five sites, Project Echo conducts a statewide training program to assist teachers to understand and use project developed materials. Another interesting facet of the Texas program is the involvement of the Texas Rehabilitation Commission in a program of occupational orientation at the project schools. This activity, in addition to providing assistance for the students, is helpful in orienting the personnel of the Rehabilitation Commission to the needs and the abilities of the learning disabled population. In turn, they play a role in informing the business community with which they regularly deal.

Summary

Project Echo, the Texas CSDC, is located in five cities in Texas. This project is actually an "echo" of an earlier, federally sponsored project at Corsicana, Texas. It is a diagnostic-prescriptive program that uses task analysis and behavior modification (contingency contracts) in an attempt to provide maximum academic success for the secondary learning disabled student. A highly valuable product

of this project is the set of 30, highly exportable minimodules in the areas of language arts, mathematics, and science. There are three learning disabilities teachers at each project site who specialize in these three academic areas. As much as possible, students pursue these minimodules within the regular class setting, but, as needed, additional help is provided in the resource room. Texas, like many other states, initiated programs for the learning disabled, discovered that nearly all were structured for elementary age children, and then had to provide secondary level programs. Project Echo, because of the relative ease of replication of program structure and the high degree of exportability of its basic teaching modules, is an ideal program for use throughout the state.

ESSENTIAL COMPONENTS IN THE ESTABLISHMENT OF EFFECTIVE, BROAD-SCOPE, SECONDARY PROGRAMS FOR THE LEARNING DISABLED

Establishment of an effective program for the various types and degrees of learning disabilities that may be found in a large high school population, taking into consideration the various levels of motivation, ability, earlier training, and vocational goals of the students involved, is a complex task. However, it is possible, and if the intent of existing state and federal legislation is to be recognized and realized, it must be accomplished. Rather than describe an idealized program in lengthy narration, we will outline the components and subcomponents that should be included in such a program. In some cases we refer to earlier sections of this text for a more complete explanation of the component. In other instances we will describe the component in considerable detail in this section.

Trained, specialized personnel

In a smaller high school, it is possible that one learning disabilities specialist *who is very well trained and who is familiar with the secondary school* (preferably an individual who has taught regular classes in the secondary school) will be all the *full-time*, special staff that is required. This one specialist may be enough *if:* (1) there is a good attitude on the part of the rest of the staff, (2) there is adequate diagnostic assistance available, and (3) there is someone else who can and will help with career education components and with work-experience placements. There must be the services (part-time will do in most instances) of a qualified diagnostician, of a secondary school counselor who is well informed regarding learning disabilities and is willing to "go the extra mile" in scheduling and in planning with the total staff, and of a special education administrator to represent the program with the central administration and to ensure provision of an adequate budget.

In larger high schools, there may be the need for two to four learning disabilities specialists, each assigned to specific subject areas and each responsible for assisting regular classroom teachers in providing adapted programs in the regular classroom and for teaching some modified classes for those students whose learning difficulties are too great

to permit inclusion in the regular class in certain academic areas. In such schools there will likely be the need for a full-time teacher to teach the career education components within the school and to plan, coordinate, and supervise the work-experience placements. It is also possible, though not too common, that there will be a need for one teacher to instruct the severely learning disabled (who may also be hyperactive, have moderate emotional problems, and so forth) in a class setting that is essentially self-contained.

Program, subject, skill area components

The program must make specific provision for adaptation and accommodation, plus remedial components for at least some students. The major emphasis should be toward compensatory teaching (as opposed to remedial teaching), and the total range of accommodative techniques outlined on pp. 85-99 should be utilized. Specific remedial efforts may be beneficial in some instances, particu-

larly as directed toward learning certain practical skills, but for the most part the program emphasis must be that of effectively using existing skills. (Note that such skills as knowing how to take lecture notes more effectively and how to prepare for tests are *not* considered remedial. These do not remediate reading difficulties. They *do* permit more effective use of reading skills already developed, and, insofar as they may build academic self-confidence, they may assist in the development of higher level reading skills.)

Vocational/occupational readiness must be an integral part of the program and should be provided at two levels. Information *about* jobs, how to apply for jobs, job futures, and the like must be deliberately *taught* on a purely informational level. This should be accomplished in separate job/career oriented modules of instruction and should also be included as a part of other academic areas when possible. At a more advanced level, *students must learn about jobs by working.* For the learning disabled student, this may be one of the most important aspects of the secondary school program. Some learning disabled students will go on to college, and some will go on to advanced vocational/technical programs after high school. But many will *not* go on after high school graduation, and they need specific help in integrating information they possess about the world of work. They need to *experience* what is required of them in employment. Where this type of program has been included in secondary level programming for the learning disabled, it has proved to be of significant value.

Subject area content and emphasis must be determined on an individual basis. Factors to consider include: (1) specific requirements for graduation, (2) basic skill strengths and deficits of the student, (3) educational/vocational goals of the student, (4) existing course structure and content (what is already provided by other teachers in the school) including *what is taught, how the teacher teaches*, and *how he or she accepts learning disabled students*, (5) how, and in which courses, the special classroom teacher can provide materials, learning modules, and

other services to the regular classroom teacher to permit adaptation within the regular class, and (6) which courses or elements must be taught by the learning disabilities teacher on a segregated, special program basis.

Diagnosis, assessment, and reassessment

Diagnosis of basic strengths and weaknesses is essential. If a student is to benefit from special program placement, as much as possible about their level of basic skill development, academic area strengths and weaknesses, and personality assets and liabilities must be known. In addition, there must be regular reassessment of the present level of development in certain of these areas as the basis for program redirection. Some reassessment is needed at least weekly; some of the better secondary school learning disabilities programs complete such reassessment biweekly in academic and basic skill areas.

Such assessment is of limited value if it leads only to statements of grade level achievement in mathematics or reading or if it is primarily a compilation of facts about strengths and weaknesses. *Diagnosis and assessment is important for use as the basis for establishing goals (for longer periods of time) and objectives (for short-term emphasis and focus) that become the basic program guides.*

Special materials and equipment

Traditionally, the high school orders materials, library books, equipment, and the like on the basis of some standard budget ratio and in relation to the presumed reading and mathematics level (or range) of students in the regular school program. For the learning disabled student, these materials and library books are likely to be inappropriate. These students must have materials that fit *their level*, and this may require special budgetary provision. High school administrators may dislike spending what they see as a disproportionate amount of their total budget on a limited number of students who may be regarded as the school misfits. However, if there is a special budget provided for this purpose, the entire program will be somewhat easier to "sell." In a similar manner, the high school "standard equipment list" is not likely to provide one tape recorder for each student enrolled, but this may be a real need for many of the learning disabled students. This type of equipment, just like the materials and books, must be specifically provided. (A blind student may be provided a tape recorder almost automatically for it is obvious that he cannot learn through the visual channel. The learning disabled student may also need a tape recorder, but there are so many more learning disabled students and their need is not so obvious, so specific budgetary authorizations must be made.)

Motivational efforts, including reward systems

Careful attention should be given to the motivational aspects of the program. With lowered self-esteem, which is almost certain to exist in the learning disabled adolescent, any system that will give the student a *reason* to try or a motivation to attempt to overcome the failure syndrome should be carefully considered. Some teachers have difficulty believing that a student who is, for example, the class clown, can feel so insecure in the academic area. The clowning is obviously a compensatory activity, and the degree to which this activity convinces the teacher that the student is "secure" is often a direct measure of the strong need to compensate for academic deficiencies.

A variety of reward systems and contracts are available and effective at the secondary level. These systems are outlined and discussed on pp. 120-145. In all cases, these systems or techniques are most effective when used in conjunction with other approaches. The goal is to assist the student to demonstrate to himself and to the teacher that he can succeed. But we must know enough about the student, his present level of abilities, and his academic needs to make the tasks that are assigned appropriate and within the range of possibility.

In-service efforts

Assistance from the entire school staff (or at least from a majority of the staff) is highly important. To accomplish this, in-service efforts are of value, but timing is of the essence. *Imposed in-service will probably be ineffective or even counterproductive.* With cooperation from the administration and with the application of a reward system (applied to the rest of the staff), perhaps the situation can be manipulated to have other staff members, or department heads, request such in-service. One possible alternative is giving college credit or salary schedule credit through an extension course with coordinated efforts of a nearby college or university. If the learning disabilities specialist can provide certain needed materials for some classroom teachers, the word will soon get around and another type of in-service can be implemented.

In conversations with secondary school learning disabilities specialists, we have heard that when the teacher can demonstrate success with a few students, success that is obvious to the regular classroom teacher, then an informal, in-service type relationship can often be established (see the case study on pp. 142-144). At any rate, some type of in-service is essential, but the type and the timing of such efforts must be tailored to the individual situation.

Advisory groups

There are many types of advisory groups as illustrated by the six programs outlined in this chapter. An advisory group within the school can prove to be of assistance in establishing the in-service efforts recommended in the previous program component description. If advisory groups are composed primarily of those individuals who have a genuine interest in providing meaningful programs for the learning disabled, it can be assumed that they will be of positive public relations value. Within the school, one member from each major academic department should be chosen to serve as spokesperson for the learning disabilities program within each department. As these individuals become involved in learning more about learning disabilities and in making program recommendations, which inevitably involve interrelationships with others in the school, academic requirements, granting of credit, and so forth, many will become advocates for the learning disabilities program. The old adage about familiarity and contempt does *not* apply here. Instead, familiarity leads to understanding, which leads to at least limited support. This of course assumes that the program is worthy of support.

In addition to an advisory group of educators from within each secondary school, there should be an advisory group that represents the entire local system and deliberately represents elementary and secondary schools, teachers, administrators, and parents. This is essential in providing continued feedback on program articulation. If the programs at the elementary and the secondary level are not conducted to be complementary, children will suffer. Therefore, this advisory group must focus on how the total system functions with particular attention to any program gaps or disharmony.

Other advisory groups are also important. A community advisory group dealing primarily with work-experience and work placement needs is essential. In some instances this should be a separate committee or task force, but in many cases the community-wide advisory committee has a subcommittee that relates specifically to job experiences, job placement, and the like.

In addition to local advisory groups, representation on state level groups can be of value, particularly as the state groups may effect new state regulations or pending legislation. The degree of involvement at this level depends on a number of factors that are too complex to attempt to analyze here. Many of these are political and may be best analyzed with the assistance of the local special education director.

The key word is "involvement"; involvement of other educators, involvement of business leaders, and involvement of parents. There may also be certain local leaders who do not "fit" any of the three categories just mentioned, but who can become major contributors to the success of the program. They too should be provided a way in which to become involved.

Learning disabilities programs in the secondary schools can be successful, but most learning disabilities authorities seem to agree that programming for the adolescent with learning disabilities is more complex and involves many more established "road blocks" than programming at the elementary school level. Careful planning, with wise use of the components outlined in this section, can lead to success for the learning disabled student in the secondary school. This is the mandate of P.L. 94-142 and of many existing state laws. This is the duty and responsibility of educators. Special educators, because of their unique and specialized training, must lead the way.

DISCUSSION QUESTIONS

1. Compare and contrast the identification and diagnostic procedures, including referral processes, of each of the Child Service Demonstration Centers summarized in this chapter.
2. Study the means of delivery of services (educational programming) of the six Child Service Demonstration Centers summarized in this chapter. Compare and contrast the role of the resource room teacher in each of these.
3. List and briefly discuss the value of the six components considered by the authors to be essential to the establishment of effective secondary programs for learning disabled students.
4. Expand on the distinction made by the authors between the role of the learning disability specialist in a small school and in a large school.
5. What factors would be (or should be) involved in your selection of an advisory board? That is, how would you select your board, who might be included, and for what reasons?

REFERENCES AND READINGS

Catalogue of Child Service Demonstration Centers: 1975-1976, Merrimac, Mass., The National Learning Disabilities Assistance Project, The Network, 1976.

Scranton, T., and Downs, M. Elementary and secondary learning disabilities programs in the U.S.: A survey, *Journal of Learning Disabilities*, 1975, 8(6), 394-399.

CHAPTER 12

Postsecondary education for the learning disabled

INTRODUCTION

While this book was in the planning stage, it seemed obvious that there should be some discussion of postsecondary education for the learning disabled student. It seemed likely that there would not be a large amount of information through which to sift to determine just what would be included. But because other authors had mentioned college level programs for the learning disabled, because there was a national directory of college programs for the learning disabled, and because there are special provisions for high school students with special needs to enter many colleges, we assumed that there would be sufficient information for a separate chapter. We were wrong! Although there is not really enough to warrant a chapter with similar scope and content as the others in this book, we decided to include this discussion primarily to point out this area of need. We will indicate what is presently available and will speculate as to why such programs are so limited. We will also suggest types of programs that may be effective, but we ask the reader to recognize that these suggestions are based on current conditions and the current level of development of secondary programs. We will *not* do any more than this, for to do so would truly be much ado about nothing.

POSTSECONDARY PROGRAMS NOW IN OPERATION

A differentiation between *programs available*, inferring some *special provision* for the learning disabled, and *schools that will admit the learning disabled*, indicating only that the learning disabled student *will be admitted*, must be made at the outset. The existence of *A National Directory of Four-Year Colleges, Two-Year Colleges, and Post-High School Training Programs for Young People with Learning Disabilities* (Fielding, 1975) would lead one to believe that there are many programs that recognize the special needs of the student with learning disabilities and that provide special programs and services that assist the student to learn effectively, despite the learning disabilities. This directory is a useful reference source, and the Department of Special Education at East Texas State University and the Association for Children with Learning Disabilities (both of which were involved in the original 1971 version of this publication) provided a valuable service in making this information available. However, later studies have indicated that many colleges, junior colleges, and technical schools apparently do little more than agree to let learning disabled students in the front door. Stated another way, these schools (at least when they were originally surveyed) will admit the learning disabled, some provide some special help for such students, and a few have someone on the college staff who has special training in learning disabilities. These conclusions may be drawn from two studies of these institutions, conducted since the original publication of the directory in 1971. The first, by Wells (1973), involved a questionnaire that was sent to the chairpersons of the English departments of 387 of the 4-year and 2-year colleges listed in the 1971 directory. Wells received 153 responses, and, along with other information, it was discovered that only 20 of these 153 schools indicated that they had a staff member with special training in learning disabilities. This, of course, does *not* mean that the other schools did not have adequate special programs, but since the study related to writing

skills, and experience indicates that this is a major problem encountered by learning disabled students in college, it would seem to imply that organized efforts by college staff members who are knowledgeable in the area of learning disabilities are few and far between.

A second study by May (1977) was a follow-up of one segment of the Wells study. This study was to determine whether special services were being provided and, if so, what type. Fifteen of the 20 colleges listed in the Wells study as having a staff member trained in learning disabilities replied to the May questionnaire. Of the 15 that responded, four, or 27%, indicated that they had no special program for the learning disabled student. We do not know about those that did not reply to this request for information, but would wonder how many have established programs.

The May study did lead to information regarding services that are provided by the 11 schools that indicated that they provide a special program. Those services included the following:

Counseling services available to (diagnosed) learning disabled students

	Number of schools	*Percent*
Special program planning assistance	8	73
Selection of instructors who indicate a willingness to work with the learning disabled student	7	64
Special counseling to assist the student to learn to manifest appropriate behavioral characteristics in the classroom	10	91

Special provisions made for poor readers

	Number of schools	*Percent*
Taped textbooks	3	27
Readers	4	36
Cassettes for recording class notes	8	73
Tutorial assistance	10	91

Instruction by learning disabilities specialist	1	9
Instruction by reading specialist	2	18

Special provisions in the testing situation for learning disabled students

	Number of schools	Percent
Oral testing	8	73
Readers	4	36
Use of typewriters	3	27
Taped tests and allowance for taped responses	1	9

In terms of counseling services available, it is noteworthy that all but one of the schools provided special counseling to assist the student to learn how to "act" in the classroom. This could be interpreted in a number of ways and without precise information about what exactly took place in such counseling sessions, it would be difficult to interpret much beyond the fact that, for whatever reasons, these students were not doing those things in the classroom (attending, taking notes, or whatever) that were prerequisites to success. The wording of this category of reply, in the May study, was "counseling to assist the student in manifesting appropriate behavioral characteristics for performance in the classroom." Special program planning (8 out of 11 schools) and special selection of "willing" instructors (7 out of 11 schools) are other adaptive techniques that are common in the secondary school and apparently considered important in college programming also.

Specific provisions made to assist learning disabled students with reading included tutorial assistance (10 of the 11 schools) and cassettes for recording class notes (8 of 11 schools) as the only provisions utilized by a majority of the schools responding. Other special provisions included the use of readers and taped textbooks (both techniques commonly used with the blind) and instruction by reading specialists and/or learning disabilities specialists. In the testing situation, oral testing was a provision reported by a majority (8 of 11) of the schools. Other provisions, also in the testing situation, were the use of readers, typewriters, and taped tests with the allowance for taped responses. It is noteworthy that with regard to both reading difficulties and the difficulties brought on by poor reading, as these might relate to meaningful testing, methods regularly used with visually disabled students are in common use with learning disabled students.

The May study also included information on types of tests used by the postsecondary programs to attempt to project success in vocational areas or in some academic subject or subjects. Achievement tests and aptitude tests were used by 6 of the 11 schools, a personality profile of some sort was used by 8 of the 11 schools, and a vocational interest inventory was used by 5 of the 11 schools. Other tests included intelligence tests and tests of specific language disorders. For purposes of entrance to the program (information considered *prior* to admission), all schools considered the high school transcripts, 9 of the 11 schools regularly requested and used special tests (psychological, aptitude, achievement, and so forth) given in high school, and 6 of the 11 schools considered records of previous behavioral characteristics manifested while in high school.

An interesting question in the May study concerned the source of funding for any special services for the learning disabled. Three schools did not respond to this question, and only two reported the use of special funds (these were vocational education funds and specified, special state funds). The other six indicated that they had to rely on the regular institutional budget for special costs of programming for the learning disabled. In this respect, the colleges are very unlike public school, precollege programs. In all (or nearly all) public secondary school programs, there are special categorical funds provided through the state education agency to encourage the development of special programs for the learning disabled. These may actually be federal funds, but in most cases they are made available through the state educational agency. The matter of funding for college level programs requires further study.

It would be an error to leave the impres-

sion that the above 11 programs described by May are all that are available for the postsecondary learning disabled student. Though the names of these programs could have been given (as could the names of the programs included in the Wells study), this would be of limited value. The fact is that postsecondary education for the learning disabled is poorly developed, and program provision may change with a new head of the local counseling center, the dean of a college, or the head of a department. However, the very fact that one or two persons can make a considerable difference in a negative direction means that one or two persons can make a difference in a positive direction. In visiting with teachers in a number of 2-year colleges (particularly those with strong vocational or technical orientation), we discovered that even though no formal, recognized program exists, a number of learning disabled students are receiving meaningful help and

genuine understanding from instructors who care. Many, particularly those in the vocational and/or technical areas, are less academically biased and can readily see the potential talent in some learning disabled students. They make provisions for them—often makeshift provisions to be sure—and the most common provision appears to be oral teaching and the opportunity for the student to show what he knows with his hands (as in technical and mechanical areas) and through oral feedback to the instructor. Liberal arts–oriented instructors tend more toward the traditional bias that implies that if a student can't write it, he doesn't know it. Another effort we have seen in some of these 2-year schools is the extensive use of tutorial help. This is not directed toward remediation, but toward assisting the learning disabled student to learn content, even though he does not read effectively. One middle-aged instructor in a vocational/technical college put it quite succinctly. He said, "What the hell—I didn't read too well when I was just a kid either." His students may not appreciate the "kid" part of his point of view, but the remainder has led to organizing some meaningful, effective oral teaching, oral testing, tutorially assisted programs for students who would likely be academic failures in other schools with very similar educational goals, but very different instructors. The problem with this type of provision is obvious. If this instructor leaves, the program may be gone also.

WHY THE SHORTAGE OF POSTSECONDARY PROGRAMS?

There are a number of reasons why there are so few organized, stable programs for the learning disabled at the postsecondary level. *A major reason is that any specialized effort is more costly than "standard" or "normal" program efforts, and thus there must be special provision of funds to assist such programs.* In the case of secondary schools, if the schools determine that such an effort is needed, the states provide state level special funding. This relieves the local educational agency budget of most, if not all, of the extra cost, and special programs are thus more simple to "sell" to local boards of directors. A subaspect of this fund or cost-related reason is that the federal government, which has provided significant funds for the elementary and secondary schools, has not become involved in the field of postsecondary education to any significant extent.

A second reason relates to mandatory attendance laws and the concept of providing a high school education for all persons. If learning disabled students are to receive an education, it is only reasonable to provide a program that is appropriate to their needs. As noted in previous chapters, in some states children may end their formal education at the end of the eighth grade or at age 16, but much of the general public seems to believe that all children should at least finish high school. *On the other hand, college is not yet conceived to be essential for all, and since it is viewed as an academic setting, some citizens are not sympathetic toward the idea of providing more academic work for students who, by definition, are not successful at academics.* Some of these same citizens change their minds quite quickly when the learning disabled student is their child.

A third reason relates to the nature of the postsecondary academic community—the instructors, professors, deans, and so forth. *If concern for academic excellence is overly prized in the secondary schools and is a stumbling block to the provision of meaningful programs there, it certainly is more of a stumbling block at the postsecondary level.* It appears that instructors in vocational/technical type schools have less concern with this concept of academic excellence and more orientation toward the ability to perform specific tasks toward which their training programs are directed. A learning disabled student about to graduate from high school should be aware of this situation, but it should not be the only factor that affects his decision about possible postsecondary program entrance.

A fourth, and relatively recent, reason is the effect of the law that states that the public schools must provide a free, appropriate public education to all children and youth. The national law, P.L. 94-142, has been discussed in various places in this book, and Appendix A summarizes the involvement of the federal government in education for the handicapped. Most states have similar laws, and this legal statement of responsibility is probably the most compelling reason why secondary schools are involved in attempting to provide programs for the learning disabled. For the present at least, this law, and the various state laws, do not apply to the postsecondary level. The federal law, however, may be interpreted as applying to postsecondary programs in states that provide postsecondary programs to students free of cost as an extension of the secondary program.

It is worth noting that the recent guidelines pertaining to Section 504 of the Rehabilitation Act of 1973, effective on June 1, 1977, apply specifically to universities and other postsecondary schools. Although the Act does not permit direct funding of programs of specific concern to the learning disabled, it does prescribe that all such institutions shall make accommodations for handicapped students by constructing or altering facilities, providing flexibility in requirements for degree programs, and in the manner in which students are instructed and evaluated in the program.

A final reason is lack of awareness on the part of many college program personnel. Elementary teachers and administrators cannot avoid this problem—the children are there and must be educated. Provision of a program may cause some small headaches, but it usually solves more problems than it creates. Secondary school teachers and administrators have tried to avoid the problem for some time and some have been successful, but to an increasing extent they have admitted the existence of the learning disabled because more and more such students have remained in the schools. Some believe that such students are not really their responsibility, but as they have realized that these students are not just "lazy" and that behavior problems may be a secondary problem caused by the learning disability, many have accepted the problem as one with which they must deal. Also, there is the presence of a department of special education in most local education agencies, and thus there is a spokesperson for the learning disabled as they leave the elementary schools and enter the secondary schools. But most college personnel have only very recently begun to recognize the existence of this type of problem, and it may take a concerted awareness program to accomplish any significant level of interest and concern for the learning disabled.

There are other reasons that might be enumerated, but most relate in a fairly obvious manner to those already listed. The high degree of subject area orientation of the college program, the emphasis on research and writing ability, and the tendency toward an ivory tower setting—insulated from the real world—of the college or university all militate against understanding or appreciating the problems of the learning disabled. But awareness is slowly increasing, and the future may hold at least some promise. Factors such as the state of the economy and any future redefinition of the role of the college may be among the more significant factors.

PROGRAM IDEAS THAT MAY BE EFFECTIVE

There is every reason to believe that some of the program provisions that are proving to be effective at the secondary level may also be effective at the postsecondary level. However, we must not slip into the same error that occurred at the secondary level when personnel there attempted to adopt the elementary program in toto. Evidence available from the few postsecondary programs that do exist plus knowledge of the structure of the various types of postsecondary schools that are in operation suggest that remedial programs may prove to be even less effective at the postsecondary level than at the secondary level. The emphasis must be on accommodation and on the various adaptive and compensatory techniques that this suggests. Specifically, the following procedures or components should be considered:

1. The use of tape recorders for recording notes and for responding to class assignments will be of concrete value to many students. Similarly, taped tests and a provision for taped responses to test questions will be of assistance in many cases.

2. Peer tutoring, not for remediation but for communicating content and concepts, will likely be even more practical (because of the nature of class schedules and the structure of the school day) at the postsecondary level than at the secondary level.*

3. Special counseling, both as regards program planning (related to vocational goals) and behavioral counseling, may pay big dividends with specific students.

---

*There were some excellent examples of peer tutoring in the review of some of the informally organized programs in 2-year colleges. This is sometimes done for credit (under the supervision of college faculty) and sometimes simply as a service project.

4. Specific instruction in "how to study" skills will likely be effective with some students. This is one activity that may be accomplished through group instruction. It may be most effective if students are shown the variety of ways in which different individuals learn, and then are provided specific, guided practice in a variety of techniques.

5. A cadre of instructors who indicate a willingness to work with learning disabled students, to adjust the way they expect written work to be submitted, and to make other modifications and adaptations may be established. Although many college instructors are even more academically oriented than high school teachers, there is also a possibility that there will be more "mavericks" among the faculty who will exercise their academic freedom through making such adaptations—perhaps in part to elicit comments from their colleagues. The fact that there are fewer institutionally imposed regulations and limitations on instructional style, methods of evaluation, and the like (at the college level as opposed to the high school level) may be an advantage to the learning disabled student.

6. Finally, and most important of all, *for any of the above to take place, and to be part of a consistent plan or program, there must be a person, and an office or department of the college, responsible for such programs.* This requires a specific assignment of this responsibility and allowance of funds and faculty for this purpose. This may be the most critical single requirement for successful college programming for the learning disabled.

IMPLICATIONS OF LEGISLATIVE ACTIONS

As we were about to send in the completed manuscript for this text, an interesting UPI press release made headlines—or at least achieved front-page status—in a number of newspapers in our geographical area. Perhaps it is purely a regional phenomenon,

but we doubt it. Unfortunately, it is more likely a surfacing of feelings and an indication of difficulties to come, which have implications on a national basis. The news release made front-page news because the legislator responsible is one who is a leading candidate for the governorship in his state. Here is the story.

In the state involved (which shall remain unnamed), several state universities have been providing remedial programs for college students who apparently need them. However, the students who enrolled in such courses were not receiving college credit for them. A group of students staged a sit-in at the offices of certain university officials at one university and demanded that they receive credit toward their college degree for the remedial courses. Eventually they received approval from the administration, and their remedial courses now count toward their degree. Some would question whether all (or any) such remedial courses should count toward a degree, and we would suggest that there may be a major difference between *remedial* courses and *adapted* or *compensatory* courses where the learning goals are the same as for other (similar) courses, with only the *manner* in which they are taught changed. However, the "credit or no credit" question was not the crux of the issue as far as this political leader was concerned. *His concern was that high schools were graduating students who still needed remedial assistance.* He wanted to find out from which high schools those students were coming, *so that the state might penalize those school districts by taking away some of their tax dollars.*

Other statements included in this news article indicated the same type of feelings that we often hear about the high schools—"ridiculous to graduate students who have difficulty reading college entrance exams," and "they just don't make kids learn in school any more." Apparently we can expect these kinds of sentiments forever, but the suggestion that schools be penalized financially if they graduate students who are "inferior" academically is one that must be carefully watched.

If this type of sentiment were to gain solid acceptance, we would be moving backward several decades. It could easily lead to the time-tested procedure of "counseling" students to drop-out of high school and to rejection of high school programs for the learning disabled, the mentally handicapped, or any other student who could not achieve as well as some hypothetical norm. In an age of increased enlightenment regarding the unique needs of students with learning problems and the right of all students to a free, appropriate public education, we must apparently remain alert to the fact that all leaders and policymakers are not equally enlightened.

SUMMARY

Although there is a directory of postsecondary programs that will admit learning disabled students and a nationally recognized provision for modified college entrance exams, there is a severe shortage of *organized programs designed to fulfill the need for college programs for learning disabled students.* Available evidence indicates that many of the accommodative techniques in use in the secondary schools may work to good advantage at the postsecondary level, but we must be careful to apply such techniques under conditions of careful monitoring. Because of lack of specific funding for programs for the learning disabled at the college level, such programs that have existed often disappear after a key person leaves or takes some assignment that makes it difficult or impossible to continue the former program. The single, most important factor in any such program may be the provision of staff time and the assignment of this program to a specific office or department in the college. Parallel with this factor is the recruiting of a staff member who is both knowledgeable and interested in the effective development and continuation of such a program. The potential is great, but the future is in doubt, when it comes to programming for postsecondary learning disabled students.

DISCUSSION QUESTIONS

1. Make two lists of the reasons why learning disabled students *should* and *should not* be enrolled in college. Can the reasons in each list be justified by other than traditional values?
2. What college careers might students pursue if they are extremely deficient in reading although provided with support and accommodation?
3. Are there any careers or occupations that would seem to be able to justify the exclusion of learning disabled candidates?
4. Is there any legal basis for the application of P.L. 94-142 to institutions of higher education?
5. Design a model support system that would ensure support for learning disabled students at a university.

REFERENCES AND READINGS

May, B. J. Unpublished survey report, University of Arkansas, Fayetteville, Ark., 1977.

Fielding, P. (Ed.). *A national directory of four-year colleges, two-year colleges, and post-high school training programs for young people with learning disabilities.* Tulsa, Okla., Partners in Publishing, 1975.

Webb, G. M. The neurologically impaired youth goes to college. In R. Weber (Ed.), *Handbook on learning disabilities.* Englewood Cliffs, N.J., Prentice-Hall, Inc., 1974.

Wells, L. *Writing disorders in the learning disabilities student in the college classroom.* Unpublished doctoral dissertation, Northwestern University, Evanston, Ill., August, 1973.

Appendixes

The effect of actions of the federal government on the evolution of programs for the learning disabled

In numerous places in this text there have been references to Public Laws (91-230, 93-380, and 94-142) and to the role of the Bureau of Education for the Handicapped, which is part of the Office of Education. Rather than provide the information necessary for the reader to understand the considerable effect of actions directed by these laws and implemented by the Bureau of Education for the Handicapped in "bits and pieces" throughout the text or repeating this entire history in several places in the text, it was decided to present a condensed summary of these actions in this appendix. It was necessary to provide some detail in certain instances within the various chapters, but the sequence of significant federal legislative enactments that led to the present status of learning disabilities as it relates to responsibilities of the federal government, are presented here to permit a meaningful gestalt of this significant factor in the development of the field.

Public laws that have provided for the learning disabled

Public Law 89-10, the Elementary and Secondary Education Act of 1965, provided significant sums of money for local educational programs, some of which was used for children we would now call learning disabled. Title I of Public Law 89-10 contained the major amount of funding, and these funds were allocated to local school districts in direct proportion to the number of low-income families in the district. Some of these monies were used for children who had se-

vere reading problems, some for special class programs for "neurologically impaired" children, and other funds for a variety of classes and programs that may have included learning disabled children and youth. However, it was not the intent of this law to provide for the learning disabled, except as they were provided for incidentally as a result of meeting some other goal or purpose. The first federal law to provide specifically for the learning disabled was Public Law 91-230.

Public Law 91-230 Title VI—Education of the Handicapped (April 13, 1970)

Public Law 91-230 included many amendments, extensions, and additions to existing laws relating to elementary and secondary education. Included in P.L. 91-230 was Title VI, a title specifically related to education of handicapped children and youth. This provision for the learning disabled in P.L. 91-230 came about in a somewhat unusual way.

During 1969 and 1970, a small but relatively strong lobbying effort was carried out in behalf of federal assistance for the learning disabled. A Learning Disabilities Act was proposed and appeared to be doing fairly well, when, almost at the last minute, it was determined that it probably could not pass as a separate Act. It was therefore added to P.L. 91-230 as *Part G of Title VI—Special Programs for Children With Specific Learning Disabilities*. P.L. 91-230 was passed with a major title (Title VI) relating specifically to education of the handicapped, and with "handicapped children" defined in the law as "mentally retarded, hard of hearing, deaf, speech impaired, visually handicapped, seriously emotionally disturbed, crippled, or other health impaired children who by reason thereof require special education and related services." However, as part of this title, the learning disabled were included— thus indicating them to be part of those children who were considered as "handicapped children," even though they were *not* included in the definition of handicapped children with which this title dealt. Those unfamiliar with the way in which the federal congress operates and unfamiliar with this particular piece of legislation would likely find this situation confusing. When these facts and understandings are present, this apparently contradictory situation becomes most logical, at least as far as federal operational procedure is concerned. The content of Public Law 91-230, Title VI, Part G follows:

P.L. 91-230, TITLE VI, PART G—
SPECIAL PROGRAMS FOR CHILDREN WITH
SPECIFIC LEARNING DISABILITIES; RESEARCH,
TRAINING, AND MODEL CENTERS

SEC. 661. (a) The Commissioner is authorized to make grants to, and contracts with, institutions of higher education, state and local educational agencies, and other public and private educational and research agencies and organizations (except that no grant shall be made other than to a nonprofit agency or organization) in order to carry out a program of—

(1) research and related purposes relating to the education of children with specific learning disabilities;
(2) professional or advanced training for educational personnel who are teaching, or are preparing to be teachers of, children with specific learning disabilities, or such training for persons who are, or are preparing to be, supervisors and teachers of such personnel; and
(3) establishing and operating model centers for the improvement of education of children with specific learning disabilities, which centers shall (A) provide testing and educational evaluation to identify children with learning disabilities who have been referred to such centers, (B) develop and conduct model programs de-

signed to meet the special educational needs of such children, (C) assist appropriate educational agencies, organizations, and institutions in making such model programs available to other children with learning disabilities, and (D) disseminate new methods or techniques for overcoming learning disabilities to educational institutions, organizations, and agencies within the area served by such center and evaluate the effectiveness of the dissemination process. Such evaluation shall be conducted annually after the first year of operation of a center.

In making grants and contracts under this section the Commissioner shall give special consideration to applications which propose innovative and creative approaches to meeting the educational needs of children with specific learning disabilities, and those which emphasize the prevention and early identification of learning disabilities.

Subsequent legislation maintained the federal involvement with learning disabled children through promotion of model centers for the learning disabled (designed as a basis for possible replication in the establishment of new programs) and through training program monies provided to colleges and universities to train teachers of the learning disabled. These programs, administered by the Bureau of Education for the Handicapped (BEH) of the Office of Education, continued to be funded specifically for the learning disabled. Then, in 1974, another Public Law had a considerable impact on programs for the learning disabled. The pertinent part of P.L. 93-380 follows:

P.L. 93-380 TITLE I, PART B (AUGUST 21, 1974)
(This is an amendment to the conditions under which the states may obtain their grants for education of handicapped children. It requires that the states must:)
(12) (A) establish a goal of providing full educational opportunities to all handicapped children, and (B) provide for a procedure to assure that funds expended under this part are used to accomplish the goal set forth in (A) of this paragraph and priority in the utilization of funds under this part will be given to handicapped children who are not receiving an education; and
(13) provide procedures for insuring that handicapped children and their parents or guardians are guaranteed procedural safeguards in decisions regarding identification, evaluation

and educational placement of handicapped children including, but not limited to (A) (i) prior notice to parents or guardians of the child when the local or State educational agency proposes to change the educational placement of the child, (ii) an opportunity for the parents or guardians to obtain an impartial due process hearing, examine all relevant records with respect to the classification or educational placement of the child, and obtain an independent educational evaluation of the child, (iii) procedures to protect the rights of the child when the parents or guardians are not known, unavailable, or the child is a ward of the State including the assignment of an individual (not to be an employee of the State or local educational agency involved in the education or care of children) to act as a surrogate for the parents or guardians, and (iv) provision to insure that the decisions rendered in the impartial due process hearing required by this paragraph shall be binding on all parties subject only to appropriate administrative or judicial appeal; and (B) procedures to insure that, to the maximum extent appropriate, handicapped children, including children in public or private institutions or other care facilities, are educated with children who are not handicapped, and that special classes, separate schooling, or other removal of handicapped children from the regular education environment occurs only when the nature or severity of the handicap is such that education in regular classes with the use of supplementary aids and services cannot be achieved satisfactorily; and (C) procedures to insure the testing and evaluation materials and procedures utilized for the purposes of classification and placement of handicapped children will be selected and administered so as not to be racially or culturally discriminatory.

Public Law 93-380 further required that:

(b) (1) Any State which desires to receive a grant under this part for any fiscal year beginning after June 30, 1975, shall submit to the Commissioner for approval not later than one year after the enactment of the Education of the Handicapped Amendments of 1974, through its State educational agency an amendment to the State plan required under subsection (a), setting forth in detail the policies and procedures which the State will undertake in order to assure that—

(A) all children residing in the State who are handicapped regardless of the severity of their handicap and who are in need of special education and related services are identified, located, and evaluated, including a practical method of determining which children are currently receiving needed special education and related services and which children are not currently receiving needed special education and related services:

(B) policies and procedures will be established in accordance with detailed criteria prescribed by the Commissioner to protect the confidentiality of such data and information by the State;

(C) there is established (i) a goal of providing full educational opportunities to all handicapped children, (ii) a detailed timetable for accomplishing such a goal, and (iii) a description of the kind and number of facilities, personnel, and services necessary throughout the State to meet such a goal; and

(D) the amendment submitted by the State pursuant to this subsection shall be available to parents and other members of the general public at least thirty days prior to the date of submission of the amendment to the Commissioner.

Public Law 93-380 thus had a major influence on services provided to all handicapped children, including the learning disabled. It may have had more effect on the learning disabled in that: (1) some states (in 1974) were providing relatively little service to these children, and the law placed them on notice regarding this situation, and (2) the requirements for due process led to many children being moved out of existing programs for the mentally handicapped, with some moved directly into programs for the learning disabled.

The next Public Law that had significant influence on educational provisions for the learning disabled was Public Law 94-142, the *Education for All Handicapped Children Act of 1975*. This Public Law, unlike P.L. 91-230 and 93-380, dealt only with handicapped children. P.L. 94-142 is undoubtedly one of the most significant pieces of legislation in the history of federal support to education. P.L. 94-142 includes a number of outstanding provisions, one of the most important of which is the funding of excess costs to school districts that provide free and appropriate public education to handicapped children. Significant parts of P.L. 94-142 follow:

P.L. 94-142 (SELECTED SECTIONS AND
SUB-SECTIONS) (NOVEMBER 29, 1975)
STATEMENT OF FINDINGS AND PURPOSE

SEC. 3. (a) Section 601 of the Act (20 U.S.C. 1401) is amended by inserting "(a)" immediately before "This title" and by adding at the end thereof the following new subsections:

(b) The Congress finds that—

(1) there are more than eight million handicapped children in the United States today;

(2) the special educational needs of such children are not being fully met;

(3) more than half of the handicapped children in the United States do not receive appropriate educational services which would enable them to have full equality of opportunity;

(4) one million of the handicapped children in the United States are excluded entirely from the public school system and will not go through the educational process with their peers;

(5) there are many handicapped children throughout the United States participating in regular school programs whose handicaps prevent them from having a successful educational experience because their handicaps are undetected;

(6) because of the lack of adequate services within the public school system, families are often forced to find services outside the public school system, often at great distance from their residence and at their own expense;

(7) developments in the training of teachers and in diagnostic and instructional procedures and methods have advanced to the point that, given appropriate funding, State and local educational agencies can and will provide effective special education and related services to meet the needs of handicapped children;

(8) State and local educational agencies have a responsibility to provide education for all handicapped children, but present financial resources are inadequate to meet the special educational needs of handicapped children; and

(9) it is in the national interest that the Federal Government assist State and local efforts to provide programs to meet the educational needs of handicapped children in order to assure equal protection of the law.

(c) It is the purpose of this Act to assure that all handicapped children have available to them, within the time periods specified in section 612 (2) (B), a free appropriate public education which emphasizes special education and related services designed to meet their unique needs, to assure that the rights of handicapped children and their parents or guardians are protected, to assist States and localities to provide for the education of all handicapped children, and to assess and assure the effectiveness of efforts to educate handicapped children.

The preceding statement of purpose was the most clear and comprehensive of any such action in the history of legislation on behalf of the handicapped. It would seem that the educational needs and rights of handicapped children had finally been fully recognized by Congress.

However, in recognition of the fact that local and state educational agencies might well attempt to take advantage of federal funds by over-estimating the incidence of handicapped children, the Congress included the following limitation on numbers of children to be served:

(5) (A) In determining the allotment of each State under paragraph (1), the Commissioner may not count—

(i) handicapped children in such State under paragraph (1) (A) to the extent the number of such children is greater than 12 per centum of the number of all children aged five to seventeen, inclusive, in such State;

(ii) as part of such percentage, children with specific learning disabilities to the extent the number of such children is greater than one-sixth of such percentage; . . .

The limitation on the number of children who might be included as learning disabled was in response to concerns of various congressional committee members that children other than the learning disabled might be "left out" due to the popularity of programs for the learning disabled and the vagueness of learning disability definitions.

Also included in P.L. 94-142 was a provision designed to remove the need for this limitation to the number of children who might be served as learning disabled. How the Commissioner of Education will resolve this legislative directive remains to be seen, but it may have far-reaching effects on which children may be called learning disabled and how they will be served. It will establish acceptable diagnostic procedures for determining who is and who is not learning disabled (for purposes of federally funded programs). This part of P.L. 94-142 provides an excellent example of how funding regulations and guidelines influence services to boys and girls.

(b) (1) The Commissioner of Education shall, no later than one year after the effective date of this subsection, prescribe—

(A) regulations which establish specific criteria for determining whether a particular disorder or condition may be considered a specific learning disability for purposes of designating children with specific learning disabilities;

(B) regulations which establish and describe diagnostic procedures which shall be used in determining whether a particular child has a disorder or condition which places such child in the category of children with specific learning disabilities; and

(C) regulations which establish monitoring procedures which will be used to determine if State educational agencies, local educational agencies, and intermediate educational units are complying with the criteria established under clause (A) and clause (B).

(2) The Commissioner shall submit any proposed regulation written under paragraph (1) to the Committee on Education and Labor of the House of Representatives and the Committee on Labor and Public Welfare of the Senate, for review and comment by each such committee, at least fifteen days before such regulation is published in the Federal Register.

(3) If the Commissioner determines, as a result of the the promulgation of regulations under paragraph (1), that changes are necessary in the definition of the term "children with specific learning disabilities", as such term is defined by section 602(15) of the Act, he shall submit recommendations for legislation with respect to such changes to each House of the Congress.

(4) For purposes of this subsection:

(A) The term "children with specific learning disabilities" means those children who have a disorder in one or more of the basic psychological processes involved in understanding or in using language, spoken or written, which disorder may manifest itself in imperfect ability to listen, think, speak, read, write, spell, or do mathematical calculations. Such disorders include such conditions as perceptual handicaps, brain injury, minimal brain dysfunction, dyslexia, and developmental aphasia. Such term does not include children who have learning problems which are primarily the result of visual, hearing, or motor handicaps, of mental retardation, of emotional disturbance, or of environmental, cultural, or economic disadvantage.

Thus we see the following sequence of legislation: (1) laws which although not intended to provide for the learning disabled, did in fact provide for some limited programs, (2) the initiation of official federal assistance to the learning disabled, (3) added emphasis on the educational needs of all handicapped children, with definite benefits for the learning disabled, and (4) recognition that learning disabilities, though ill-defined, represented the major emphasis of many programs for the handicapped in the public schools of the nation. In fact, the final legislation cited (P.L. 94-142) included specific subsections designed to "protect" other programs from over-zealous advocates of programs for the learning disabled.

Fortunately, the intent of Congress in passing the legislation was to serve children and for the most part that intent has been realized. The Congress and those who have attempted to implement the program so as to carry out congressional intent should be complimented for efforts that have had a profound effect on the development of meaningful services to children who so badly need such assistance.

Publishers of professional books and suppliers of materials and equipment for learning disability programs

This alphabetical list of publishers and suppliers is a revised version of a similar list provided in *Learning Disabilities: Educational Strategies* (2nd ed.).* Publishers and suppliers whose products were appropriate *only* for the elementary age level were deleted, and some new entries were provided. Because the overwhelming number of learning disabilities programs in the nation are elementary level programs, much of the emphasis of commercial suppliers has been directed toward younger children. In fact, the majority of materials provided by most publishers and suppliers listed in this Appendix are elementary level materials, but each has something to offer secondary school programs although more are appropriate for junior high school students than senior high school students.

Requests for catalogs, brochures, supply lists, and other descriptive material can be made to these publishers and suppliers. It is usually more effective to send such requests on school letterhead stationery; however, many will reply to all requests.

Some of these companies provide audiovisual materials, learning games, equipment, and a variety of other curriculum materials. Others produce or supply only one type of product, for example, professional books. The list that follows indicates six categories of products.

AV Audiovisual materials
BK Professional books
CM Curriculum materials
EQ Equipment
GA Educational Games
TE Tests and testing equipment

Overlap among these six categories makes it difficult to "key" the list precisely, and various publishers and suppliers add to or modify their product lines regularly. The list is provided as a starting point for further investigation and does not imply qualitative endorsement.

Academic Therapy Publications AV, BK, CM,
1539 Fourth Street EQ, TE
San Rafael, Calif. 94901

Acropolis Books BK, CM
2400 17th St.
Washington, D.C. 20009

Adapt Press Inc. BK
808 West Avenue North
Sioux Falls, S.D. 57104

Addison-Wesley Publishing Co. BK, CM
2725 Sand Hill Road
Menlo Park, Calif. 94025

Allied Educational Council BK, CM, GA
Distribution Center
P.O. Box 78
Galien, Mich. 49113

Allyn & Bacon, Inc. BK, CM
470 Atlantic Avenue
Boston, Mass. 02210

American Book Co. BK
450 W. 33 Street
New York, N.Y. 10001

---

*Gearheart, B. R. St. Louis: The C. V. Mosby Co., 1977.

American Educational Publications   BK
245 Long Hill Road
Middletown, Conn. 06457

American Guidance Service   AV, BK, CM,
Publishers Building   EQ, GA, TE
Circle Pines, Minn. 55014

American Speech & Hearing   BK, CM
Assoc.
9030 Old Georgetown Road
Washington, D.C. 20014

Ann Arbor Publishers   CM
611 Church Street
Ann Arbor, Mich. 48104

Amidon, Paul S., & Associates   CM
1966 Benson Ave.
St. Paul, Minn. 55116

Appleton-Century-Crofts   BK
440 Park Ave. S.
New York, N.Y. 10016

Argus Communications   CM
7440 Natchez
Niles, Ill. 60648

Association for Childhood Education   BK, CM
3615 Wisconsin Ave. N.W.
Washington, D.C. 20016

Audio-Visual Research   CM
1317 Eighth Street S.E.
Waseca, Minn. 56093

Baggiani & Tewell   BK, CM
4 Spring Hill Court
Chevy Chase, Md. 20015

Baldridge Reading Instructional   CM
Materials
14 Grigg Street
Greenwich, Conn. 06830

Bantam Books Inc.   CM
666 Fifth Avenue
New York, N.Y. 10019

Barnell-Loft   CM
958 Church Street
Baldwin, N.Y. 11510

Barnhart, Clarence L., Inc.   CM
P.O. Box 250
Bronxville, N.Y. 10708

Basic Books, Inc.   BK
404 Park Ave. S.
New York, N.Y. 10016

Beckley-Cardy   CM, GA
1900 N. Narragansett
Chicago, Ill. 60639

Behavioral Research Laboratories   CM, GA
P.O. Box 577
Palo Alto, Calif. 94302

Bell & Howell   AV
7100 McCormick Rd.
Chicago, Ill. 60645

Benefic Press   CM, EQ
10300 W. Roosevelt Rd.
Westchester, Ill. 60153

Bobbs-Merrill Co., Inc.   BK, CM, TE
4300 West 62nd St.
Indianapolis, Ind. 46206

Book-Lab, Inc.   CM
1449 37th St.
Brooklyn, N.Y. 11218

Borg-Warner Educational Systems   CM, EQ
7450 N. Natchez Ave.
Niles, Ill. 60648

Bowmar   AV, CM, EQ
622 Rodier Dr.
Glendale, Calif. 91201

Brown, Wm. C.   BK
135 S. Locust St.
Dubuque, Iowa 52001

Burgess Publishing Co.   BK, CM
4265 6th St.
Minneapolis, Minn. 55415

California Association for   AV, BK
Neurologically Handicapped Children
P.O. Box 1526
Vista, Calif. 92083

California Test Bureau   TE
Del Monte Research Park
Monterey, Calif. 93940

Chandler Publishing Co.   BK, CM
124 Spear St.
San Francisco, Calif. 94105

Chicago (University of) Press   BK
5750 Ellis Ave.
Chicago, Ill. 60637

Children's Music Center, Inc.   AV, BK, CM
5373 West Pico Blvd.
Los Angeles, Calif. 90019

Communication Research Associates   CM
P.O. Box 110012
Salt Lake City, Utah 84109

Concept Records AV
P.O. Box 250
Center Conway, N.H. 03813

Consulting Psychologists Press BK, CM, TE
577 College Ave.
Palo Alto, Calif. 94306

Continental Press AV, CM
Elizabethtown, Pa. 17022

Control Development, Inc. GA
3166 Des Plaines Ave.
Des Plaines, Ill. 60018

Council for Exceptional Children BK, CM
1411 S. Jefferson Davis Highway
Arlington, Va. 22202

Craig Corp. & Industrial Division CM, AV
921 W. Artesia Blvd.
Compton, Calif. 90220

Creative Publications CM, GA
P.O. Box 10328
Palo Alto, Calif. 94303

Croft-NEI Publications BK
24 Rope Ferry Road
Waterford, Conn. 06386

Cuisenaire Company of America, Inc. CM
12 Church Street
New Rochelle, N.Y. 10885

Day (John) Co. BK, CM, TE
257 Park Ave. S.
New York, N.Y. 10010

Developmental Learning Materials BK, CM,
7440 Natchez Ave. EQ, GA
Niles, Ill. 60648

Dexter & Westbrook Ltd. CM
958 Church Street
Rockville Centre, N.Y. 11510

Dick Blick, Inc. CM, GA
P.O. Box 1267-F
Galesburg, Ill. 61401

Dimensions Publishing Co. BK, CM
P.O. Box 4221
San Rafael, Calif. 94903

Doubleday & Co. CM, BK
Garden City, N.Y. 11530

Dryden Press, Inc. BK
901 N. Elm
Hinsdale, Ill. 60521

The Economy Company CM
1901 N. Walnut Ave.
Oklahoma City, Okla. 74103

Edmark Associates CM
655 S. Arcas St.
Seattle, Wash. 98103

Educational Activities, Inc. AV, BK, CM
P.O. Box 392
Freeport, N.Y. 15520

Educational Development CM, GA
Laboratories
284 Pulaski St.
Huntington, N.Y. 11744

Educational Progress Corp. AV, CM
P.O. Box 45663
Tulsa, Okla. 74145

Educational Projections Corp. AV, CM
1911 Pickwick Ave.
Glenview, Ill. 60610

Educational Service, Inc. CM, GA
P.O. Box 219
Stevensville, Mich. 49127

Educational Teaching Aids CM, GA
159 W. Kinzie St.
Chicago, Ill. 60610

Educational Testing Service TE
Princeton, N.H. 08540

Educators Publishing Service AV, BK, CM,
75 Moulton St. EQ, GA, TE
Cambridge, Mass. 02138

EduKaid of Ridgewood CM, GA
1250 E. Ridgewood Ave.
Ridgewood, N.J. 07450

Electronic Future Inc. AV, EQ
57 Dodge Avenue
North Haven, Conn. 06473

Essay Press CM, TE
P.O. Box 5, Planetarium Station
New York, N.Y. 10024

Expression Co., Publishers CM, GA
Magnolia, Mass. 01903

Eye Gate House AV, CM
146-01 Archer Ave.
Jamaica, N.Y. 11435

Fearon Publishers BK, CM, TE
6 Davis Dr.
Belmont, Calif. 94002

Field Educational Publications, Inc. AV, CM
2400 Hanover St.
Palo Alto, Calif. 94304

Filmstrip House, Inc.   AV
432 Park Ave. S.
New York, N.Y. 10016

Follet Educational Corp.   BK, CM, TE
P.O. Box 5705
Chicago, Ill. 60680

Gamco Industries, Inc.   CM, EQ, GA
P.O. Box 1911
Big Springs, Tex. 79720

Garrard Publishing Co.   BK, CM
1607 N. Market St.
Champaign, Ill. 61820

General Learning Corp.   CM
250 James St.
Morristown, N.J. 07960

Ginn & Co.   BK, CM
125 Second Ave.
Waltham, Mass. 02154

Globe Book Co.   BK
175 Fifth Ave.
New York, N.Y. 10010

Grune & Stratton, Inc.   BK, TE
111 Fifth Ave.
New York, N.Y. 10003

Gryphon Press   BK, CM
220 Montgomery St.
Highland Park, N.H. 08904

Guidance Associates   TE
1526 Gilpin Ave.
Wilmington, Del. 19800

Hale, E. M., & Co., Publishers   BK
1201 S. Hastings Way
Eau Claire, Wis. 54701

Harcourt Brace Jovanovich, Inc.   BK, TE
757 Third Ave.
New York, N.Y. 10017

Harper & Row, Publishers   BK, CM
49 E. 33rd St.
New York, N.Y. 10016

Heath, D. C., & Co.   BI
125 Spring St.
Lexington, Mass. 02173

Hiskey, Marshal   TE
5640 Baldwin
Lincoln, Nebraska 68507

Hoffman Information Systems   AV, CM
5623 Peck Rd.
Arcadia, Calif. 91006

Holt, Rinehart & Winston, Inc.   BK
383 Madison Ave.
New York, N.Y. 10017

Houghton Mifflin Co.   BK, TE, CM
2 Park St.
Boston, Mass. 02107

Houston Press   TE
University of Houston
Houston, Texas 77000

Hubbard   CM
P.O. Box 105
Northbrook, Ill. 60062

Illinois (University of) Press   BK, CM, TE
Urbana, Ill. 61801

Imperial International Learning Corp.   AV, CM
P.O. Box 548
Kankakee, Ill. 60901

Incentive Products Educational   CM, TE
1902 Coral Way
Miami, Fla. 33145

Instructional Industries Inc.   CM
Executive Park
Ballston Lake, N.Y. 12019

Instructo Corp.   CM, EQ, GA
200 Cedar Hollow Road
Paoli, Pa. 19301

The Instructor Publications   CM, GA
7 Bank Street
Dansville, New York 14437

International Reading Association   BK, CM
6 Tyre St.
Newark, Del. 19711

Interstate Printers, Inc.   BK, CM
Jackson at Van Buren
Danville, Ill. 61832

The Johns Hopkins University Press   BK
Baltimore, Md. 21218

Jones-Kenilworth Co.   CM
8301 Ambassador Row
Dallas, Tex. 75247

Journal of Learning Disabilities   BK
5 N. Wabash Avenue
Chicago, Ill. 60602

Journal of Special Education   BK
433 S. Gulph Rd.
King of Prussia, Pa. 19406

Kansas (University of) Press   BK
366 Watson
Lawrence, Kan. 66044

Kenworthy Educational Service, Inc.   CM, GA
P.O. Box 3031
Buffalo, N.Y. 14205

Keystone View Co.   GA, TE
P.O. Box D
Meadville, Pa. 16335

Kingsbury Center   CM, GA
2138 Bancroft Pl.
Washington, D.C. 20008

Kismet Publishing Co.   CM, GA, TE
P.O. Box 90
South Miami, Fla. 33143

Knowledge Aid   CM
6633 W. Howard St.
Niles, Ill. 60648

Kutz Corp.   CM, GA
P.O. Box 140
McLean, Va. 22101

Laidlaw Brothers   BK, CM
Thatcher and Madison Sts.
River Forest, Ill. 60305

Language Research Associates   BK, TE
P.O. Box 95
Chicago, Ill. 60637

Lawson Book Co.   CM
9488 Sara St.
Elk Grove, Calif. 95624

Lea & Febiger   BK
600 S. Washington Square
Philadelphia, Pa. 19106

Learning Concepts   CM, TE
2501 N. Lamar
Austin, Tex. 78705

Learning Corporation of America   CM
1350 Ave. of the Americas
New York, N.Y. 10019

Learning Pathways   CM
Rt. R, Box 723
Evergreen, Colo. 80439

Learning Research Associates, Inc.   AV, CM, TE
1501 Broadway St.
New York, N.Y. 10036

Learning Systems Press   CM, GA
P.O. Box 909-E
Rantoul, Ill. 61866

Learning Trends   AV, CM, GA
115 Fifth Avenue
New York, N.Y. 10003

Leswing Press   CM
750 Adrian Way
San Rafael, Calif. 94903

Lippincott, J. B., Co.   BK
E. Washington Square
Philadelphia, Pa. 19105

Little, Brown & Co.   BK
34 Beacon St.
Boston, Mass. 02106

Litton Instructional Materials, Inc.   CM, EQ, GA
1695 W. Crescent Ave.
Anaheim, Calif. 92801

Love Publishing Co.   BK, CM
6635 E. Villanova Pl.
Denver, Colo. 80222

Macmillan Co.   BK
866 Third Ave.
New York, N.Y. 10022

Mafex   BK, CM, GA, TE
111 Barron Ave.
Johnstown, Pa. 15906

Math Media, Inc.   CM, GA
P.O. Box 345
Danbury, Conn. 06810

McCormick-Malthers Publishing Co.   CM, GA, AV
450 W. 33rd St.
New York, N.Y. 10001

McGraw-Hill, EDL   CM, EQ, GA, AV
284 Pulaski Rd.
Huntington, N.Y. 11743

McGraw-Hill/Early Learning   CM
Paoli, Pa. 19301

McKay, David, Co., Inc.   BK
750 Third Ave.
New York, N.Y. 10017

Mead Educational Services   CM, GA
245 N. Highland Ave.
Atlanta, Ga. 30307

Media   CM
P.O. Box 1355
Vista, Calif. 92083

Medical Motivation Systems   EQ
Research Park, State Rd.
Princeton, N.J. 08540

Merrill, Charles E., Publishing Co.   BK, CM
1300 Alum Creek Dr.
Columbus, Ohio 43216

Milton Bradley Co.   CM, EQ, GA
74 Park St.
Springfield, Mass. 01106

Modern Curriculum Press   CM
13900 Prospect Rd.
Cleveland, Ohio 44136

Modern Education Corporation   CM
P.O. Box 721
Tulsa, Okla. 74101

Morrow, W. C.   BK
105 Madison Ave.
New York, N.Y. 10016

Mosby, The C. V., Co.   BK
11830 Westline Industrial Dr.
St. Louis, Mo. 63141

Motivational Research Inc.   CM, GA
P.O. Box 140
McLean, Va. 22101

MultiMedia Education, Inc.   AV, CM, GA
11 West 42nd St.
New York, N.Y. 10036

National Council of Teachers of English   BK
1111 Kenyon Rd.
Urbana, Ill. 61801

National Reading Conference Inc.   BK
Reading Center, Marquette University
Milwaukee, Wis. 53233

New Readers Press   BK, CM
P.O. Box 131
Syracuse, N.Y. 13210

New York Association for Brain-Injured   BK
Children
305 Broadway
New York, N.Y. 10007

Noble & Noble, Publishers, Inc.   CM
750 Third Ave.
New York, N.Y. 10017

Northwestern University Press   BK, TE
1735 Benson Ave.
Evanston, Ill. 60201

Open Court Publishing Co.   CM
P.O. Box 599
LaSalle, Ill. 61301

Orton Society   BK
8415 Bellona Lane
Towson, Md. 21204

Owen, F. A., Publisher   BK
7 Bank St.
Dansville, N.Y. 14437

Oxford University Press   BK
200 Madison Ave.
New York, N.Y. 10016

Peek Publications   BK
P.O. Box 11065
Palo Alto, Calif. 94303

Penn Valley Publishing Co.   BK
211 W. Beaver Ave.
State College, Pa. 16801

Phonovisual Products, Inc.   CM
12217 Parklawn Dr.
Rockville, Md. 00852

Prentice-Hall, Inc.   BK, CM
Englewood Cliffs, N.J. 07632

Preston, J. S., Co.   CM, EQ, GA, TE
71 Fifth Ave.
New York, N.Y. 10003

Priority Innovations   BK, CM
P.O. Box 792
Skokie, Ill. 60076

Project Life—General Electric   AV
P.O. Box 43
Schenectady, N.Y. 12301

Pruett Publishing Co.   BK, CM
P.O. Box 1560
Boulder, Colo. 80302

The Psychological Corp.   TE
316 E. 45th St.
New York, N.Y. 10017

Psychological Test Specialists   TE
P.O. Box 1441
Missoula, Mont. 59804

Psychotechnics, Inc.   CM, EQ, GA
1900 Pickwick Ave.
Glenview, Ill. 60025

Putnam, G. P., & Sons   BK
200 Madison Ave.
New York, N.Y. 10016

Random House   BK, CM
201 E. 50th St.
New York, N.Y. 10022

Reader's Digest Services   CM, GA
Educational Division
Pleasantville, N.Y. 10570

Regents Publishing Co.   CM
Division of Simon Schuster
1 West 39th St.
New York, N.Y. 10018

Research Press Co.   BK
CFS Box 3327
Champaign, Ill. 61820

Response Systems Corp.   AV, EQ
Edgemont, Pa. 19028

Rheem Mfg. Califone Div.   EQ, CM
5922 Bowcroft St.
Los Angeles, Calif. 90016

Frank F. Richards Publishing Co.   CM
330 1st St.
Liverpool, N.Y. 13088

Scholastic Magazines, Inc.   CM, EQ
50 West 44th St.
New York, N.Y. 10036

Science Research Associates   BK, CM, GA, TE
259 E. Erie St.
Chicago, Ill. 60611

Scott, Foresman & Co.   AV, CM
11310 Gemini Lane
Dallas, Tex. 75229

Seal Inc.   CM
Dept. 2
Derbly, Conn. 06418

Silver Burdett   CM
A Division of General Learning Corp.
250 James St.
Morristown, N.J. 07960

Singer, L. W., Co.   CM
Division of Random House
201 E. 50th St.
New York, N.Y. 10022

Skill Building—Vantel Corp.   EQ
P.O. Box 6590
Orange, Calif. 92667

Slosson Educational Publications   TE
140 Pine St.
East Aurora, N.Y. 14052

Society for Visual Education, Inc.   AV, CM, GA
1345 W. Diversey Pwy.
Chicago, Ill. 60514

South-Western Publ. Co.   CM
5001 W. Harrison
Chicago, Ill. 60644

Special Child Publications   BK
4535 Union Bay Pl. N.E.
Seattle, Wash. 98105

Speech & Language Materials, Inc.   CM, GA
P.O. Box 721
Tulsa, Okla. 74101

Stanwix House, Inc.   CM, GA
3020 Chartiers Ave.
Pittsburgh, Pa. 15204

Steck-Vaughan Co.   CM, GA
P.O. Box 2028
Austin, Tex. 78767

Stoelting, C. H., Co.   BK, CM
424 N. Homan Ave.
Chicago, Ill. 60624

Stone, R. H., Products   CM
18279 Livernois
Detroit, Mich. 48221

Syracuse University Press   BK
Box 8, University Station
Syracuse, N.Y. 13210

Teachers College Press   BK, TE
1234 Amsterdam Ave.
New York, N.Y. 10027

Teachers Publishing Corp.   BK, CM
Darien, Conn. 06820

Teaching Aids   CM, GA
159 W. Kinzie St.
Chicago, Ill. 60610

Teaching Resources Corp.   AV, BK, CM, EQU,
100 Boylston St.   GA, TE
Boston, Mass. 02116

Teaching Technology Corp.   CM, GA
7471 Greenbush Ave.
North Hollywood, Calif. 91609

Telesensory Systems Inc.   CM
1889 Page Mill Rd.
Palo Alto, Calif. 94304

Thomas, Charles C, Publisher   BK
301 E. Lawrence Ave.
Springfield, Ill. 62703

3M Visual Products   CM
3M Center
St. Paul, Minn. 55101

Topaz Books   BK
5 N. Wabash Ave.
Chicago, Ill. 60602

Tweedy Transparencies   AV
208 Hollywood Ave.
East Orange, N.J. 07018

United Transparencies, Inc.   AV
P.O. Box 688
Binghamton, N.Y. 13002

Chicago (University of) Press BK
5801 Ellis Ave.
Chicago, Ill. 60637

Illinois (University of) Press BK, CM, TE
Urbana, Ill. 61801

Wadsworth Publishing Co. Inc. BK
10 Davis Drive
Belmont, Calif. 94002

Webster Division/McGraw-Hill Book Co. AV,
13955 Manchester Rd. BK, CM
Manchester, Mo. 63011

Wenkart Publishing Co. BK, CM
4 Shady Hill Sq.
Cambridge, Mass. 02138

Western Psychological Services BK, CM, EQ
12031 Wilshire Blvd. Dept. E GA, TE
Los Angeles, Calif. 90025

Westinghouse Learning Corp. CM
P.O. Box 30
Iowa City, Iowa 52240

Wiley, John, & Sons, Inc. BK
605 Third Ave.
New York, N.Y. 10016

Winston Press Inc. CM
25 Groveland Terrace
Minneapolis, Minn. 55403

Winter Haven Lions Research CM
Foundation
Box 1112
Winter Haven, Fla. 33880

Word Making Productions CM, GA, TE
P.O. Box 1858
Salt Lake City, Utah 84100

Xerox Education Publications CM
Education Center
Columbus, Ohio 43216

Zaner-Bloser Co. CM
612 North Park St.
Columbus, Ohio 43215

Index